Liking Ike

Liking Ike

EISENHOWER, ADVERTISING, AND THE RISE
OF CELEBRITY POLITICS

David Haven Blake

OXFORD
UNIVERSITY PRESS

OXFORD
UNIVERSITY PRESS

Oxford University Press is a department of the University of Oxford. It furthers
the University's objective of excellence in research, scholarship, and education
by publishing worldwide. Oxford is a registered trade mark of Oxford University
Press in the UK and certain other countries.

Published in the United States of America by Oxford University Press
198 Madison Avenue, New York, NY 10016, United States of America.

© Oxford University Press 2016

CIP data is on file at the Library of Congress
ISBN 978-0-19-027818-2

1 3 5 7 9 8 6 4 2
Printed by Sheridan Books, Inc., United States of America

For my mother and father

So sometimes, to get your story across, you gotta work a different angle or two, use a few tricks, zap it up with a bit of spectacle—I mean, what's spectacle? it's a kind of *vision*, am I right?

—ROBERT COOVER, *THE PUBLIC BURNING*

{ CONTENTS }

{ PREFACE }

On October 20, 1956, newspapers around the country published a story about an injury that President Dwight Eisenhower had incurred while campaigning in Portland, Oregon. The president's personal physician, Major General Howard McCrum Snyder, told the press that he had removed several tiny pieces of paper from the president's eye after overeager crowds had hurled confetti in his direction. "President's Left Eye Inflamed by Confetti," the story in the *New York Times* began, before reporting that the red spot in his eye would most likely remain until he returned to the White House for the weekend.[1]

Eisenhower's career was filled with stories about the ecstatic reception crowds gave him in Europe, Asia, South America, and the United States. Ike grew up in the late nineteenth century, when citizens marched in torchlight parades to support their favorite candidates. Over fifty years later, he would preside over a remarkable transformation of how Americans conducted political campaigns. As a candidate, he not only jetted from city to city, the crowds lining the streets to watch his motorcade, but the most trivial aspects of his personal life became of routine interest to the press. Sidebar stories like the encounter with confetti were relatively benign, but as Eisenhower complained, others pushed the boundaries of good taste. The president was appalled to learn that, after he suffered a heart attack in 1955, newspapers reported on the quality and frequency of his bowel movements.[2]

More than anything else, however, Eisenhower sensed that television was rapidly transforming the political scene. In his memoir *Mandate for Change*, he described having to fight his way through hordes of reporters, photographers, and curiosity seekers during the 1952 Republican National Convention to shake hands with the man he had just defeated, Ohio's Senator Robert Taft. "I returned to my hotel under circumstances much easier than my former crossing," Eisenhower recalled, but the experience would become even more perplexing. "When I entered my apartment, I saw a marvel of communications that had never occurred to me. As I reached the door of my room my eye was attracted to the television screen in the far corner. On it, startled, I saw myself, moving through my own door."[3]

Liking Ike returns us to a decade that Eisenhower himself recognized as being filled with disorienting change. Television combined instant communication with a sense of presence that suggested politicians were speaking directly to the people without the filter of newspapers and magazines.

The new access weakened the role of political parties, which for decades had played an outsized role in determining which candidates would get a public hearing. (Eisenhower's 1952 nomination was grim news for the Republican hierarchy that had supported their loyal stalwart Senator Taft.) But television also turned politicians into performers, requiring them to stage their appearances for an audience watching them far away in bars, hotel lobbies, and living rooms. Though television brought him great political success, Eisenhower greeted these changes with ambivalence, skeptical of the attention to theatrics but glad to funnel his public persona through Madison Avenue and the booming advertising industry.

Viewers of the AMC television program *Mad Men* will recognize many of the advertising agencies described in this book. While there is no Sterling Cooper, readers will encounter the agencies BBDO, Young & Rubicam, J. Walter Thompson, and that nemesis of Don Draper and Roger Sterling, McCann-Erickson. This book focuses, however, on something that the television series overlooked—that, in telling Eisenhower's story, Madison Avenue played a key role in the collective activity of "liking Ike." Following his ubiquitous campaign slogan, the agencies created a larger narrative about Eisenhower's abundant popularity: there was the man with the incandescent smile and the warm-hearted patriarch; there was the general who inspired confidence and the liberator who was universally admired; there was the president who drew ardent crowds and the candidate who waved through blizzards of confetti.

Ike's advisers were not satisfied with his being venerated across the land. It mattered who, precisely, liked Ike. Among the farmers, housewives, cab drivers, bakers, children, businessmen, and newlyweds featured in the campaign, Eisenhower's friends lined up dozens of public figures who themselves were widely admired. Actors, actresses, singers, athletes, talk show personalities: their images spread across the decade in their shared endorsement of Ike, their collective celebrity visually conveying the importance of likeability and familiarity in the new television age. Writers have praised the thirty-fourth president as a visionary warning against the military-industrial complex, a diplomat trained in the art of the bluff, and a champion of what he often called "the middle way." This book explores how Eisenhower helped usher in another cultural phenomenon of the 1950s: the growing political alliance between television, advertising, and celebrity, an alliance that radiated out of the president's tight-knit circle and influenced many politicians of the age. That alliance, despite significant changes, remains extraordinarily powerful today.

I am grateful to the many archivists, librarians, and friends who have helped bring this book into being. Over many years, Thomas Branigar, Christopher Abraham, and Kathleen Struss of the Dwight D. Eisenhower Presidential Library in Abilene, Kansas, have been tremendously patient and supportive.

I have also received valuable help from Holly Reed of the National Archives Center, Robert Clark of the Franklin Delano Roosevelt Presidential Library; Laurie Austin, Kyla Ryan, and Maryrose Grossman of the John F. Kennedy Presidential Library; Ryan Pettigrew and Jon Fletcher of the Richard Nixon Presidential Library; Steve Branch of the Ronald Reagan Presidential Library; and the Ronald Reagan Foundation.

This book would not exist without the unstinting support of librarians across the country, including Albert King of the Special Collections and University Archives at Rutgers University Libraries; Jim Liversidge of the Special and Area Studies Collections at the University of Florida; Jenifer Baldwin and Andrew Diamond of the Samuel Paley Library at Temple University; Nancy Freeman of the Women and Leadership Archives at Loyola University, Chicago; Joshua Rowley of the Hartman Center for Sales, Advertising, and Marketing History, David M. Rubenstein Library, Duke University; Amy Fitch of the Rockefeller Archive Center; Lucas R. Clawson and Lynsey Sczechowicz of the Hagley Museum and Library; Michelle Reynolds of the Syracuse University Libraries; and staff members at the New York Public Library, Division of the Performing Arts.

For permission to quote from Robert Coover's novel *The Public Burning*, I thank the author and Georges Borchardt, Inc.

Ms. Shannon Honl and Brigadier General Carl Reddel, US Air Force (Ret.), the Executive Director of the Eisenhower Memorial Commission, supplied invaluable assistance as this project neared completion.

My grateful appreciation goes out to Fred Davis of Strategic Perception Inc.; Marciarose Shestack; and the late Preston Wood for taking the time to share their stories and reflections with me.

I have benefitted from the tremendous insights of numerous scholars who looked at some of these materials before me, including Craig Allen of Arizona State University, William L. Bird, Jr. of the Smithsonian Institution, Cynthia Meyers of the College of Mount Saint Vincent, and Richard Fried of the University of Illinois, Chicago. Audiences at Yale University, Washington University in St. Louis, and the University of Nottingham helped me refine my ideas, and I am particularly indebted to Robert Milder, Steven Zwicker, and Robin Vandome for their insights.

The library staff at my home institution, The College of New Jersey (TCNJ), has been consistently helpful and creative in helping me find materials. I especially appreciate the aid of Elizabeth Maziarz, and my friend and research assistant Emily Witkowski.

Critical support for this book was provided by three deans of TCNJ's School of Humanities and Social Sciences, Susan Albertine, Ben Rifkin, and John Sisko, and by the committee on faculty scholarship which generously awarded me time to research and write from 2006 to 2015.

I am grateful for the interest and support of many friends and family members, including Peter Balakian, Peter Blake, Jonathan Blake and Liz Shriver-Blake, Jo Carney, Cindy Curtis, Celia Colbeth, Scott Dierks, Christopher Fisher, Ellen Friedman, Ameen and Jen Ghannam, Paulette LaBar, Andy Loesberg, Emilie Lounsberry, Rob McGreevey, Amanda Norvell, Michelle Ordini, Rosa Rodriguez, Ralph Savarese, and Kevin Warner. My colleague Gary Woodward provided exceptionally helpful feedback on many of these chapters.

My agent, Jessica Papin, has warmly supported this book for many years. I owe special thanks to my fellow author and childhood friend Philip Beard for leading me to her.

The people at Oxford University Press have been a pleasure to work with, especially my editor, Brendan O'Neill, his assistants Stephen Bradley and Alexa Marcon, and Sasirekka Gopalakrishnan of NewGen KnowledgeWorks. I also thank the two anonymous reviewers who provided many useful suggestions toward its revision.

Michael Robertson has given wise and generous counsel from the beginning of this project, poring over some of these chapters multiple times and always encouraging me to think bigger than the moment seemed to demand. I could not ask for a more supportive colleague.

Ed Schwarzschild has been the most constant of readers and friends, not only reading this manuscript several times but enthusiastically discussing its premise in cafes, restaurants, clubs, city parks, tennis stadiums, and a Brooklyn opera house.

My immediate family have lived through the many stages of this project even as they have gone on to develop their own academic and political lives. I've come to depend on sharp, keen insights into the problem of celebrity politics over email, text, Face Time, and sometimes even in person from my wife, Julie, and my children, Eva and Eben.

Part of my attraction to this project was the opportunity to recreate a world that existed just before my memory. Born in the early 1960s, I learned something about the 1950s from old magazines and the black and white reruns I saw on TV. My interest in the decade, however, comes mostly from my parents, who grew up dancing to Elvis, fearing *Sputnik*, and making their own transitions from the Eisenhowers to the Kennedys. In their very different ways, they fed my fascination with celebrity politics, from the classic movies my mother and I watched on winter afternoons to the political science textbooks my father casually left around the house soon after I could read. With great love and appreciation, this book is dedicated to them.

Liking Ike

{ Introduction }

EISENHOWER, TELEVISED AND MEMORIALIZED

In March of 2010, Frank Gehry unveiled his new plans for the Dwight D. Eisenhower Memorial across from the National Mall in Washington, DC. A bipartisan public commission had selected Gehry, one of the world's most acclaimed architects, to memorialize the man who led the Allied Forces during World War II and then became the thirty-fourth president of the United States. From the outset, the commission sought a design that would both honor Eisenhower and "inspire generations with his devotion to public service, leadership, integrity, [and] life-long work ethic." It was equally important, the commission stated, that the design reflect Eisenhower's "total devotion to the values and processes of democracy," the implication being that, of all his accomplishments, perhaps the greatest was his respect for the grassroots participation that makes up a democratic society.[1]

Some memorials are made to commemorate, others to tell a story. Gehry's proposal ignited controversy when the Eisenhower family publicly objected to the "romantic Horatio Alger notion" at the heart of his design.[2] Although he would revise his plans multiple times, Gehry held fast to a narrative depiction of Ike's life. In contrast to Abraham Lincoln and Thomas Jefferson, who heroically tower over the visitors to their memorials, Eisenhower appears in the most recent design as a young man sitting on a stone ledge with an image of the Kansas prairie behind him. From this informal perch, he looks upon two massive stone blocks, each one the backdrop for a sculpted scene from his adult life. In one, he is a general talking to troops before D-Day; in the other, he stands symbolically between representatives of the military and civilian needs of the country.[3] From the beginning, the project design called for a digital component (called the E-Memorial) that would feature multiple images and video of Eisenhower and his times: cadets doing mathematics on a West Point blackboard, soldiers walking through the French countryside, the president waving to the crowds from a Cadillac El Dorado after his 1953

FIGURE I.1 *An overview of the proposed Eisenhower Memorial.*
Courtesy of Gehry Partners, LLP, 2015.

inauguration ceremony. With the aid of wireless electronics, these images would trace how this modest young man rose from the heartland to have an enormous impact on the twentieth century.

Among the ancillary images included in the E-memorial, a worthy addition would be an image of Eisenhower surrounded by celebrities. The designers could depict Eisenhower and a group of stars singing around a piano during the 1952 presidential campaign or Eisenhower's filmed appearance on the *Colgate Comedy Hour* to kick off 1955's Armed Forces Week. Then there is Eisenhower in white tie, grinning with Bob Hope, Jane Powell, and Pearl Bailey, or Eisenhower laughing with Arnold Palmer on the grounds of Augusta National Golf Club. In no way, of course, should these images rival the attention given to Eisenhower's great achievements: the victory over European fascism, the peace in Korea, the booming postwar economy. However Eisenhower and his stars deserve their own commemorative treatment. Though the commission or his family might not agree, the images are as much a part of Eisenhower's presidency as they are of the scrapbooks of these departed celebrities. As this book explains, they go hand-in-hand with Eisenhower's commitment to the values and processes of democracy. They, too, should be engraved in our cultural memory.

To many, Dwight Eisenhower would be a surprising, even shocking, addition to the pantheon of celebrity-infused presidents and political campaigns. A humble plainsman, a soldier-citizen, a steadfast and grandfatherly head of state, he seems worlds away from such Hollywood-tinged presidents as John F. Kennedy, Ronald Reagan, and Bill Clinton. When we see Ike's grainy black-and-white image reviewing American troops in London, when we recall his warnings about the military-industrial complex, we are inclined to see a model of integrity and foresight rather than theatrical charm. And yet,

FIGURE I.2 *President Eisenhower at the June 7, 1956 dinner of the White House News Photographers Association in Washington, DC. With him* (from left to right) *are Raymond Mouriks, Antonina Murio, Vic Damone, Jane Powell, Bob Hope, Pearl Bailey, and Leonard Pennario.*

Courtesy of National Park Service and Dwight D. Eisenhower Presidential Library and Museum.

no matter how durable his accomplishments, no matter how penetrating his vision, Eisenhower gave celebrities a curious role in promoting him as a political candidate. Guided by television pioneers and Madison Avenue advertising executives whom insiders dubbed "Mad Men," he cultivated scores of famous supporters as a way of building the kind of broad-based support that had eluded Republicans for twenty years.

Eisenhower's presidential campaigns were so saturated with stardom that they would astonish many Americans today. Broadway stars performed at jam-packed Madison Square Garden rallies designed to drum up enthusiasm for his candidacy. Roy Disney created an animated television commercial, and Irving Berlin composed a campaign theme song, turning the phrase "I Like Ike" into the most memorable political slogan in American history. Popular figures from the world of sports appeared at fundraising dinners and in television commercials touting Eisenhower's record. Working with Madison Avenue executives, actors and actresses gave press conferences extolling the benefits of an Eisenhower presidency. Critics complained that all the advertisements and endorsements risked turning Eisenhower into a commodity, as if he were a carton of Lucky Strike cigarettes being plugged by comedian Jack Benny. Far from objecting, Ike's advisers invited such comparisons. As they described it, their job was to merchandise the man who was at once their client, their product, and their candidate. Television advertising, they explained, simply extended the reach of democracy.

During the same period, Eisenhower himself was developing into a congenial, media-savvy performer. Initially flustered by the tedium and distractions of being on camera, he grew to understand the demands of the presidency in the television age. He worked with Robert Montgomery, the former president of the Screen Actors Guild and the popular host of an eponymous hour-long drama series on NBC, to help improve his televised interviews and speeches. As producers, directors, and cameramen were figuring out how to maneuver their heavy equipment through the White House windows and hallways, Montgomery was teaching the president how to read from a teleprompter and appear more open and engaging. From his office in the West Wing, he developed camera angles and poses that would help Eisenhower seem youthful, invigorated, and authoritative on TV. Although he had been famous for well over a decade and had hired advisers to improve his communication skills, it was television that transformed Ike into a media celebrity. The Academy of Television Arts and Sciences awarded the president an honorary Emmy for his innovative use of the medium to communicate with the American people.[4]

This book tells the story of how Eisenhower's celebrity politics was developed on Madison Avenue, practiced in the White House, debated in the press, protested by his opponents, and then remade by subsequent generations of politicians and stars. It analyzes the ways that this most respected of leaders, a hero throughout much of the world, was drawn into the conflux of television, advertising, and political glamour that emerged in the 1950s. Not willing to stand purely on his credentials, Eisenhower agreed to the same set of promotional strategies that advertisers used to sell products like laundry detergent and shaving cream. Although they may seem obvious to us now, the systematic efforts to decorate a candidate with stardust were then perceived as being radically new, and the glitz surrounding Eisenhower's campaigns aroused consternation and concern. To some at the time, the image-making seemed more appropriate for a movie star or talk show host than the Supreme Commander of the North Atlantic Treaty Organization (NATO). "Get rid of the vaudeville, pretty-girl" embroidery, one editorialist advised, "and conduct the campaign on a level commensurate with the General's intelligence and position."[5] But to leading Republicans and the advertising executives they hired, television made the power of celebrity endorsements appealing, and they were confident that this softer, glamorized version of politics would attract votes. The result was a vision of American politics in which publicity would become a principal site of democracy and voters would soon identify themselves as both an electorate and an audience. The rise of Eisenhower's "star strategy" made for an odd historical juxtaposition. At the same time that Congress was investigating the influence of Communists in Hollywood and the film and broadcasting industries were blacklisting alleged subversives, advertising executives were seeking ways to bring conservative performers into the political spotlight. The irony did not trouble the advertising agencies that worked on Ike's campaigns, for as they saw it, their task was not to politicize entertainment but to make politics more entertaining.

Gehry's proposed memorial seems well attuned to the significance of a media-inflected Ike. Millions of Americans experienced Eisenhower's heroism through newsreels and photographs, and the proposal brilliantly ties his devotion to public service and democracy to his representation in the media. We might briefly consider Gehry's Eisenhower next to the statue of Abraham Lincoln that presides over the National Mall. Although he studied dozens of portraits and photographs, the sculptor Daniel Chester French ultimately chose to depict Lincoln as being outside history, a timeless figure who sits in judgment on his Roman-style throne. Visitors don't see Lincoln meeting with his military staff at Antietam or delivering his inaugural address. The memorial honors Lincoln in a wholly imagined and ahistorical pose, one that suits the godlike proportions French gave him. Gehry's design does not imagine Eisenhower as much as it recalls and recreates him. The proposed D-Day sculpture reenacts a well-known moment from Eisenhower's career as a soldier and a statesman. In recreating this iconic image, the sculpture brings the media's role in documenting and publicizing Eisenhower's life directly into its narrative. Indeed, part of the Horatio Alger narrative concerns an obscure young man who looks out upon images of his democratic service and fame. Eisenhower was not a creation of the media, and Gehry does not depict Ike's fame as being one of his accomplishments. The proposed memorial makes it clear, however, that the president's power, his impact, was inextricable from his visibility.

We live in an age in which politicians regularly appear on late-night television, and entertainers use Twitter to share their political commentary. The media's focus on celebrity has transformed our sense of politics, shifting attention from evaluating policy to following the rise and fall of political personalities. From the *Washington Post* to *People* magazine, politicians customarily receive what Neal Gabler has called the "celebrity treatment"—the "breathless glamorization" the media applies to virtually every individual it covers.[6] We read about this candidate's favorite (or least favorite) vegetable and that Cabinet member's Nantucket vacation home. Family backgrounds loom over these stories, so that even high-profile columnists such as Maureen Dowd end up casting their analyses as if they were lessons from *Freud for Dummies*. The intense focus on personality has accelerated the tabloidization of American life and the elevation of scandal and controversy over rational political debate. President Barack Obama spoke for many when he

FIGURE 1.3 *The proposed sculptural grouping of Eisenhower speaking to US troops before D-Day.*
Courtesy of Gehry Partners, LLP, 2015.

nostalgically compared the "instant commentary and celebrity gossip" that occupies journalism today with the "hard news and investigative journalism" that Walter Cronkite championed. Speaking at Cronkite's funeral, he lamented this fusion of news and entertainment: "The public debate cheapens. The public trust falters. We fail to understand our world or one another as well as we should."[7] The irony of these comments did not escape the White House press corps, which has complained that Obama himself frequently bypasses news conferences in favor of celebrity-themed interviews on both broadcast and digital media.[8]

The influence of celebrity on American politics, however, has a longer, more complicated history than we might think. Although the nineteenth century produced a handful of celebrities who either ran for office or helped elect others, it was during the 1920s that Broadway and Hollywood stars began to attract significant publicity to presidential campaigns. The singer Al Jolson led dozens of Broadway entertainers in support of Republican candidates Warren G. Harding and Calvin Coolidge. Movie studio moguls such as Louis B. Mayer worked behind the scenes to support specific causes and candidates, dispatching stars to perform at rallies or have their photographs taken with tired-looking politicos in need of some glamour and stardust. As they grew over the next decades, Hollywood and Broadway would become sites of intense activism, powerful enthusiasms, and careful image-making. Although he tended to keep them at a distance, Franklin Roosevelt enjoyed the support of hundreds of artists and entertainers during his presidential campaigns. These supporters produced radio programs, appeared at rallies, and barnstormed across the country in pro-Roosevelt shows.

What makes Eisenhower such an interesting case is that for the first time we begin to see a large-scale coordinated effort to professionalize celebrity politics. At the behest of such groups as Citizens for Eisenhower and the Republican Party, advertising agencies developed a vision of how stardom could be used to sell a presidential candidate. This was not simply an issue of like-minded entertainers working together to pursue an ideological goal, nor was it about studio executives using the tools at their disposal to advance their commercial and political interests. Eisenhower's star strategy was developed on Madison Avenue by men and women who regarded him as both a friend and a political commodity. Hoping to make politics palatable and even charming, these advisers created celebrity-themed shows and events that they hoped would generate mass appeal. They reasoned that, like so many products of the time period, Eisenhower would benefit from the warmth and admiration Americans had for celebrities. Formed into committees, they drafted television scripts, pursued endorsements, and researched the partisan affiliations of leading personalities, entertainers, and athletes, all in an effort to attract independents and swing-voting Democrats. The work of these advisers was remarkably prescient. With both outrage and dismay, the journalist Chris Hedges writes that today's celebrity culture avoids political conflict and debate in favor of narratives, images, and commodities.[9] Over sixty years ago, the people who ran the Eisenhower campaigns aimed for precisely that effect, using celebrities to overwhelm the opposition with glamour and likeability.

Like many critics, Hedges would have been at home in Adlai Stevenson's presidential campaigns, as Stevenson regularly denounced the role of advertising in politics. Known more for his eloquence than his marketing appeal, the popular Illinois governor ran against Eisenhower in both 1952 and 1956. Both times he failed miserably, never winning over 45 percent of the popular vote and never winning his home state.[10] To be sure, the governor faced a nearly impossible task in running against Ike. Not only was Eisenhower one of the world's most admired men, but after twenty years of Democrats in the White House, many voters agreed that it was time for a change. Stevenson frequently campaigned with Hollywood couple Lauren Bacall and Humphrey Bogart, but their presence did not alter his dim view of glamour and advertising in a presidential race. The governor's objection to Republican image-making was consistent with his desire to "talk sense" to the American people, but his reluctance to incorporate the new promotional techniques ultimately impaired both of his campaigns.[11]

In many ways, it was television that made the 1950s such a vibrant period in the history of celebrity politics. In 1950, only 9 percent of American homes had a television set; ten years later, the number had risen to 90 percent.[12] The new medium was rapidly transforming American political life, changing the role of advertising, the nature of campaigning, and the goals for nominating conventions. With its direct appeal to viewers, television threatened to weaken the power of party bosses to select their favorite candidates, making the home, not the precinct, the focus of every campaign. Observers noted that the presence of cameras altered the conduct of lawmakers during two key proceedings: Tennessee senator Estes Kefauver's 1950–1951 hearings about the impact of organized crime on interstate commerce, and Wisconsin senator Joseph McCarthy's 1954 investigation into the presence of Communists in the Department of Defense. Commentators from all parts of the political spectrum worried about these changes, and reporters, scholars, and politicians studied the medium's impact on their fellow citizens.[13] The *New York Times* television critic Jack Gould published a seven-part series titled *What TV Is Doing to Us*, in which he surveyed the medium's effect on different aspects of American life, including education, sports, culture, and politics.[14] The Brookings Institution published monographs on the campaigns of 1952 and 1956, breaking down everything from viewing patterns to the number of affiliate stations that carried live political programming.[15] Writing in the *Christian Science Monitor*, film critic Richard Dyer MacCann worried that the modern politician would become "more and dependent on the man who can manipulate the impersonal forces of the mass media."[16] Massachusetts senator John F. Kennedy made the same point in an essay he wrote for *TV Guide*, but he also praised television's capacity to expose deception and dishonesty.[17]

At the same time, television was giving advertisers a powerful new medium to extend their sway over consumers. Not only did Madison Avenue foster more liberal attitudes about consumption; it also seized the new commercial sphere to turn advertising into one of the culture's most dominant forces. By the decade's end, as historian Lizabeth Cohen has shown, television accounted for over half the total revenues at most of the major advertising agencies. More importantly, television was fundamentally redefining social relations. As an NBC promotional film put it, the industry had successfully put a "selling machine in every living room," one that gave companies the opportunity to turn "strangers into customers."[18]

Finally, with its capacity to bring visual entertainment into people's homes, television facilitated a genuine explosion in the growth and significance of celebrity to a nation that had a long history of exalting individual personalities. Entertainers became objects of veneration, makers of fashion, and generational icons. As if summoned by magic, celebrities appeared directly in the home as one was dusting furniture, ironing work shirts, or reading the newspaper in the evening. Aware that television was changing public tastes toward the spectacular and revealing, publishers unleashed a torrent of magazines such as *Confidential* and *Hush-Hush* that delivered gossip about politicians and celebrities to ever-hungry readers.[19] By the end of the decade, even mainstream magazines like *Life* had expanded the number of pages they dedicated to glossy, intimate profiles of the nation's leading personalities.

Glamour "moves and persuades not through words," Virginia Postrel tells us, "but through images, concepts, totems." Though the movies increased the visibility of glamour in the 1930s, television extended its power over large segments of the population.[20]

The prevalence of celebrity in our own time can lead us to forget that each age sees the famous differently. While certain perspectives carry across decades and centuries, how the public views celebrity tends to be grounded in culture and history. Two key themes emerge from celebrity culture in the 1950s. The first is that the limited number of television stations and motion picture studios created a common and coherent viewing experience. Adults and children may have followed different performers, but they knew the stars each group admired. With our tablet computers, streaming video feeds, and fan-designed websites, we are accustomed to niche celebrities—figures who capture the attention of very specific populations. Our popular culture is so fragmented that subscribers to *Wired, Rolling Stone, Sports Illustrated*, and *Good Housekeeping* may not recognize the celebrity faces on the covers of the other magazines. But fame in the 1950s imparted a sense of stability that fed even the most rebellious stars back into the mainstream. Many commentators regarded Elvis Presley's June 5, 1956 appearance on *The Milton Berle Show* as both radical and offensive. The *New York Daily News* objected to the singer's "animalism," and the Catholic magazine *America* warned its readers, "Beware of Elvis Presley."[21] But less than five months later, shortly before Election Day, the singer appeared on *The Ed Sullivan Show* alongside the ventriloquist Señor Wences and an Irish children's choir.[22] Elvis must have appeared shockingly subversive next to these acts, but the format of the show also helped to contain and domesticate whatever rebelliousness his swiveling hips conveyed.

The era's second distinctive trait is that, in the 1950s, celebrities enjoyed a form of respect that came from their remoteness and singularity. Gossip magazines were popular because, to most Americans, celebrity still represented a combination of achievement and individuality. The magazines titillated readers who were eager to learn about a star's bouts with alcohol or adultery, but even the most controversial information betrayed a troubled but still glamorous personality. For example, though studios combated them with payoffs, legal action, and their own PR-driven fictions, whispers about a star's sexuality could have a surprisingly limited impact on a career. The former teen idol Tab Hunter remarked in his autobiography that only months after a cover story in Robert Harrison's *Confidential* hinted at his homosexuality, he won the 1955 Audience Award for Most Promising New Personality. In subsequent years he would record hit songs and appear as a romantic lead in popular movies.[23] Hunter and others obviously felt oppressed by such magazines, and Hollywood insiders snickered about its "lavender lads" and "baritone babes." But such rumors tended to reinforce the mysterious attraction that fans experienced as they watched these figures on the television and movie

FIGURE I.4 *A cover story in the September 1955* Confidential *magazine exposed the entertainer Tab Hunter's 1950 arrest for attending an all-male "pajama party" in Los Angeles. Private Collection.*

screen. In the 1950s, the institution of celebrity produced votaries, spectators, and hatchet men rather than today's meme-producing masters of irony.[24]

Perhaps because our own age is so steeped in it, any serious discussion of celebrity has to combat a prevailing skepticism about politically active stars. Putting aside the slick, gossipy coverage of *Gawker* or *People* magazine, media discussions of celebrity politics have generally been shrill and alarmist, the consensus being that this star's activism or that star's candidacy has put democracy at risk. "Shut Up and Sing," the radio host Laura Ingraham told entertainers like Barbra Streisand and the Dixie Chicks in her diatribe against the so-called cultural elite.[25] Although they would target a different group of celebrities, many leftist critics would heartily agree.

The tone is regrettable because scholars and journalists have done a superb job excavating the rich history of celebrity politics in the United States. The foundation of this growing field has been Ronald Brownstein's *The Power and the Glitter: The Hollywood-Washington Connection*. Writing in the wake of the Reagan presidency, Brownstein demonstrated that, since the moguls of the 1920s, power has long shuttled between the halls of government and studio offices in Los Angeles. The appearance of entertainers in political campaigns has been only one part of the deep, institutional alliance Hollywood has forged with Washington, DC. More recently, Stephen J. Ross's *Hollywood Left and Right: How Movie Stars Shaped American Politics* recounts the stories of ten Hollywood personalities who involved themselves in political life. Interlacing biography, film criticism, and political history, Ross forcefully corrects widespread assumptions about the "liberal entertainment industry" in demonstrating that conservative entertainers have been remarkably successful in turning their celebrity into actual political power. Republicans may now be in short supply at Academy Awards ceremonies, but historically they exerted much more influence over Washington (and Sacramento) than their Democratic counterparts.[26]

Brownstein and Ross present the history of celebrity politics on an epic scale with stars like Charlie Chaplin, Charlton Heston, and Jane Fonda putting in impressive performances. Stars and politicians fill the pages of these books, their manifold stories serving both to broaden the historical record and frame a new field of study. As our understanding of celebrity grows, however, and as we see its meaning change across the decades, commentators can begin closely examining the strategies and tactics behind individual campaigns. In switching our focus from coverage to depth, we can ask a different set of questions about the production of celebrity politics: Who designed such appearances and events, and why were they eager to match stars with their candidates? How did political operatives find working with these stars, and did they see risk in gilding their campaigns with the hoopla and values of show business? How did specific stars function as cultural symbols, as codes that elegantly conveyed larger meanings to the audience and the electorate? How did parties launch counteroffensives, using their own celebrities to neutralize the argument and charm of their opponents? How did advertising agencies, and the companies they represented, use stardom to promote political agendas that would shape American society for decades? Probing the details of individual campaigns invites us to treat the history of celebrity politics as less a sequence of biographical studies, and more a set of richly textured civic texts.

Liking Ike examines the 1950s from multiple perspectives and points of view. It delves into the memos, committee minutes, and press releases that connected Eisenhower with Madison Avenue executives, Hollywood supporters, and grassroots organizations across the nation. It traces the blacklisting of liberal television performers to some of Eisenhower's most loyal advisers in the advertising industry, executives who were also engaged in grooming Ronald Reagan's conservatism. At the same time, the book recounts the Democrats' difficulty in adjusting to the television age. While Adlai Stevenson attracted enthusiastic supporters such as Bette Davis and Henry Fonda, he refused to prepare for the great waves of publicity that washed over his presidential campaigns. His flummoxed approach left some Democrats questioning whether he would have been better suited to earlier decades. *Liking Ike*, in this respect, is an act of historical recovery and dilation. It resurrects the forgotten details of a revolutionary set of campaigns and offers a new vantage point on what has long been regarded as a familiar story. In haunting prose, the *New Yorker* writer George W.S. Trow described the experience of growing up "under the aesthetic of Dwight David Eisenhower."[27] *Liking Ike* explores the people who defined and disseminated that aesthetic, the people who made it work.

Eisenhower and his advisers left a remarkable archive of his television productions and advertising. From New York governor Nelson Rockefeller to Young & Rubicam president Sigurd Larmon, Ike's supporters believed that publicity had played a crucial role in his quest for the presidency, and they ensured that an astonishingly wide range of materials survived. Film scripts, project proposals, tips on how to celebrate the candidate in the home; telegrams, television treatments, advertisements for *TV Guide*; Nielsen ratings, program reviews, commendations from the Oval Office; fan mail, voter scrolls, notes from Ike's chief of staff; executive summaries, press releases, the results of internal polls—all these documents help us reconstruct celebrity politics in the 1950s; all of them give a new window into the president's alliances and his times.

Eisenhower's contemporaries engaged in a spirited public debate about how Madison Avenue was changing the nation. With its capacity to reach such far-off places as Hartford, Dallas, and Albuquerque, television was creating a national audience—and, indeed, a national storyline—for the presidential race. From a commercial perspective, the beauty of the medium was that it allowed advertisers to address different segments of the population while drawing them into a common experience. Fans of the Cheerios Kid typically did not purchase Brylcreem, but they probably recognized the hair gel's jingle and knew that "a little dab" would "do ya" and leave the ladies eager "to run their fingers through your hair." The same unifying effect could be found in American politics. Previous presidential candidates had undertaken grueling whistle-stop campaigns in which they traveled around the country, addressed regional concerns, and hoped for favorable coverage in the local press. Ike had traveled extensively in 1952, and throughout the decade, the Grand Old Party (GOP) ingeniously staged numerous events that brought the presidential race to local communities. But after his heart attack in 1955, Eisenhower and his advisers seized upon television as a way to conduct a national campaign without the physical toll of constantly leaving Washington, DC. The result was a profusion of commentary from writers, academics, and journalists who questioned what the new political advertisements revealed about democracy in the television age. Leading them all was Stevenson, who predicted in 1956 that candidates would become increasingly isolated by TV. As Stevenson saw it, the medium allowed politicians to be seen and heard by millions while never having to listen to what those millions hoped and feared.[28]

The relationship between politics and celebrity figured prominently in these discussions. As Congress investigated the leftist activities of writers and directors, as actors Bob Hope and Danny Thomas encouraged Americans to go to the polls, it became harder to ignore the power of fame in American life. Politicians flocked to televised news programs, and commentators worried that the medium was reducing complex issues to theatrics and personal style. Novelists and filmmakers noted the glassy-eyed stupor that television induced in its viewers and feared that its influence would lead to more sinister forms of manipulation. (One Cold War intellectual admonished his readers that mass culture threatened "not merely to cretinize our taste, but to brutalize our senses while paving the way to totalitarianism.")[29] Across the country, there was a growing sense that while most Americans *watched*, others were *scrutinized* and *observed*. "All those who succeed in America are likely to become involved in the world of celebrity," the sociologist C. Wright Mills argued in 1956.[30] Entertainers, athletes, and leaders in business, the sciences, and the arts—they had all become members of a national elite that ruled the public's fortunes and attention. Mills joined his contemporaries in warning that politicians would find it difficult to resist the system of prestige that was spreading across the nation.[31]

Enlisting stars for Ike was not just a matter of finding ideologically compatible personalities: it was about expanding the campaign in more collaborative directions. As radio veterans and TV pioneers, Eisenhower's advisers were well-schooled in performance, and they knew how small aesthetic choices could help create a coherent and compelling message about their candidate. They knew that stars helped produce narratives not only about Eisenhower and the Republican Party, but perhaps more importantly, about the public's own interests and desires. Ralph Waldo Emerson once touted the creative and symbol-making capacity of Americans by pointing to "the power of badges and emblems" in their political campaigns. "Witness the cider-barrel, the log-cabin, the hickory-stick, the palmetto," Emerson wrote in 1843, amazed at how such national symbols rose organically from the populace.[32] Taking their place among the donkeys, elephants, and lesser-known roosters and eagles, Eisenhower's stars functioned as key symbols in his presidential campaigns. Unlike Emerson's palmetto and hickory stick, however, these symbols did not emerge from the masses. They were coordinated, staged, and broadcast by advertising agencies.

One of these symbols was "Ike Day." On October 13, 1956, supporters across the nation gathered to celebrate the president's sixty-sixth birthday with locally organized parades, dances, rallies, and charity events. The festivities culminated that evening in a star-studded television program on CBS featuring Jimmy Stewart, Nat King Cole, and Helen Hayes. With its fusion of grassroots volunteerism and Hollywood glamour, Ike Day captured the populist tone that made celebrity politics useful in the 1950s. The model proved to be adaptable to different contexts and personalities. As we will see, Ronald Reagan's emergence as a conservative firebrand had its roots in the Eisenhower era when Batten, Barton, Durstin, and Osborne (BBDO) hired the actor both to host *General Electric Theater* on NBC and to tour General Electric (GE) factories as part of its employee outreach and education program. With its close ties to the president and the Republican Party, BBDO took charge of promoting Reagan as a popular corporate spokesman and critic of government bureaucracy.

Despite Stevenson's resistance, the Democrats simultaneously developed their own model of celebrity politics. We find an interesting counterpart to Ike Day in the 1962 fundraiser that Democrats held for John F. Kennedy in Madison Square Garden. The event is largely remembered for Marilyn Monroe's show-stopping rendition of "Happy Birthday, Mr. President." With all its breathy exaggeration, there was nothing "political" about Monroe's performance, yet the moment signaled something new on the cultural landscape: the erotic charge of politics in the television age. Of course, there were inklings of this eroticism in the 1950s, but as Dwight and Mamie gave way to Jack and Jackie, public life became increasingly stylized and oriented toward pleasing and stimulating the eye. Monroe's performance in Madison Square Garden captured America's attraction to the glossy antics of the Kennedy family, but it also suggested the degree to which television rooted political life in the pleasures of spectacle and publicity.

We have become so habituated to spectacle that many of the activities that alarmed Eisenhower's critics are commonplace today. Hardly anyone questions the practice of marketing politicians, and the news industry thrives on the image-making it once scorned, focusing more on political performance than on questions of policy and governance. As if irony were the most fitting response to a media-saturated age, young Americans have turned to late-night comedians for their political news, and the politicians have eagerly followed, scrambling to appear with the very entertainers who mock and deride them nightly. To be a national politician is to become a national celebrity, to submit oneself to the carnival of popular culture and the unblinking gaze of publicity. And yet, even as they glamorize politicians and pay extraordinary attention to celebrity candidates, many Americans remain remarkably suspicious of actors and musicians who express strong opinions or offer polemical entertainment.

It is hard to know what the bright young man depicted in Gehry's memorial would have thought about the Broadway songs and television shows that eventually decorated his path to the presidency. Even more incomprehensible is how he would have responded to politics in the twenty-first-century United States, with its Malibu fundraisers, *Saturday Night Live* skits, and celebrity Twitterstorms. One thing we can say with certainty, however, is that the path to these contemporary activities runs directly through him. As the public rediscovers Eisenhower as a figure of surprisingly contemporary significance, as it continues to examine his long-tranquil legacy, it will want to consider his role in the making of our spectacle democracy. The television show celebrating the president's sixty-sixth birthday is a good place to begin.

Ike Day

There had been pom poms, jingles, motorcades, interviews, press releases, and televised endorsements from across the United States. Six bandwagons had toured the country, and at selected towns, slews of young women had spilled out of buses, their dresses and twirling parasols emblazoned with the president's nickname. In a series of five-minute programs titled "You and Your Government," key Cabinet members had described the administration's success, aiming to prove that, despite their millions, they were still in touch with Main Street. There was a "people's news conference," a World Series appearance, and a commercial touting the president's popular wife. The president was an "experienced quarterback," said Frank Leahy, the former Notre Dame football coach, in a television spot directed at the youth vote.[1]

But to many in the press, the televised birthday celebration had been one of the most inspired moments of the reelection campaign. The policy handbooks, convention speeches, and questions about the challenger's inexperience were no match for the star-studded presidential tribute that aired three weeks before Election Day. The newspaper reviews gathered for the president's secretary offered admiration and praise. *Variety* marveled at how the event "subtly wrapped a political pitch in terms of an entertainment for an ostensibly non-partisan occasion." The *Washington Post* concluded that "without a single plea for partisan votes, it was the most politically effective program of the week." "As a demonstration of how to win friends and influence voters," the *Philadelphia Inquirer* commented, "it was worth dozens of speeches."[2] The genius of the program was that it hardly acknowledged its role in the presidential campaign.

On October 13, 1956, the Republican National Committee (RNC) recognized Dwight D. Eisenhower's upcoming birthday with a coast-to-coast celebration organized under the banner "Ike Day." Eisenhower had spent his momentous sixty-fifth birthday recuperating from a heart attack in a Denver military hospital, and as the president received greetings from well-wishers around the world, the RNC anxiously speculated whether he would run for a second term. Though questions about his health would plague him over the coming months, the president eventually agreed to seek reelection, with the goal of rebuilding a Republican Party that, insiders confessed, was badly underfunded, lacked organization, and had recently lost control of both houses of Congress.³ In the late summer of 1956, the RNC created the National Ike Day Committee to turn the sixty-sixth birthday into a major campaign event.

The heart of the celebration was a thirty-minute tribute that aired on CBS at 10:00 p.m. Loosely based on the popular shows *Person to Person* and *This Is Your Life*, the program interspersed scenes from Eisenhower's youth with musical performances from some of the era's leading entertainers. Actor Jimmy Stewart hosted the program from Hollywood, and his opening remarks made it clear that, while partisanship would never be mentioned, politics was on everyone's mind. Ike Day, he said, "is more than just a birthday celebration. It is a nationwide tribute to a man who has devoted almost all of his adult life to the service of his country." The sense of a collective, national celebration was built into the broadcast itself, which shuttled between Hollywood, New York, Abilene, Kansas, and two sites in Washington, DC. Stewart seemed almost winded by the experience of being a transcontinental host—breathlessly introducing Helen Hayes in Washington, Nat King Cole in Hollywood, and the president himself, who sat with his family, watching the tribute in the White House library.⁴

Stewart may have been the ideal host for a program that so earnestly trucked in sentiment. Taking viewers on a video tour of Abilene, the president's hometown, he spoke with wistful reverence of how the town's atmosphere had produced such a great man. Abilene was at the "crossroads of America," Stewart said, and "one of the biggest little cities in the Midwest." Addressing the president, he described how the locals still pointed with pride to "the creamery where you worked and the old swimming hole you used to enjoy." "It's almost dried up today though," Stewart added, as if resigning himself to the poignancy of change. With its pictures of boyhood friends, tree-lined streets, and the family church, the Abilene montage nimbly prefaced a visit to a replica of the Eisenhower family home where Howard Keel and Kathryn Grayson welcomed viewers around the parlor piano to hear a few of President and Mrs. Eisenhower's favorite songs. Ike had met Mamie in San Antonio, Texas, where he was stationed as a young lieutenant. In the program's breezy sweep from boy- to manhood, however, the songs of courtship became tender expressions of family and hearth. Even the somewhat feverish lyrics of "Down Among the Sheltering Palms" ("How my love is burning, burning, burning / How my heart is yearning, yearning, yearning") seem as charmingly stripped of carnality as the image of old creameries and dried-up swimming holes.

From the moral comforts of Abilene, the broadcast moved to the Statler Hotel in Washington, DC, where a key component of the Ike Day celebration was already in progress: a party organized by a number of college and Young Republican groups titled "Youth Salutes the President." The overflow crowd of several thousand partygoers had been treated to an evening of entertainment including speeches by leading Republicans, choral performances by Fred Waring and the Pennsylvanians, and a 32-foot, 2000-pound cake depicting various moments of Eisenhower's career.[5] When the television cameras joined the festivities, Stewart introduced Hayes as "one of the first ladies of American theater." Hayes would soon reprise her definitive role as Amanda in the Broadway production of Tennessee Williams's play *The Glass Menagerie*, but on this night, she would appear as the president's charismatic champion. Whatever glamour she lent the proceedings, her role in the television program was neatly confined to the humble task of cutting a piece of cake. "Here Mr. President, for you, a slice of your favorite cake, for your birthday," she announced to the cameras, before warning its young courier, a boy named Johnny Cross, not to drop the plate en route to the White House.

The entertainers appearing on Eisenhower's behalf were selected for both their star power and their potential to invoke important political values and constituencies. Stewart prefaced Eddie Fisher's performance of "Count Your Blessings" with a reminder that the president had asked him to sing the song at a 1954 ceremony marking the 300th anniversary of the Jewish people in America. The appearance of Fisher, known as "the Jewish Sinatra," must have had special meaning for voters in 1956 who nervously awaited the administration's response to conflicts over the Suez Canal with Egypt. Performances by Nat King Cole and the gospel choir Voices of Victory reached out to African Americans even as civil rights legislation was delayed until after the November elections.[6] Two of the songs—"Swing Low, Sweet Chariot" and "The World Is Waiting for the Sunrise"—seemed to counsel optimism and patience.[7] Recorded on newsreel cameras, James Cagney joined Irene Dunne, co-chairman of the National Ike Day Committee, in sending their birthday greetings while serving cake at a children's hospital in Los Angeles.

From the program's beginning, Ike had presented himself as a genial patriarch. (In his opening discussion with Stewart, he agreeably explained that, while his two older grandchildren had been permitted to join the broadcast, the others were properly asleep in their beds.) The heart of Eisenhower's reputation, however, was his celebrated military leadership. Upon graduating from West Point in 1915, he embarked on a military career that took him from Panama to the Philippines. Eisenhower never saw combat directly (much to his disappointment, he spent World War I training soldiers stateside), but in the ensuing decades, he gained a reputation for administrative excellence. In 1941, he was put in charge of developing US war plans. Seven months after

FIGURE 1.1 *A publicity photo for the Ike Day telecast featured the president surrounded by (clockwise from top left) Irene Dunne, Jimmy Stewart, James Cagney, Helen Hayes, Gordon MacRae, and Eddie Fisher.*
Courtesy of Special Collections and University Archives, Rutgers University Libraries.

the bombing of Pearl Harbor, he assumed command of the Army's European Theater of Operations, then headquartered in London. As a lieutenant general, Eisenhower planned the invasions of North Africa in 1943 and Normandy the year after, both of which were critical to the Allied forces' gaining control of Europe. By the time he presided over the surrender of the German army in Reims, France, in 1945, Eisenhower enjoyed worldwide affection and popularity. He would go on to serve as Chief of Staff of the US Army from 1945–1948. After a brief stint as president of Columbia University, the famed general became Supreme Commander of NATO forces in Europe. He resigned his commission in June 1952 in his quest to become the Republican presidential candidate.

One of the most significant achievements of Eisenhower's first term was that he had brokered a peace agreement in Korea, and by 1956, the campaign was reluctant to showcase him as a war hero. The broadcast solved this problem by focusing on the formative years at West Point. Shifting back to the Statler Hotel party, Stewart introduced Fred Waring and the Pennsylvanians with their rendition of the West Point hymn "The Corps." As the choir sang of the "long gray line" of cadets stretching across generations, images filled the screen—monuments, buildings, Eisenhower's yearbook portrait, and rows of crisply marching cadets. The images obscured the realities of fear and sacrifice with nostalgia and romanticism. The nation's dead were replaced with vigorous pride and youthful promise.

The program's ability to incorporate camera feed from around the country was remarkable for its day, and reviewers commented on the excellence of the production.[8] The broadcast featured Eisenhower as a viewer, an honored member of the audience enjoying the entertainment on screen. As the show neared its end, however, the White House became the center of interest. Following Stewart's cue from Hollywood, the president's grandchildren opened the library door, where Johnny Cross was waiting to present him with a slice of birthday cake. Stewart then introduced Charles Percy, chairman of the Ike Day Committee, who echoed the host in saying that no man had given so much of himself to the country and to the world. Percy delivered to Eisenhower one of the several thousand scrolls that citizens had signed pledging to vote in the upcoming election, a gift he enthusiastically accepted.

As Percy joined the family members sitting on the couch, Ike looked to the camera and thanked the organizers for arranging such a wonderful evening. He offered his deep gratitude to all the entertainers and viewers who had participated in the party. Responding to Percy's gift, the president reserved special thanks for the many Americans who "signed their names that they are determined to do their duty this fall in determining the course of America and are going to get their friends to do the same." Led by Waring's Pennsylvanians, the guests at the Statler Hotel sang "Happy Birthday" with Ike and Mamie looking on. As the program wound down, balloons fell into the ballroom's cheering crowd, an image that resembled nothing so much as the climax of a nominating convention.

A Lovely Glow upon the Family

Over half a century separates us from Ike Day, a span of time that has brought fundamental changes to how we understand television, politics, and fame.

To those of us raised on a steady diet of jump cuts, sound bites, and spe-cial effects, the tribute to Eisenhower may seem as dry and predictable as the Abilene it portrays. And yet, at the time, this transcontinental variety show was lauded as a major political event, one that successfully attracted average viewers as well as diehard Republicans. Although planned in only six weeks, the program turned out to be a critical and popular success. In 1956, 37 mil-lion households had television sets in the United States, yet an astonishing 20 million people tuned in to see the Ike Day festivities; 20 million watching Mamie join the crowd at the Statler Hotel in singing "Happy Birthday" to the president; 20 million watching Ike explain his aversion to eating breakfast in bed.[9] The figure represents nearly one-third of the 61,613,224 Americans who would vote in the November election.[10] One wonders how many view-ers actively supported Eisenhower and how many tuned in expecting to find James Arness and *Gunsmoke.*

Although virtually forgotten today, the televised tribute is a fitting intro-duction to celebrity politics in the Eisenhower era. Politicians had long asso-ciated themselves with entertainers, and from the days of abolition to the New Deal, it was not uncommon for political rallies to include popular singers performing songs and hymns meant to engage the crowd in the cause at hand.

FIGURE 1.2 *The Eisenhower family watches the Ike Day television show in the White House Library on October 13, 1956.*

Courtesy of National Park Service and Dwight D. Eisenhower Presidential Library and Museum.

In the late 1940s, television provided a similarly public experience, as viewers gathered in hotels and bars to root during a boxing match, laugh along with Milton Berle, or follow a program on current affairs. In 1950, the advertising agency BBDO calculated that "on a typical day, 11% of those without a TV and 9% of those with a TV at home" spent two hours watching television outside their home.[11] Television regularly drew viewers into an independent public sphere, a place of revelry, discussion, and debate.

With falling prices and increased consumption, however, the predominance of "tavern television" ended quickly. By 1956, nearly 72 percent of Americans had a unit in their home, and watching television became the kind of family activity that the Eisenhowers modeled on screen.[12] Television's ability to politicize domestic settings had surfaced in 1952 when Richard Nixon delivered his famous "Checkers" speech and saved his position as Eisenhower's running mate. Accompanied by his wife and speaking from a soundstage made to look like a home office or living room, Nixon opened his family's finances to a national audience that, as historian Kevin Mattson has shown, welcomed the campaign melodrama as if it were a soap opera.[13] Emphasizing the way that prudence and parenthood served as bulwarks against communism, the speech contributed to the general valorization of family life that permeated the 1950s.[14]

Four years later, the Republicans would again politicize the domestic associations of television, this time using the president's family to mirror the audience at home. When Keel and Grayson sang of their burning hearts in 1956, they were not like-minded singers providing a rousing anthem between political discussions. They were entertainers engaged in the task of completing Eisenhower's transition into the living rooms of the United States. Although ostensibly performing *for* the president, Keel and Grayson were implicitly asking viewers to connect their performance *with* the president and his wife—both the young lieutenant and his bride, whose picture graced the piano behind them, and the distinguished couple sitting in front of the White House TV. The Ike Day special brought vigor and style to the political campaign, heralding a world in which television and star power could capture the attention of potential voters in a way that politicians could not. Although no policies were discussed, the Ike Day tribute espoused a politics based on the merging of two distinct groups—the audience and the electorate. The politics of identification temporarily linked up with the politics of associative prestige.

The organizers of Ike Day were at the forefront of thinking about how to use televised entertainment as a political tool, and they hoped the program would build on the warmth and affection Americans already had for the president. As if they were fitfully aware that critics might charge them with trivializing the presidency, they sometimes downplayed the glamour that celebrities brought to the campaign. Lightly editing a press release, for example, one adviser gave the program a little more heft by eliminating references to Jimmy Stewart as a "film star" and changing "Hollywood" to "Los Angeles." A week later, however, the more neutral language disappeared, and an updated release boasted of the "gallaxy [*sic*] of stars" that would appear on the president's behalf.[15] While they struggled to come up with a consistent tone, the advisers were committed to the common goal of designing a campaign that did not forsake policy as much as it periodically exploited the advantages of withholding it.

Eisenhower's advisers had good reason to believe that their strategy would work. When Harriet Van Horne, the television critic for the *New York World-Telegram*, reviewed the program, her fascination far outweighed any wariness. The birthday tribute "may have been, as the Republicans were at pains to state, entirely non-political," she reported. "But it's hard to imagine a more effective piece of campaign strategy than the picture of the Eisenhower family, gathered in the White House library—an atmosphere at once intimate and suspicious—happily watching the TV screen."[16] Van Horne noted how effective—and composed—the setting had been, and as the phrase "intimate and suspicious" suggests, the combination led to some skepticism. But whatever misgivings the program raised, there seemed to be little doubt that this new brand of politics would survive beyond 1956. For Van Horne at least, the television placed in the library was not a source of alarm but intrigue. "This may have been a nonpolitical broadcast, but it cast a lovely glow upon the first family of the land." "The GOP," she concluded, "can consider its money well spent."[17] What Van Horne did not disclose was that she knew all about the money that had poured into the event. Her husband, David Lowe, had produced the telecast for CBS.[18]

Writing in *The Society of the Spectacle* in 1968, the influential French theorist Guy Debord railed against the domination that advertising and media capitalism had achieved in Western Europe and the United States. "The spectacle," he wrote, "is capital accumulated to the point where it becomes image."[19] In the onslaught of television, film, and magazines, Debord saw not just a collection of images but "a social relationship between people that is mediated by images."[20] From this perspective, the planning of Ike Day offers a brilliant window into the various organizations and relationships that went into celebrity politics in the Eisenhower age. Behind the president were teams of fundraisers, party officials, public relations specialists, and advertising executives eager to use the glitziest, most spectacular aspects of television to define and brand his candidacy. Although designed as a partisan celebration, Ike Day was ultimately a strategic self-portrait of the Eisenhower elite. The stars, the balloons, the oversize cake—such images not only conveyed how Ike's advisers wanted his campaign to be seen, they also established a reverent, yet seemingly familiar relationship between the public and the presidency. Ike Day captures a moment when the gathering forces of stardom, television, and advertising began to form an increasingly dominant alliance, one in which the unifying power of images could strategically supplant political dialogue and debate.

The National Ike Day Committee

Shortly after its nominating convention, the Republican Party announced the creation of the National Ike Day Committee and charged it with planning a celebration of Eisenhower's birthday that would span all forty-eight states. Coordinating with the White House, the RNC, state organizations, and the national press, the committee drew upon such publicity-driven volunteers that even their working lunch of "Eisenhower Stew" at the Mayflower Hotel generated a press release. As chairman and co-chairman, respectively, Charles Percy and Irene Dunne formed an impressive team. A four-time Academy Award nominee, Dunne had appeared in over thirty films, including the classics *Show Boat* (1936) and *I Remember Mama* (1948). A devout Catholic, she retired from the movies in 1952 and was devoting herself to television dramas and church-related charity work when she agreed to take part in the Eisenhower campaign.[21] While Dunne represented the stylish side of celebrity politics, the image at the heart of spectacle, Percy represented its moneyed interests. Percy was well known as a corporate "whiz kid," one of the many young men who came out of World War II eager to get ahead. By the age of twenty-nine, he had become the president and chief executive officer of Bell & Howell, the Chicago-based producer of phonographs, film, and movie cameras. During the fourteen years he led the company, Bell & Howell saw its sales numbers climb from $13 million to $160 million annually.[22] Eisenhower took a special interest in Percy and encouraged his political activities. When the Republicans lost seats in the 1958 midterm congressional elections, he tapped Percy to lead a committee to chart a future course for the party.[23] Dunne's reward would come more quickly. Ten months after Ike Day, the president appointed the actress as a special delegate to the United Nations General Assembly.[24]

In addition to the usual array of politicians, party supporters, and federal appointees, the twenty-one-person Ike Day Committee included some striking names. Spencer T. Olin, the heir to a conglomerate of Midwestern chemical and explosives companies, served as the finance chairman. Joining Olin was another representative of the chemical industry, Mrs. Francis V. DuPont, whose husband played a key role in inventing the interstate highway system. (Both the Olin and DuPont corporations had large contracts with the Department of Defense, though as an avid hunter and marksman, Eisenhower must have been pleased by their connection to two legendary brands of American firearms, Remington and Winchester.) General John Reed Kilpatrick, the colorful chairman of National Citizens for Eisenhower,

also served on the committee. Kilpatrick had first come to the nation's attention as an All-American football player at Yale University before serving in
World War I. He temporarily gave up his position as president of Madison
Square Garden and the New York Rangers to serve as a brigadier general in
the Second World War. Kilpatrick was joined on the committee by his fellow
Yale alumnus and MGM actor George Murphy, the man whom Steven Ross
credits with "preparing Republican politicians for the new media age."[25]

The day-to-day leadership for Ike Day fell to Tracy Voorhees, the vice chairman and director. Voorhees had left his Manhattan law firm during World
War II to accept a commission in the Judge Advocate General's office. He
quickly rose up the ranks, heading missions "to reorganize the medical supply systems" in Europe and Asia and overseeing the establishment of hospital
facilities in the United States. In 1949, President Truman nominated Voorhees
to be the Under Secretary of the Army, a post he held for four years. During
that time, he led the Army's emergency relief efforts for demobilized soldiers
and worked to set up postwar policies with Germany and Japan.[26]

In September 1956, however, Voorhees was immersed in the very different
challenge of planning a coast-to-coast celebration of the president's birthday.
From the committee's offices at 1625 I Street, a block away from the United
States Chamber of Commerce and two blocks from the White House, he
oversaw an eclectic range of responsibilities: coordinating with state organizations, directing payments, approving television scripts and publicity; and
communicating with the president, the president's wife, and the president's
press secretary. "If any one person was to be singled out for recognition,"
Percy wrote him in the weeks after Ike Day, "it would be Tracy Voorhees!
Your complete devotion for this project and willingness to work 24 hours a
day under extreme pressure made it possible for the program to be the success
that it was." As if Voorhees were one of the stars, Percy proclaimed, "My hat
is off to you for a magnificent performance!"[27]

Among Voorhees's responsibilities, perhaps the most important was hiring
the McCann-Erickson advertising agency. In contrast to Young & Rubicam
and BBDO, which put together multiple campaign events and promotional
materials, McCann-Erickson focused on Ike Day. In 1956, the agency was
well on its way to becoming the second-largest advertising company in the
country. Like Bell & Howell, McCann-Erickson owed much of its success to
its ambitious young president. Dubbed the "Hurry-Up Man" by *Time* magazine, Marion Harper had worked his way up from the mailroom to become
president of the agency at the age of thirty-two.[28] A studious, low-key executive more partial to seminars at Yale than cocktails on Madison Avenue,
he made his employees study the emerging field of semantics and stressed
the value of social science research in testing consumer behavior. By 1956,
McCann-Erickson had acquired dozens of new agencies and held such lucrative accounts as Buick, Coca-Cola, Westinghouse, Bulova, and NBC. At the

FIGURE 1.3 *Marion Harper, the president of McCann-Erickson, in 1951.*
Courtesy of McCann-Erickson.

time of Ike Day, its annual billings topped $200 million, doubling what they
were only three years earlier.[29]

On September 14, 1956, Harper and his team met with Langhorne
Washburn, the director of Eisenhower's Bandwagon Operations, to figure
out how to integrate the many local events into a unified national celebration. They settled on a series of standard operating procedures that would
send a consistent message and reach out to supporters beyond the Republican
faithful. The foremost of these activities involved the voter scrolls that played
such a key role in the television program. McCann-Erickson agreed to design
and print the scrolls (charging $21,957.97 in the process), while the League of
Women Voters distributed them across the country.[30] At supermarkets, football games, rallies, and harvest festivals, volunteers collected signatures from
an estimated three million citizens who, in honor of the president's birthday,
had pledged that they would vote. The Day itself involved thousands of public celebrations and pageants. At the White House, a boy from Naugatuck,
Connecticut presented the president with the world's largest birthday card.
Back home in Connecticut, 169 towns and cities were decorated with bunting
and posters. In Virginia, the Young Republicans held a congratulatory square

dance. At college football games in Ohio and Texas, students hung banners, yelled cheers, and sang along to the marching band tributes.[31] At the World War Memorial in Indianapolis, supporters lit candles on 1,066 birthday cakes, while 1,500 onlookers waved sparklers and sang "Happy Birthday."[32] As one might expect from his title, Washburn was attracted to large motorcades and parades, and he proposed a nationwide competition for the best float depicting the president's life of national service. Leaving no detail to chance, he insisted to Voorhees that "the word parade is ill defined unless it includes several marching bands."[33]

The task of transforming what were essentially campaign events into acts of celebration and charity fell to Katherine Howard, a longtime Eisenhower supporter and one of the committee's vice chairmen. A graduate of Smith College and the daughter of an R.J. Reynolds tobacco company executive, Howard had a long résumé of political activity. She had been Secretary of the Republican National Convention, a special adviser to the Federal Civil Defense Administration, and a US delegate to NATO, but in a sign of the times, the committee regularly listed her as "Mrs. Charles P. Howard." Under Howard's guidance, newspapers from Boston to Amarillo had printed Mamie Eisenhower's special recipe for chocolate cake with vanilla icing. State by state, women baked cakes according to the recipe and brought them to the wards of hospitals, senior homes, and veterans' institutions. The committee carefully used celebrities to publicize their civic volunteerism. Photographers captured the Chicago White Sox second baseman Nellie Fox visiting the children's ward of his hometown hospital in central Pennsylvania. Dunne was photographed decorating one of the cakes she would take to a Los Angeles children's hospital. The day concluded with a final act of collective celebration. Supporters across the country threw television parties in which friends gathered to watch the tribute and eat a slice of the president's favorite cake.[34]

The plans for some of the local parties were ambitious. In Wisconsin, Minnesota, and Connecticut, supporters rented halls for youth-oriented dances and filled them with television sets, voter registration booths, and refreshments. A member of Washburn's staff put together a handbook for state and local committees, urging them to be both pragmatic and creative in seeking corporate sponsorship. "Try to have some bakery donate as large a cake as possible to be presented during the festivities," she advised. "If possible, get some company like Pepsi Cola to donate drinks." (Anticipating skepticism, she added, "This *is* possible.") In addition to dancing, door prizes, and fashion shows, the celebrations featured politically themed carnival games: pin the tail on the (Democratic) donkey, throw a dart at an Adlai Stevenson balloon, knock the trademark coonskin cap off of his running mate, Estes Kefauver. With their elaborate organizational structure—there were decorations committees, sign committees, pastry and jewelry booth chairmen—the parties seemed to represent the best of grassroots volunteerism, middle America

FIGURE 1.4 *The National Ike Day Committee combined the media appeal of celebrity with an extensive grassroots outreach program.*
Nelson Rockefeller Collection, Courtesy of the Rockefeller Archive Center.

arranged into responsibility charts and devoted to the common enterprise of publicly liking Ike. And yet, amid all the folksy resourcefulness, the RNC hoped that glamour would magically descend on towns like Duluth and Green Bay and that, at some point in the evening, the program committee would introduce the "famous personalities and celebrities and honored guests."[35]

Organized under the banner "Youth Salutes the President," the celebration in Washington, DC, was more elaborate. In a widely read editorial, the *New York Herald Tribune* had suggested that Republicans needed to identify themselves with youth and the future of the country. The organizers of the DC event (which included Mamie's nephew) seized upon the editorial in proposing that they personally come to the White House, in the company of six Ike Girls and the press, to deliver the president's invitation to their party. Over the next two weeks, Washburn helped the organization plan its events with the aim of maximizing publicity and reminding the nation of Ike's service. The festivities began on October 13 with a parade in which college groups from Washington, DC, New York, Maryland, Virginia, Massachusetts, and Illinois built floats depicting different phases of Eisenhower's life. The political class had little patience for rock 'n' roll, but in a nod to youth culture, the parade culminated not in a duet by Keel and Grayson but in a live "jam session" with the Booker Coleman Jazzmen.[36]

Following Washburn's recommendations, the evening gala at the Statler Hotel also focused on Young Republican and college groups. In addition to Fred Waring and the Pennsylvanians, the Barnee Breeskin orchestra played throughout the party. Although Washburn had to scale back his hopes of recruiting Bob Hope and Ed Sullivan for the job, a pair of roving reporters interviewed people in the crowd, some famous such as Helen Hayes and Eddie Fisher, others less well-known, such as the identical twins from Rock Island, Illinois, who would sing at the president's inauguration.[37] From the beginning, Washburn insisted that Ike Day should "strike the hearts and minds of all Americans," and he designed the gala to reinforce that aim. At 9:05, violinists on special scaffolding spelled out the word "Eisenhower" with fluorescent lights. At 9:20, two 20-foot portraits of the president and his wife were unveiled. At 9:33, a seven-minute film, which Washburn described as an "impact vehicle," traced Eisenhower's "singular life of service" and injected "near spiritual content" into the evening.[38]

In the end, however, Washburn's efforts to spiritualize Eisenhower were no match for the party's most spectacular feature. With their bandstands decorated to look like birthday candles, the Barnee Breeskin orchestra played on top of a massive 2,000-pound cake, which, at the rate of one revolution per minute, turned throughout the evening. Donated by a local baker and prepared according to Mamie's recipe, the cake was a stunningly garish symbol of the thousands of cakes that volunteers had distributed throughout the country. Extending from eight feet tall to thirty feet wide, the giant confection undoubtedly caused many logistical headaches, but Washburn took pride in the attention it received. "We have heard from the White House and the Republican National Committee," he wrote a colleague, "and from many people who were in the audience that the highlight of the evening was the dramatic rendition of music and singing which emanated from the revolving cake."[39]

FIGURE 1.5 *Irene Dunne posing with a birthday cake prepared according to Mamie Eisenhower's special recipe.*
Courtesy of National Park Service and Dwight D. Eisenhower Presidential Library and Museum.

Although it consulted with Washburn on many of these details, McCann-Erickson primarily focused on writing, producing, and promoting the half-hour program that aired on CBS. Harper and his staff knew the promotional value of entertainment, and they convinced the Ike Day Committee that a variety show with musical acts would do better in the Nielsen ratings than a film clip designed to deepen the nation's affection for Ike.[40] In addition to meeting the president's approval, the tactic fit with the idea that the program should separate the civic ritual of voting from active electioneering, and that the entertainment should be free of partisan content. Written by McCann-Erickson's Robert Smock and produced by CBS's David Lowe, the program assiduously followed these guidelines as it integrated the Hollywood and Statler Hotel performances with the White House family interviews. Although the agency did not presume to write the president's speech, it scripted lines for Percy, Stewart, Hayes, and everyone else who appeared on screen. The cost of all these services—script writing, news releases, press kits, poster design and production, hotels, entertainment, multiple flights to Los Angeles and Washington, DC quickly added up. In the end, the bill came to $218, 412.46, roughly $1.8 million today.[41]

Democracy in Action

Undergirding all the puffery and spectacle of Ike Day lay a surprisingly firm foundation of capital and fundraising. Having served as Eisenhower's Special Assistant for Foreign Affairs from 1954–1956, Nelson Rockefeller was in regular touch with the committee, and his long history with McCann-Erickson may have led to the agency's being hired. McCann-Erickson had handled the Rockefeller Center account for years, and its offices were housed in the complex, just minutes away from the family's headquarters. An heir to the Standard Oil fortune, Rockefeller played a critical role in fundraising. After consulting with their accountant, he and his family donated over $9,000 to the Ike Day celebration—besting the Olin family, which contributed $6,000. The committee insisted that it was not a political organization, but "out of excess of caution," it submitted a list of its major backers to Congress in accord with the Federal Corrupt Practices Acts. The list included the head of General Mills, the head of Owens-Corning Fiberglass, the head of the Spencer Chemical Company, and the DuPont family. Overall, the committee collected some $200,000 in donations, enough to broadcast on 189 television and 360 radio stations.[42]

The money and attention affirmed political bonds that would extend into the next decade. Displaying the personal touch that had endeared him to many successful men and women, Ike wrote Rockefeller directly, saying that he was "not only highly complimented, but greatly pleased" that the Rockefeller family had contributed so much to the birthday party. "As always," he wrote, "I am indebted to you—and I hope you will pass along to your brothers an expression of my deep thanks."[43] Rockefeller's response was equally gushing. "No one but you, in the midst of a magnificent campaign and the most extraordinary world situation, would be so thoughtful as to write as you did." "All of our thoughts are with you," Rockefeller closed, "in these days of trial and triumph."[44]

No matter how frivolous the final product, the committee proved to be a veritable training ground for political and government careers. Rockefeller himself would serve as Governor of New York from 1959–1973 and succeed Gerald Ford as Vice President in 1974. Actor George Murphy had been involved in Republican politics since the 1940s. Serving on the Ike Day Committee and arranging talent for the television program added to his long list of campaign activities. After frequently joking that politicians were ill equipped for the public stage, he himself ran for office in 1964, winning a Senate seat from California. Katherine Howard remained with the Civil Defense Administration through the end of the year, but in 1957, Eisenhower named her the Deputy US Commissioner General to the Brussels World Fair. In the latter days of the presidential campaign, news of the Budapest uprising in Hungary began to rock the world, and on November 4, the Soviet military entered the city to dispel the demonstrations. The invasion sent several hundred thousand refugees into Austria and Yugoslavia. Fresh off the logistical challenges of Ike Day, Voorhees was appointed Eisenhower's personal representative for Hungarian Refugee Relief. Working across international, federal, and state agencies, he would oversee the evacuation and relocation of 32,000 refugees to Camp Kilmer, New Jersey. In six months, Voorhees helped all of them settle in communities across the United States.[45]

Eisenhower took a particular interest in helping young men such as Percy and Harper who had rapidly advanced in their careers. Perhaps because they reminded him of his own life story, he looked for ways to bring executives with modest beginnings into positions of greater and greater responsibility. With the president's blessing, Percy would become chairman of the 1960 Republican platform committee and would soon contemplate running for office. After a failed gubernatorial bid, he was elected to the US Senate, representing Illinois, in 1966 and served for eighteen years, the last four of which he chaired the Senate Foreign Relations Committee. Ike Day's other whiz kid, Marion Harper, earned Eisenhower's admiration for a series of *New York Times* advertisements his agency had created promoting better science education and funding in the aftermath of the Soviet Union's launching of the satellite *Sputnik*.[46] Though he had few political allegiances and was not close to the president, Harper used the Ike Day telecast to connect with Republicans across the country. McCann-Erickson would go on to develop advertisements for Nelson Rockefeller's and Ronald Reagan's gubernatorial campaigns.[47]

An event such as Ike Day may seem like a diversion from actual politics, but spectacles are not simply a trick of bread and circuses. As Debord describes them, spectacles embody the power relations they seem to escape; they provide new, receptive arenas in which commercial and political interests can operate. "By means of the spectacle," he explains, "the ruling order discourses endlessly upon itself in an uninterrupted monologue of self-praise."[48] On the most basic level, Ike Day was a pleasant addition to the campaign and a harmless way to keep presidential and corporate power in place. At the same time, it promoted a vision of wealth and success in the United States that neatly matched the trajectory of entrepreneurs such as Percy and Harper. Although it was partially funded by members of the Rockefeller, DuPont, and Olin families, the Ike Day telecast praised Eisenhower's rise from humble roots to his leading role on the world stage. The picture of the family homes in Denison and Abilene, the shots of the creamery where he worked and the church where he prayed, even the photograph of him punting a football on the West Point team—all these images conveyed a vision of Ike as the standard bearer of upward mobility. Juxtaposed with his presence in the White House library, they suggested how a life of humble service could lead to international renown and grave responsibilities. Though the grandfatherly Ike was

FIGURE 1.6 *Charles Percy presents President Eisenhower with* Decisions for a Better America, *a report from the special committee he chaired that was charged with charting a new path for the Republican Party. With them on the left is Kentucky senator Thurston Morton.*

Courtesy of National Park Service and Dwight D. Eisenhower Presidential Library and Museum.

not a whiz kid like the men who publicized his birthday, he was seemingly eager to build an America in which young talents could rise to the top of their fields, creating wealth and opportunity for themselves and their country. At the heart of Ike Day lay the dream of bureaucratic capitalism: the organization man who rises from the mailroom to the boardroom to the highest offices in Washington, DC.

Ike's associates recognized the ideological value of the broadcast, and they readily concluded that this story of affection and aspiration was a story that the United States would want to tell about itself—not just to viewers in San Francisco and Kansas City, but around the world. In the heady, congratulatory weeks after it aired, the organizers talked about how the program could be used internationally. Percy showed the tribute to some visiting English friends who commented on "the magical effect of the Eisenhower name in England and how the British are always looking for the human interest aspects of their own royalty and other world leaders." From his office in Chicago, he asked Voorhees to send a kinescope to England for broadcast over the BBC.[49] Eight days later, Voorhees reported to Rockefeller that he was preparing to give the program to the United States Information Service for broadcast overseas, where viewers would appreciate its portrait of "democracy in action and the warmer side of the US and its President."[50] Voorhees couldn't have found a better audience for this news. Rockefeller had been a strong advocate for "public diplomacy" since the 1930s, when he took a job in the Roosevelt Administration distributing pro-US advertisements in Latin America. Now the Ike Day telecast was taking its place as part of the Cold War propaganda machine.[51]

The keys to integrating all these power relations and ideological themes were celebrities, the media stars whom Debord described as "spectacular representations of living human beings."[52] In contrast to other well-known Republicans such as the comic Bob Hope or the leathery cowboy John Wayne, the choice of Jimmy Stewart to host the Ike Day television special suited the campaign's desire to associate the president with humility, consensus, and grassroots democracy. As both a political symbol and box office attraction, Stewart possessed tremendous marquee value. In 1940, he won an Oscar for *The Philadelphia Story*, and since then, he had become one of the United States's most admired actors. As effective in a Hitchcock thriller as he was in a Western, he lent Ike Day a combination of respect and likeability that few stars could provide. But Stewart brought more to the program than stardust. To many he seemed a quintessentially decent and honest American, the epitome of small-town values.

Although he rarely talked about it, the actor had enlisted in the Army Air Corps after the bombing of Pearl Harbor and insisted that he be sent overseas. Piloting a B-24 bomber, he flew combat missions over Germany and later participated in the liberation of France. Stewart returned from Europe a decorated war hero and newly promoted colonel. Recent scholarship suggests that the war had a bigger impact on Stewart's selection of roles than was previously thought and that we see its effects in such highly acclaimed films as *Rope* (1948), *Rear Window* (1954), and the incomparable *Vertigo* (1958).[53] The actor took significant pains, however, to reinforce his image as a self-effacing common man. When he returned from World War II, he promptly took the role of George Bailey in *It's a Wonderful Life* (1946). Bailey, we will remember, struggles to understand that his humble dedication to the people of Bedford Falls has been as valuable and heroic as the military valor of his younger brother. After seeing the film, President Harry Truman remarked, "If Bess and I had a son, we'd want him to be just like Jimmy Stewart."[54]

By 1956, Jimmy Stewart was a cultural icon whose image tapped into a network of patriotic memories and values. His participation in the Ike Day tribute effectively lent the Eisenhower campaign the virtuous, Everyman persona that had been the hallmark of his movie career. While there are traces of George Bailey in his syrupy description of Abilene, Stewart would have reminded viewers of another Frank Capra film: *Mr. Smith Goes to Washington*

(1939). The role of Jefferson Smith epitomized the tendency of studios to cast Stewart as "the upholder of community values, the character who," as Jim Cullen puts it, carries the "torch of institutionalism" in the film.[55]

With Stewart as its host, the Ike Day tribute was infused with *Mr. Smith*'s story of an idealistic young senator whose faith in the nation's founding principles exposes a corrupt political machine. Like countless politicians after him, Eisenhower must have been eager to associate himself with Stewart's inspirational character. The script turns Jefferson Smith into an amalgam of appealing cultural archetypes—he is David fighting Goliath; he is Daniel Boone in the wilderness; and perhaps most significantly, he is the defender of Jeffersonian idealism in cynical Washington. Awakened to cronyism, graft, and an irresponsible press, Smith continues to revere the democratic vision of Washington, Jefferson, and Lincoln. Though the insiders treat it as a joke, we know to trust Smith when he goes on a pilgrimage to George Washington's Mount Vernon estate before his first day in the Senate. At a bleak moment later in the film, he makes a late-night visit to the Lincoln Memorial where he resolves to fight the forces conspiring against him. Steadied by his respect for history and ethics, Smith manages to cleanse the Senate of its impurities and create hope for political renewal.

That hope is captured in the film's repeated confidence in boys. Back home in the West, Smith was the leader of the Boy Rangers, and in Washington, the pages immediately gravitate to him. Not unlike Stewart (who was regularly addressed as Jimmy), Jefferson Smith embodies the unsullied charm of the simple, almost boyish man. He arrives in Washington with carrier pigeons for a schoolboy experiment. He naïvely entertains the press corps with his birdcalls and whistles. Capra and Stewart knew how to turn Smith's sexual inexperience into a sign of genuineness and sincerity. He hems, haws, and fiddles with his hat when he talks to a pretty girl. He unwittingly courts his hard-boiled secretary, Clarissa Saunders (Jean Arthur), when he speaks about his mother's homemade jam.

Smith's virtue is contagious in a fraudulent Washington, and his political idealism revives a youthful, patriotic innocence. In the film's climactic scene, Smith delivers a marathon filibuster that ends in his collapse, but it also provokes a corrupt politician (played by Claude Rains) to publicly acknowledge his sins. Smith succeeds at both redeeming the Senate and winning Clarissa's heart, but she does not reward him with a romantic kiss. Seated among the pageboys cheering for "good old Jeff," Clarissa delivers the movie's final line— the exuberant, childlike exclamation "Yippee!"

Stewart contributed some of this faith in youth and boyhood to the Ike Day telecast. With its cake-bearing nine-year old, dried-up swimming hole, and alluring movie stars, the program fused a nostalgia for a lost past with an appreciation for the vigor and vitality of commercial life. In the voices of Keel and Grayson, warbling across a replica of the Eisenhower family home,

FIGURE 1.7 *Jimmy Stewart talks with President Eisenhower on the Ike Day television broadcast on CBS.*
Courtesy of Special Collections and University Archives, Rutgers University Libraries.

the audience heard capitalism's seemingly endless capacity to reinvent itself, to present consumers with new and improved products for new and improved desires.

While McCann-Erickson knew how to emphasize a product's superior effectiveness, they used celebrities to move the president away from partisan politics and toward the broader appeal of spectacle and consumption. As did their counterparts on Madison Avenue, the executives assumed that electing a president was as much a choice of lifestyle as it was a choice of policy. Although Stewart refrained from playing the wide-eyed Mr. Smith during the Ike Day program, his presence recalled the film's sentimental ideals. With his easy charm and all-American manner, he reinforced the president's image as a trans-political man, a grandfather who smiled upon the endless vitality of the nation's citizens and spectators. As Jefferson Smith, Stewart embodied how celebrity politics would function in Eisenhower's campaigns. Exchanging the divisiveness of federal policy for the idealism of television and the movies, events such as Ike Day did not represent a step away from contests of democratic power and legitimacy: they represented a moment when politicians came to recognize the advantage of waging politics by other, more glamorous means.

The RNC viewed the famous as potential weapons in a battle they pretended not to fight, the battle to make popular culture an expression of political allegiance. Stewart, Cagney, Dunne, and Hayes lent the campaign vibrancy, fashion, and a certain familiarity.[56] They offered the president a form of populist endorsement that was rooted in the orientation of an audience that would take that endorsement seriously. Stardom created the illusion that the nation was coming together in gratitude for the president's lifelong service. Although few had trouble seeing through the ruse, their skepticism had little effect. Around the country, commentators recognized that something new was taking place. Television, advertising, and celebrity had changed the game of electioneering, and the Republicans were far ahead. As a reporter from *Variety* put it, the changes were here to stay: "Just what the Dems can do to counter this is a toughie, but they'd better do something."[57]

Riding the Roosevelt Special

Speaking to the Women's National Democratic Club on October 15, 1956, George Ball objected to the hoopla surrounding Ike Day. The Republicans, he argued, were substituting a "cult of personality" for "earnest debate," and never before had their attitude toward average Americans been so clear: "Let 'em eat cake." Ball coordinated public relations for Adlai Stevenson's presidential campaign, and as he led his audience through the many television programs the Republicans had broadcast over the previous two weeks, he contrasted what he called the "incense" arising from Ike Day with the annual birthday parties held from 1934–1945 to honor Franklin D. Roosevelt. "President Roosevelt's birthday," he noted, "was celebrated by the nation for the first time in a non-election year. And it was celebrated to start a drive against polio." Recalling that the FDR celebrations helped fund the March of Dimes and Dr. Jonas Salk's discovery of a polio vaccine, Ball asked (and then informed) his audience what the meaning of Ike's "birthday Saturnalia" had been. "It has been played strictly for hearts and flowers; and it has had but one purpose—the glorification of one of the Republican candidates at a time when his party leaders know that he is facing a very tough fight."[1]

Ball was being optimistic in claiming that Eisenhower was in for a battle; by the middle of October, the president had a commanding lead and was ready to dismiss Stevenson outright. "This fellow's licked," he told his son before heading off to the World Series, "and what's more he knows it!"[2] Sure enough, when November arrived, Eisenhower won comfortably with 457 votes in the Electoral College and 57 percent of the popular vote.[3] However, the contrast Ball set up between the two presidents was illuminating, for the Eisenhower tribute was closely modeled after the charity birthday balls that arose during Roosevelt's presidency. As with Ike Day, the FDR celebrations involved a network of local events that stretched across the country. As with Ike Day, they were anchored by a series of well-publicized, celebrity-themed parties in Washington, DC. Ball believed that, in fêting Eisenhower on national television, the Republicans were adapting a popular Democratic idea to a powerful new medium that substituted glamour and stagecraft for altruism and authenticity. The distinctions between the FDR and Ike events, he argued, offered insight into each party's priorities: one focused on helping the unfortunate, the other on worshipping personalities.

Roosevelt became involved in raising money for polio research after he was diagnosed with the disease in 1921, at the age of 39. In 1927, he established a care facility for polio victims in Warm Springs, Georgia. Like many charitable foundations, the facility faced serious financial difficulties throughout the 1930s. As president, Roosevelt gave his blessing to a group of supporters who wanted to organize a network of birthday balls to honor him by raising funds for polio research and treatment. Each January, they hosted balls in Washington, DC and, with the help of local postmasters, thousands of communities held their own birthday festivities, keeping a portion of the funds for local efforts and sending the rest to the national committee. The events were successful, and even though it was the height of the Depression, the January 1934 event netted $1,016,444.[4] As the events grew more elaborate and the focus expanded beyond Warm Springs, the President's Birthday Ball Commission evolved into the National Foundation for Infantile Paralysis and then later the March of Dimes. The Birthday Ball in Washington expanded to include lunches, dinners, entertainment, and research panels.

Many individuals and organizations contributed to the Foundation's success. In 1944, for example, the Bakers International Union provided a cake for the Washington Ball, with fifty-nine candles, each containing a check for $100. Eddie Cantor, the radio comedian who coined the phrase "march of dimes," dedicated hours of airtime to the cause. Hollywood played an important role in raising money, and Joseph Schenck, the chairman of the board of Twentieth Century Fox, was a member of the Foundation's organizing committee. Movie studios contributed short films about the polio threat, and theater owners collected contributions from their patrons. In 1944, they gave $4,667,520.56 to the National Foundation and its local chapters.[5]

A key part of each birthday celebration was a benefit show in which stars such as Guy Lombardo, Margaret Sullavan, Mickey Rooney, Gene Autry, Betty Grable, and Lucille Ball appeared. Commensurate with the emerging significance of motion pictures in American life, the reception for the participating stars grew each year. In 1938, Eleanor Roosevelt hosted a Saturday luncheon for thirteen movie stars. In 1941, fifty-nine stars and their guests were invited, and the president himself attended. By 1944, the luncheon had grown to about eighty people, and a formal seating chart indicated that the president was to be seated between opera singer Lily Pons and silent film star Mary Pickford. From their inception, the parties culminated in a dinner that focused on the achievement of doctors and researchers; the stars, in fact, were not included in this event. In 1944, the Foundation changed course, adding a new event titled "A Dinner for Movie Stars," hosted by Red Skelton. The

FIGURE 2.1 *Eleanor Roosevelt and celebrity guests at one of the Birthday Balls created to raise money for polio research in 1944. Guests include Red Skelton, William Douglas, Lucille Ball, and John Garfield.*

Courtesy of National Park Service and Franklin D. Roosevelt Presidential Library and Museum, 72-18-325.

evening's slickly produced program featured publicity photographs of the talented men and women attending.[6]

Ike Day transferred the charitable spirit of the Birthday Balls to the heat of the presidential race. Several of Eisenhower's most prominent supporters were alumni of the polio crusade. Walt Disney produced a cartoon in which Mickey Mouse led a parade of animated characters singing "Hi Ho, Hi Ho / We'll lick that polio"; Edgar Guest read poems about the polio fight on his weekly NBC radio program. Jimmy Stewart would have known how closely the glittering performances and charity work of Ike Day resembled FDR's Birthday Balls. In 1942, Stewart had attended the White House luncheon in his military uniform, and later that evening, he appeared at one of the benefit galas taking place across Washington, DC. Among the stars joining him was Robert Montgomery, the actor who eventually became Eisenhower's television consultant and one of Ronald Reagan's mentors. As the White House staff certainly knew, in 1940 Montgomery had been an organizing member of Hollywood's "We the People Committee" that supported Republican presidential nominee, Wendell Willkie.[7]

This bipartisan roster underscored the fact that Roosevelt's birthday galas were not tied to the election calendar and the stars were not invited to brand him as a candidate. Stars like Rooney, Grable, and Stewart were useful in raising money and public consciousness, but they saw their efforts as being altruistic rather than partisan, focused more on children and medicine than on the president. Roosevelt himself was careful to maintain his distance from the festivities. He rarely attended the dinners and performances, and he appeared at the star luncheons infrequently. Taking its cue from the president, the press focused less on the presence of stars than on the children who had fallen victim to the disease. Celebrities may have been useful in attracting local attention, but in the hierarchy of White House social planning and publicity, doctors, researchers, and juvenile victims were the most honored guests.

Though the Democrats claimed otherwise, FDR's birthday parties were not apolitical events. The members of the Birthday Commission had strong ties to the president, and the postmasters who ran the local community balls were political appointees, well-ensconced members of the Democratic machine. In the midst of all the charitable fundraising, Republicans vociferously objected to the coupling of a national cause with the valorization of a highly controversial president. The wife of one leading Republican commented that she would give money to the March of Dimes any day of the year *but* Roosevelt's birthday, which she considered to be "a sad day in American history."[8]

Ball's comments were especially misleading, however, in implying that celebrities had not played a role in Roosevelt's presidential campaigns. Even as he poked fun at Stewart, Waring, and Hayes, Ball said nothing about the many stars who had regularly come to Roosevelt's aid, a list that included Bette Davis, Frank Sinatra, Orson Welles, Humphrey Bogart, Benny Goodman, Helen Gahagan Douglas, and Count Basie. Driven by strong ideological commitments, they supported the New Deal and the fight against fascism overseas. They appeared in radio broadcasts. They performed and gave speeches at political rallies to support their candidate. Hidden in the background of Ball's political swipes was the fact that since 1947, when Republicans took control of Congress, the House Un-American Activities Committee (HUAC) had been investigating the activities of liberal celebrities during the Roosevelt administration.[9] Events such as Ike Day challenged nearly two decades of highly partisan activity from both right- and left-wing celebrities.

The Rise of Hollywood

Before the highly coordinated media productions arranged for Roosevelt and Eisenhower, a Chicago advertising executive named Albert Lasker came up with the idea that celebrities could make presidential campaigns more entertaining and appealing for newspaper reporters.[10] An impresario as much as he was an executive, Lasker was the force behind the morning of August 24, 1920, when jazz singer Al Jolson led a group of fifty Broadway stars to Marion, Ohio, where Warren Harding, the Republican presidential nominee, was in the midst of his Front Porch campaign. Republicans had developed the Front Porch campaign in 1896 when William McKinley was running for office. The basic strategy was for the candidate to stay at home while his opponent spent millions of dollars traveling the country seeking votes. Front Porch campaigns made a show of a candidate's appearing folksy and low-key, though they only worked if the national press reported his responses to a steady stream of visitors. When Lasker brought the Chicago Cubs to visit Harding, the *New York Times* dutifully printed the candidate's baseball-themed attack on Woodrow Wilson; Harding claimed Wilson had "struck out" during the peace negotiations at Versailles.[11]

Merging the tradition of the circus and political parades, Jolson's appearance in Marion, Ohio, earned considerable publicity. At the encouragement of Harding's wife, Florence, the performers had taken the train from New York City, and at the Marion train station, they met up with a 100-piece marching band from Chicago.[12] After breakfast, the crew of singers, dancers, and musicians paraded to Harding's home on Mount Vernon Avenue, where three to four thousand people were waiting.[13] The *Washington Post* noted that the crowd extended for over a hundred yards, and the trees were filled with children perched on the branches to get a better look at the festivities. As president of the "Harding and Coolidge Theatrical League," Jolson served as the emcee for a two-hour show that included songs, impersonations, and theatrical stunts. At the end, he debuted a song he had composed for the occasion:

> We think the country's ready for a man like Teddy.
> One who is a fighter through and through;
> We need another Lincoln to do the nation's thinking—
> And Mr. Harding we've selected you.

The crowd joined in on the chorus:

> Harding lead the GOP;
> Harding, on to victory.
> We're here to make a fuss;
> Mr. Harding you're the man for us.[14]

The *Washington Post* praised Jolson's visit as "one of the most remarkable demonstrations perhaps that has ever come to a nominee for President."[15] Although the newspapers buzzed about his "Jazz Campaign," Harding explained his platform in theatrical terms.[16] With Jolson standing beside him, he spoke of the "great likeness between political life under popular government and many of our most successful productions on the stage." "Our American popular government,"

Harding continued, "ought not to be a one-lead or a one-star drama of modern civilization." Drawing on his experience as an amateur actor, he offered a critique of Wilson's foreign policy. "We have been drifting lately under one-lead activities, and I am sure the American people are going to welcome a change of the bill." Harding concluded that both politics and theater required an ensemble of talents working together rather than a few self-important stars. A successful company, like a successful administration, depended on everyone doing their part.[17] Although the metaphor may have been forced, Harding tapped into a long-standing idea that American politics was a show created by and for the democratic masses. As president, he promised, he would supply an "all-star cast presenting America to all the world."[18]

The *New York Times's* reaction to the visit was willfully positive. The paper devoted a sixty-line editorial to parsing the significance of the "Harding and Coolidge Theatrical League." It found the performers "charming" and the afternoon a "blithesome interlude" in the campaign, though it strained to find hidden ironies in Jolson's lyrics. As if it were a dark cloud on the horizon, the *Times* acknowledged that critics might see in Harding's remarks a fitting metaphor for the Senate's faded stars. "A jaundiced caviler might suggest that Mr. Harding's idea of popular government is the old reliable Senate stock company, full of veteran, robustious players, and differing from all other troupes in that it insists on managing, not being managed." The *Times* had little patience for such skepticism and dismay. "Away with such leaden-paced and crabbed thoughts!" it commanded. "Marion's Players Day was a vision, a delight and a desire." But the writers may have been suffering from star fever themselves. After the festivities, the Harding campaign had invited reporters to join the Broadway visitors for a chicken dinner. As if the afternoon promised only healing and good will, they held the picnic at a homeopathic sanatorium.[19]

Jolson was convinced that theater groups could make useful contributions to presidential campaigns. Four years later, he led another Broadway contingent to the White House to greet Calvin Coolidge, who had taken office after Harding's untimely death. Sounding a theme that artists would return to through the years, Jolson speculated, "We members of the theatre are perhaps in more intimate touch with the people than any other profession." In Jolson's version of celebrity politics, actors and actresses made their living by understanding human emotion and enacting it on stage. Their endorsement carried weight because, unlike the members of other professions, they were engaged in the fundamentally populist activity of mirroring the human activity they explored each day. Jolson's vision may strike us as naïve and self-flattering, especially in its assumption that acting superseded other forms of political communication, but the Republican National Committee obviously valued his support. A congressional investigation later revealed that, having seen Jolson's success in Ohio, the committee had secretly funded the trip.[20]

Although the tone of celebrity politics would change considerably, Jolson's trips to Ohio and Washington, anticipated the kind of organized political support that celebrities would offer politicians throughout the twentieth century. As if he were contending for a dual legacy, this founding member of the Republican Theatrical League joined scores of Broadway and Hollywood stars eight years later in openly backing Roosevelt. The president's larger-than-life personality, combined with his tenure in office, helped him establish a close relationship with the burgeoning industry. Hollywood was eager to help the president out of respect for the battles he seemed personally to wage against infantile paralysis, economic collapse, and fascism in Europe. To many, his political fortunes dramatically aligned with the fate of American life.

Roosevelt's correspondence reveals Hollywood's extraordinary hunger for recognition and the president's skill in using that hunger to his advantage. The Academy of Motion Picture Arts and Sciences, for example, repeatedly invited Roosevelt to participate in its annual awards show, but year after year, he declined. In a surprising move, he agreed to deliver a radio address as part of the thirteenth annual Academy Awards in February 1941. The crisis in Europe had been weighing heavily on the president's mind. German bombers had been attacking Great Britain for months, most recently obliterating the Swansea town center. The Nazis had opened Auschwitz the previous year, and the deportation of Europe's Jews had begun. Roosevelt used the Awards ceremony to talk about the value of motion pictures in projecting an image of democracy overseas: "We have seen the American motion picture become foremost in the world," Roosevelt remarked. "We have seen it reflect our civilization throughout the rest of the world—the aims and aspirations and ideals of a free people and of freedom." Tying the film industry to national defense, he praised the Academy for the service it could render "in promoting solidarity among all the people of the Americas." Hollywood, he suggested, could have a quasi-diplomatic role in providing an important ideological complement to the military's might. The film industry joyfully embraced this vision of itself, and by October, a string of Detroit theaters had secured the White House's permission to use excerpts from the address in a promotional trailer.[21]

The speech was a prelude to Roosevelt's decision after Pearl Harbor to turn Hollywood into a wartime industry by organizing the studios under the Office of the Coordinator of Government Films. Almost immediately, studios began to produce war-themed movies that promoted the virtues of American democracy and rallied citizens at home. (These films starred a number of celebrities who would assume prominent roles in the politics of the next decade, including Humphrey Bogart in 1942's drama *Casablanca* and Irving Berlin, Ronald Reagan, and George Murphy in the 1943 musical comedy *This Is the Army*.) Stars also participated in massive fundraising efforts. Bob Hope headlined a short that included Judy Garland, Dorothy Lamour, Frank Sinatra, and Harpo Marx, all encouraging Americans to buy war bonds.[22]

Bette Davis proposed that the United Service Organizations (USO) could sell pictures of stars for a penny and autographs for a nickel to raise money for the troops.[23] Pin-up photographs of actresses such as Betty Grable and Ava Gardner were sold to GIs. In what amounted to the first USO tour in American history, Jolson logged some 40,000 miles traveling from Alaska, to Sicily, to Morocco to entertain troops at military bases. On the domestic front, the Hollywood Victory Caravan toured the country, putting on benefit shows. At their request, the president wired the group his gratitude for their service, claiming that their optimism was the spirit that would help him win the war.[24]

Celebrity Partisans

Celebrities stepped up their involvement in Roosevelt's political campaigns after his decision to seek an unprecedented third term met with substantial resistance. Representing nearly 200 actors, actresses, directors, producers, and industry executives, the Hollywood for Roosevelt Committee organized a stunning range of activities in support of the president's controversial reelection. The committee placed advertisements in the New York, Chicago, and Los Angeles newspapers and supplied screen personalities for private and public events. Edward G. Robinson and his wife, Gladys, hosted a campaign reception at their Beverly Hills home, while movie stars were dispatched to mass meetings in Long Beach, Santa Barbara, and Riverside. Although it focused on California, the committee sent speakers such as Dorothy Parker, Douglas Fairbanks, Jr., and John Garfield to cities outside the state. Claude Rains gave radio addresses in New York, Chicago, and Philadelphia, while Melvyn Douglas toured the country giving speeches.[25]

Douglas's wife, former actress Helen Gahagan Douglas, threw herself into the 1940 campaign like no other, and by one estimate, she gave over 250 speeches on behalf of the Roosevelt-Wallace ticket.[26] Helen had been one of Broadway's shining stars in the 1920s and early 1930s, and she followed up her success by becoming a professional opera singer in Europe. When she and her husband, Melvyn, moved to California to join the film industry, they became deeply involved in the Democratic Party. FDR admired Douglas's political instincts, and with his encouragement, she ran for Congress in 1944, winning the seat which represented the largely black and Hispanic district of downtown Los Angeles. Despite the objections of Los Angeles newspapers (which characterized her as a Hollywood carpetbagger), Douglas was a formidable member of Congress, and she won reelection in 1946 and 1948 before losing a highly contested senate race against a Red-baiting Richard Nixon.[27]

The Roosevelt campaign did not oversee the Hollywood for Roosevelt Committee, but as with the studio heads, the committee hoped the president would acknowledge their special contribution. They sent FDR copies of their advertisement in the *New York Times*. They sought special congratulatory telegrams to read at their victory dinners. Six weeks after the election, the Motion Picture Division of the Democratic National Committee sent FDR a certificate naming him an honorary member of his own presidential campaign. Each of these letters produced a perfunctory response, with the president offering his Hollywood supporters the same gratitude and appreciation he offered other labor organizations. The letter dispatched to the Hollywood for Roosevelt Committee was nearly identical to the ones Roosevelt sent to the United Taxi Council of Greater New York and the United Retail, Wholesale, and Department Store Employees of America. The message was that every supporter and every industry deserved the same expression of gratitude.[28]

While Roosevelt was not inclined to court famous supporters, the country itself had become accustomed to highly partisan, activist stars. The experience of the Great Depression and the rising significance of fascism and communism overseas had politicized American cultural life, producing an abundance of notable men and women who openly identified themselves as political beings. From Charlie Chaplin to Oscar Hammerstein, a large number of cultural figures associated with the broad-based leftist movement known as the Popular Front. The Popular Front was especially strong in California, and many of Roosevelt's Hollywood supporters found a political home in this loose coalition of anti-fascists, fervent New Dealers, workers, unionists, liberals, progressives, radicals, Communist sympathizers and party operatives. Other Americans such as Gary Cooper, Cecil B. DeMille, and Hedda Hopper affiliated themselves with right-wing movements.[29] Charles Lindbergh, who had charmed the world in 1927 when he flew across the Atlantic Ocean, made several highly publicized trips to Nazi Germany.

The most prominent Hollywood conservative of the period was Louis B. Mayer, the head of Metro-Goldwyn-Mayer (MGM) studios. Steven Ross has described Mayer as the man "who brought the Republican Party to Hollywood and Hollywood to the Republican Party."[30] A Russian immigrant who claimed he was born on the Fourth of July, Mayer forged a strong relationship with Republican politicians during the 1920s. He frequently invited political figures—such as Calvin Coolidge, Herbert Hoover, and Winston Churchill—to tour the MGM studios, and he increased their exposure by having them photographed with its leading stars.[31] Mayer had close ties to Hoover. Not only did he chair the California Republican Party in 1928, but trying to engage a radio audience, he staged the Republican National Convention that nominated Hoover for the presidency. During the fall campaign, the man described as the nation's "first political mogul" dispatched such MGM stars as Jackie Cooper, Wallace Beery, and Ethel and Lionel Barrymore to appear at rallies.[32] Mayer celebrated Hoover's victory by taking out an MGM advertisement in *Variety* congratulating the president-elect and announcing, "The Stars predict prosperity!" As soon as he took office, a grateful Hoover invited Mayer and his family to be his first guests at the White House.[33]

Mayer had bitterly opposed Roosevelt in 1932, and the Democrat's landslide victory was a grave disappointment. Nonetheless, he quickly turned to the task of building a strong Republican Party in California. In 1934, the mogul notoriously required his MGM stars to contribute to Frank Merriam's California gubernatorial campaign when his Democratic opponent, Upton Sinclair, began to talk of creating a special tax on the movie industry.[34] The more the New Deal disappointed him, the more Mayer focused on the long game. MGM became "a training ground for GOP activists," as Ross puts it, with Mayer hosting elaborate luncheons in which figures like Stewart, Montgomery, and George Murphy were seated next to visiting politicians and activists. His associate Ida Koverman supplied the stars with lessons in politics, economics, and speech-making, as she prepared them to talk about political ideas both simply and powerfully.[35] It was on the MGM lot that many of the celebrities who made prominent contributions to Eisenhower's campaigns got their first political training.

The fruits of this labor appeared in 1940 when Montgomery formed the "We the People" movement, which organized against the president's decision to seek a third term. So many stars had publicly announced themselves for Roosevelt that the organization had to combat the impression that Hollywood had gone entirely Democratic. In New York, Gloria Swanson and Ayn Rand rented a theater to show campaign films for Wendell Willkie, the Republican presidential candidate.[36] The day before the election, supporters placed a corrective advertisement in the *New York Times*. "The TRUTH is," the ad declared, "We of Hollywood . . . are opposed to the New Deal and the Third Term!" The advertisement proclaimed that 164 prominent Hollywood figures were going to vote for Willkie—among them, W.C. Fields, Walt Disney, Fred Astaire, Gary Cooper, Cecil B. DeMille, and Mrs. Spencer Tracy.[37] The politics of endorsement were not about who would perform a song and dance routine or provide comic relief. They weren't about a Broadway entertainer parading down Main Street with children high up in the trees. In this new formulation of celebrity politics, writers, actresses, actors, composers, and singers viewed themselves as vibrant political beings whose opinions and preferences were relevant to their public identity. Political engagement was rooted in citizenship and one's responsibility to exercise free speech. Even with Mayer's outsized presence, the MGM lot was known for its lively and polemical atmosphere. Just as FDR would later host Stewart, Montgomery, and Pickford (all of whom supported his opponents), lunchtime brought conservative executives, liberal writers, and actors of all political stripes to MGM's famous commissary for turbulent discussion and debate.[38]

The politicization of American celebrity was especially apparent in the Democrats' 1940 Election Eve radio broadcast on NBC. The two-hour show was put together by the Hollywood for Roosevelt Committee in conjunction with the Democratic State Committee of New York. Like the Ike Day television special, the broadcast spanned the continent, moving from Manhattan's Carnegie Hall, to Hollywood, to Washington, DC, to Roosevelt's home in Hyde Park, to Chicago, and back to Carnegie Hall again. New York's Republican mayor Fiorello La Guardia hosted the evening, introducing the Pins and Needles Chorus (all members of the International Ladies' Garment Workers Union) singing "The Franklin Roosevelt Way" with Bill "Bojangles" Robinson tap-dancing in the background. The song was followed by a denunciation of the *New York Times* and its publisher, Arthur Sulzberger, for having long disparaged Roosevelt. Benny Goodman and Count Basie's band then collaborated on a song they dedicated to Wendell Willkie, "Gone with What Wind?"[39]

While Ike Day hid its politics in glittering musical set pieces, the Salute to Roosevelt was openly partisan and confrontational. La Guardia introduced Bill Robinson by saying he tap-danced like "a utility man trying to get a higher rate." He prefaced the performances by Marian Anderson and Irving Berlin with statements that they were great Americans who suffered from the "racial and religious hatreds" that the utility companies were injecting into the campaign. Such comments made for an ideologically seamless transition to the public policy speeches. Marian Anderson's rendition of "God Bless America," for example, preceded publisher Marshall Field's speech about economic and military affairs.

Most of the program's Hollywood actors gave political speeches. Fresh off his Oscar-winning performance in the 1939 film *Stagecoach*, Thomas Mitchell recited Abraham Lincoln's speech on the occasion of leaving Springfield for Washington, DC.[40] Melvyn Douglas read a letter from George Washington to the Marquis de Lafayette about the impropriety of limiting the president to a specific number of terms. Douglas Fairbanks, Jr., delivered a blistering attack on the men who would likely serve in Willkie's Cabinet. Walter Huston sang "Uncle Sam Gets Around," depicting the government as a New Deal uncle lending the people a helping hand. The Hollywood speeches prefaced the addresses by Henry Wallace, the Secretary of Agriculture and Vice Presidential candidate; Cordell Hull, the Secretary of State; and Roosevelt himself from his home in Hyde Park. Just before the program ended with another song from the Pins and Needles Chorus, poet Carl Sandburg ruminated on the congressional opposition to Abraham Lincoln's serving a second term.

The Salute to Roosevelt emanated from a different vision of celebrity politics than Ike Day did. Not only did the program overtly address politics, it went out of its way to politicize entertainment. The garment workers performed more songs than Anderson; Fairbanks offered a polemic rather than a sketch or tribute. While the producers of Ike Day used celebrities to deny the program's political content, the FDR program showcased celebrity activism. As Huston remarked, so many people wanted to speak on Roosevelt's behalf that the entertainers had to draw lots to decide who could appear on the broadcast. Political work was as natural to the occupation of an actor or entertainer as it was to the union laborer. Democracy involved strong opinions and partisan rhetoric, whether it was from conservative journalist Dorothy Thompson (who had famously switched her support to FDR mid-campaign) or the actress Katharine Hepburn.

Saving Democracy from Politicians

By 1944, the United States had entered the war in Europe and Japan, and an ailing Roosevelt was seeking a fourth term. His entrance into the presidential race brought hundreds of notables and celebrities into the campaign. Roosevelt benefited from the emergence of the Independent Voters Committee of the Arts and Sciences, a Manhattan-based organization that was dedicated to supporting the president's reelection. Founded in July 1944 by sculptor Jo Davidson and twelve other artists and writers, the committee grew in less than six weeks to include "more than fifteen hundred of the country's leading artists, writers, musicians, scientists, actors, educators, physicians and engineers." "This honor roll of the Arts, Sciences, and Professions," the committee boasted to its members, "brought a fresh and vigorous influence into our national life."[41]

The committee's activities spanned everything from putting on a voter registration parade to sponsoring an art exhibit in honor of the Roosevelts. Under the name "Broadway Limited," groups of actors, actresses, writers, and radio personalities barnstormed through Connecticut, New York, and New Jersey giving speeches and performances. Photographs of such notables as Duke Ellington, Bette Davis, Albert Einstein, and Olivia de Havilland appeared in pro-Roosevelt advertisements in the New York papers, as well as the "Negro, labor, and foreign language weeklies." The committee sent 206 "glamour speakers" to 173 meetings and rallies in the Northeast, drawing upon such diverse talent as Frank Sinatra, Helen Keller, Howard Fast, and Rockwell Kent. The committee was proud of its September 21, 1944, Madison Square Garden rally in which 20,000 people paid to hear a dozen or so celebrities join the vice president in launching the Roosevelt campaign "in a dramatic, attention-compelling way."[42]

The most fervent star to campaign for FDR in 1944 was Orson Welles, the maverick director and actor who starred in his 1941 classic, *Citizen Kane*. A longtime political activist, Welles hit the campaign trail for Roosevelt in 1944, giving speeches and attracting media attention in New York, Los Angeles, Florida, West Virginia, and Boston. Working with the Independent Voters Committee, Welles introduced Vice President Henry Wallace at the Madison Square Garden rally. He later joined Roosevelt for a final campaign rally in Boston the night before Election Day. Roosevelt felt indebted to Welles and wrote him on November 25, 1944, two weeks after the victory: "I may be a prejudiced spectator who had a special interest in the action but I want to thank you for the splendid role you played in the recent campaign." Sounding a note similar to the one Harding made to Jolson in 1920, he added, "I cannot recall any campaign in which actors and artists were so effective in the unrehearsed realities of the drama of the American future."[43]

Frank Sinatra developed into one of Roosevelt's most popular and controversial spokesmen during the 1944 campaign. If Welles provided gravitas and uncompromising intellectualism, Sinatra provided youthful energy. Roosevelt was fond of the young singer from Hoboken who seemed to create mobs of excited young women wherever he appeared. Republicans were skeptical of Sinatra, and they criticized the president after he invited the bobbysoxers' idol to the White House early in the campaign. Sinatra responded by incorporating their attacks into his performance at the Paramount Theater later that week, changing the lyrics to "Everything Happens to Me" to address his friendship with the president.[44] At a time when Roosevelt was gravely ill and becoming increasingly weak, Sinatra added vigor and vitality to his campaign. Several days before Election Day, Sinatra participated in a parade through Brooklyn that led to a rally at the Academy of Music. According to the *New York Times*, Sinatra "stole the show." "Fifty 'teen-age girls, non-voters, whose only candidate is Sinatra, thronged about his taxicab and followed it to the hall, their ranks swelling with other kiss-throwing and singing bobbysoxers as the parade moved along. At the hall a sergeant and six patrolmen had to rescue Sinatra from 1000 of his admirers."[45]

Sinatra's fan base had little in common with the people who might have been swayed by other members of the Independent Voters Committee. It is unlikely that poet Mark Van Doren or novelist Fannie Hurst produced a similar frenzy when they campaigned for FDR. But the central dynamic of the singer's Brooklyn appearance was woven into the committee's mission to offer a fresh approach to politics. Flush with Roosevelt's victory, the committee sent its members a final congratulatory report, assuring them that "as high as government offices go," their efforts were regarded as being crucial to the president's success. "Millions of people were directly reached by the Committee," the report boasted, and the results demonstrated "that we people in America can have the effective government we want if we want it enough to work for it."[46]

Like many supporting groups, the Committee of Independent Voters exaggerated its impact. The committee's final report presented its work as being

FIGURE 2.2 *Eleanor Roosevelt and Frank Sinatra at the Jackson Day Dinner in Los Angeles, California in 1947.*

Courtesy of National Park Service and Franklin D. Roosevelt Presidential Library and Museum, 63111.

vital not only to FDR's victory, but to democracy itself. "The most important thing about this election has been the remarkable demonstration that thousands upon thousands of people have already taken a part in the processes of politics which have heretofore been left solely in the hands of professional politicians."[47] In the same way that *Mr. Smith Goes to Washington* strove to transform its viewers into newly invigorated citizens, the committee associated its honor roll of notables with the resurgence of grassroots democracy. Celebrities like Welles and Sinatra served as bridges between politicians and the people; they ushered voters into the political system and made government accountable to the public will. The committee took its independence as a charter to maintain the republic's righteousness and health as if fame were a force equivalent to the courts and the press. Combined with the renown of its members, the group's *independence* was meant to certify its sincerity and public-mindedness.

While the Independent Voters focused their attentions on the East Coast, the Hollywood for Roosevelt Committee organized events in the West. Sensing a shift in public opinion away from the president, the committee worked with the Biow Company, Milton Biow's advertising agency, to produce a sixty-minute radio program that was broadcast nationwide. Proud of his reputation for building a "tonnage" agency (meaning he focused on selling to the "mass, not the class"), Biow was eager to apply his skills to the world of celebrity politics.[48] Whether selling Bulova watches, Pepsi-Cola, or Philip Morris cigarettes, he had followed one central dictum throughout his career: "Don't tell people how good you make your goods. Tell them how good your goods make them."[49] The trick was finding a way to use the Hollywood volunteers to create a message in which everyday people would recognize the benefits of a fourth Roosevelt term.

Though various organizations squabbled over who controlled the program, Norman Corwin, whom historian David Everitt described as "the great standard bearer for Popular Front radio," created the script in three feverish weeks.[50] Humphrey Bogart was recruited to host the program, Judy Garland to sing. James Cagney, Groucho Marx, and Keenan Wynn collaborated on a satirical sketch about how sentimental they were for the good old Depression-era Hoovervilles. In between testimonials from voters around the country—a Tennessee farmer, a brakeman on the New York Central railroad, a Michigan housewife, a sailor with the merchant marine—Garland would lead a chorus in buoyantly singing that the way to win the war, create jobs, and improve the world was simple: "You gotta get out to vote."[51] The message smacked of Biow. Vote for Roosevelt, the lyrics implied, for the good results a fourth term would bring.

The program's climax came when Bogart encouraged all Americans to join the "millions and millions of people riding on the Roosevelt special." To the sound of a locomotive gaining speed, dozens of famous men and women came to the microphone in Hollywood and New York, offering their brief endorsements of the Roosevelt administration. Danny Kaye, Gene Kelly, Irving Berlin, Rita Hayworth, Lana Turner, Jane Wyman, John Dewey, Dorothy Parker, Fay Ray, Milton Berle, Frank Sinatra—the voices went on and on as if they were passengers on a massive victory train that spanned the entire continent. Interweaving celebrity voices, citizen testimonials, and the aural effect of a rushing train, Corwin created a unified effect in which celebrities were responsible for grassroots democracy. Like their humble compatriots struggling across the country, they were an essential part of the populist movement behind the president's fourth term. Celebrity did not signify a glamorous, isolated being. It prepared the way for a guy like Joe Hamilla, a World War I veteran and self-described "Nobody." Hamilla also had his ticket for the Roosevelt Special; he, too, was boarding the train—right behind Berle and Sinatra.

A number of themes emerge from the Roosevelt campaigns that would shape celebrity politics in the 1950s. The first is how, from Garland's refrain to Ike Day's scrolls, celebrity politics frequently centered on getting out the vote. Stars became agents of mobilization, advocates and preservers of an essential civic responsibility. At once frivolous and important, this new role portended a world in which the illusory relationships forged through entertainment would become a critical part of national identity. By the 1950s, being American would somehow involve cheering for Joe DiMaggio, listening to Dinah Shore, or watching Bob Hope in a musical comedy. The association of celebrity with getting out the vote was no doubt helped by the surprising number of stars who remained politically active through several long and tortuous decades. Some, such as Robert Montgomery, traced their political awakening to the ideological battles of the 1930s and saw both their interest and their influence grow over time. Others, such as Helen Hayes, Irving Berlin, and James Cagney, switched their party allegiance—either because their worldviews had changed or because they found themselves less attracted to an ideology than to a particular candidate. What united all these stars, however, was that they saw their fame as an invitation to become leading voices in the ongoing conversation about the future of the United States.

Corwin's script has been justly recognized for its power to move the listener, but it also suggests a valuable contrast to the 1940 production with its political songs and dry political speeches.[52] The 1944 radio program did more than deliver information and rally listeners with expressions of political sympathy; it turned political persuasion into an aesthetic experience. Bogart's and Sinatra's, Garland's and Berle's: the voices offered the sensation of belonging to a dramatic, unstoppable force. In 1940, Roosevelt's campaign created distance around its listeners; it allowed them the space to smile, dance, and sing along—but also to listen and think. By 1944, the Hollywood Democratic Committee was trying to fill the nation's living rooms with a grassroots aestheticism. Compared to Ike Day, the program was openly political, its opinions patently clear. When the broadcast turned to the president speaking from Hyde Park, no one could doubt that there was more to this program than lighthearted entertainment. But as the chorus chanted "Vote, Vote, Vote, Vote" and the locomotive gained steam, there was also a step toward what the Eisenhower celebrities would come to represent—the effort to make politics so emotionally and aesthetically satisfying that its content seemed almost beside the point. Glamour and celebrity served as powerful substitutes for an ailing president who was unable to travel around the country. Eisenhower's supporters returned to this lesson in 1952 as they promoted a candidate whose positions were unknown and whose overseas duties prevented him from joining his own campaign.

The Coriolanus Candidate

Dwight Eisenhower's entrance into the 1952 presidential race was as prolonged as it was complicated. Americans were used to politicians such as Franklin Roosevelt and Harry Truman pursuing the office with zeal, but with Eisenhower they faced a kind of political detachment that they had not seen in years. Amid rampant speculation about his political leanings and ambitions, Eisenhower left the United States in 1951 to take the position of Supreme Allied Commander of NATO in Europe. In his absence, two young businessmen, Stanley Rumbough, Jr., and Charles F. Willis, Jr., established Ike Clubs across the nation in an effort to draft the general as a presidential candidate. The Ike Clubs sought to create the kind of grassroots enthusiasm and infrastructure that would be necessary for a campaign—if only Eisenhower would agree to one.[1] On January 6, 1952, Massachusetts senator Henry Cabot Lodge announced that he had entered the general's name into the New Hampshire primary. Still stationed in Paris, Eisenhower privately seethed at Lodge's unauthorized announcement and the media firestorm it produced. "Time and again," he wrote in his diary, "I've told anyone who'd listen I will not seek a nomination. I don't give a d—how impossible a 'draft' may be. I'm willing to go part way in trying to recognize a 'duty,' but I do not have to seek one, and I will not."[2]

Publicly, however, Ike was forced to release a statement clarifying his intentions: he would continue to serve as the Allied Commander, and he refused to engage in any form of campaigning. At the same time, he would not repudiate the Republican nomination if it were offered to him at the national convention in July.[3] Although mild and noncommittal, the statement was enough to convince supporters that their efforts were not in vain, and the local Ike Clubs were gathered under the organization Citizens for Eisenhower, a bipartisan group that developed close ties to a national organization led by Senator Lodge that had the mission of securing the Republican nomination. Much to the consternation of some backers and the press, Eisenhower maintained his distance from the campaign until he returned from Europe on June 1 and resigned his commission. Asked to explain Ike's puzzling detachment from the race, an adviser referenced one of Shakespeare's most brutal political plays. "His attitude would be that of Coriolanus," the anonymous campaign official told the *New York Times*, quoting a passage in which the Roman general questions whether political honors are tarnished by their pursuit.[4] Although the reporter found it highly problematic, the comparison was revealing. For much of the 1952 primary season, Eisenhower was the Coriolanus candidate.

Shakespeare's *Coriolanus* tells the story of a Roman general who struggles to turn his military fame into political power. Having captured the Volscian city of Corioli and brought its treasures home, he quickly becomes the sensation of Roman society. "All tongues speak of him," a hostile tribune reports, and all eyes earnestly seek him out.[5] When Coriolanus parades through the capitol, the city welcomes him with a fanfare bordering on ecstasy. Mothers fling their gloves into the procession, maids their handkerchiefs and scarves. The commoners greet the general with thunderous shouts, and the nobles bow as if he were a statue of Jove.[6] Impressed by this reception, Coriolanus's fellow patricians encourage him to run for the position of consul, a political office that would give him extraordinary powers.

It is a time of reform, however, and custom dictates that Coriolanus has to seek the people's favor. He must wear a cloak of humility in the public square and show the plebiscite his wounds in asking for their support. The practice offends him to the bone, for from the play's beginning, he has expressed nothing but scorn for the crowd. "He that depends / Upon your favours swims with fins of lead," he tells a group of mutinous citizens in the play's opening scene.[7] Coriolanus's appearance in the marketplace proves to be a disaster, as the qualities that made him such a fearsome warrior make him a terrible politician. With overweening pride, he insults the assembled citizens, telling them that they don't deserve their powers. The uproar over his comments only enrages him more. He will not counterfeit affection for the people nor cover his "stout heart" in asking for their support. Coriolanus's mother begs him to temper his warlike tongue and supplicate the commoners, his "knee bussing the stones."[8] But Coriolanus's desire to be the "author of himself," as he puts it in the final act, is incompatible with a republic in which even the least heroic citizens have a ceremonial voice.[9] The most popular man soon becomes the most loathed. In a stunning reversal, Coriolanus is eventually exiled and dies after threatening to lead the Volscian army against his native Rome.

Shakespeare found the story of Coriolanus in Plutarch's *Lives*, but to the basic plot points of heroism, banishment, and revenge, he added his own reflections on the relationship between fame and power. To him we owe the conflict of a highly celebrated warrior who refuses to seek the favor of a people he regards as unaccomplished and unheroic.[10] To him we owe the tragedy of a fiercely self-reliant man who will not submit to a political environment that requires publicity, persuasion, and stagecraft. Coriolanus may wear his wounds as if they were medals, but he loathes the prospect of using them for votes.

Since the late 1940s, Eisenhower's supporters had resembled the Roman patricians who tried to capitalize on Coriolanus's fame. Although known more for his ability to build coalitions than for his performance on the battlefield, Eisenhower was a conquering hero who had been celebrated around the globe. From Paris and London to New York and Abilene, he had been paraded through cities and at countless events. His reputation as a professional soldier of nearly universal appeal led many to see him as an ideal presidential candidate. Businessmen befriended him. Publishers and media executives gave him tips. Delegations of Republicans and Democrats visited the general, trying to woo him to their side. In 1948, Harry Truman secretly offered to return to the vice presidency if Eisenhower would top the Democratic ticket.[11]

Eisenhower, of course, had a different temperament than Coriolanus. Humble, gracious, quick to smile, he displayed profound respect for the lives of common Americans. Although he preferred the company of corporate titans and could be stern and impatient with his underlings, he was no elitist. He himself had come from modest circumstances, with a father who had provided for his six sons by working as a mechanic. Until he was awarded entrance into West Point, he and his brother Edgar had set up an elaborate arrangement in which each would work to put the other through college.[12] Merriman Smith, known to contemporaries as the "Dean of White House reporters," thought Eisenhower exemplified what Thomas Jefferson called the "natural aristocracy," that is, individuals whose virtue and talents would help them rise to positions of leadership throughout the Republic.[13]

And yet, the soldier in Eisenhower led him to distrust the publicity and hype surrounding his presidential candidacy. Like Coriolanus, he was wary of the insincerity and rhetoric of political campaigns. Eisenhower had long valued the American military doctrine that required soldiers to remain nonpartisan, and he grew indignant when pressed about his presidential ambitions. "Look, son," he rebuked a persistent reporter in 1948, "I cannot conceive of any circumstance that could drag out of me permission to consider me for any political post, from dog-catcher to Grand High Supreme King of the Universe."[14] Although four years later his position had changed, he continued to regard political office as a duty and sacrifice: he would accept a call to office, but under no circumstances would he pursue it himself. To strive for the presidency, to actively seek public favor, was to engage in the kind of ambitious self-promotion that he, like Coriolanus, found beneath him.

Rooted in both tradition and personal belief, these convictions made it difficult for Ike to accept the requirements of a modern media campaign. He had a hard time speaking with a teleprompter and for months insisted on reading his speeches from the page. When advisers tried to coach his media appearances, he grew caustic and weary. "Why don't you just get an actor?" he told a

CBS correspondent trying to help him. "That's what you really want."[15] Again and again, Eisenhower emphasized the disparity between his military background and campaign publicity. When asked to wear makeup before a television appearance in Abilene, he resisted by explaining, "An old soldier doesn't feel very good under that sort of thing."[16] In the midst of an exhausting day taping television commercials, he shook his head, muttering, "To think that an old soldier has come to this."[17]

The irony of this resistance was that Ike could afford to be such a detached politician because he had entered the campaign with fame. As his supporters and detractors agreed, celebrity gave him license to bypass the partisan maneuvering that occupied his opponents. At the same time, Eisenhower's absence created a hole at rallies and events that entertainers happily filled. When he returned to the United States, the tenor of the campaign had already been established, and he needed only to step into the role that others had prepared for him. Eisenhower's skepticism makes his conversion to celebrity politics all the more interesting. He not only learned to tolerate the cosmetic aspects of the campaign, but he came to acknowledge what Shakespeare's Coriolanus could not: his knees had to kiss the stones. The emergence of television meant that he had to accept, if not downright embrace, the spectacle of political showmanship. Significant portions of his campaign were subsequently given over to advertising agencies whose primary job was to nurture and promote his image. At every stage, the politics of fame differentiated and elevated his candidacy.

They Like Ike

Perhaps the most important step in the movement to draft Eisenhower into the 1952 presidential race began at the Imperial Theater in New York City. In October 1950, Irving Berlin premiered a new musical titled *Call Me Madam,* with Ethel Merman starring as a Washington socialite who becomes the American ambassador to the fictional country of Lichtenburg. Although the focus remains with Merman's character, Sally Adams, the show featured a catchy tune midway through the second act in which two senators and a congressman speculate about the upcoming presidential race. As the Democrats boast that the combative Truman would hold the White House for another term, the Republican asserts that his party has set their sights on running a more affable candidate:

> They like Ike
> And Ike is good on a mike.
> They like Ike.

When the Democrats interrupt, "—But Ike says he don't wanna," the congressman wittily replies:

> That makes Ike
> The kind of fella they like!
> And what's more
> They seem to think he's gonna.

In each verse, the Democrats list various reasons why Truman will win, but the chorus always comes back to the simple Republican theme: "They like Ike."

Call Me Madam was a hit. Both Merman and Berlin won Tony Awards, and the show ran for 644 consecutive performances, closing in May 1952.[18] After a month in Washington's National Theater, the production went on the road—moving from city to city during the height of the fall election season. (MGM would release a film version of *Call Me Madam* in March 1953, only months after Eisenhower's inauguration.) Although Merman aficionados prized her show-stopping duet with Russell Nype, "You're Just in Love," the power of the Eisenhower song was immediately evident. In fact, soon after the show opened, syndicated columnist Inez Robb compared Berlin's efforts to that of another Ike supporter, New York governor Thomas Dewey:

> I think the man who has done the most to place the general in nomination will eventually be listed as Irving Berlin. In his new musical comedy, *Call Me Madam*, he has written a rollicky tune "They Like Ike," which may alone and unaided sweep the general into the White House by acclamation. This song is one of the greatest political windfalls ever to fall like manna upon a presidential possibility. If Ike makes it, mebbe he ought to consider Irving for [Secretary of] State.[19]

Robb possessed enviable foresight. The phrase "They like Ike" had occurred to Berlin when he met Eisenhower in London in 1944, and since then he had been eager to use it in a song. *Call Me Madam* provided just the opportunity, although the song itself had nothing to do with the story line. Once Lodge entered Eisenhower in the New Hampshire primary, the lyrics took on new significance. Audiences began to applaud as soon as they heard the chorus, and Berlin rushed to New York from the Bahamas to work on a revision, inviting a reporter from the *New Yorker* to check in on his progress.[20] The result was a bit of lyric genius:

> I like Ike
> I'll shout it over a mike
> Or a phone
> Or from the highest steeple

> I like Ike
> And Ike is easy to like
> Stands alone
> The choice of We the People.

Berlin cleverly transformed Ike's media experience (he's "good on a mike") into the speaker's enthusiasm for his candidacy. Over the course of the campaign and, indeed, over the next sixteen years, Berlin would use the song to reflect on changing political circumstances. When Joseph McCarthy endorsed Eisenhower's chief Republican opponent, Ohio senator Robert Taft, Berlin instructed the *Call Me Madam* cast to sing: "McCarthy's backing Taft? / That's the kiss of death!"[21] After Ike's victory in November, the disillusioned Democrats bemoaned "how many changed their minds down at the polls."[22] As late as 1968, Berlin was changing the lyrics to address Lyndon Johnson, the Vietnam War, and the wide-open primary contests. While the verses comically weighed the chances of Hubert Humphrey, Eugene McCarthy, Bobby Kennedy, Richard Nixon, Nelson Rockefeller, and Ronald Reagan, the chorus stubbornly clung to a candidate from the 1950s: "We still like Ike."[23]

Berlin's song helped popularize the most memorable political slogan in the history of the United States. Only days after the general's victory in New Hampshire, the Radio Corporation of America (RCA) released the new version of "I Like Ike," and the phrase promptly became part of national consciousness.[24] The three short words gave Eisenhower a new, less formal identity, a nickname perfectly suited to retail politics. The slogan, as George Trow pointed out, shifted attention from "General Eisenhower" to a new, seemingly familiar person named "Ike," the "like" in the middle becoming the shared emotional preference of a broader national community.[25] Comparing its sonic complexity to the sonnets of John Keats, a prominent linguist noted how the slogan's compressed rhymes effectively absorbed Ike into the feelings he inspired.[26] Advertisers loved the phrase, and supporters could soon find it on everything from pocket combs, matchbooks, and swizzle sticks, to sunglasses, bow ties, and poodle skirts.[27] Herbert Brownell, who served as Attorney General during Eisenhower's first term, would later conclude that the public's response to Berlin's song was a major factor in convincing the general that the time was right for a presidential bid.[28]

In contrast to Coriolanus, who expressed his political discomfort through rage, Eisenhower's ambivalence made him appear statesmanlike and, in fact, enhanced his political desirability. The more he resisted, as Berlin put it, the more he became the "kind of fella" that his supporters keenly liked. From January to June of 1952, two campaigns unfurled simultaneously—one, a campaign to persuade the general that the nation both wanted and needed an Eisenhower presidency, and the other, to persuade the Republican Party

FIGURE 3.1 *Attending the Al Smith Dinner on October 16, 1952, General Eisenhower heard a rendition of "I Like Ike" from key members of his campaign's National Arts and Sports Committee. From left to right, Gene Tunney, Eddie Eagan, Robert Montgomery, Happy Felton, Dorothy Fields, Bob Christenberry, Bill Gaxton, and New Hampshire Gov. Sherman Adams. Irving Berlin and Helen Hayes are seated at the piano.*
Courtesy of the Associated Press.

that Ike was its man. Only days after Lodge's announcement, executives at the Young & Rubicam advertising agency met to define a central theme for both of these campaigns. What they settled on was as flattering as it was amorphous—"Here is the only man who can literally save this nation"—and they set about discussing a series of radio spots that might bring Arthur Godfrey, Bob Hope, and Helen Hayes into the effort. Godfrey was one of the first radio stars to make it big in television, and in the winter of 1952, he had the top-rated show on the new medium. The agency hoped Godfrey would cut some twenty-second spots for both radio and television and that "as a public service" he would pay for these contributions himself.[29]

As the agency of record for Citizens for Eisenhower, Young & Rubicam was also involved in planning a February 8 rally in Madison Square Garden that had the dual purpose of persuading the general to commit to the race and of raising funds for his potential candidacy. Led by the husband-and-wife talk show team Tex McCrary and Jinx Falkenburg, the rally had to contend with a packed Garden calendar, including a series of regularly scheduled boxing matches on

Friday evenings. McCrary decided to begin the event at 11:30 p.m. after the box-ing fans had departed the building and over 15,000 Eisenhower supporters had flooded in. Working within these constraints, Young & Rubicam began looking for famous boxers to showcase, while McCrary and Falkenburg figured out how to adapt to the peculiar space and timing. In the end, they billed the program as "A Midnight Serenade to Eisenhower" and called upon a bevy of stars to get the overflowing crowd involved and excited. In an effort to create "grass roots inter-est," various state and local delegations were introduced to the hall throughout the night—the Eisenhower Club of Taft, Texas; the Ike Club of Mount Holyoke College; Greek Americans from Brooklyn; the Mummers from Philadelphia.[30] A representative of the earliest primary, Miss New Hampshire, went first, lead-ing her state delegation in a bathing suit. In between these demonstrations of support, Fred Waring led a choral rendition of "When in America." Clark Gable spoke. The Brooklyn Dodgers symphony band performed. By means of a short-wave radio hookup, Mary Martin addressed the crowd from overseas where she was starring in the London production of *South Pacific*. With Richard Rodgers playing the piano in New York, she dedicated her performance—"I'm in Love with a Wonderful Guy"—to Ike.[31]

The cast of *Call Me Madam* played a prominent role in the festivities. As the curtain fell at the Imperial Theater, several cast members headed to Madison Square Garden to provide entertainment and support. Ethel Merman belted out her signature piece "There's No Business Like Show Business" and, to much applause, danced with the chorus master Waring. Berlin debuted his new version of "I Like Ike" and made sure the revised lyrics were printed in the newspapers. In a crowd-pleasing stunt, the actor who played Harry Truman in the musical appeared in costume as Berlin's song wound down, provoking applause and laughter among the faithful. As if politics were a combination of pugilism and show business, all the performances and speeches took place within the confines of the Madison Square Garden boxing ring.[32]

NBC broadcast the rally on radio nationwide and on television as far west as Chicago. The show produced significant backlash in the press. Calling it the beginning of a "mummer's campaign," conservative George Sokolsky denounced the event as an insult to Eisenhower. "It was cheap," he wrote. "It was vulgar." From the left, Arthur Schlesinger, Jr., described the rally as "an expression of really outrageous cynicism" and argued that if the Eisenhower campaign were going to succeed, then someone "must take it out of the hands of advertising men and jack it up to the level of a ten-year-old intelligence." The *New Bedford Standard Times* acknowledged what the rally had intended to hide: "Horseplay and lavish star-studded spectacles are no substitute for a candidate or a program."[33] The reviews from theater critics were so hostile that Lodge himself would later dismiss the rally as "a very mediocre effort."[34]

The viewing audience, however, responded to the show enthusiastically. With some sixty-five operators standing by to take donations, the program raised over

$3 million—a substantial sum, considering that, for much of the audience, it was the middle of the night.[35] News of the rally made it into local papers, which, from Spokane, Washington, to Austin, Texas, to Portsmouth, New Hampshire, all commented on the size and vigor of the crowd. As far back as January 8, Young & Rubicam was planning to distribute films of the rally "throughout key cities for indoctrination and arousing enthusiasm in local workers."[36]

Although someone had arranged for a radio hookup to Paris, Eisenhower decided to sleep through the festivities.[37] With McCrary's encouragement, famous pilot Jacqueline (Jackie) Cochran had volunteered to take a three-hour kinescope of the rally overseas so Ike and Mamie could witness the enthusiasm Americans had for his candidacy. An aviation pioneer who had started the Women's Airforce Service Pilots (WASPs) during the Second World War, Cochran was an ardent Republican and a leading member of the Citizens for Eisenhower committee.[38] As Cochran rested after her journey, Eisenhower anticipated the program with strong but mixed feelings. "I am to see the whole business this evening," he wrote in his diary. "Undoubtedly some publicity will be generated out of my mere viewing it." Whatever weariness and skepticism the statement betrayed, those feelings quickly gave way to a sense of humble astonishment. "The performance at the Garden is not only something to make an American genuinely proud—it is something to increase his humility, his sense of his own unworthiness to fulfill the spoken and unspoken desires and aspirations of so many thousands of humans."[39] The next morning, Ike returned to his diary to record how overwhelming the experience had been:

> The picture brought by Miss Cochran was very elaborate and long. Viewing it finally developed into a real emotional experience for Mamie and me. I've not been so upset in years. Clearly to be seen is the mass longing of Americans for some kind of reasonable solution for her nagging, persistent, and almost terrifying problems. It's a real experience to realize that one would become a symbol for many thousands of the hope they have.[40]

The entry was the only time Eisenhower wrote in his diary about the primaries, the convention, or the fall campaign.

Ike was an ideal hero to tap for the presidency, for as political scientist Samuel L. Popkin suggests, his experience and commitment to the public good seemed well matched to the problems of the age.[41] After his victory in New Hampshire, Eisenhower would have a strong showing in Minnesota, where, despite not being on the ballot and running against a former home state governor, he received over 100,000 write-in votes.[42] And in April, he swept three important primary states: New Jersey, Pennsylvania, and Massachusetts. Although he was not an official candidate, the victories confirmed the general's persistent stature in the United States. The Second World War had made Eisenhower a household name, and praise for his leadership was a steady topic on radio and in the newspapers. Polls revealed him to be one of the most admired men in the nation, and for many Americans, Ike was the public face of a military effort that had spanned every continent but Antarctica. Over the past fifteen years, they had come to know that face from the covers of magazines and the newsreels that preceded feature attractions in movie theaters. The general's ubiquity did not trivialize his reputation nor reduce him to a matinee idol. In the dark of the theater, Eisenhower's low-key demeanor took on the aura of a cinematic hero. This aura was enough to keep him competitive until he returned from Europe and publicly took hold of his campaign.

The Madison Avenue Candidate

In significant ways, Eisenhower's aversion to campaigning harked back to previous presidential candidates. The most important predecessor to Eisenhower's Coriolanus candidacy was the last general to occupy the White House, Ulysses S. Grant. Like Eisenhower, Grant was buoyed by his previously won fame and therefore could allow others to make his case for him. Touring the Western states five months before the 1868 presidential election, he made a point of greeting voters in town after town and then declining to make a speech or engage in any form of politicking. The *New York Times* repeatedly editorialized against Grant's opponent, former New York governor Horatio Seymour, for "lowering his dignity" and "electioneering for himself" rather than retiring to the country—as Grant had done in Illinois.[43] Defending the general from Democratic attacks, the *Times* argued that Grant showed "his uncommon common sense in *not* 'starring' it through the country on speech-making tours." Seymour, the editorial implied, had overstepped the line separating actors from politicians.[44]

The dawn of the television age meant that advisers could finesse Ike's absence through the careful use of image-making. In this regard, Eisenhower's path to the presidency was paved by the many friends in the media and advertising that he met after moving to New York City in 1948. Executives quickly surrounded the new president of Columbia University, eager to promote his broad appeal. From advertising, there were Bruce Barton and Ben Duffy of BBDO and Sigurd Larmon of Young & Rubicam. From the press, there was William Robinson, the publisher of the *New York Herald Tribune,* who had arranged for the publication of Eisenhower's 1948 memoir, *Crusade in Europe.* An early confidante, publisher Henry Luce, was with the general in Paris on the day Cochran arrived from New York, and in fact, two of his men—on loan from *Fortune* and *Life*—eventually crafted Ike's momentous pledge to go to Korea and personally broker a peace agreement.[45] Representing television were David Sarnoff of NBC and William Paley of CBS, a network that raised the ire of anti-Communist crusaders but seemed to have an unusually close relationship with Eisenhower over the years.[46] These friendships sent a clear signal to industry professionals about how to turn a military hero into a viable presidential candidate.

As early as December 1951, a group of nine advertising and television executives (five from NBC alone) began secretly meeting in New York's Commodore Hotel to develop strategies for what they called "IKE-TV." Without the knowledge of their employers, they reported directly to Lodge, who concealed their existence, even from the advertising agencies working for different branches of the campaign. The efforts of the TV Plans Board were far-reaching. In addition to advising Lodge on the production of the Madison Square Garden rally, the board also shaped the way local news stations covered the proceedings. Its members cleverly arranged for news stories that emphasized the "spontaneous Eisenhower effort," by which they meant the impression that thousands, even millions, of Americans were enthusiastically calling for his candidacy without professional calculation or influence.[47] Cultivating this impression was as important to wooing Eisenhower as it was the general public, and when Cochran wrote the general in 1952, she described the rally as "the greatest spontaneous ovation that has ever been received in the history of our country" by a potential presidential candidate. Lest he be concerned that the crowd was there for the entertainment rather than the politics, she noted that "we only informed the public three days before the rally that any stars would be present."[48]

Sig Larmon was particularly close to Eisenhower, and although BBDO received the contract with the GOP, Young & Rubicam did the advertising, public relations, and program development work for Citizens for Eisenhower in 1952. Throughout the campaign, he encouraged Eisenhower to make good use of broadcast media, tutoring him in the value of professional communications techniques. "The public relations phases of this campaign," he wrote in a private letter, "call for the same careful planning and strategy as you and your staff employed in setting up the invasion of Normandy, and the same careful planning that we, in our business, employ in order to ensure the successful introduction of a new product."[49] What Larmon envisioned was a kind of media-promotional alliance in which agencies would coordinate radio and television as Eisenhower began to conquer (some Republicans would say "liberate") the land.

Citizens for Eisenhower was a nonpartisan group distinct from the Republican Party that sought ways to broaden the candidate's appeal. This put Young & Rubicam in an unusual position because most advisers believed that winning the nomination would be more challenging than winning the presidency. "THE IMMEDIATE AND MOST DIFFICULT TASK IS TO GET EISENHOWER NOMINATED," an internal Young & Rubicam document announced in January 1952. A recent Gallup poll had revealed that not only was Senator Taft's appeal rising among rank-and-file voters, but among 1,727 GOP County leaders, 1,027 preferred Taft, 375 preferred Eisenhower, and 94 the former Minnesota governor Harold Stassen. The numbers meant that, despite Eisenhower's popularity among independents, there was a lot of work ahead.[50] "Most 'professional politicians' are not enthusiastic about a non-political candidate," the Young & Rubicam report explained, "for if such a man secures the nomination on the basis of his own personality and ability they are not in a position to exact patronage and favors in return for their support."[51]

The agency recognized the tensions between these two modes of candidacy: the experienced politician who had risen through party and government ranks and the political amateur whose name recognition and media persona appealed to the broader electorate. Taft represented the conservative wing of a Republican Party that had lost five straight presidential elections. He was a fierce opponent of the New Deal and had an isolationist streak that put him squarely at odds with the Supreme Commander of NATO. The eldest son of President William Howard Taft, he was known as "Mr. Republican" for both his ideological purity and his party loyalties. Taft was a steady and trusted ally to the thousands of Republicans who worked in federal, state, and local politics and looked forward to the spoils coming their way. Eisenhower was something of a mystery, for until Lodge disclosed it in January, few even knew his party affiliation. Facing these constraints, Young & Rubicam chose not to focus on county executives and other party operatives. Instead, they went directly to the voters in the hopes that "public sentiment" would "compel" the delegates to support Ike.[52]

Larmon turned to Frederick A. Zaghi to oversee the Citizens for Eisenhower account. Known by his colleagues as "Tony," Zaghi was an unusual choice. The business manager of Young & Rubicam's Television and Radio Department, he expected to fill in for only three weeks while Larmon's regular assistant was away. Zaghi jumped at the opportunity to take on such new responsibilities as developing print and broadcast materials with the creative team; overseeing the distribution of folders, brochures, newspaper mats, and money to the states; and buying time on radio and television.[53] "We were real neophytes when we started," Zaghi recalled, and the learning curve was steep as both he and the agency tried to figure out how to adapt their product expertise to a political campaign in the midst of the hectic New Hampshire primary. The three-week replacement position turned into eleven months, and Zaghi found himself moving to the agency's executive floor in an office directly adjacent to Larmon's. News of Zaghi's success got around, and he was gratified when, years later, the president warmly greeted him at a White House dinner, "Holy gee I know you, you're Sig Larmon's deputy."[54]

As Zaghi traveled from state to state working with local Citizens groups, he saw an ever-widening gap between the party-based politics of Taft's campaign and the personality-based campaign of Ike's. A key part of his job was recognizing where the politics of personality would work and where they wouldn't. In West Virginia, he was told there was such fervent support for Taft that he should remove his Eisenhower pin or else he would be tarred, feathered, and run out of town. The campaign reconciled itself to losing the state. In South Dakota, Zaghi discovered a tight but winnable race and asked the Finance Committee for funds to expand the reach of a radio commercial featuring Kate Smith. The singer had been a popular radio and television personality for nearly three decades and had recorded the signature version of Berlin's "God Bless America" in 1939. (Well known for her spirited patriotism, she sold over $600 million worth of war bonds during a series of marathon radio programs in 1943 and 1944.)[55] To Zaghi's mind, Smith's endorsement could make a difference in peeling voters away from Taft, and he hoped to "counteract the effect of the big name politicians" the senator was bringing into South Dakota by running her commercials more heavily on the largest stations in the state. The committee denied Zaghi's request, and Eisenhower lost the state by 600 votes.[56] To Zaghi and his colleagues, the beginnings of an overarching strategy were evident. Celebrities provided an appealing and oftentimes effective antidote to party bureaucracies. More pertinently, they could be useful as proxies when candidates were not ready (or able) to seek votes themselves.

In the weeks leading up to the Chicago convention, Young & Rubicam continued to use radio and television to build popular enthusiasm for Ike, though not without some stumbles. Advisers had carefully choreographed the general's return to the United States, setting up a series of media-friendly events to mark his becoming an active candidate. With its seventeen-gun salute and performance by an Army band, Ike's arrival at Washington's National Airport was broadcast live on NBC, ABC, and the soon-to-be-defunct Dumont network. A press conference at the Pentagon two days later earned the general high marks from the *New York Times* television critic Jack Gould, who described the performance as "a model illustration of how to act in front of the cameras."[57] Only days later, however, a freshly decommissioned Eisenhower was in Abilene for a homecoming ceremony that was meant to kick off his abbreviated campaign. Steady rain, an inattentive audience, and Eisenhower's own poor delivery ruined the nationally broadcast speech. As if the change into civilian clothes had reversed his fortunes, the event inevitably drew attention to the way that Ike's time overseas had burnished his image. "The onetime supreme commander wore a nondescript raincoat and the wayward breeze mussed his hair," Lodge lamented, regretting television's ability to capture the ordinariness of his candidate. "The groundswell of public opinion which had been building flattened out," and the special prestige associated with Eisenhower began to fade.[58]

Television and the New Kingmakers

With the candidates largely offstage, the action at the Chicago convention came down to a battle over whether Eisenhower's advertising executives could outmaneuver the Taft machine. Neither candidate had a decisive lead going into the convention, though Taft was the clear choice of professional Republicans. The senator led among party officials in every region of the country, especially the South and Midwest, and since January, the percentage of county chairman supporting Taft had actually risen to 61 percent.[59] Amid the debates over Eisenhower's legitimacy as a Republican and over US involvement overseas, a cultural battle was shaping up about the role of personality in the presidential campaign. All sides seemed to recognize that television was creating a drama between a career politician with deep Republican roots and an image-oriented hero. In challenging the power of party bureaucrats, television challenged the very processes through which political decisions were made. Young & Rubicam shrewdly used the medium to tell stories about the popular celebrations that seemed to make the general's candidacy a reality. Perfect for buttons, "I Like Ike" also made for compelling TV.

The most significant conflict in the 1952 Republican National Convention was the controversy surrounding which delegation from Texas would be seated. Eisenhower had performed well in the local and county caucuses, but Taft supporters charged that his victories came from the large number of Democrats and independents ("Republicans for a day") who had been recruited to participate in the meetings. A truly Republican electorate, they argued, would have selected a more conservative candidate. Taft's supporters controlled Texas's Republican machinery, and thus, at the state convention, party officials replaced a number of pro-Eisenhower delegations with ones from 1948. Similar steamrolling tactics had taken place in Georgia and Louisiana as state officials refused to approve their pro-Eisenhower delegates. Eisenhower's campaign labeled these tactics "the Texas Steal," and at the convention's beginning, Lodge proposed a "Fair Play" rule that would disqualify contested delegates from approving the credentials of others.

The legal and political machinations surrounding the "Texas Steal" have received volumes of commentary. What matters for this discussion is how the participants shaped the controversy into a battle between diehard, militant Republicans and their seemingly bipartisan, media-friendly opponents. As far back as December 1951, Taft's campaign manager David Ingalls had been preparing for such a conflict, publicly dismissing Eisenhower as a "glamour" candidate whose viability was rooted in "hero worship" and "sex appeal." Suggesting that the general's nomination would result in the death of the GOP, he argued, "We don't want to turn the party over to a good looking mortician."[60] While still emphasizing his substance and experience, Eisenhower's advisers essentially accepted the terms of this conflict in that they positioned the attractiveness and likeability of their candidate as virtues capable of breaking down partisan manipulation and secrecy. From the halls outside committee meetings to the convention floor itself, Young & Rubicam was instrumental in orchestrating events to underscore these two different visions of American politics. No job was too trivial or too weighty to carry the message forward. Agency workers set up display tables in hotel lobbies; they spoke with uncommitted delegates, they developed strategies for getting around the roadblocks meant to thwart the campaign. Zaghi told Ike's leadership that they needed "to ridicule all of Taft's claims and at the same time, build up an impression of a successful Eisenhower campaign."[61] He sent groups of attractive young women to the delegates' hotel rooms at two or three o'clock in the morning to give them the latest literature on the Texas situation. Although these late-night visits aroused suspicion among the doormen, the combination of sex appeal and information won out, and the delegates found the materials waiting for them the next morning.[62]

The gulf between the two campaigns was apparent in their different attitudes toward television. Again and again, Taft's supporters tried to restrict the access of television and radio to committee meetings where officials were deliberating which delegates would be seated. Dominated by Taft supporters, the Republican National Committee voted 60–40 to bar radio and television from the pre-convention hearings. CBS broadcast its report outside the locked door, the camera dwelling on three imposing security guards as Walter Cronkite repeatedly referred to the secret discussions underway. The image of a clandestine meeting did not sit well with either the viewers or the delegates, and Taft found himself looking more like a machine politician than a statesman. The scene "could leave only one impression," Gould wrote in his *Times* column. "There was something someone wanted to hide." "The Taft 'steamroller' had blacked out TV."[63]

Although they themselves had been wary of televised press conferences only weeks before, leaders like Lodge and Dewey instantly praised television as an instrument of democracy. "Let the people see and hear the evidence," Governor Dewey proclaimed to the press.[64] When the Credentials Committee met in Chicago, Zaghi arranged—without its knowledge—to have television reporters show up at the meeting.[65] Some Taft supporters again tried to keep cameras out of the proceedings, but the reaction against the RNC's decision had been so strong that their efforts were in vain. As the public looked on, the committee awarded a majority of the disputed delegates to Taft. "Like Banquo's ghost and the blood-spot on Lady Macbeth's finger," one observer wrote, "the issue of political corruption in the South refused to go away."[66] A floor vote reversed the decision and seated the Eisenhower delegations instead.

Helped by their opponents' mistakes, the Eisenhower campaign skillfully tied open television coverage to fair and democratic proceedings. If Taft's power appeared to reside in loyalty, patronage, and backroom agreements, Eisenhower's lay in exposure, publicity, and public celebrations of his candidacy. The more viewers and delegates saw the crowds supporting Ike, the more momentum he had behind him. With good reason, the Taft forces worried that the excitement around Eisenhower would give him an air of inevitability. Knowing what television might convey, they tried to prevent a lengthy parade when the general's name was put into nomination. David Levy, a Young & Rubicam executive who headed up the television/radio committee for Citizens for Eisenhower, worked with the networks to make sure the celebration took place:

> The Taft people didn't want an Eisenhower rally when he was nominated, so they tried to clear the hall of his supporters. I had about six or seven credentials. I gave 'em to one of my advisors and said, "Get six people in." As soon as six came in, we passed the credentials out again and again. The networks let us stash these people around the hall as extra cameramen, makeup people. We even put them in closets. We brought in maybe 150 people, and they put on a big parade for Eisenhower's nomination.[67]

Levy's trickery underscored a central point: what was good for Ike was good for TV. After all the rancor and controversy, he won on the first ballot and became the nominee.

The maneuvering left many conservatives outraged. They marveled at the way Lodge had agitated the nation with his accusations against Taft, and they bitterly complained about the media glamour surrounding the general. In the days leading up to the convention, the *Chicago Daily Tribune* lambasted Darryl F. Zanuck, the head of Twentieth Century Fox, for bringing Humphrey Bogart and Susan Hayward to an Eisenhower rally in Denver the previous week.[68] The *Tribune* was a bastion of conservative thought, and under the editorship of Robert McCormick, it promoted a brand of isolationism that had little room for NATO and Ike. Zanuck had already challenged the California Republican establishment when he joined forces with Samuel Goldwyn and Jack Warner to promote Eisenhower's nonpartisan appeal.[69] Their efforts became a natural target for the *Tribune*'s frustrated Taft supporters. As tensions rose in Chicago, the paper described Zanuck as being one of "Hollywood's strutting colonels" whose service during World War II was nothing more than a show. With Eisenhower in office, it charged, Zanuck expected to profit enormously from movie sales abroad. As if trying to draw him into a HUAC investigation, the paper accused him of being "long friendly to internationalist and leftist causes" and having attended a pro-Communist Writers' Congress in 1943. Amid these scattershot accusations, however, there was one central concern: Zanuck and the "internationalist Hollywood movie colony" were vigorously picking up "movie money for the general's backers to spend." Angered by the smears, Zanuck fired off a lengthy, point-by-point response demanding a retraction.[70]

Other opponents argued that, with friends who controlled the nation's leading television stations, news magazines, and advertising agencies, Ike won the nomination on the basis of a staged controversy. Launching her first salvo into public life, conservative writer Phyllis Schlafly included the 1952 convention in her attack on Republican kingmakers for selecting candidates who were out of step with rank-and-file party members. She excoriated the New York elite for using the media and advertising industries to dupe the nation into believing that Taft couldn't win the general election and, worse, that he had cheated. Schlafly did not blame Eisenhower for these machinations, largely because she thought he was an "amateur in politics" and "did not have the slightest idea of the tactics used by the little clique determined to steal the nomination and push him into the Presidency."[71] To Schlafly, a well-orchestrated media machine had produced the Texas delegation fight. "Suddenly, as if someone had pushed a button, the whole propaganda apparatus of our country went into action to slander the character of the most honorable man in public life."[72]

Throughout her discussion, Schlafly used the epithet "kingmakers" to refer to the men who supported more liberal and internationalist Republican candidates. The "kingmakers" were the center of Schlafly's theory that New York media and financial elites had conspired to control the Republican electorate through propaganda, publicity, and image-making. Schlafly appropriated the term from an older mode of American politics that had groomed and supported candidates such as Senator Taft. Commentators usually use the word "kingmaker" to refer to party bosses like Big Tim Sullivan of New York or Matthew Quay of Pennsylvania who oversaw the distribution of offices and rewards in a self-perpetuating system. The 1952 Republican convention made a significant crack in the ward- and county-based politics that had dominated American elections for over one hundred years. Eisenhower was suited to the television age, not because he was especially good-looking or charismatic or interesting to watch on screen. He was suited to the television age because his heroism had made him famous. A latter-day Coriolanus, Eisenhower could delay his visit to the marketplace because his image had successfully preceded him.

With its emphasis on fame and publicity, television was a powerful force in breaking down the insularity, one might even say tribalism, that had long influenced the nomination of candidates. Although he was a veteran of Sunday news programs, Taft was suspicious of television and recoiled from its power to disrupt the political establishment. A revealing moment came when he entered the convention hall and was mobbed by supporters. Some candidates would enjoy the attention; others would merely tolerate it. Taft found the whole business distasteful. Still smarting from his public opinion beating the previous week, he blamed the commotion on the new medium. "That is a good example of why we don't have TV at national committee meetings," he snapped as he moved away.[73]

Taft was not alone in worrying about the effects of television. Charles A. H. Thompson, a scholar with the Brookings Institution, released a report demonstrating that, in its political coverage, television did a better job of showcasing personalities than issues, an imbalance that reflected the influence of advertising agencies as well as the networks.[74] In a landmark study of the 1952 conventions, University of Chicago sociologists Kurt and Gladys Lang found that television's focus on drama and personality gave viewers a false impression of the key power players in the delegate fight.[75] As the campaign evolved, the politicians began to understand how they could harness the emphasis on drama and personality. Nixon's iconic "Checkers" speech ultimately saved his spot on the Republican ticket not because he dispersed all the questions about his secret political fund but because he used the medium so effectively. Funded by three Republican organizations and arranged by BBDO, the broadcast went out over sixty four NBC television stations after *The Milton Berle Show*.[76] Nixon later acknowledged that he selected the timing of the speech for aesthetic reasons. "We wanted to create suspense," he explained, so he consequently delayed his speech from a Sunday to a Tuesday.[77] Zanuck was a near-constant (and sometimes annoying) presence in the Eisenhower campaign, sending missive after missive about how to improve the general's appearances.[78] When he congratulated Nixon after the "Checkers" speech, however, he had nothing but praise. He told the young senator it was "the most tremendous performance I've ever seen."[79]

While television introduced superficial values into the process, it also succeeded in achieving an important goal for any minority party: expanding and opening up the electorate. The 1952 convention had been a battle for the heart of the GOP. As Schlafly's attack made clear, the party's kingmakers and core philosophy had changed, but with that change came the chance of a November victory. Personality and likeability, whatever their limitations, were precisely the bipartisan qualities that Ike's advisers thought they would be, strong enough to draw Democrats and independents into Republican caucuses and primaries. Thomson held television responsible for the jump in voter participation from 48.8 percent in 1948 to 61.3 percent in 1952. (The last time the US had seen such a dramatic increase, he argued, was after the introduction of radio.)[80] In the end, the insiders Schlafly revered would continue to feel threatened until they adapted to the new age. By 1955, the new chairman of the Republican National Committee, Leonard Hall, was urging party members to think differently about their presidential nominees. As he told a group of activists, "We must choose able and personable candidates who can 'sell themselves' because TV has changed the course of campaigns."[81]

Merchandising Ike

After the July convention, a number of advertising agencies helped expand Eisenhower's campaign to the general election. Chief among these was BBDO, one of the largest and most comprehensive agencies in the nation. In 1952, BBDO became the agency of record for the Republican Party, adding it to a list of clients that included US Steel, DuPont, and General Motors. BBDO was headed by two standard-bearers of the industry. Bruce Barton had started the company in 1918 with Alex Osborn and Roy Durstine. Barton had served as BBDO's chairman of the board since its merger with the Batten Agency in 1928, overseeing its expansion into radio and television. To Barton, advertising was more than a commercial practice: it was a discourse, a language that structured the way people knew the world. The son of a Congregationalist minister, he had a deeply spiritual vein, and, among numerous books, he published *The Man Nobody Knows* (1925) which praised Jesus's use of sales and advertising techniques. A best-seller when it was first released, the book sold over 725,000 copies in the United States by 1959. The book's popularity contributed to the sanctification of business that historians have observed in mid-century American culture.[82]

FIGURE 3.2 BBDO's Bruce Barton with movie director Cecil B. DeMille. DeMille holds a copy of Barton's *The Man Nobody Knows*, a biography of Jesus that influenced the director's 1927 film *The King of Kings*. The inscription reads, in part, "Bruce, If nobody knows him when we are through, it will be because they are blind and deaf."

Courtesy of Wisconsin Historical Society, 32701.

Barton was a veteran of Republican politics. He had advised Calvin Coolidge and Herbert Hoover during their presidential campaigns, working to soften their public image and present them as well-rounded candidates. (In addition to writing parts of speeches, one of Barton's suggestions was to distribute a series of Hoover photographs—one with his wife, another while fishing or chopping down a tree, "something that shows him a human being."[83]) After consulting with the Republican National Committee on the mid-term elections, Barton ran for Congress in 1937, winning a seat representing New York's Upper West Side in a special election.[84] He held the seat for three years before losing a campaign for the Senate. Although he was something of an isolationist, Barton had enjoyed a warm friendship with Eisenhower since the general had arrived at Columbia University, and the two exchanged familiar, self-deprecating letters. ("I'm still doing a pretty fair job dodging speeches," Eisenhower wrote in 1950, "—but I'm booked for a four-network, twelve and half a minute affair on Monday night—Labor Day. I'm speaking in favor of the 'Crusade for Freedom,' which is something on the order of being against sin!")[85] Although he remained torn between Taft and Eisenhower during the primaries, Barton supported the general "with gusto" once he received the nomination and would remain part of his advisory circle during the presidency.[86] The fact that he had long coached candidates that they "must appear to be 'above the place of partisan politics'" made him an exceptionally compatible member of Eisenhower's team.[87]

At Barton's side was the president of BBDO, Ben Duffy, who had taken on the day-to-day operations of the agency since 1947. In the ten years that Duffy served as president, BBDO quadrupled its billings from $50 to $200 million.[88] In contrast to Barton, who had gone to prep school and then Amherst College, Duffy was a self-made man. He had started at the agency when he was just seventeen years old, and he enjoyed the business so much that he dropped out of college to continue. By 1942, he had become the president of the agency and would proceed to build it into one of the most formidable in the world.

BBDO's approach to the Eisenhower campaign was simple: selling Eisenhower and Nixon by focusing on their personalities. As the official "Campaign Plan" put it, the agency had to get the candidates "into the homes of America by every means possible so that the warmth of their personalities can be felt."[89] Barton made this approach practical when he sketched an appeal sent to Republican women encouraging them to donate to a television fund for Ike:

> If General Eisenhower could go personally into every home in the United States he would be elected overwhelmingly. His charm, his integrity, and his forthrightness are almost irresistible.

> He can't, of course, go into every home in person, but we can take him into 38 million homes by television—and the cost is less than one cent a home.

Will you take him into a hundred homes by sending us $1.00? Or into
10 thousand homes by sending us $100?[90]

When explaining his agency's approach, Duffy offered no apologies about
selling Ike's personality as if it were a consumer product: BBDO would focus
its efforts on "merchandising Eisenhower's frankness, honesty, and integrity,
his sincere and wholesome approach."[91]

As Duffy and Barton conceived it, Eisenhower's personality was not just
the sum of his personal qualities. It was also about the warm reception he
inspired in others. Eisenhower was a great and trusted leader, but more
importantly, he was *liked*. When properly conveyed to donors and voters, he
was "almost irresistible," as Barton put it, so the task was to think of ways
to communicate the enthusiasm others felt for him. BBDO had been one of
the first agencies to incorporate "brainstorming" into their creative process,
and memos sailed around the office about how to promote Ike's popularity.[92]
Barton suggested putting a microphone in the audience during Eisenhower's
speeches so that the applause would seem more dramatic and powerful.[93] He
talked with Duffy about incorporating rhetorical questions into the text that
would produce a unified, fervent response. Thus Eisenhower might say, " 'Do
you want your boy to die in some far off Korea; in a war you never voted
for?' 'No. No. No.' " "The audience feels that it is advising the speaker," Barton
explained, and the unseen television audience "feels that all the people in the
country are shouting approval."[94]

At times, clients and supporters also sent their ideas to BBDO. The
Pittsburgh-based company Westinghouse Electric had been the primary
sponsor of the Republican and Democratic national conventions; its spokes-
woman, Betty Furness, had become a celebrity in her own right, appearing in over four-and-a-half hours of live commercials each week. In early
September, Andrew Robertson, the Westinghouse chairman of the board,
called Barton with some ideas for the campaign. "It would be very effective if
we could get a group of endorsements of Eisenhower by well-known people
for special use in the out of town areas. We who live in big cities tend to
underestimate the influence of such names in the smaller towns and rural
communities."[95] Whether prompted by Robertson's phone call or not, an
organization named "Sportsmen for Eisenhower–Nixon" surfaced to promote the GOP ticket. Suggesting that there was an essential bond between
athletic competition and Americanism, the committee included some eighty
"World Sports Champions," including boxer Gene Tunney, baseball players
Ty Cobb and Mickey Mantle, and Olympic gold medalists Dorothy Poynton
and Bob Mathias.[96]

At first glance, the most talked-about advertisements of the 1952 campaign
had nothing to do with celebrity; they were a series of thirty-second spots that
Rosser Reeves, an executive with Ted Bates & Company developed for Citizens

for Eisenhower–Nixon. Reeves was notorious for developing the "hard sell," a strategy that concentrated less on creating brand image than on repeating a single, uncheckable claim meant to differentiate a product from its competitors. M&M candies "melt in your mouth, not in your hands" was one Reeves formulation. "Anacin for Fast Pain Relief" was another. Both slogans followed what Reeves called his "Unique Selling Proposition," or USP, in which the advertisement pits the qualities of its product against the implied deficiencies of unnamed competitors.[97] As one of Reeves' most famous advertisements put it, "Only Anacin of the four leading headache remedies has special ingredients to relieve pain FAST, help overcome depression FAST, relax tension FAST." In part a response to the tremendous proliferation of products in the 1950s, in part an expression of skepticism about more entertaining (and expensive) kinds of advertising, Reeves's hard-sell techniques were so insistent that they were often accused of creating headaches themselves. And yet the repetition, crude graphics, and faux mysteries (caffeine and aspirin are Anacin's "special distinctive" ingredients) worked miraculously. As Reeves liked to boast, his advertisements "made more money for the producers of Anacin in seven years than 'Gone With the Wind' did for David O. Selznick and M-G-M in a quarter of a century."[98]

Reeves's techniques set him apart from the more genteel stream of Madison Avenue advertising. His brother-in-law was David Ogilvy, an Englishman who made his advertising fortune promoting prestige brands such as Hathaway shirts, Schweppes soda, and Rolls-Royce luxury automobiles. Known as the "Prince of the Hard Sell," Reeves promoted everyday packaged goods that one could find in medicine cabinets across the United States. Friends questioned Reeves's crude, rudimentary approach, but he took pride in the effectiveness of the USP and his personal ability to move products off the shelves. As other agencies began cloaking their advertisements in glamour and sex, Reeves focused on the products themselves, using strident pronouncements and somewhat harsh lighting. Talking to the *New Yorker* magazine, he boasted about how he had helped Rolaids overcome Tums as the nation's leading antacid. The Tums commercial had begun with a long, slow shot of a beautiful woman diving into a swimming pool. As she smiles into the camera, her ample cleavage visible in the water, she is beset by crippling stomach pains. Tums soothes the pain and restores the visual fantasy. Reeves's commercial featured a man with a hole-ridden handkerchief meant to represent the effects of acid on the stomach lining. Rolaids, the man announces, "absorbs *forty-seven times* its own weight in stomach acid."[99]

With funding from three wealthy oilmen, Reeves borrowed a technique that Milton Biow had first used on the radio: he produced a collection of twenty- to sixty-second Eisenhower commercials that appeared between popular television programs.[100] These spot advertisements highlighted specific aspects of Eisenhower's platform and life. "The Man from Abilene," one

FIGURE 3.3 *An executive with the Ted Bates agency, Rosser Reeves designed the*
"Eisenhower Answers America" TV spots for the 1952 campaign.
Courtesy Wisconsin Historical Society, 83073.

spot began, with the voice of an announcer blaring through the commercial
as if he were summoning a superhero with a megaphone. For a series of spots
titled "Eisenhower Answers America," Reeves spent a day recording the candidate's answers to questions about the war in Korea, the cost of living, and
government corruption. Reeves had written the responses on giant cue cards,
and with minimal revisions, Eisenhower read the pithy, resolute answers in
a New York studio. Only after filming some forty Eisenhower answers did
Reeves go to Rockefeller Center and invite tourists to read the pre-scripted
questions themselves. The effect was rather jarring. "General, I'd like to get
married," a young man asks off-camera, "but we couldn't live on the salary
I get after taxes." "Well," Eisenhower responded, "the Democrats are sinking
deeper into a bottomless sea of debt and demanding more taxes to keep their
confused heads above water. Let's put on a sturdy life boat in November." With
its contorted metaphors (how does one "put on" a life boat?) and overzealous
response, the advertisement made little sense, but the illusion of give-and-
take was enough to grab the electorate's attention and set the critics ablaze.[101]

In an age in which corporations purchased entire television programs to advertise their wares, Reeves's idea was perceived as radical and revolutionary. Rumors about the advertisements had journalists buzzing for weeks, and the Democrats immediately cited the spots as evidence that Eisenhower was a shill for corporate interests. In many ways, the spots had the opposite effect of the celebrity-themed events that avoided politics and softened Eisenhower with entertainment and glamour. Supervised by the director of the *March of Time* newsreel programs, Reeves's spots were all politics and featured a flinty, plain-spoken Eisenhower barking out the words that Reeves had written on the cue cards. Though Reeves claimed the spots were "ideally suited to his warm personality," the man who emerged seemed as wooden and uncomfortable as Coriolanus in the marketplace.[102]

What remains largely unacknowledged, however, is that Reeves designed the Eisenhower spots to capitalize on the American fascination with celebrity. Although they struck a different tone than Ike Day, the spots were just as tactical in positioning the general alongside show business celebrities. In a confidential memo titled "PROGRAM TO GUARANTEE AN EISENHOWER VICTORY," Reeves touted this "new way of campaigning":

A big advertiser, for example, puts on a one-hour net-work television show. It may cost him $75,000 . . . for that one hour. Immediately after, another big advertiser follows it with another big expensive show. Jack Benny! Martin and Lewis! Eddie Cantor! Fred Allen! Edgar Bergen and Charlie McCarthy! Or dozens of other big-time stars. THESE BIG ADVERTISERS SPEND MILLIONS—WITH TOP TALENT AND GLITTERING NAMES—TO BUILD A BIG AUDIENCE!

But—between the two shows comes the humble 'spot.'

If you can run your advertisement in this 'spot,' for a very small sum YOU GET THE AUDIENCE BUILT AT HUGE COSTS BY OTHER PEOPLE. It's a form of 'ju jitsu', whereby a little pressure gets some startling results.[103]

Rather than seek celebrity endorsements as Young & Rubicam and BBDO were already doing, Reeves developed a campaign that adhered to his hard-sell techniques—"Eisenhower Answers America"—but piggybacked on popular culture and celebrity. The tactic made sense, for as interested as Americans were in television and politics, they much preferred entertainment. The Nielsen ratings from the period made this preference clear. In July 1952, over 13 million people viewed the Republican National Convention; 14.5 million tuned in to see the Democrats the next week. In January 1953, 29 million watched Ike's inauguration. The week before, the leading episode of *I Love Lucy* attracted 44 million viewers.[104]

In Reeves's plan, Eisenhower would be carried into the homes of millions of Americans by the likes of Jerry Lewis and Jack Benny. As if they were products, politicians would go where they would find the most consumers; whether they followed a comedy or a drama did not matter, as long as they received maximum exposure. Not only did the Reeves spots attract attention, but their careful placement put them far ahead of the Democrats, who continued to buy up popular broadcast times for special programs and speeches. Eisenhower's team made this mistake once and quickly learned to use celebrity rather than replace it. Adlai Stevenson's advisers seemed oblivious to the fact that they were continually preempting America's favorite shows for their 30-minute political programs. Their disregard earned the rancor of viewers across the country, one of whom wrote the Stevenson campaign, "I Love Lucy, I like Ike, drop dead."[105]

Throughout the 1952 campaign, an important voice of dissent came from within the general's ranks: actor George Murphy. A veteran of dozens of MGM musicals and a former head of the Screen Actors Guild, Murphy had come from a traditionally Democratic family before falling out with the party after FDR tried to increase the size of the Supreme Court to protect his New Deal policies. Nicknamed the Ziegfeld of the Republican Party, Murphy was frequently asked to organize shows and rallies for Republican candidates.[106] In 1940, he joined "We the People," the Wendell Willkie organization that counted among its 200 supporters Robert Montgomery, Ginger Rogers, and Irene Dunne.[107] Over the years, Murphy would organize everything from anti-Communist rallies at the Hollywood Bowl, to USO tours of South Korea. He found that "bringing in Hollywood 'names,' increased Republican audiences." "It was all a matter of staging," Murphy said. "It was like building a show with an all-star cast. I discovered that if a congressman was going to make a speech and you could advertise that actors like John Wayne were also going to be on the platform, it would double the audience."[108]

Murphy came from the conservative wing of the Republican Party. The actor's close association with Louis B. Mayer at MGM had put him in contact with high-level politicians for over a decade, and he had learned much from the executive and his assistant Ida Koverman. As Donald T. Critchlow has demonstrated, he joined many Hollywood Republicans (including Cecil B. DeMille, Hedda Hopper, Mary Pickford, and Adolphe Menjou) in arguing that Robert Taft would make a better president than Ike. Although as a member of the California delegation he was bound to support Earl Warren in 1952, Murphy always found Warren too moderate for his tastes, and he was more than happy to back Ike, a candidate he saw as a winner.[109] After the convention, Murphy worked with Zanuck to bridge the divisions between the Eisenhower and Taft supporters in Hollywood, the two camps agreeing to focus on different sets of California voters—independents, Ike-leaning Democrats, and hardcore members of the GOP.[110] In mid-September, Murphy organized a jam-packed rally in Los Angeles that Ike attended and admired. When an Eisenhower aide asked him to join the campaign, he replied that his contract with MGM prevented him from accepting. The next day, he learned that the studio had altered his contract and that he was "assigned to General Eisenhower for the duration of the campaign." The actor spent the rest of the fall organizing Ike's rallies, scheduling entertainment, shortening political speeches, and making sure the speakers and microphones were in the proper places.[111] Eisenhower admired Murphy so much that he twice asked him to join the Administration's public relations team. "I must say I am more than impressed with him," he wrote the chairman of the RNC's finance committee in 1953. Several months later, he again praised the actor's expertise: "I for one would certainly be delighted if we could find a way to integrate him more closely into the staff family."[112]

What made Murphy a voice of dissent during the campaign was his impatience with Eisenhower's Madison Avenue advisers. Both confident and frank, Murphy was quick to dismiss politicians and advertising executives for not knowing anything about public relations and show business. "He can

FIGURE 3.4 *Eisenhower admired the work of Republican actor and activist George Murphy. Here the two meet during Murphy's 1964 Senate campaign.*
Courtesy of National Park Service and Dwight D. Eisenhower Presidential Library and Museum.

never be anybody's man but his own," Mayer put it, "and as such, he has great value in Hollywood. He has never been afraid to tell us the truth, whether it will be popular or not. It is not in him."[113] This attitude led Murphy to clash with the people at Young & Rubicam and BBDO who didn't seem to recognize Eisenhower's poor performance on TV. "His voice was flat," Murphy complained, "he looked like an old man on TV because his light hair and eyebrows did not show up, giving an impression of blankness; his rimless glasses registered as two blobs of light on the tv screen."[114] With remarkable brio, Murphy dismissed the executives who had been working for Ike with the line, "You don't know anything about" television and "you won't handle it."[115] It was under Murphy's guidance that Eisenhower received help from Robert Montgomery and started to become a television-savvy candidate. That viewers told pollsters that Eisenhower seemed "good-natured, sincere, honest, cheerful, and clear-headed" seemed like a victory not just to the ever-confident Murphy but also to the advisers who had been working for the general since the winter of 1951.[116]

The campaign to draft Eisenhower—to secure for him the nomination while not involving him in politics, and then to win the presidency itself—proved to be a long and complicated effort, as a wide range of individuals adapted to the new medium of television and its emphasis on personality and fame. The campaign had arguably begun in the least likely of settings—the boxing ring of Madison Square Garden—and it ended on the night before the election in another events arena, the Boston Garden. A Wild West rodeo show had preceded the rally that Young & Rubicam organized for Ike, and the stench of the animals permeated the building as the Republicans prepared for the final television rally of the campaign.

While the admen prepared for the television show, vaudeville acts entertained the crowd until the top-flight entertainers like Fred Waring arrived from New York. As Murphy describes it in his memoir, a tense moment occurred when Cabot Lodge wanted to make a few remarks before introducing Dwight and Mamie later in the evening. Like all politicians, Lodge thought the evening was about speech-making, and though Murphy had cut all the speeches in half, the Massachusetts senator continued to resist: he wanted to read his statement in its entirety. When the time came to introduce the Eisenhowers, however, the noise from the excited crowd was deafening. Lodge fumbled as he tried to read his introductory speech, but he soon realized that no one was listening. The cheers for Ike kept coming. Murphy looked on with satisfaction. Knowing he had been right, he slowly walked to the center of the stage. "Cabot, I don't think you have to say anything," he whispered. "They know the General is in the hall."[117] And as Lodge stepped away from the microphone, a transition began to take place—for Eisenhower and for the nation.

The Spectacle Campaign

On the afternoon of March 22, 1956, CBS broadcast a rather extraordinary television program: "Happy Birthday to Our First Lady—With Music." The program involved live music and dance performances from a studio in New York and a luncheon hosted by the "Wives of the Federal Independent Agencies of the United States Government" in Washington, DC. Heavy on strings and sentiment, the music featured nearly a dozen numbers. Choreographer John Butler had created dances to accompany each of the songs, his troupe providing a stylish, often romantic atmosphere for such tunes as Martha Wright's "'Til We Meet Again" and Robert Rounseville's "I Dreamt I Dwelt in Marble Halls." Conceived on Madison Avenue, the program relied on selections from what we might regard as the Eisenhower family canon. Marion Marlow sang "I'm in Love with a Wonderful Guy" from *South Pacific* and "It's a Lovely Day" from *Call Me Madam*. Mahalia Jackson offered "Swing Low, Sweet Chariot," and Wright, "Down Among the Sheltering Palms," both of which later appeared in the Ike Day show that CBS televised in October.[1] What made "Happy Birthday to the First Lady" extraordinary, however, was not its relationship to Ike Day or its frothy attention to the well-heeled women having lunch at the Willard Hotel. What made the program extraordinary was its timing. The broadcast honoring Mrs. Eisenhower's birthday came four months too late. She had turned fifty-nine on November 14, 1955.

Among the many successes they felt in the spring of 1956, the Republicans would have been pleased to know how nettlesome the Democrats found this program to be. The sudden appearance of a birthday show left Democrats angry and suspicious, especially since Dwight Eisenhower had announced his intent to seek reelection only three weeks before. Cy Anderson, the rough-spoken leader of the Railway Labor Union, had seen advertisements for the Mamie broadcast and called the Democratic National Committee to complain. The DNC chairman, Paul Butler, rifled off a note to his staff: "Please investigate this report and advise whether this is a *network* or local program. Who is responsible for its *production* and presentation? Is this a

Robert Montgomery show? Is it planned and placed on the TV facilities by B.B.D. and O?"[2] Six days after the show had aired, Reggie Schuebel reported that the request for time had gone directly to Frank Stanton, the president of CBS and a longtime Eisenhower adviser. "On the face of it, this was a non-political broadcast," she acknowledged, "but when you consider that Mrs. Eisenhower's birthday was last year—that this party was arranged after the President's public declaration of his candidacy—and that the luncheon was given by the wives of 61 appointees of the President—it smells very much like Republican politics." The frustration kept growing. Not only did CBS seem to violate federal laws about giving candidates equal airtime, but the Republicans were hiding their campaign activities behind a veil of entertainment. "This television thing," Anderson fumed to Butler's secretary, "has gone beyond all reason."[3]

In many ways, the 1956 presidential race looked back to the previous campaign. Eisenhower and Adlai Stevenson ran against each other a second time, and on the Republican side, the major advertising agencies and political consultants remained the same. Critics still struggled with the idea of televised spots that Rosser Reeves had developed, and celebrities were still willing to promote Eisenhower's candidacy. BBDO returned as the agency of record for the Republican Party, and as Butler suspected, it was responsible for the belated celebration of Mamie's birthday. In 1952, however, the alliance between Madison Avenue, television, and celebrity was only beginning to coalesce. The partnerships were tentative, and the major players were improvising to keep up with new technologies and opportunities. While observers noted the important shifts taking place, it took another four years to recognize that the many incremental changes were producing a new paradigm for political campaigns. By 1956, the burgeoning alliance had become a powerful cultural force. The agencies had grown, their revenues had skyrocketed, and their executives had spent three years playing golf and cards with the president. The DNC's frustration conveyed their fear of being left behind.[4]

Of all the proponents of television in politics, perhaps the most surprising was Eisenhower himself. The president had suffered a heart attack while vacationing in Colorado in September 1955, and he had spent seven weeks in a Denver military hospital convalescing. The experience left him reluctant to embark on a cross-country campaign, and once he decided to seek reelection, he hoped television would relieve him of such trips. Ike was happy to exchange the locomotive and whistle-stop speeches he had employed in 1952 for a series of staged events in Washington and New York. Television would allow him to speak to both regional and national audiences without the exhaustion of traveling. Television "can replace much of the physical exertion of campaigning," his TV Plans Board explained in the proposal they submitted before Ike had declared his candidacy. Perhaps more importantly, it could "most persuasively present Eisenhower's beliefs to the American people."[5]

The president and his advisers had good reason to be confident about the use of television in his reelection campaign. As the board explained, the medium's explosive growth created more opportunities (and challenges) than existed when the Citizens for Eisenhower group was battling Taft for open committee meetings in Chicago. In 1952, 40 percent of American homes had a television set; by 1956, that number had almost doubled, to 76 percent. Over the same four years, television had made its way into smaller cities and rural communities, and the number of broadcasting stations in the United States rose from 109 to 450. All this expansion meant more choice and more content. Early in the decade, the networks had begun to inch away from their reliance on live programming, and as the transition to film and video accelerated, Hollywood movie studios began to produce their own series. In 1952, television provided 11,000 hours of programming per week. Four years later, there were 54,000 program hours each week, and the competition for viewers had grown more expensive and intense.[6] While publishers continued to lobby for the newspaper as the cornerstone of political communications, advertising agencies were directing their clients toward TV. In October 1956, BBDO's vice president, Carroll Newton, reported to the Senate Subcommittee on Privileges and Elections that the agency had spent $26,160 buying space for print advertising and $17,192 buying radio time for the Republican National Committee. With less than a month to go before Election Day, they had put $218,958 into purchasing television time for the Eisenhower–Nixon ticket and $416,194 toward Republican Senate candidates. The disparity was remarkable, especially considering that these numbers did not include the high production costs associated with TV.[7]

The addition of Robert Montgomery to the White House staff in 1954 also explains Eisenhower's growing enthusiasm for the way the medium had changed the political landscape. George Murphy had brought his fellow MGM actor into the 1952 campaign, but midway through his first term, the president asked Montgomery to join him permanently. A two-time Academy Award nominee and a highly successful leading man, Montgomery had retired from acting in 1952 and was producing the weekly drama "Robert Montgomery Presents" on NBC. Sensitive to how Ike's opponents might depict the invitation, he accepted the appointment with little fanfare and no pay. After hosting the Monday evening broadcast in New York, the actor traveled to Washington where he spent two or three days each week working out of his second-floor White House office.[8] As Eisenhower's media consultant, Montgomery focused on helping the president adapt to the peculiar demands of television. Some of his innovations were as simple as adjusting the length of the podium or getting Eisenhower to wear darker suits and trade in his dark-rimmed glasses for ones with clearer frames.[9] Improving the president's timing and delivery required practice. Television cameras were large and unwieldy pieces of equipment in the 1950s, and Montgomery noticed that

Eisenhower grew distracted by all the movement and commotion involved in producing live TV. His solution was to drape black curtains over the set so Ike had nothing to see but the lenses filming him.[10] Over time, Montgomery would play a bigger role in developing programs he thought were suitable for the president. He adapted Franklin Roosevelt's "fireside chats" to television and instituted the practice of broadcasting live press conferences, the latter of which made an indelible mark on the way Americans view the presidency. It was Montgomery who encouraged the president to ad-lib his calming remarks on April 5, 1954, urging Americans not to "fall prey to hysterical thinking" about the Cold War and the hydrogen bomb.[11]

FIGURE 4.1 *Actor Robert Montgomery advising the president before a televised address on March 15, 1954.*

Courtesy of National Park Service and Dwight D. Eisenhower Presidential Library and Museum.

No one was more pleased with Montgomery's contribution than the members of the resurrected Eisenhower TV Plans Board. Although the board recommended some targeted changes to press secretary Jim Hagerty's office, they unequivocally praised Montgomery as being "invaluable" to the campaign. In fact, their only suggestion was to use him as much as possible:

> This Board believes that the television techniques that will be used in the coming campaign will differ greatly from the last campaign—basically in tending to the "*spectacular*" approach. Thus, Montgomery's combined background of Hollywood motion pictures and network television uniquely fit him as the *creative producer* type needed for specific political telecasts.

> His advice should be sought on all strategy matters which pertain specifically to the President appearing before network television cameras.[12]

Long before the campaign got underway, the TV Plans Board was pushing the Eisenhower administration to use television as a medium for image-crafting, not just delivering speeches. Montgomery fit their plans nicely. They did not expect him to appear before the cameras like other conservative celebrities; they wanted him behind the scenes where he could make the campaign as visually appealing and effective as it could be.

As the board presented it, the major change from 1952 was a shift away from merely garnering publicity to finding ways to attach the campaign to the lavish and spectacular. Since the earliest days of the Draft Eisenhower movement, the Republicans had done an excellent job of drawing attention to how much voters liked their candidate, and they expanded some of their previous efforts to bolster that excitement. The fleet of six bandwagons they sent around the country was designed precisely to have "maximum impact," leaving the cities they visited "with an atmosphere of Eisenhower and a spirit of enthusiasm and opportunism."[13] Langhorne Washburn oversaw the operation and proved to be ingenious in turning each stop into an extravagant public display. With their matching outfits and parasols, the Ike Girls entertained the crowds, dancing and cheering as canvassers distributed information about Ike's positions and upcoming appearances on television. Having served as a blimp pilot in the Navy, Washburn equipped each bandwagon with a searchlight and an inflatable 40-foot barrage balloon so that individuals could see the bandwagon's presence at night and from blocks away.[14]

The board hoped to begin staging such spectacles directly on TV. Building on the popularity of what network executives termed "spectaculars"—lavish entertainments that featured multiple performers in visually striking environments—they set about to create programs that would rally both voters and volunteers around the president. A fundraising program broadcast on closed-circuit television in January 1956 aimed for such an effect as it moved from Fred Waring's choir in Chicago, to Jimmy Stewart in California, to Olympic gold medalist Dick Button ice skating into a darkened Madison Square Garden, carrying an American flag. Even Ike was swept into the enthusiasm, marveling at how the "magic carpet of TV" made such a night possible.[15] The Plans Board saw a clear distinction taking place. If the primary television concern in 1952 was to gain coverage, four years later the election had become a battle of techniques.[16] The programs celebrating Ike's and Mamie's birthdays showcased where the board expected the battle was heading.

Network time and production costs were expensive, however, and advisers looked for ways to get television advertising for free. Hugh Foster of National Citizens for Eisenhower proposed that groups could buy up tickets for Steve Allen's *Tonight Show* and then stage an on-air rally that demonstrated their support for Ike. (If the network complained, he hinted, the rally could be explained as a Youth for Eisenhower stunt.)[17] The Plans Board saw the creation of programs like Ike Day as a budgetary priority, but they, too, looked for ways to create " 'pro-Eisenhower impressions' at *no cost.*" They strategized about whom to place on news shows and concluded that "new personalities with warm earnest appeal" would supplement the " 'marquee star value' of the established political names." They listed the producers and phone numbers of fourteen panel interview programs—from Edward R. Murrow's *Person to Person* to Groucho Marx's *You Bet Your Life*—so that once the campaign began, advisers could start trying to get Eisenhower supporters on air.[18]

The members of the TV Plans Board were interested in what they termed "Spectacular Hitch-hikes" in which stars and politicians could become part of an extravagant entertainment program that brought the campaign good publicity. Both Eisenhower and Nixon had been featured on such programs during their first term, and the advisers wanted to see more of these guest appearances. The board noted that Eisenhower came off as warm and friendly during his fireside chat at the end of David O. Selznick's *Light's Diamond Jubilee*, a two-hour television spectacular sponsored by General Electric that celebrated the seventy-fifth anniversary of electric light. Ever the Cold Warrior, Nixon had done a cameo appearance on the televised version of Arthur Koestler's anti-Soviet novel, *Darkness at Noon.* The fact that one in five Americans had seen the program and heard the Vice President's remarks made the board hungry for more. "The spectacular approach is here to stay," they counseled, and recommended that the campaign begin to pursue opportunities on the more than one hundred such programs scheduled for 1956.[19]

One advantage of these "behemoth" formats was that they brought an attentive and diverse audience. As the board pointed out, more people saw Eisenhower on television during the GE program than had ever seen a president at any single moment in the nation's history. The real payoff, however, was that the program offered what the board called the "inferred integration of the political personality."[20] When Eisenhower appeared on the same show as Lauren Bacall, Joseph Cotton, and Debbie Reynolds, when he became another player in Selznick's epic undertaking, he seemed to be drawn out of politics and into the company of people known for their charm and likeability. Eisenhower's opinions, his policies, and his political identity were momentarily integrated into the pleasurable surface of performance and entertainment. In turning the president into a figure of both admiration and inspiration, television partially stripped the audience of its critical capacity. The staged setting of the fireside chat gave an aura of nostalgic intimacy to a program that was celebrating the partnership of American capitalism and modern technology. Once Eisenhower was integrated into the virtual community, once the context had mitigated his difference from other famous people, he became the nation's grandfather rather than an architect of Western power.

It was up to the best advertising agencies to make these visions a reality, and the Plans Board offered their robust support for BBDO and Young & Rubicam. The agencies were large enough that they could put eight to ten people on the account and bring their full "corporate weight" into planning. Not only were the agency presidents Ben Duffy and Sig Larmon longtime Eisenhower supporters, but they had served as unofficial advisers during his first term. In January 1954, Larmon declined the president's request that he join the administration to help develop and coordinate its Cold War and psychological warfare programs.[21] The TV Plans Board had to work harder to convince Young & Rubicam than it did BBDO. The agency was reluctant to become too identified with one political party, so Citizens for Eisenhower–Nixon turned to J. Walter Thompson to handle the task of attracting independents and swing-voting Democrats. Midway through the summer of 1956, however, the Citizens group had returned to Young & Rubicam, asking the agency to reconsider and take over parts of the television account. By August, Young & Rubicam was writing scripts, making recommendations, and scouring the nation for personalities they could bring into the campaign.[22]

The Star Committee

In many ways, Young & Rubicam was an ideal agency to bring a sense of spectacle to the Citizens account. The agency was steeped in tradition and yet ready to adopt new technologies and ways of thinking. Among the many supporters and hangers-on, Eisenhower had real fondness for Larmon and considered him a close friend. The adman frequently attended the president's "stag" weekends of hunting, golf, and bridge. A graduate of Dartmouth College, he had joined Young & Rubicam in 1929, just three years after it had moved to Manhattan from Philadelphia. Taking over as its president in 1942 and chairman in 1944, he oversaw two decades of growth in which the agency opened branch offices, added over 2,000 employees, and increased its annual billings from $40 million to $280 million.[23] From its headquarters at 285 Madison Avenue, Young & Rubicam was poised to become a leader in an increasingly powerful and profitable industry. Part of that success lay in the sense of camaraderie and loyalty that Larmon nurtured among his employees. He instituted bonuses, benefits, and scholarships for continued education. As men were shipped off to the Korean War, he assured them that the agency would look out for their families and that, when they returned, their jobs would be waiting. Workers pointed with pride to the fact that the employees' trust fund was the agency's largest stockholder.[24]

Larmon oversaw advertising's transition from print-based to broadcast-based media. In an era when agencies independently produced radio and television programs for their sponsors, Young & Rubicam employed directors, script writers, cameramen, and producers, all of whom had to meet the challenge of creating live television. The Television and Radio Department occupied the entire third floor at 285 Madison Avenue. It was a highly dynamic environment, as technological changes created a steady stream of new jobs and opportunities. Insiders nicknamed the third floor "Young and Move Again" because the people working in television moved from office to office,

FIGURE 4.2 *Young & Rubicam's Sigurd Larmon was one of President Eisenhower's closest advisers in the advertising industry.*
Courtesy of Young & Rubicam.

and title to title, so frequently. The environment appealed to ambitious young men who liked seeing their names on the frosted glass of the office doors and took pride in their rapid advancement. Once the office manager alerted them of an imminent promotion, they would slip into their new office later in the evening, pacing off the size to determine their new stature in the agency's ever-changing hierarchy. But the real action on the third floor took place in the hallways where, at any given hour, a half-dozen directors or staff members would be talking about production—how they choreographed camera angles or snaked the heavy television cables into a narrow room. "Production was all a novelty to us," a Young & Rubicam alumnus explains. For each account, the agency's creative vision developed alongside the opportunities and restrictions posed by the new technology.[25]

Returning to Citizens in 1956, Larmon appointed David Levy to lead his team in preparing a series of five- and one-minute commercials and special televised events. Levy was a former naval officer and a graduate of the Wharton School of the University of Pennsylvania. In the clubby environment of what C. Wright Mills called America's "power elite," he had worked with Eisenhower previously. The general had hired Levy in the late 1940s to help him with a series of radio broadcasts in which he encouraged Americans to support the Marshall Plan for rebuilding Europe.[26] He would rely on Levy's expertise again. During the 1952 campaign, it was Levy who controlled Young & Rubicam's television operations on the floor of the Republican National Convention where he worked to emphasize the inevitable nomination of the crowd-pleasing Ike.

As the head of the agency's Television and Radio Department in 1956, Levy saw the recruitment of celebrities as being crucial to the goal of attracting Democratic and independent voters to the Republican ticket. On September 4, 1956, he asked his colleagues for help "in getting names of any and all pro Eisenhower personalities," tying his request to Larmon himself. "I do not need to emphasize to you the importance of this to Mr. Larmon and Young & Rubicam and the need for urgent action."[27] Eight days later, the staff sent him a list of eighty-three celebrities with notes indicating who intended "to vote and talk Rep[ublican]," who would "give money and possibly appear," and who would "really get out and work." The responses are fascinating. Jack Benny was one of the few stars who promised nothing more than his opinions and vote. Among the actors who pledged money and said they would possibly appear were Bud Abbott, Fred Astaire, Gene Autry, Lou Costello, Bing Crosby, Clark Gable, Bob Hope, Ozzie Nelson, and William Powell. The list of stars committed to working hard for the candidate included some of the most prominent names in mid-century media and show business: Irving Berlin, Cecil B. DeMille, Hedda Hopper, The King's Men, Dorothy Lamour, Claire Luce, Mary Pickford, Red Skelton, John Wayne, Esther Williams, and Robert Young. The campaign did not use all of these celebrities for the Citizens' events, but their pledges of support were duly recorded, and as was the case with Wayne, a few would assume prominent roles in later campaigns.[28]

Young & Rubicam was not able to land all of the dignitaries it desired. As part of the agency's designated "star committee," Mildred Fox wrote a daily progress report for executives working on the Citizens account, and her September 12 report listed a number of people whom the agency had unsuccessfully tried to join their ranks. Perry Como and Billy Graham replied that they were pro-Eisenhower, but they felt the need to be neutral publicly. Ernest Hemingway avoided political entanglements by being "in Europe for [an] indefinite stay." The writers John O'Hara, Thornton Wilder, and Anne Lindbergh could not be reached—neither could the painter Grandma Moses, whom the campaign seemed eager to enlist. Richard Rodgers, Carl Sandburg, and the 1951 Miss America, Yolande Betbeze, all responded that they supported Stevenson. Professor Frank Baxter, the host of an Emmy-award-winning program titled "Shakespeare on T.V.," replied that he was not "voting Republican because of Nixon"—voicing a fear that had vexed party leaders throughout the early summer.[29]

Two days later, the people at Young & Rubicam increased their efforts to bring new celebrities into the fold. "It is of utmost importance that we supplement our lists of names that we are trying to contact," Richard Dana wrote his colleagues, as he assigned them different periodicals that "should be religiously covered" for evidence of a star's political leanings. *Sports Illustrated, Variety, Billboard*, and the major news magazines topped the list.[30] Levy had asked for these names to determine who might travel to New York in the campaign's final weeks to participate in its television and radio programs. In early September, his group had sketched plans for numerous television programs, many of which featured celebrity appearances: a series of five-minute discussions that would be integrated into preceding programs; a thirty-minute film to be narrated by Gary Cooper which would provide "a swiftly moving cavalcade" of the president's first term; and a coast-to-coast Election Eve rally hosted by Ed Sullivan and including some of Hollywood's "top stars." Each of these events would undergo revision as the election neared, but from the beginning, Levy was committed to using stardom to create the kind of spectacle that Larmon and others wanted to incorporate into the campaign.[31]

The partnership between spectacle and celebrity was on full display during the massive rally that Young & Rubicam helped stage at Madison Square Garden on October 25, 1956. Advisers from across the campaign had planned the event meticulously, knowing that the site would recall the 1952 midnight rally when supporters first gathered to draft Ike into the New Hampshire primary.[32] With lots of time to plan and a good chance at victory, the organizers arranged for a series of attention-grabbing stunts and activities. At 12:20 p.m., Eisenhower arrived at Pennsylvania Station, where he was greeted by the Valley Stream High School band, the Ike Girls, and the

Eisenhower bandwagon. After participating in a presidential motorcade to the Commodore Hotel, the bandwagon and Ike Girls set up their display on 49th Street, just outside Madison Square Garden. At 5:30 p.m., the Garden doors opened and thousands flooded in. The evening featured speeches from cross-voting Democrats, performances by twenty bands, group singing lessons from choral leader Fred Waring, and a choreographed-for-television card-turning trick in which the Republican faithful did their best to imitate the student section at a Big Ten football game. The rally must have been a stage-master's nightmare in which even people became props: among the necessary items were three walkie-talkies, four searchlights, six spotlights, twelve fixed mikes, fifty-eight ushers, "1,000 negro voices," "1,100 little flags for women," 1,200–2,000 singers, 4,000 thumbtacks, 5,000 red, white, and blue cards, and a room furnished with a sofa, chairs, and roses for the First Lady and President.[33]

The celebrity interviews played a key role in raising the level of excitement, and Young & Rubicam provided Ike with a brilliant supporting cast. Actors Peggy Wood, Lillian Gish, and Ralph Bellamy agreed to have their names announced as supporting the president, as did soprano Lily Pons and cartoonist Peter Arno. Perhaps in recognition that the Garden was an appropriate site for athletic endorsements, professional boxers Gene Tunney and Jack Dempsey joined New York baseball legends Phil Rizzuto and Leo Durocher in publicly declaring for Ike. African-American fullback and businessman Fritz Pollard sent his support, along with "Little Dynamite"—the famous Notre Dame runner Greg Rice.[34] Broadway fixtures Billy Gaxton and Victor Moore each addressed the audience, as did a veteran of the 1952 rally, talk show personality Jinx Falkenburg.[35] At 7:50 p.m., actor Wendell Cory and gossip columnist Walter Winchell took over as "roving reporters," moving through the Garden to interview some of the famous guests and prepare for the climax of the evening: an address by the president himself that would be carried live on 124 NBC affiliates across the country and shown again the next afternoon on CBS.[36]

Working on the principle of "planned spontaneity," Levy, Montgomery, and Washburn carefully brought the crowd to a fever pitch by the time Eisenhower took the stage. To ensure a good audience, the campaign had developed an intricate ticket distribution scheme in which they created the impression of scarcity and then offered more tickets than there were seats. Thus after announcing that the rally would be a first-come, first-served event, the campaign distributed over three times as many tickets as the arena could accommodate, leaving them with a jam-packed building and 10,000 supporters on the street.[37] As the choir rehearsed and the card turners practiced, as Winchell and Corey moved from celebrity to politician to celebrity, the crowd was reminded how important it was for the television cameras to capture their response to Eisenhower's appearance on stage. Levy and Montgomery had planned for precisely two and a half minutes of televised pandemonium before the crowd had to settle down and let the president speak; at their direction, the master of ceremonies, John Roosevelt, announced these instructions in advance.[38] All the preparation and practice worked. The television program began, and for the twenty-first time that evening, the crowd sang "We Like Ike" at the top of their lungs. The president approached the podium to a wall of deafening sound. Writing for *The Guardian*, the British-born journalist Alistair Cooke tried to recreate what he heard: "It was the kind of cheer, from 20,000 crowing idolaters, that sizzles like a plague of grasshoppers and rattles the ear drums."[39]

Leavening the Loaf

The most prominent and influential star at the Garden rally was Helen Hayes. Introduced by Walter Winchell (whose television show she would visit the next week), this previous Roosevelt Democrat was a particularly valuable spokesperson who had deep roots in the 1952 campaign. With much fanfare, Hayes returned from England (where she had been filming *Anastasia*) in August 1956 to co-chair the newly formed Committee of the Arts and Sciences for Eisenhower, a group she jokingly dubbed "Eggheads for Ike." The office rounded out a collection of other responsibilities she had assumed for Citizens for Eisenhower–Nixon, including Financial Chairman and Women's National Chairman.[40]

The ubiquitous Fred Waring and his Pennsylvanians offered a different kind of support than Hayes. Often billed as "America's Singing Master," Waring was one of the nation's most popular and adaptable entertainers. Since the 1920s, his orchestra and choir had starred in hit shows on Broadway, radio, and television. In between, they tirelessly traveled the nation, giving live performances and offering workshops on choral techniques. Waring had pioneered the concept of televised musical spectaculars, and he knew how to turn large-scale events into boisterous but also intimate experiences. He had proudly been with the Eisenhower campaign since the beginning. "People who happen to be in show business have been advised not to get mixed up in politics," he yelled to the crowd during the 1952 midnight rally. "I'm speaking for the Pennsylvanians and myself. We are not mixed up. We know exactly what we are doing. We're for Eisenhower."[41] Over the years, Waring's wholesome energy and enthusiasm had made him an ideal fixture at events that emphasized the kind of spectacle and showmanship that Washburn and Murphy specialized in creating.[42]

Hayes was given a more substantial role than Waring. The most outspoken of the Eisenhower stars, she dedicated several months to the presidential race, and with stops in California, Massachusetts, Washington, DC,

Pennsylvania, and New York, her speaking engagements drew enviable publicity. Not only did she participate in the Garden rally and Ike Day tribute, but Young & Rubicam successfully placed her on David Garroway's television program "Wide, Wide World" which hosted a series of guests speaking about the upcoming election.[43] Although she wore Ike- and GOP elephant-themed jewelry, reporters were curious about Hayes' political past, and after some initial dissembling, she reluctantly acknowledged that she had voted for Roosevelt in 1932 "because she was caught up in the desire for a change." "I reformed quick," she insisted to the Washington Post, "and started thinking hard and working hard."[44] Like many Hollywood Republicans, she described her enthusiasm for Roosevelt as a sign of youthful naïveté rather than changing world circumstances.

Hayes's glamour could be unnerving in a political context, and she worked to present herself as a common citizen. She confessed to being nervous when campaigning, pointing out that, while acting allowed her to conceal her "fuzzy thinking," there was so much at stake in a presidential race and so much emphasis on her words.[45] "I am always afraid the interview will come out looking like 'Idiots for Eisenhower.'" Her most effective stance was that of a concerned parent who wanted "to keep the administration of the country in the hands of a man who has the ability to lead in both war and peace." When a reporter from the Los Angeles Times asked why she campaigned for Ike, she replied that she was speaking not as an actress or politician but "as a mother making a last gesture to secure the welfare of my 18-year-old son who is now at Harvard and will soon be out of my hands."[46] The identity fit her well. In 1952, Hayes had starred in the film My Son John about a mother whose indulgence of her intellectual son helps pave the way for his becoming a Communist spy and traitor to the United States. A classic of Cold War fearmongering, My Son John was predicated on the widespread concern that overbearing (and over-sentimentalized) mothers were the weak link in the nation's defense against Communist ideology. Having dramatized the threat of what was known as "Momism" on screen, Hayes campaigned as an exemplary parent and patriot, a humble American mother who, nonetheless, knew how to apply her theater experience to politics. As she told Richard Coe at the Washington Post, "I believe in being brief, prepared, and dramatic!"[47]

The Young & Rubicam advisers viewed Hayes as one of their most reliable representatives, even as they sought an array of semi-prominent personalities whose function seemed to be more window-dressing. Young & Rubicam earnestly tried to track down the top winners of television's $64,000 Question to see if they would speak on Ike's behalf. One of the winners, a seventy-eight-year-old self-taught investment whiz named Alice Morgan, had become so popular that she had difficulty fitting the campaign into her lecture schedule.[48] The agency put special emphasis on featuring "distinguished Democrats

FIGURE 4.3 *One of the most active of the Eisenhower stars, Helen Hayes presented the president with a giant birthday card from Hollywood as part of the Ike Day festivities.*
Courtesy of National Park Service and Dwight D. Eisenhower Presidential Library and Museum.

and independents" who had decided to vote for Ike. A five-minute program aired on October 30 featured a pro-Eisenhower conversation between Lewis Douglas, a former ambassador under Harry Truman; John Roosevelt, the son of FDR who had emceed the rally; Mrs. Emily Smith Warner, the daughter of the legendary New York Democrat Alfred Smith; poet Ogden Nash; Harry Carman, dean emeritus at Columbia University; and Mrs. Babe Ruth. The rationale behind such discussions seemed to be twofold: to select people whose prominence gave them a respected platform from which they could speak and to select others whose lives were so well-known that voters might identify with them. Thus, while Douglas and Roosevelt ruminated on the unrest in Eastern Europe, Mrs. Babe Ruth was given the lines that perhaps most represented the electorate's perspective: "Mr. Douglas, my whole family knows I'm for Ike and while I'm supposed to know a great deal about baseball, my politics is a little weak. Has there been as much bi-partisanship under Eisenhower as in the past?"[49]

Eisenhower's advisers developed competing theories about what celebrity brought to the presidential race. Washburn believed that all the bandwagon and celebrity events created a helpful environment for raising money and reaching out to supporters. The aim in distributing propaganda, he wrote, "should be to create a backdrop of public enthusiasm against which the political activities of this organization may best be accomplished."[50] From celebrity interviews to television spectaculars, the events created an air of passion and excitement around the Eisenhower–Nixon team. Because supporters enjoyed and rallied behind such activities, they were "strongly conducive to the fundraising activity of the organization."[51] Washburn differentiated the celebratory aspects of his position from the messaging part of the campaign. Parades of Ike Girls and sports stars would not change voters' minds, neither would elaborate birthday parties. These operations entertained the public so that the political message could come through. Washburn saw himself engaging with an audience; it was up to the politicians to convert them into an electorate.

The executives at Young & Rubicam, however, thought figures such as Hayes could be effective in actually convincing voters that they should back the GOP. In a memo to Levy, Wood argued that the agency should include show business personalities in the interviews they were creating with prominent Democrats and labor leaders going for Ike. Emphasizing the importance of tone and setting—"All very informal and *low key*, the very opposite of the set political speech"—he concluded that interviewing people in their homes would draw the interest of ordinary citizens and move the campaign away from partisan politics. "An audience," he wrote, "would be attracted and held by curiosity to see a celebrity and his home. We should see—quickly—enough of the home in each case to satisfy this curiosity."

The goal of these interviews, as Wood envisioned them, was to counteract the points "most frequently held against Eisenhower—military background, rich friends, etc." Wood urged his colleagues not to underestimate the "value an endorsement always carries with it. I think that an intelligent endorsement by prominent personalities will carry tremendous weight." Leave policies and principles to the National Committee, he argued. "I feel, we are on strong ground in letting a movie star say 'my son went to Korea to fight during a Democratic administration. Eisenhower brought him home.'"[52] Six weeks later, Hayes would sound precisely this theme when she remarked at a Los Angeles press conference that she trusted Ike to keep her son in college rather than ship him off to war.[53] The tight scripting of celebrity endorsements continued throughout the fall campaign. When Hayes appeared on Garroway's "Wide, Wide World," Young & Rubicam assured her that "there will be no weighty discussion of Mr. Eisenhower's principles, nor any questions involving controversial, or major, political issues." In case the actress had any last-minute Eisenhower questions, they asked Wood to be with her backstage.[54]

The solution was surprising, for, as Preston Wood remembers it, his professional life was so full, he barely followed politics in the 1950s. "It was hard to look up and see what was going on." Wood had arrived at Young & Rubicam in 1948. As a student at the University of Florida, he had worked extensively with the college radio station. After serving in the army, he moved to New York where he wrote scripts for a number of musical comedies. At Young & Rubicam, he found a thriving company that rewarded its most talented employees with an ever-changing roster of new jobs and responsibilities. He quickly became in demand after he wrote a jingle that saved the lucrative Life Savers account. The agency then sent him to work with *Life Magazine* on its coverage of the 1948 presidential nominating conventions, both of which were held in Philadelphia. Wood spent the next decade writing scripts for radio and television, but he also became deeply involved in television production. He directed *The Bigelow Show* and *Open House*, a late-night comedy show with a rotating host. When Arthur Godfrey welcomed Harry Truman as his guest in a 1950 episode, Wood wrote the script.[55]

In 1952, he became the director of *We, the People*, a program sponsored by Gulf Oil that featured stories on celebrities, public leaders, and "everyday Americans." Among the usual parade of entertainers and sports stars, guests on *We, the People* included Nobel Prize winners, members of the Newark Fire Department, and Supreme Court Justice William O. Douglas.[56] The program devoted thirteen episodes to the presidential election. This background made Wood an ideal person to work on the Eisenhower campaign, for he already knew how to turn political discussion into a human interest story. Eisenhower had appeared on *We, the People* that summer, and in his memo to Levy, Wood commented that the candidate had been "tremendously effective" when he spoke from a standing position. (Wood's perception matched that of Montgomery and the advisers who produced the Ike Day program, all of whom thought he was a more natural speaker when standing or walking.)

Two years after the Eisenhower–Nixon campaign, Wood would leave Young & Rubicam to become a program development executive with NBC. By 1961 he had moved to California where he returned to writing television scripts full time. Although Preston Wood is not a household name, he had a long and active career writing for such programs as *Gunsmoke, Bonanza, Hawaii 5-0*, and *Quincy*, as well as the popular Jack Webb dramas *Dragnet, Adam-12*, and *Emergency!* Wood also wrote screenplays for Levy when he became the executive producer of the sitcom *The Addams Family*. The shift from working on a presidential campaign to writing for a television series may be surprising, but it also makes warped sense. Until recently, writing for a television series required one to create a story that was engaging enough to entertain but still held the characters in stasis, a story that consistently reaffirmed character rather than deepened or examined it. Political advertisements depended on a relatively similar formula.

Wood's memo to Levy envisioned a campaign in which celebrities would buff the icon of presidential character rather than delve into policy. The value of figures such as Gene Tunney and Dorothy Lamour lay in their ability to vouch for Eisenhower's likeability without revealing his complexities. Wood argued that Young & Rubicam should focus on associating their candidate with the satisfying, nonpartisan realm of show business. "We should attempt to leaven the loaf of political content with as much entertainment as possible," Wood wrote.

> I sincerely doubt that the lukewarm Democrat, the independent (which is another way frequently, of saying "disinterested") voter and others in the group which we are aiming for actually listen to set Republican speeches of the strongly partisan variety. I believe that the bulk of the audience in such cases consists of already converted and convinced Republicans.[57]

Wood contended that the values of stardom and entertainment could assist the GOP by encouraging moderates to forget that Eisenhower the candidate was a partisan creation with pronounced partisan loyalties. The trick was to present him as you would a character on a long-running television series— "The Man from Abilene" rather than "The Republican from Washington, DC."

The reality of this star strategy turned out to be quite different. The bipartisan veneer of Eisenhower's celebrity politics obscured a concerted effort to rebuild and strengthen the GOP. Political scientist Daniel Galvin has demonstrated the extent to which Eisenhower used his presidency to solidify the reach and organization of the Republican Party. Ike himself exhorted the members of the independent Citizens group to join the GOP, and according to Galvin, the 1956 campaign was more integrated into the RNC than had ever been the case with an incumbent president and a national party.[58] For all the bipartisan appeal of its celebrity guests, the January closed circuit broadcast brought in $5.5 million for Republican candidates, and in a bid to wrest Congress from the Democrats, the Garden rally explicitly promoted the Republicans running for New York's House and Senate seats.[59] The emphasis on converting independents played itself out on an individual level, too. Singer Dinah Shore came to the White House for an evening performance in 1953. Before she arrived, Murphy urged the president to use the occasion to "influence Miss Shore to the point where she would declare herself for the party."[60]

Young & Rubicam had an important role in this process by selling a vision of Ike that was meant to persuade Democrats and independents to give the president their votes. To make Eisenhower a symbol of consensus, as Wood explained it, the campaign would have "to leaven the loaf of political content."[61] The metaphor suggests that, because politics is flat and distasteful, the agency had to improve its product with the yeast of entertainment. Washburn saw the spectacle as softening viewers for a political message to come. Wood thought the interviews and televised visits would make the Eisenhower campaign seem lighter, airier, more appetizing to the public at large. His job was to feed the masses rather than the converts.

Celebrities and the "Little People"

One of the great ironies of celebrity politics in the United States is how frequently it is meant to express the candidate's populist sympathies. Campaigning with musicians, actresses, and athletes, even the most insulated leaders hope to appear more human and down-to-earth than they would in the company of fellow politicians. Eisenhower was vulnerable to charges that he had surrounded himself with rich friends, and critics liked to point out that millionaire businessmen dominated his Cabinet. The executives at Young & Rubicam and BBDO were confident that surrounding Ike with celebrities would make him appear more accessible and welcoming. The strategy may seem counterintuitive, particularly if we associate stardom with luxury and excess. To many, television and film stars were as rich and removed from common life as the heads of General Motors and General Mills. Looking back on the period, however, Preston Wood explained that television had changed the nature of fame for a public that was "not accustomed to face recognition."[62] In 1956, Young & Rubicam counted on the public to view the stars as familiar, trustworthy friends, ordinary folk whose recommendation they valued and respected.[63] The strategy turned on a notion of persuasive identification in which the most popular and visible celebrities would help the candidate seem more natural and ordinary. Once the stars were assembled for the Ike Day broadcast, the president could celebrate his birthday like everyone else—watching television and eating cake.

Young & Rubicam worked hard, throughout the campaign, to surround the president with regular citizens. As the agency developed proposals for new television programs and commercials, they routinely focused on "the little people," a term they used to signify working men and women who traditionally voted Democratic. A particularly memorable advertisement featured a fictional Washington taxi driver walking his dog late at night. Pointing to the lights still shining in the White House, the man takes comfort in the fact that the president is up late, working for people like him. "I've got a feeling he's thinking of me," the man says. "In times like these, so full of perils and problems, I'll be honest with you, I need him."[64] Young & Rubicam wanted to cultivate a similar folksiness with their celebrity supporters. At one point they proposed a televised talent show with Wood's old colleague Arthur Godfrey serving as the host. Seven "little people," each matched with a well-known politician, would join Godfrey and his special guest, Richard Nixon. Each group would introduce a "big" entertainer who would announce his or her endorsement of the GOP ticket.[65] Celebrities would serve as the glue for the "little people," the substance that bound them together, as well as to the Republican Party.

The most successful grassroots program created by Young & Rubicam was the People's Press Conference that was televised live on Friday, October 12, 1956, the night before the Ike Day celebration. Although the program was advertised as a chance for Eisenhower to hear directly from voters, the participants were carefully selected to represent the kinds of "little people" the campaign wanted to attract: among them, a Democrat from Virginia, an African-American pastor from Chicago, a dairy farmer from New York, and an auto worker from Detroit. The speakers asked Eisenhower about a variety of issues, ranging from his support for families and unions, to the constitutionality of developing a spiritual guidance curriculum in the public schools. The people were less interested in asking questions than in expressing their admiration. As the *Chicago Daily News* put it, "Their questions were really little after-thoughts, postscripts to short speeches on why they 'like Ike.' "[66] The only curve ball of the evening came when a New York garment worker wondered about all the "big shots" in the Cabinet. Though many newspapers chose to focus on this unexpected question, it did not seem to register with the television audience.

The People's Press Conference was an outstanding success. Congratulatory telegrams and messages arrived at the White House the following morning. A Mrs. J. H. Odin from Maple Park, Illinois, wrote the president enthusiastically:

> We have enjoyed the different radio and television programs wherein you have taken part. Especially, the other night when you allowed the people to ask questions, and you, in turn, would answer them. . . . It thrilled our hearts to hear the people give you so much for your praise. . . . I try to pray every day that the people's eyes will be opened to the truth, and will not be clouded over by the untruth stated by the opposite party.[67]

Flush with his sense of triumph, Eisenhower wrote Larmon about the "terrific success" and thanked the agency for coming up with the format. The president had long been concerned about Nixon's unpopularity and had spoken with the Vice President directly about creating "a crash program for building you up."[68] Perhaps Young & Rubicam could create a similar program for Dick Nixon, Ike wrote Larmon, "since one of the criticisms about him is that he does not like and understand people."[69] Although the program focused on the voices of the "little people," Young & Rubicam felt compelled to include figures who would be familiar to the viewing audience. Lewis Douglass explained his support for Eisenhower before asking about European perceptions of US foreign policy. Stephen Frolich, a winner on *The $64,000 Question*, used his knowledge of history to ask the president about his faith in Nixon. An early script reveals that Young & Rubicam had wanted Yankee infielder Phil Rizzuto to provide some levity by asking about the president's golf game.[70]

If the People's Press Conference amounted to a flirtation between grassroots politics and celebrity, events like the Garden rally and Ike Day were full-blown love affairs. They provided a ritual of shared engagement, a way for Americans to ground themselves in a civic activity that connected citizen to

FIGURE 4.4 *Robert Montgomery before an Oval Office speech with Eisenhower and the assembled media.*
Courtesy of National Park Service and Dwight D. Eisenhower Presidential Library and Museum.

citizen, and citizen to star and head of state. In 1956, Ike's advisers used celebrities to bring visibility to average Americans who honored their president by baking cakes for patients in veterans' hospitals or joining 3,000 volunteers in spelling out his name on giant cards. In this formulation, celebrity politics was democratic politics, for it offered Eisenhower's inspirational public service as a model for committing to civic life.

The actual situation was more complicated. Although Irene Dunne served as co-chairman of the National Ike Day Committee, Katherine Howard privately complained that the actress "took no part whatsoever" in planning the event, "other than appearing in the TV show."[71] The White House fretted when Youth Salutes the President requested that Eisenhower give Hayes a special letter of commendation that would effectively distinguish her efforts from those of the other celebrity participants.[72] But, as presented by the press, Ike's celebrity admirers seemed wholly integrated into the Republican grassroots campaign; they served as nodes of public attention, each one representing thousands of like-minded citizens. Television was critical to creating this sense of community, for it transformed local events into coast-to-coast extravaganzas. Millions of viewers observed the president's birthday simply by watching him on TV. Sociologist Chris Rojek has written that celebrities "offer peculiarly powerful affirmations of belonging, recognition, and meaning in the midst of the lives of their audiences."[73] From the campaign's perspective, the benefit of political spectaculars was that they created a formal structure that both extended and politicized that sense of belonging, oftentimes by brazenly avoiding or lightening political content.

Celebrities helped root these many events in good feelings rather than policy. In this respect, they were consistent with Young & Rubicam's parallel project of cultivating an emotional connection with the president among voters who traditionally did not vote Republican. The agency's September 1956 report for the National Citizens for Eisenhower–Nixon emphasized that the focus of its television campaign should be "the appeal of the Eisenhower personality, its warmth, its integrity, its guiding principles and its leadership." Levy believed that "*the public generally votes more with its heart* than with its reasoned mental conclusions," and thus, in developing a strategy for network television, he concluded that the agency's "first and most important aim should be for an emotional preference for Eisenhower and his principles, for Eisenhower the great leader, the great human being."[74]

Levy's thinking assumed what many analysts were concluding at the time, that voters were not rational in their decision-making.[75] In a projected rematch with Adlai Stevenson, for example, Eisenhower saw his Gallup poll numbers go up five points in the months following his heart attack. The *New York Times* columnist James Reston was baffled by the result and wryly wondered whether the majority of Americans felt a heart attack improved one's capacity to be president.[76] As he prepared for the fall campaign, Levy concluded that the development of star-studded programs would strengthen this emotional connection and result in a landslide victory for Ike. No single event, of course, would change a voter's mind or result in a radically different vision of the president. To borrow a phrase from the TV Plans Board, the campaign aimed to produce "cumulative commercial impressions" of the president, each one directed at nurturing and extending this emotional bond.[77] Sending a consistent promotional message through a range of familiar spokesmen and women, Levy, Montgomery, and their colleagues subtly integrated the president and his policies into the world of Broadway, Hollywood, and Madison Avenue. At once vibrant, youthful, and energetic, this new context would present the likeable Ike as a creature of spectacle rather than an agent of history.

Corn Flakes

The analysis of Dwight Eisenhower's popularity began long before he ran for office or even committed himself to a political party. In 1950, the sociologist David Riesman published his groundbreaking book *The Lonely Crowd* in which he argued that the American character was undergoing a fundamental change. Americans, he explained, were increasingly driven by external forces such as markets and media rather than the internal forces of family, goals, and faith. Noting the role of commercialism in elections and campaigning, Riesman asserted that, just as it had taken over the sale and production of commodities, glamour had become a key feature of American political life. The new emphasis on consumption and packaging encouraged voters to become indifferent, to substitute the allure of charisma for acting in their own self-interest. "Wherever we see glamour in the object of attention," he concluded, "we must suspect a basic apathy in the spectator."[1]

By way of example, Riesman looked to the beginnings of the Draft Eisenhower movement in the 1948 presidential campaign. To an electorate that found Harry Truman out of date and Thomas Dewey insincere and lacking sympathy, the general was "irresistible" and seemed to have "everything." But Riesman saw something beyond the good-natured, modern outlook that supporters championed in Ike. (His political positions, we might remember, were virtually unknown at the time.) What Eisenhower represented was a political commodity wrapped up in attractive packaging. "The spontaneous elements in the Eisenhower movement," Riesman wrote, "were to a large degree a tribute to people's desperate search for glamour." Having been tutored by popular culture, these supporters found in Ike both a source of attraction and, paradoxically, an end to the apathy such attraction helped create.[2]

Riesman's brief but withering assessment obviously did not damage Eisenhower's political prospects, but his analysis of the American character established an important touchstone for mid-century intellectual life. A sociological study written for the classroom, *The Lonely Crowd* became an unlikely best-seller, and over the next decades, it would sell more than

1.4 million copies in numerous trade and scholarly editions.[3] The book conveyed such a popular, compelling vision that by 1967, Bob Dylan would allude to it in his song "I Shall Be Released."[4] Although his analysis was more complex, Riesman's description of an increasingly bored, other-directed society prompted a wide-ranging public discussion with astonishing reach. Margaret Mead reviewed the book in the *American Journal of Sociology* and then, ten years later, wrote an essay on its significance.[5] *Time* magazine did a cover story on Riesman in 1954, complete with illustrations of inner- and outer-directed men.[6] And on Madison Avenue, executives treated the book's sober academic analysis as a blueprint for understanding the new personality-type of American consumers. We see something of Riesman in Preston Wood's suggestion that Young & Rubicam use celebrity interviews to attract independent and "disinterested" voters to the Eisenhower–Nixon ticket. The broader the electorate a candidate needed to reach, Riesman had concluded, the more glamour was required.[7]

Thinking about Riesman can remind us that politics and celebrity have a historically contingent relationship. In 1920, there was little concern about Al Jolson's endorsement of Warren Harding, and journalists responded to his Ohio visit with a warmer, more amused attitude than their counterparts would today. Although his friendship with Franklin Delano Roosevelt elicited some Republican carping, the commotion Frank Sinatra's fans caused outside a Brooklyn rally was thought to reveal more about popular culture than the presidency.[8] With the advent of television and the boom in advertising, however, commentators began to see the glamorization of presidential politics as an insidious threat to democracy. Riesman stands at the forefront of a wide variety of scholars and creative artists who studied and often railed against the growing alliance between politics, publicity, and what Dwight MacDonald called the "senseless and routinized" world of television.[9] Their response to celebrity politics encompassed a range of postwar anxieties and fears: the synthetic production of fame, the individuals' vulnerability to propaganda in both entertainment and publicity, the power of television to amplify personality, and the way that fame can quickly turn to demagoguery.

The most obvious and pressing concern in the 1950s, however, was the threat of advertising. In an age in which radio and television programs were owned and produced by corporate brands, celebrities were not just performers. They were living commercials, the glamorous, entertaining package through which the benefits of detergents, cigarettes, and motor oil were displayed. As critics presented it, broadcast communications had given birth to an empire of advertising, and Washington seemed destined to become Madison Avenue's most prized colony. They consistently returned to the question of what happened to democracy when it was run by the principles of promotion and consumption found in a marketplace.

One of the first to tackle this question was George Ball, who in 1952 served as the executive director of National Volunteers for Adlai Stevenson. Overwhelmed by the Republican onslaught but genuinely concerned about what it meant for American politics, Ball would become a trenchant and rueful critic of advertising's influence on the presidential race. His highly publicized October 1, 1952, speech titled "The Corn Flakes Campaign" derided the Republican plans for spot advertisements leading up to Election Day.[10] Bemoaning the Republicans' ability to attract funding from wealthy families like the Rockefellers and the DuPonts, he pleaded for increased donations to the Democratic National Committee (DNC). "We are broke," he confessed. "We are broke from day to day and every day." Ball charged his opponents with using their funds to invent "a new kind of campaign—a campaign conceived not by men who want us to face the crucial issues of this crucial day, but by the high-powered hucksters of Madison Avenue." Sensing that the election was slipping away, he aimed to discredit Eisenhower and Nixon by questioning their promotional machine.

> They have conceived not an election campaign in the usual sense but a super colossal, multi-million dollar production designed to sell an inadequate ticket to the American people in precisely the way they sell soap, ammoniated toothpaste, hair tonic or bubble gum. They guarantee their candidates to be 99 4/10% pure; whether or not they will float remains to be seen.[11]

The problem, as Ball presented it, was that the Republicans were promoting their candidates as if they were commodities. The resultant glamour cheapened the political process, making it difficult to discern substantive ideas from marketing. Speaking to a conference of Stevenson volunteers, Ball tried to find a positive message, eventually settling on the notion that voters could see through the barrage of image-making. "No matter how much gold goes into it," he willfully concluded, "the Republican campaign is still coming out cornflakes."

Ball's speech was both witty and memorable, but it was not especially revealing. Ike's advisers had been frank about their eagerness to use Madison Avenue techniques since he had won the nomination. The campaign had leaked news of these plans in early September, and two weeks later, the Citizens for Eisenhower group had outlined their tactics at a public meeting. Although Ball succeeded in getting his protest into the press, he made little headway against opponents who proudly touted their expertise. As we saw in Chapter 3, Ben Duffy candidly declared that BBDO was focused on "merchandising Eisenhower's frankness, honesty, and integrity, his sincere and wholesome approach."[12] And Rosser Reeves, the Ted Bates agency executive whose spots became the bête noire of the Stevenson campaign, contended that political advertising was no more meaningful than

FIGURE 5.1 *Kellogg's released this special election-themed cereal box in October 1952, the same month that Adlai Stevenson's campaign adviser George Ball criticized Eisenhower for running a "Corn Flakes Campaign."*

Courtesy of Kellogg North America Company.

the launch of a hygiene product. "I think of a man in the voting booth who hesitates between two levers as if he were pausing between competing tubes of toothpaste in a drugstore. The brand that has made the highest penetration on his brain will win his choice."[13] A sense of competition (and envy) led Ball to lament that "from morning to night the air waves and the TV screens will be filled by the omnipresent General Eisenhower."[14] By the time he wrote his memoirs, however, Ball realized that Ike had merely been the first candidate to wallow in the excess of publicity and that 1952 offered a glimpse into the threats to democracy that would become endemic in subsequent years. "Presidential candidates would thereafter be presented as commodities, market-tested and packaged to satisfy individual markets." With "the attrition of serious dialogue," all politics would be akin to selling cereal and toothpaste.[15] Harry Truman expressed the sentiment more bluntly, dismissing BBDO as standing for "Bunko, Bull, Deceit, and Obfuscation."[16]

Eisenhower's landslide victory brought considerable attention to Madison Avenue's influence in the presidential race. The writer Marya Mannes echoed Ball's concerns in a piece of doggerel she published in *The Reporter*, a liberal weekly out of Washington. With her characteristic wit, she wryly titled the poem "Sales Campaign":

> Hail to BBD&O
> It told the nation how to go;
> It managed by advertisement
> To sell us a new President.
>
> Eisenhower hits the spot
> One full General, that's a lot.
>
> Feeling sluggish, feeling sick?
> Take a dose of Ike and Dick.
>
> Philip Morris, Lucky Strike,
> Alka Seltzer, I like Ike.[17]

Mannes's imagery drew upon the pop sensibility of contemporary products and the wild, therapeutic claims of the old patent medicine industry. Eisenhower was refreshing like Pepsi (which in 1949 unleashed the jingle "Pepsi-Cola hits the spot. / 12 full ounces, that's a lot! / Twice as much for a nickel, too. / Pepsi-Cola is the drink for you!")[18] At the same time, he had the restorative capacity of a drug, a politician who would cure what ailed the United States. Like Ball, Mannes's satire dismissed the hucksters for lacking the gravity and propriety that seemed crucial to a stable democracy. With their catchy jingles and inflated claims, they threatened to tarnish both the voters and the candidates. Reeves' brother-in-law, David Ogilvy, was more brusque. His agency refused to bid on all political accounts for the simple reason that "the use of advertising to sell statesmen is the ultimate vulgarity."[19]

Over the next four years, a cottage industry arose of writers and thinkers ruminating about the effects of the 1952 campaign. The pace of publication increased as the country's attention turned to the upcoming presidential race. In 1956 alone, a slew of new essays and books offered a behind the scenes look at American politics, especially as it involved glamour, television, and advertising. These included articles in trade newspapers like *Nation's Business* and respected academic studies such as Stanley Kelly's *Professional Public Relations and Political Power* and John Charles A. H. Thomson's *Television and Presidential Politics*. The list extended to two of the year's top sellers, C. Wright Mills' sociological study *The Power Elite* and Eugene Burdick's novel of political manipulation, *The Ninth Wave*. It was as if Ball's allies had arrived four years too late.

Amid the considerable hand-wringing of his contemporaries, a former advertising executive named John G. Schneider wrote *The Golden Kazoo* (1956), a satirical account of the 1960 presidential election. Rather than lament the changes taking place, however, Schneider was amused by the notion that rather humdrum political candidates could be dressed up as commodities. Set in the offices of Batten and Reade, a fictional advertising agency, *The Golden Kazoo* tells the story of Blade Reade, the former boy wonder of Madison Avenue, whose agency handles the account of a Republican presidential candidate, Henry Clay Adams. The novel is filled with stock characters (the egghead pollster dependent on his wheezing computer, the sex-kitten talk-show host who realizes she's in love with Reade), and its comedy often outstrips the veneer of believability. A persistent subplot is Reade's plan to convince the electorate that Adams's forty-two-year-old wife is pregnant with the couple's first child.

But *The Golden Kazoo* is compelling in its unapologetic portrait of candidates as commodities. By way of an interior monologue, Schneider gives us insight into a pollster's private thinking:

> [The year 1952] first found admen in the very highest policy-making councils of both parties: for the first time, candidates became "merchandise," political campaigns were "sales promotion jobs," the electorate was a "market." . . . Never again after '52 would a major political party be so abysmally stupid as to attempt a sales campaign on its own, an amateur job without professional merchandising know-how.[20]

At one time or another, Eisenhower, Taft, and Stevenson, all complained about having to submit to a public-relations makeover. As Schneider envisioned it, by 1960, the equilibrium would change: the admen would be issuing orders, and the politicians would line themselves up for instructions and glamour treatments.

The novel offers a hyperbolic portrait of Ike, Duffy, and Reeves. Reade demands that his team think in new, more modern ways, that they find a way to sell their product—even if he isn't "a five-star general who looks like Papa to the whole damned human race."[21] "The business of advertising is to *sell*," Reade tells a resistant staff member. "Adams may look like a lousy product. Well, it won't be the first time you've sold some junk that you personally wouldn't buy at half the price. He's our product. Sell him."[22] Schneider describes a series of promotional gimmicks to turn Governor and Mrs. Adams into appealing commodities. The agency releases Mrs. Adams's "Old Harvest Table Recipes" and arranges for her to "give birth" on afternoon TV. In an update to the Ike Girls, Reade dispenses with actual speeches at rallies and instead surrounds Adams with attractive young women dressed in shorts and cowboy hats. "Please try to get it through your heads," he tells the twenty-six people working on the campaign, "that a product never is sold until the customer has shelled out his money, or his vote."[23]

The Golden Kazoo unsentimentally chronicles the triumph of advertising politics over ward politics, depicting its candidates as naïve bumpkins who need to be slicked up for consumption on Election Day. The novel is hardly a sophisticated work of political commentary, but with its broad-brush strokes and amped-up comedy, it takes as an obvious truth that democracy involves salesmanship and performance, that it requires leaders to mold themselves into pleasing public shapes. Although keenly aware of Madison Avenue excess, Schneider viewed politicians as being an obstacle to an effective campaign. Writing in *The Nation* in late November, he "reviewed" the recent election and found all the participants wanting. Touching upon the People's Press Conference and the Ike Day birthday party, he concluded that the entertainment was mediocre, but the salesmanship even worse. The GOP was so proud of its showcase product—the magnificent Thunderbird of Ike—that it forgot to sell its entry-level vehicles—all those Republican congressional candidates.[24]

The Democrats did not share Schneider's satirical glee in the confusion of political categories. By the summer of 1956, they had embraced the anti-advertising theme as if it were a central platform plank. When Stevenson accepted the Democratic nomination for a rematch with Ike, he wasted no time in recalling Ball's comparison of cereal with presidential candidates:

The men who run the Eisenhower administration evidently believe that the minds of Americans can be manipulated by shows, slogans and the arts of advertising. And that conviction will, I dare say, be backed up by the greatest torrent of money ever poured out to influence an American election—poured out by men who fear nothing so much as change and who want everything to stay as it is—only more so.

This idea that you can merchandise candidates for high office like breakfast cereal—that you can gather votes like box tops—is, I think, the ultimate indignity to the democratic process.[25]

Stevenson treated the Republican blitz of publicity as an affront to national values, a well-coordinated attempt to manipulate the American mind. According to political scientist Elvin T. Lim, Eisenhower worried so much about sounding like a highbrow intellectual that he cultivated his reputation for being inarticulate.[26] Offended by the new emphasis on political style, Stevenson viewed his campaign as an opportunity to educate the people and be educated by them in return. To paraphrase Stevenson biographer Jean Baker, the Illinois governor believed that running for president was like leading a vast moving seminar in which policies were clarified and explained.[27] With the advent of Madison Avenue politics, however, he feared that Americans would no longer weigh options and ideas; they were attracted to candidates who had merged show business and public relations with electioneering. The combination of money and manipulation had created "the ultimate indignity to the democratic process," draining the nation of the honest, rational dialogue that was at the heart of self-government.

Two months later, Ball would follow Stevenson's earnest pleading with his own sarcastic jabs at the GOP's promotion-heavy campaign. Aided by BBDO and Young & Rubicam, the Republicans had built a cult of personality around the president to the extent that their platform consisted of three simple words—the vaporous *I Like Ike*. Ball conveyed a bitter fascination with the events of Ike Day and the filming of Republican commercials around Washington, DC. Recalling the presence of Jimmy Stewart and Helen Hayes at the birthday party, he questioned the role of likeability in the campaign. "Some people like Elvis Presley," Ball commented, "and I like Marilyn Monroe, but I doubt that is sufficient reason for electing either President."[28] Ball's critique went beyond the question of merchandising candidates. He charged the Republicans with deceiving the public by using actors as stand-ins for real people in their television commercials. "What the Republican campaign adds up to, it seems to me, is an attempt to replace journalism by bad melodrama." There would be no "false aura" around the Democratic candidates, he promised, no effort to create false impressions of the party. "We do not feel that the electorate needs to be recruited from the Central Casting Bureau," Ball stated, fearing that the commodification of the president was fast becoming the commodification of the electorate.

The debate over salesmanship and promotion reflected the uncertainty among left-leaning intellectuals about the meaning of postwar prosperity. After years of economic depression followed by the Second World War, consumerism and affluence were undoubtedly good problems to have, but the proliferation of mass-produced commodities—and the subsequent commercialization of social life—posed thorny questions about the direction of American democracy.[29] On one hand there was the argument that Richard Nixon would offer to the Soviet Union's premier Nikita Khrushchev during the famous Kitchen Debate of 1959: that national progress was tied to the production of affordable appliances and color television sets. From this perspective, advertising functioned as the language of freedom and choice, providing the means by which information was packaged for consumers and voters alike. The counterargument questioned whether the glamour of such products hid the encroachment of commercial values on the nation's most sacred political institutions and rites. Glamour created a false aura around products and candidates, an aura that masked a growing apathy and indifference. As Khrushchev suggested to Nixon, that glamour also masked the nation's actual economic conditions; namely, its disregard for people living in poverty.[30]

Beyond these concerns, however, there was persistent anxiety about the public's relationship with the president. Few would dispute that the general's service and achievements were exemplary. But like some of his contemporaries, Ball mistrusted the way Eisenhower had exploited a promotional environment that subjected washing machines, cereal, and politicians to market testing and popularity. History had proven Eisenhower's *character*. It took Robert Montgomery and Madison Avenue to merchandise his *personality* for an electorate impressed with stature, prestige, and likeability. According to Riesman, Eisenhower's supporters believed that the candidate they so ardently liked "would surely know" what they themselves needed.[31] "I've got a feeling he's thinking of me," the cab driver says of Eisenhower in the 1956 commercial. "I'll be honest with you, I need him."[32] This wasn't a case of advertisers simply distracting voters with the illusory intimacy at the heart of political and celebrity culture. Television and advertising had created a public that saw glamour as an attractive, even necessary quality in political candidates. In the face of this promotional frenzy, commentators expanded their critique beyond Eisenhower and his advisers to question the voters' capacity to resist.

Zombies

Writing in *Saturday Review*, John Steinbeck criticized advertising's effect on political life. Long before the 1956 presidential election had gotten underway, Steinbeck responded to both parties' plans to run five-minute commercials at the end of popular television programs. The novelist must have had *The Jackie Gleason Show* in mind when he described television's effect on its audience:

> Let us say there is a fat comedian who is so admired that when his show goes on X millions of television screens welcome him. His admirers gather

by families, by clans. Bars with TV are jammed. So funny is this man that people laugh before he speaks because they know how funny he is going to be. They feel close to him and also they feel indebted to him to the extent of rushing out to buy the product he endorses.[33]

Steinbeck appreciated the merriment, but he cautioned that television left viewers "half-hypnotized" and "in a will-less, helpless state." This was precisely the frame of mind, he argued, that advertisers hoped to create and precisely the reason the fat comedian was on TV: once the audience was stunned and mentally asleep, they were powerless to resist the commercials that emanated from the screen.

As Steinbeck saw it, with their slackened mouths and glazed eyes, the audience was "captive" to a medium that undermined its reason and sense of choice. And while it was one thing to purchase breakfast cereal in such a docile, biddable state, it was another to choose a politician. The political commercial was premised on the hope that, after twenty-four minutes of clowning from Jackie Gleason or Milton Berle, the audience "will be so conditioned that it will be drawn with zombie inevitability to the Republicans' or Democrats' side of the ballot." "If they will buy the things they are told to buy," the logic goes, "then they will vote the way they are told to vote." The problem, as Steinbeck presented it, was that in their confusion, viewers had trouble distinguishing products from political personalities, "Squeakies— the body-building bran dust" seemed to merge with "Elmer Flandangle," the senate candidate. Whatever anxieties he felt about these potential mix-ups, Steinbeck took refuge in wit, noting that in the previous year, a cleansing powder had been elected to three public offices and a convertible automobile had won a governorship. He wondered whether voters would be able to resist a chocolate-coated candidate or one with sugar and cream in his hair.[34]

Steinbeck's absurdist comedy betrays the agitation with which intellectuals greeted televised advertising in the 1950s. From novelists and filmmakers to journalists and sociologists, attempts to understand the emergence of this new technology were inflected with a strongly hyperbolic and paranoid strain. While consumers welcomed the role of celebrities in promoting the bonanza of new commodities, writers such as Steinbeck warned how manipulative advertising could be. They saw consumers not as independent agents happily exercising their freedom of choice (a perspective zealously championed by the advertising industry) but as will-less members of a vast crowd, longing for social acceptance and vulnerable to commercial bureaucracies.[35]

The public is generally much savvier about advertisements and celebrity than critics thought in the 1950s. Rather than passively absorbing the media landscape, consumers tend to sift through commercial claims and imagery, pragmatically tailoring them to fit their individual needs. For several generations, researchers both in and out of the advertising industry have studied the way that consumers function as collectors rather than zombies, exercising a range of choices without regard for whether they cohere with mass sensibilities. Historian Lizabeth Cohen and others have shown that demographic research into consumer behavior began in the 1950s, and though the notion of market segmentation did not make its way into popular consciousness for another decade, it was already operating in the more innovative US boardrooms during Eisenhower's presidency. Consumer preferences shaped American corporations as much as corporations shaped individual taste. As Eisenhower himself put it, free economies were built on the consumer's "sovereign right of choice." "One of the hopeful developments of recent years," he continued, "is that new knowledge is rapidly being accumulated about the aspirations and wants and motivations of our people."[36] Eisenhower's friend General Lucius Clay offered a different perspective in comparing the experience of watching European and American television. In Europe, "you get this constant repeated propaganda without advertising and without break," he observed, but in the United States, "the advertising gives you a direct feeling of assurance that you haven't got propaganda in the program being thrown at you."[37]

News of these developments was slow to reach critics such as Steinbeck. Some of the most prominent books of the postwar period conveyed the sense that things were not as they seemed and that Americans were vulnerable to secret forces that sapped their independent thinking. The titles alone suggest a growing paranoia about the self's ability to withstand the dehumanizing effects of mass society. To *The Lonely Crowd* (1950) and *The Power Elite* (1956), we might add such studies as William H. Whyte's *The Organization Man* (1956) and Riesman's *Individualism Reconsidered* (1954). While Red Scare politicians fumed about the mental and emotional consequences of Soviet domination, others feared that capitalism was sowing its own demise. According to this parallel narrative, advertising secretly threatened to turn the public into a mob of all-consuming zombies. To borrow the title of Edward Bernays's influential 1947 essay, "the engineering of consent" seemed destined (if not designed) to overwhelm individual decision-making.[38] Americans have "TOO MANY THINGS," Steinbeck wrote Stevenson after the scandal about rigged quiz shows broke. "They spend their hours and money on the couch searching for a soul."[39]

Vance Packard's 1957 book *The Hidden Persuaders* helped popularize this view. Written after the second Eisenhower campaign, the book excoriated the manipulative nature of advertising. Packard focused on the development of the "depth approach" in which advertising and public-relations executives used psychology and motivational research to appeal to the public's secret desires. As Packard explained it, corporations systematically tried to persuade Americans—not through reason and rational arguments, but through symbolism and Freudian theory. "Preferences generally are determined by factors of which the individual is not conscious," one market researcher explained.[40] With the aid of psychologists and other social scientists, advertisers developed techniques to tap into consumers' subconscious fears and desires. Thus, convertibles were sold as symbolic "mistresses," insurance as the purchase of immortality, and wine as a connection to family roots. Cigarettes, as one might expect, were forms of oral gratification—"pacifiers for grown-ups," one psychiatrist explained.[41] Eisenhower presented the interest in consumer behavior as a new stage of democratic power; others saw it as cause for concern. "If I wanted to destroy a nation," Steinbeck warned Stevenson, "I would give it too much, and I would have it on its knees."[42]

Packard's power lay in his remarkable access to insiders who proudly explained their techniques. In 1956, an estimated $12 million was spent on motivational research, and major agencies were either consulting with independent experts or hiring their own teams of social scientists.[43] One of Packard's most memorable guides was the president of the Institute for Motivational Research, Dr. Ernest Dichter. *The Hidden Persuaders* follows the cheerful Viennese immigrant through the Institute's offices atop a mountain overlooking the Hudson River. We learn about the Institute's "psychopanel" of several hundred families who participate in its studies and visit the room where researchers record the reactions of children watching TV. Dichter expressed remarkable enthusiasm for a profession that many would find unsettling, and Packard shrewdly gave him ample room to explain. A successful advertising agency, Dichter boasts to clients, "manipulates human motivations and desires and develops a need for goods with which the public has at one time been unfamiliar—perhaps even undesirous of purchasing."[44] Noting the latent Puritanism in American attitudes toward consumption, Dichter counsels, "One of the main jobs of the advertiser in this conflict between pleasure and guilt is not so much to sell the product as to give moral permission to have fun without guilt."[45]

Packard badly overemphasized the role that subliminal messages and motivational research played in mid-century advertising. Historian Stephen Fox has criticized Packard for taking the comments of figures such as Dichter too literally, confusing their self-promotional claims for corporate fact. In introducing a recent edition of *The Hidden Persuaders*, media scholar Mark Crispin Miller has described the book as being "naïve by current academic standards" and offering a portrait of advertising that was "completely ahistorical and apolitical."[46] Whatever it lacked in accuracy, however, Packard's portrait of secret forces stripping people of their individuality touched a cultural nerve. The public was already fascinated by newspaper and magazine accounts of Communist brainwashing during the Korean War, and Hollywood had fed this interest with a series of popular prisoner-of-war films such as the 1956 Paul Newman vehicle *The Rack*.[47] That winter, science-fiction fans had begun flocking to the highly publicized film *Invasion of the Body Snatchers*, awed by

FIGURE 5.2 *The president of the Institute for Motivational Research, Dr. Ernest Dichter produced several influential reports that applied motivational research to US presidential campaigns.*

Ernest Dichter Photograph and Sound Recording Collection, Courtesy Hagley Museum and Library, P20101012 001.

the prospect of alien life silently replacing the regular citizens of a California town. When *The Hidden Persuaders* appeared the following year, it quickly attracted attention. The book spent a year on the *New York Times* bestseller list and eventually extended to over 3 million copies in print.[48]

Packard's discussion took on particular urgency when he addressed the application of motivational research to political campaigns. Tracing the roots of "effective political manipulation" to the works of Pavlov, Freud, Riesman, and the mass-merchandising lore of BBDO, he argued that democratic discourse during the 1952 and 1956 presidential races had given way to the science of image-making. To readers who had seen only scattered reports in newspapers and magazines, Packard provided a compelling (and sinister) context for understanding the GOP's enthusiasm for Robert Montgomery, Madison Avenue, and the commodification of candidates. Packard wrote from a liberal perspective, but his revelations appealed to a wide audience. Conservative commentator Phyllis Schlafly was so convinced by Packard's analysis that she later charged Republican moderates with using hidden persuaders to damage Robert Taft during the 1952 Republican National Convention. Eisenhower had won the nomination, she concluded, not because the "New York kingmakers" had propagandized on his behalf but because the "vicious and dishonest 'hidden persuaders'" had duped the nation into believing that Taft was secretive and corrupt.[49]

Packard's most startling find, perhaps, was that researchers had determined that "voters could not be counted on to be rational" and that independents often switched their votes for trivial reasons. As the agencies perceived it, their task was to use depth and projection techniques to determine the "underlying emotional tones of voter preference" in preparing strategy for their campaign.[50] Packard singled out Young & Rubicam and McCann-Erickson as the New York agencies that were uniquely committed to developing depth techniques. The agencies had built experienced research departments and conducted scores of motivational studies. Like most of his contemporaries, Packard focused so intensively on the GOP's relationship with BBDO that he never addressed the contributions other agencies made to the Eisenhower campaign. Evidence suggests, however, that both Young & Rubicam and McCann-Erickson used Dichter's research in planning their celebrity-themed campaign events. In 1956, the Institute tested a panel of 300 Americans on the emotional dependence, affection, admiration, and trust they felt toward the presidential candidates. Eisenhower beat Stevenson in every category, but the study revealed considerable anxiety about whether the president's health problems would affect his second term.[51] Shortly after the Republican National Convention, Young & Rubicam's David Levy directly referred to these anxieties in challenging his colleagues to improve Eisenhower's television appearance "which has *never* reflected *his own* healthy and vigorous look." His recommendation focused on cosmetics: the agency should "find a 'stand in'—a man whose skin texture is like the President's and test him under various conditions as Hollywood does for its stars."[52]

The Institute may also have informed Levy's decision to organize the Citizens television campaign around the goal of establishing "an emotional preference for Eisenhower."[53] Dichter's research had concluded that the election would be determined not by issues but "by the emotional reactions of the voters to the candidates."[54] As we saw in Chapter 4, Young & Rubicam premised their strategy on the belief that "*the public generally votes more with its heart* than with its reasoned mental conclusions."[55] In a subsequent series of memos, Levy and his colleague Preston Wood determined that celebrity appearances would establish this emotional connection in a way that standard political content could not. If the mission was to reach independent voters, then it was better to have the glamorous Helen Hayes talk about Eisenhower's bringing the boys home from Korea than to feature a foreign policy official, an academic expert, or simply an anonymous announcer's voice. Dichter had concluded in 1952 that the ego-involvement of viewers is enhanced when they receive information from a person who is easy to recognize and with whom they experience a gratifying, seemingly personal bond.[56]

As prepared by McCann-Erickson, the script for the Ike Day telecast took the question of relationships and identification a step further in placing the president in the domestic setting of the White House library. Fascinated by the arts of political manipulation, the University of California political scientist and novelist Eugene Burdick completed a study of the qualities the public felt would make up a "perfect president." Having interviewed hundreds of voters, Burdick concluded that a president "becomes great . . . to the degree that he becomes a 'father image' in our minds."[57] A man of warmth, confidence, and humor, the perfect president was seen less as a partisan warrior or highly gifted manager and more as a protector of the nation. The personality type corresponded to a shift that pollsters had noticed in the summer of 1956. Voters no longer viewed Eisenhower as the vigorous man of action they had elected in 1952; the average American household now regarded him as a wise and compassionate patriarch, "a grandfather of the Republic."[58] McCann-Erickson made sure that the Ike Day telecast created numerous opportunities to enhance the president's paternal role. Surrounded by his children and grandchildren, gently enforcing his grandchildren's bedtime, the president emerged from the program as a beloved and exemplary patriarch, a man who attended to the smallest details with both kindness and conviction. Mulling over his results, Burdick questioned the public's desire to select a president on the basis of personality rather than an issues-oriented debate. As he asked a reporter from *This Week*, "Are Americans in their dislike for politicians looking for a heroic leader of the totalitarian type?"[59]

The answer to Burdick's question lay somewhere in between. There seemed to be a complex calculus between what consumers desired, what market researchers deduced that they desired, and the way those desires appeared in advertisements. The image and the perception of the image reinforced each other in a self-defining loop. In the April 30, 1956, issue of *Advertising Age*, Margaret Mead compared the industry's influence on American life to "a silkworm that spins silk out of the inside of itself and wraps itself up in it." The confusion made it impossible to tell what was authentically American and what came from advertisements. Mead's sobering assessment was that there was "not a culture of the US but a culture of Madison Avenue."[60]

Five years after the 1956 presidential election, Daniel Boorstin introduced the term "pseudo-event" to explain how this disorientation was taking over public life. A historian at the University of Chicago, he had grown troubled by the effort to glamorize politics by staging happenings that had the primary function of garnering media attention. Boorstin's book *The Image: A Guide to Pseudo-Events in America* springs from the work of Riesman, Whyte, and Packard, but it moves the conversation from advertising and commodities to public relations and the "de-valuation" of reality. As Boorstin described it, a "flood of pseudo-events" was washing over the United States, appearing in everything from news leaks, to awards ceremonies, to the opening of shopping malls. In contrast to real events (a coup succeeds, an official resigns, a trade agreement falls through), pseudo-events are designed to be reported, designed to *make* news.[61] News events had become "dramatic performances" in which public officials acted out their prepared script. Boorstin argued that, in the minds of many Americans, pseudo-events had begun to overshadow the significance of real ones. Charmed by the drama and iridescence of the staged event, drawn to its consolatory power, the public had chosen to deceive itself in a contrived world.

Long before Eisenhower came to office, political campaigns included events that were made to be both experienced and reported. The union rally, the whistle-stop speech, the Labor Day parade—all these events packaged candidates for easy public consumption. Boorstin argued, however, that with the rise of television, the public had begun to prefer events that recognized the media as a primary constituent. As it became more embedded in American life, the pseudo-event created expectations and desires that only other, presumably larger pseudo-events could fulfill. Eisenhower had refused to debate Stevenson in 1956, so Boorstin's chief example was the 1960 presidential debates between Kennedy and Nixon. We like to think of presidential debates as nobly descending from the 1858 Lincoln–Douglas Illinois senatorial race, but Boorstin gave them a humbler, more embarrassing source: the television quiz show. The candidates square off as contestants in a battle of mental quickness and television cool. The public, in turn, evaluates the performance, with discussion focusing on questions of lighting, makeup, and vocal intonation rather than policy and leadership.[62] "In a democracy, reality tends to conform to the pseudo-event," Boorstin wrote. "Nature imitates art."[63] The self-fulfilling quality to the pseudo-event results in politicians who are skilled at image-making and citizens who are savvy spectators and critics.

Although he does not mention it, an event such as Ike Day was a textbook case of Boorstin's pseudo-event. Not only was it fashioned for the purposes of public relations, but it required the public to participate in what was arguably one of the most contrived episodes of the 1956 campaign. Filled with the satisfaction of do-gooder volunteerism, thrilled with the flurry of parties and parades, Ike's supporters successfully transformed their real activities into a spectacle of simulation and stagecraft, one in which the president joined 20 million Americans in staring into a *replica* of his boyhood living room. The program's courtship of celebrity gave Ike Day a surreal quality, turning it into a pseudo-event of startling proportions. The celebrity, Boorstin famously wrote, is "the human pseudo-event, a person who is known for his well-knownness."[64] As figments of the media, celebrities are endowed with public identities that hinge not on personal achievements but their ability to attract publicity. By surrounding the president with this fleeting prestige, the Eisenhower campaign downplayed his actual heroism in favor of giving him the celebrity treatment. He no longer represented a magnified version of the electorate; rather, he reflected the personality that the campaign and the media had worked to create.

Packard hoped to expose the forces that conspired against individual autonomy. By his account, advertising researchers and executives lurked in the shadows, using Freudian techniques to persuade Americans to think, vote, and consume as corporate powers wished. Like Steinbeck and Ball, he ultimately possessed rather simplistic fears about advertising's relation to the world. Consumers emerge in his analysis as victims of a well-funded scheme to dupe them of both their money and their will. For all its sense of anxiety, there was something comforting in such a Manichaean narrative, for it absolved the public of any responsibility for the secret manipulations going on. That absolution was key, for as the historian Daniel Horowitz has shown, Packard did not expose Dichter so much as he turned him into a national celebrity. By the decade's end, the Viennese analyst had opened franchises in more than a dozen American cities.[65]

Boorstin's vision was darker than what readers found in *The Hidden Persuaders*. The image industry had transformed the American environment to the extent that people struggled to know themselves outside the comfortable, mediated world. In Boorstin's analysis, individuals had become part of the alliance among politics, advertising, and celebrity, full participants in the rise of the pseudo-event as the principal mode of public life. He notably included both his readers and himself in the failures rising up around them: "We have become eager accessories to the greatest hoaxes of our age."[66]

The Two-Headed God

The most comprehensive critique of celebrity politics in the Eisenhower era came from two Academy Award-winners who had been deeply involved in progressive causes since the 1930s. In May 1957, director Elia Kazan and screenwriter Budd Schulberg released *A Face in the Crowd*, their searing portrait of a charismatic television star named Lonesome Rhodes who uses his popularity to spread reactionary ideas to millions of admirers.[67] Contemporary viewers will see traces of Rhodes in such right-wing media personalities as Donald Trump, Rush Limbaugh, and Glenn Beck, but although rarely acknowledged as such, the film was steeped in the debates about glamorized politics in the 1950s. Not only did the film echo the title of Riesman's companion volume to *The Lonely Crowd* (the 1952 collection of case studies, *Faces in the Crowd*), but the filmmakers had gone to both Madison Avenue and Washington to research the changes they saw taking place.

We might regard *A Face in the Crowd* as a cinematic partner to Boorstin's *The Image* and Packard's *The Hidden Persuaders* in its casting a cold and skeptical eye on the promotions-based industries. Despite strong protest from Madison Avenue insiders, mid-century Americans were surrounded by novels and movies about the alluring but shallow lives of public relations and advertising executives.[68] What linked Clark Gable in *The Hucksters* (1947), Gregory Peck in *The Man in the Gray Flannel Suit* (1956), and even Cary Grant in *North by Northwest* (1959) was the sense that beneath the protagonist's urbane surface was an individual suffering from a corrosive, disorienting industry.[69] Like *The Hidden Persuaders*, *A Face in the Crowd* had little interest in exploring the doubts of disillusioned Mad Men. The film's unsentimental critique makes it a useful cultural marker of the Eisenhower years and a movie worth exploring at length. As Kazan and Schulberg presented it, the manipulative powers of television, advertising, and celebrity were creating a dangerously authoritarian environment within the United States.

A Face in the Crowd tells the story of Lonesome Rhodes, a drunken roustabout played by a young Andy Griffith. Discovered in a small-town jail by an ambitious radio producer, Marcia Jeffries (Patricia O'Neill), Rhodes experiences overnight success as an Arkansas radio personality. A brief sojourn in Memphis and a move to New York City turn him into a television sensation and guitar-picking American icon. With the help of a retired general whose vitamin company sponsors his show, Lonesome Rhodes evolves into a wielder of national opinion. By the end of the film, he is advising a presidential contender and commenting widely on public affairs.

Though Jeffries is responsible for creating "Lonesome Rhodes" at each stage of his career, his comprehension of television runs deep, and he uses the medium to advance his vision to over 65 million viewers each week. But the more power he exerts over his audience, the more contemptuous he becomes. Appalled at his cornpone demagoguery (and her own complicity in it), Jeffries secretly broadcasts the star deriding his followers as "stupid idiots" and "miserable slobs." The audience revolts; backers turn away; Rhodes's empire collapses; and in the final scene, he is left drunkenly addressing an imaginary nation. The ending is not redemptive, however, for the menace of television remains. As his former writer Mel Miller (Walter Matthau) reminds us, there are other faces in the crowd ready to take Rhodes's place.

Although they shared an abiding commitment to leftist causes, Schulberg and Kazan will forever be remembered for their 1952 appearance as "friendly witnesses" before the House Un-American Activities Committee. Hating the witch hunts, but convinced that the Soviet Union had become a genuine threat to the United States, these former members of the Communist Party cooperated with HUAC and "named names." In the aftermath, they used the story of a gritty, proletarian hero to represent their rather erudite political views. With Marlon Brando playing the dockworker Terry Malloy, they created *On the Waterfront*, which won eight Academy Awards, including Best Picture, in 1954. Kazan later acknowledged that he saw his own story in Malloy's—that of a longshoreman who, despite pressure and physical threats, decides to inform the government about his corrupt union boss, the provocatively named Johnny Friendly.[70]

Kazan began shooting *A Face in the Crowd* in the summer of 1956 as the Republicans and Democrats were gathering for their nominating conventions. At the time, the press was abuzz with the news that representatives from the same Hollywood studio would be producing both conventions for a television audience. In Chicago, the Democrats had turned to the production chief of MGM, Dore Schary, who had overseen the making of such films as *Showboat* (1936), *Father of the Bride* (1950), and *Singin' in the Rain* (1952). Their program featured a skit in which well-known contestants from *The $64,000 Question* were quizzed about politics and world affairs. Meeting in San Francisco later that August, the Republicans entrusted their proceedings to George Murphy, then working as the director of public relations for MGM. Struck by the convention's "slick performance," the *New York Times* described Murphy standing conspicuously at the back of the rostrum in his suit and dark glasses, moving the program along and complaining that the politicians "think you just ad-lib everything."[71] As they shot on location in the hot and dusty town of Piggot, Arkansas, Schulberg and Kazan must have congratulated each other on the timeliness of their project. With its bitter satire and propulsive filmmaking, *A Face in the Crowd* was destined to be a revealing counterpart to the congenial telecasts from Chicago and San Francisco.

Lonesome Rhodes was an unlikely vehicle for thinking about the Eisenhower presidency. With his aw-shucks charm and maniacal energy, he could never be mistaken for the mild, soft-spoken patriarch who regularly appeared on the nation's TV screens. Schulberg had originally based the character on Will Rogers, whose son had confided that the popular entertainer "was so full of shit" because he pretended to be a folksy man of the people while his best friends were really bankers and power brokers.[72] As the project developed, however, he and Kazan began to focus on television personalities such as Arthur Godfrey, whose shows combined a family atmosphere with music and yarn-spinning commentary. Godfrey's programs enjoyed a tremendous following—Eisenhower himself was a fan—and they introduced an easy, down-home quality to the medium that other entertainers imitated.[73] "We took cognizance of the new synthetic folksiness that saturated certain programs," Kazan later remarked, "and the excursion into political waters by these 'I-don't-know-anything-but-I-know-what-I-think' guys.'"[74] References to Godfrey and Rogers appear throughout *A Face in the*

FIGURE 5.3 *Elia Kazan and Andy Griffith on the set of* A Face in the Crowd.
Courtesy Photofest.

Crowd, with Rhodes even suggesting that Godfrey might fill in for him when he travels to Mexico.

Although Rhodes's countrified swagger and anti-establishment airs would have appalled Eisenhower's golfing buddies, his story squarely took on the politics of the 1950s. The theme linking the two was what Schulberg described as "the two-headed god of public persuasion, television and advertising."[75] A master of the promotional spot, Godfrey had a low-key, down-to-earth manner that made him a favorite among politicians, sponsors, and audiences. (In 1952, Ernest Dichter quoted one viewer's admiration of Godfrey's "special way of talking that makes you think he is talking just to you.")[76] Not only did Young & Rubicam hope to enlist him in their work for Ike, but there is some evidence that Montgomery tried to adapt the entertainer's style and delivery to the president's own television appearances.[77] Like Steinbeck before him, Kazan saw television as "an almost hypnotic terrible force." "We knew television was selling 'personality' because we had Eisenhower up there on TV all the time," he explained. "You looked at him, and there was Grandpappy. And everyone wants to be nice to Grandpappy. But if you listened to him, he was saying nothing."[78] Leadership has always involved a certain measure of stagecraft and personality—this is one of Shakespeare's central themes in *Coriolanus*—but television made those requirements more elaborate and dangerous than before. After seeing *A Face in the Crowd*, French filmmaker Francois Truffaut remarked, "In America, politics always overlaps show business, as show business overlaps advertising."[79]

With the access granted to Academy Award winners, Kazan and Schulberg went to Washington and met with Stuart Symington and Lyndon Johnson, both of whom, at the time, were Democratic presidential candidates. Television had made politics "a whole new ballgame," the senators confessed, and they now understood that "'one false move' could undo all their preparation."[80] Hoping to skewer the culture of Madison Avenue, the filmmakers spent days talking with people at Young & Rubicam.[81] The summer before it began working on the 1956 Eisenhower–Nixon campaign, the agency invited its Hollywood visitors into product meetings, knowing that they were doing research for a new film.[82] "We went to Madison Avenue like explorers going into a strange country," Kazan wrote in his introduction to the published screenplay.[83] They attended conferences about how to photograph a ketchup bottle and how to capture the briskness of Lipton Iced Tea. By the time filming began, Kazan found himself enraged. "This has to be directed in anger," he wrote in the production notebooks, "anger at the Fraud, the general Fraud in our advertising surrounded lives."[84] He would later adopt a more lighthearted, though no less critical, tone. "The discussions were really ludicrous," he told Michael Ciment in 1974; "you could hardly keep a straight face."[85]

The advertising sequence in *A Face in the Crowd* memorably intersects with many of the themes that appear in Packard's and Riesman's work. It begins in a Memphis television station when Rhodes picks a fight with his sponsor, the owner of a mattress company, and although the on-air mockery provides great publicity, he is promptly fired. The public backlash is so strong that Rhodes is quickly signed as the new face of a humdrum medicine pill called Vitajex. He moves to New York and interrupts a meeting in which advertising executives are tepidly pondering how to increase the pill's declining sales. Rhodes recommends changing the pills from white to yellow, "the color of sunshine and energy—gives a feller that git-up 'n-go that sets 'em up with the ladies." He gobbles up a couple. His eye brows rise, his mouth opens into a teeth-baring grin. "Hoo-wee," he declares, "I am ready. I mean I am in the mood. My personality undergoes a startling change." Chasing a pretty secretary around the office, he exhibits the promise of sexual vitality that has occupied pharmaceutical advertisements from liver pills to Viagra. The account executive is appalled, but the members of the television department revel in their discovery. They gaze with admiration as Rhodes improvises a blues-inflected jingle that will become the heart of their new campaign: "Oh, Vitajex whatcha doin' to me? / Oh, Vitajex whatcha doin' to me? / You fill me full of oomph and ecstasy."

From there, the film breaks into a series of Vitajex commercials on Lonesome Rhodes's variety show. With the (now) rock 'n' roll jingle playing in the background, the montage features a string of clips in which the pill turns men into sexual animals and women into appreciative lust objects. Three scantily clad beauties dance on an oversized Vitajex, singing the pill's benefits and urging "Do it again. Do it again." A sickly-looking Rhodes takes a pill from one of three fawning women, he breaks into a wide grin, and the women begin to kiss him. A live audience of men, women, and children offers a collective "Oomph" and then chants with increasing speed that Vitajex makes them want to "GO, GO, GO!" A Marilyn Monroe lookalike coos from her unmade bed that she's bought her boyfriend a ten-year supply, fondling the massive bottle as she seductively turns out the light. In a nod to body builder Charles Atlas, who promised to transform the nation's "97-pound weaklings" into men, an animated pig gets no attention from a cute, bikini-clad sow until he gulps a sun-sized Vitajex. His body hardens, his tail stiffens with a boing!, and he takes on the head of a salivating wolf. His girlfriend faints with anticipatory pleasure.

While one could never describe the montage as subtle, Kazan and Schulberg may have been justified in their aesthetic approach. Beneath the hyperbole is some sober thinking about the appeal of advertisements and the ways in which personalities like Rhodes can overwhelm and revolutionize an

FIGURE 5.4 *After attending Young & Rubicam product meetings in New York City, Elia Kazan and Budd Schulberg satirized television advertising in* A Face in the Crowd. Warner Brothers.

industry. The accounts executive complains that the star does not care that the agency has "spent tens of thousands of dollars to find out the key words, like bracing and zestful," but he fails to understand that Rhodes's stardom fulfills advertising's promise to be a magnetic, visceral force. "In the end," Kazan remarked, "what it came down to is that what you sell in America is not what's in the product but what's in the ad."[86] With his residual concern for text, the executive completely misses how television has given him better tools for manipulation—the celebrity and the image.

A Face in the Crowd stands at the head of a long line of films that question and satirize television. From Sidney Lumet's Network (1976) to Spike Lee's Bamboozled (2000), a film dedicated to Schulberg, Hollywood has consistently depicted television as a comic but insidious threat to the reason, decorum, and valuable perspective apparently offered by the movies. Television emerges as cinema's vivacious younger sibling, a giggling adolescent who offers no apologies for being popular, scatterbrained, and indiscriminate. Kazan and Schulberg understood the rise of television in political terms, and they were amazed at its ability to overwhelm the nation with "easy, comforting lies." Television manipulated its viewers "in the crudest way," Kazan remarked, and betrayed the public voice it was supposed to represent.[87] The parade of stars and commodities masked an industry that was relentlessly taking over American life. To these two former Communists, television was the epitome of false consciousness, for it depicted social relations through the lens of entertainment and publicity.[88]

A Face in the Crowd does much to expose the manipulative aspects of television, and as Denise Mann has argued, the film bears the influence of German playwright Bertolt Brecht, whom Kazan had met the decade before. In his desire to create a genuinely Marxist theater, Brecht had developed the "Alienation-effect" (sometimes called the "V-effect") in which he sought ways to interrupt the audience's identification with the action or characters in a play and thus teach them to analyze the issues it raised. A Face in the Crowd may present us with the rags-to-riches story of Lonesome Rhodes, but Kazan pays exceptional attention to the production of Rhodes's stardom.[89] He shows us monitors, cameras, cables, soundboards, writers, and directors. At one point, Rhodes asks his cameraman to focus on his close-up in a monitor, thus inviting the Memphis viewers to see how his image appears on the sound stage. The shot of screen within screen, as Mann informs us, creates a moment of self-consciousness, forcing the movie audience to reflect on the ways in which television produces and mediates experience.[90]

Eisenhower's advisers sought to eliminate the critical distance that Kazan hoped to create. Rhodes seeks the names of the contraptions that broadcast his image across the airwaves, the question subtly pushing viewers to consider the powers behind him. As it moved from Los Angeles, to Washington, to Abilene, the Ike Day broadcast celebrated the seamlessness of transcontinental broadcasting. McCann-Erickson and the GOP fundraising team were as absent from "A Salute to Eisenhower" as cables, monitors, and make-up artists. The politics of concealment, of removing the program's frame, would become especially pertinent on Election Eve in 1956 when Young & Rubicam produced a coast-to-coast televised rally that featured live reports from San Francisco, Philadelphia, Chicago, Washington, and Boston. David Levy directed the program and smoothly integrated the camera feed—not from a Manhattan studio but from a White House women's bathroom.[91]

While Rhodes's furious energy made a great subject for filmmaking, it was Ike's easy, comfortable salesmanship that had Kazan and his collaborators worried. "Remember," he explained, "this was Eisenhower's time, and Eisenhower won the elections because everybody looked at him and said: 'There's Grandpa!' We're trying to say: never mind what he looks like, never mind what he reminds you of, listen to what he's saying!"[92] Televised image making, they warned, was already producing disturbing personal power. Ignoring the many other reasons why voters might have preferred the president, the filmmakers joined the chorus of Democrats who complained that liking Ike was a flimsy, even dangerous basis for giving him their vote.

Democrats were not the only ones who feared that the commodification of the president was leading to a cult of personality. After Ike's heart attack in 1955, a group of liberals and conservatives began to call for a national unity ticket in which Eisenhower would receive the presidential nomination for both the Republican and Democratic parties. The idea seemed ludicrous to the thirty-one-year-old conservative William F. Buckley, Jr., who ridiculed the proposal in his fledgling magazine, *National Review*: "There is abroad in the land a spirit of blind submission whose political expression is the attempt to Caesarize Dwight Eisenhower, with or without his cooperation. There seems to be a deep yearning in some quarters of America for a benevolent monarch or, *mutatis mutandis*, a reigning chairman-of-the-board."[93] Nearly a year before Election Day, Buckley observed an inexplicable desire to move beyond politics, to turn the stricken Eisenhower into a trans-partisan personality whose sheer likeability put him beyond contest and debate.

As we know, the executives at Young & Rubicam aimed to capitalize precisely on this sentiment, wooing independents and crossover Democrats with the trademark promise of a genial, warmhearted Ike. The spontaneous enthusiasm that Levy, Montgomery, and Langhorne Washburn did so much to coordinate at the October 1956 Madison Square Garden rally made for great television, but some observers found the hero-worship alarming. Alistair Cooke's report in *The Guardian* showcased the risks and rewards of building Eisenhower into a monumental personality. Buckley had condemned the spirit of blind submission that was circulating about the country. Eleven months later, Cooke saw evidence of idolatry as, awash in the charm of celebrities and confident in the prospects of victory, 20,000 men and women cheered for their candidate as he left the stage:

> He is the all-American granddad. He knows it, and they know it and it makes for a tumult of content. On his way out, while the cheers rolled on and on, he would pause and turn to some obscure balcony and lift both hands. The privileged section would rise at him and for this favour its inmates would throw their arms high in a hypnotized imitation of him. Trance is the state of the people who have seen Ike. The men glow, the women weep, and then he is gone to saddle up good old Donner and Blitzen again.[94]

Santa Claus, Caesar, a Republican Baal—Ike emerges from these contemporary reports as an unstoppable cultural force, a patriarch who brings ecstasy and meaning to civic life. Without comment, Cooke closes with a chilling image: six Communists from the Soviet Union and Romania observing the rally from special reserved seats.

As one can tell from the metaphors—trance, hypnosis, and idolatry—Schulberg and Kazan contributed to the broadening fear that political glamour could lead to the kind of mind control that mid-century Americans associated with authoritarian regimes. Lonesome Rhodes arises out of the concern that American populism, celebrity, and television could combine to produce what Kazan described as "native grass-roots fascism."[95] A Face in the Crowd, Richard Schickel has written, "openly acknowledges, as never before, [Kazan's] fear of the American mass, his sense that its fundamental good nature, its lack of historical sense, its feckless need for idle amusement, always leaves it open to some form of baronial (mis)leadership, to some form of benignly presented fascism."[96] The true fear of the movie is that Americans won't recognize fascism when it arrives via the smiling faces on their television sets, a problem Truffaut saw rippling out of the United States and into Europe.[97] People didn't fear that Eisenhower himself was a fascist. That would have been a preposterous charge to level at the man who led the fight against Hitler and Mussolini. But to critics who remembered how radio contributed to the rise of those dictatorial regimes, the manipulative power of television and advertising was more frightening. The "two-headed god" threatened to manufacture both exalted personalities and the spectators who would worship them.

A Face in the Crowd ultimately places these fears not in the ferocious Lonesome Rhodes but in mild-mannered and balding General Haynesworth, who owns the Vitajex company. Pleased by his booming business, Haynesworth sees an opportunity to use the star for his reactionary purposes. In a speech that is at once disgusting to Jeffries and revelatory to Rhodes, Haynesworth describes a plan to develop the iconic entertainer into a right-wing spokesman:

> Right now Lonesome is merely popular, oh-oh very popular. But Lonesome Rhodes could be made into an influence, a wielder of opinion, an institution

positively sacred to this country like the Washington monument.... My study of history has convinced me that in every strong healthy society from the Egyptians on, the masses had to be guided with a strong hand by a responsible elite. Let us not forget that in TV we have the greatest instrument for mass persuasion in the history of the world.

Haynesworth, we might say, is the hidden persuader in an economy based on promotion and visibility. Echoing Edward Bernays' argument that democratic leaders should use mass communications "in leading the public through the engineering of consent to socially constructive goals and values," he swiftly incorporates the magnetism of celebrities into his authoritarian theory of politics.[98] Stardom becomes a valuable tool for manipulating the masses into supporting the opinions of an invisible elite. Kazan follows the general's announcement with a montage that shows the effects of Haynesworth's image-making: Rhodes appears on the cover of *Life* magazine; he christens a naval vessel the USS *Rhodes*; he holds a telethon for crippled children; he contrives a sentimental yarn about his mom and pop for the ultra-right-wing newspaper, the *New York Journal American*. And ultimately, he serves as an adviser to Worthington Fuller, the priggish senator who General Haynesworth wants to run for the presidency, a senator who needs to develop the kind of down-home personality that viewers admire in Lonesome Rhodes.

Compared to the general's conspiratorial designs, Rhodes himself never amounts to a serious threat. With his swipes at Social Security and lurking isolationism, his politics sound less like Joseph McCarthy and more like Robert Taft. Broadcast across the country, his rant against the viewers—he calls them guinea pigs and slobs—injures their pride more than democracy, and the film swiftly punishes the transgression. Within minutes, the network switchboard lights up, the show's popularity plummets, and Haynesworth cancels the Vitajex sponsorship. Senator Fuller moves on to new backers and personalities, and the film ends with Rhodes screaming into the night, his populist power disintegrated into drunken megalomania. As Miller reminds him, demagogues in denim are easily replaced.

But even with Rhodes's demise, a more sinister threat remains—namely, the growing alliance between elites like General Haynesworth and what J. Hoberman has described as the beginnings of the National Entertainment State.[99] Although Rhodes initially baffled the advertising executives, the institutional power that they represent would historically overwhelm both leaders and celebrities. Perhaps the film's most ominous exchange directly echoes Reeves's infamous description of candidates as commodities. Speaking about Senator Fuller, General Haynesworth explains, "The majority in this country don't see eye to eye with him. We've got to find 35 million buyers for the product we call Worthington Fuller." Rhodes extends his sponsor's comment, bluntly embracing the analogy that had repelled Steinbeck, Packard, Ball, and Stevenson. "Did you ever hear of anyone buying a product—beer, hair rinse, tissues—because they respect it?" He challenges the reluctant senator, "You've got to be *loved*, man, *loved*!" How else, he asks, are the people going to "buy him for that big job on Pennsylvania Avenue?"[100]

With all his charismatic charm, Rhodes was a compelling way to dramatize the amorphous threat of television, advertising, and celebrity politics. But as mid-century intellectuals looked to the changes taking place, the real challenge was how to depict those less-outspoken personalities, the leaders and stars who exhibited the quiet affability and air of trust that corporations and advertising agencies were coming to prefer. As captivating as it might be, the critique of *A Face in the Crowd* could seem overblown, and the conservative magazine *Counterattack* dismissed the film as offering nothing more than hackneyed complaints: Kazan and Schulberg were just mainstream liberals selling "profitable bunk" about "conformity and thought-control" in mass society.[101] Though Kazan dismissed this (and more liberal) reviews as being "incredibly stupid," they attest to the prevalence of fear and paranoia about the rise of a commercial demagoguery. As Cold War commentators reflected on the Second World War, as they assessed the rise of Joseph Stalin in the Soviet Union and Mao Zedong in China, they started to fear the vulnerability of democratic capitalism to the personalities it created. What happened when members of the lonely crowd sought guidance and direction from the media and the public relations industries? How would one recognize the shift from social norming to corporate manipulation? In a passage that Packard made famous, political theorist Kenneth Boulding warned that "a world of unseen dictatorship is conceivable, still using the forms of democratic government."[102] That assessment may have seemed alarmist and hyperbolically partisan in the 1950s. By 1968, however, even Robert Montgomery was willing to concede that television's capacity to exalt personality could make it "the strong right arm of dictatorship" in the USA.[103]

Madly for Adlai

Adlai Stevenson disliked campaigning so much that he ran for president only three times, twice as the Democratic nominee and once as the lionized party stalwart hoping to be drafted if the 1960 frontrunners stumbled. Stevenson's mockery of the Republicans' Corn Flakes campaign and the merchandising of candidates was consistent with his general aversion to television. Eisenhower may have been a reluctant convert to the new medium, but Stevenson turned resistance into an ethic, a sign that, in his high-minded and serious way, he would "talk sense to the American people."[1] The erudite, low-key governor prided himself on public speaking and believed that campaigns offered him the chance to speak rationally about the United States' position in the world. He cultivated the image of a wise, empathic statesman whose dislike for theatrics permeated him to the core. To a party struggling to find itself seven years after Franklin Roosevelt's death, Stevenson was a genuine, cool-headed progressive when being progressive brought great distrust. "In this generation he has stood apart," Walter Lippmann eulogized in 1965, "not only for his deeds and his words and his wit and his lovableness, but as somehow a living specimen of the kind of American that Americans themselves, and the great mass of mankind, would like to think that Americans are."[2]

Stevenson's path to the 1952 and 1956 nominations was almost as predictable as it was surprising. His maternal grandfather, Jesse W. Fell, had been one of Abraham Lincoln's most trusted confidantes, and as owner of *The Bloomington Pantagraph* newspaper, he played a key role in encouraging Lincoln's debates with Stephen Douglas and bid for the presidency. Stevenson's paternal grandfather, also named Adlai, served as Vice President under Grover Cleveland and bequeathed his descendants a network of Democratic connections throughout Illinois and the nation. At the age of twelve, Stevenson traveled with his father to Sea Girt, New Jersey, to meet with Woodrow Wilson, who was then planning his own presidential campaign. Inspired by Wilson, Stevenson attended Princeton University, and after graduating, he moved on to law school at Harvard.[3] Midway through his studies, however, he returned home to run *The Pantagraph*, an occupation that helped him polish his eloquent writing style. Stevenson would eventually finish his legal training at Northwestern University and practice law in Chicago before joining the Roosevelt administration during World War II, first as a legal adviser to the Secretary of the Navy, and then as an aide to the US delegation at the founding of the United Nations.

Stevenson was elected governor of Illinois in 1948, and in that role, he welcomed party members to the 1952 Democratic National Convention in Chicago. At once witty, thoughtful, and stirring, the speech immediately put him in the spotlight as a potential nominee. Though he had not assembled a campaign, nor run in a single primary, Stevenson won on the third ballot. As he later told the convention, "I would not seek your nomination for the Presidency because the burdens of that office stagger the imagination. Its potential for good or evil, now and in the years of our lives, smothers exultation and converts vanity to prayer." Like Eisenhower, Stevenson saw the presidency as an awesome responsibility, one for which he had not prepared. "I have asked the Merciful Father," he continued, "to let this cup pass from me, but from such dreaded responsibility one does not shrink in fear, in self-interest, or in false humility. So, 'If this cup may not pass from me, except I drink it, Thy will be done.'"[4]

Though hardly humble, Stevenson's comparison to Jesus Christ in Gethsemane fit the circumstance, as he faced a grueling task in taking on one of the world's most admired men. The governor brought significant personal weaknesses to his campaigns: he had limited experience; he had been divorced in 1949; and he was easily caricatured as a patrician intellectual who lacked the common touch. A host of historical factors worked against Stevenson as well. Democrats had controlled the Executive branch for nearly twenty years, and over time, the cronyism had run rampant. In 1951, Truman's White House became the center of controversy when investigators discovered that leading aides and advisers had taken luxury goods in exchange for political favors. Later that year, a similar influence-peddling scheme erupted at the Internal Revenue Bureau leading to the dismissal of 166 officials.[5] As alarming as they were, the controversies were overshadowed by the public's growing weariness with the Korean War, which showed no signs of progress after two bloody years. Although the battle against communism had stalled overseas, it seemed to be taking over every corner of American society. The anti-Red fervor frightened traditional liberals to the extent that even politicians began to modify their public comments for fear of being the subject of House or Senate inquiries. In this polarized climate, Stevenson was fated to run against a man that many Americans regarded as a proven and likeable leader. In 1945, 12,209,238 men and women were serving in the Armed Forces, many of them under General Eisenhower's command.[6] Seven years later, they looked to him as a potential Commander-in-Chief.

A candidate's relationship to Hollywood obviously does not make or break his or her political career. At the same time, Stevenson's campaigns were unusual in that, for many years, Democrats had an advantage when it came to the mixture of politics and entertainment. Although Truman had little interest in Hollywood, Roosevelt had come to enjoy its assistance. He delighted in the contrast between the peppy Election Eve special his supporters had broadcast in 1944 and the dull Republican program that followed it. As the GOP proclaimed its preference for politics over show business, as it filled the airwaves with "monotonous and deadly talk," Roosevelt pointed to Fala, his beloved Scottish terrier, and mirthfully boasted, "They even put my dog to sleep."[7] By 1952, the advantage had swung the other way. The rise of blacklists in Hollywood and New York had limited the number of stars who would publicly support Democratic candidates. And of course, Eisenhower's stature made him a safe and appealing choice for stars such as Ronald Reagan and James Cagney, who had previously endorsed Democrats.

Despite—or perhaps because of—the many challenges facing his campaign, Stevenson inspired an unusually fervent response among Hollywood liberals. Discouraged from pursuing social justice issues through film and activism, the celebrities who worked for him did so with remarkable passion and commitment. Stevenson possessed an unusual gift in personally connecting with his supporters, drawing them out of their own busy lives and into his intellectual and emotional orbit. "He was so charming and so urbane and friendly," screenwriter and director Philip Dunne recalled, "that you just felt that you really meant something to him." Bette Davis was not alone in praising Stevenson as "a beautiful egghead."[8] From Greta Garbo and Marlene Dietrich to Tallulah Bankhead and Lauren Bacall, a series of actresses found themselves entranced by the Illinois governor. He was an improbable object for such attention and fantasizing. Stooped, bald, sporting a trademark hole in the sole of his shoe, he seemed more equipped for a conference of voting rights attorneys than Hollywood stars. And yet, Stevenson produced a somewhat erotic attachment in his followers that left many puzzled but no less enthusiastic. "One knew why some adored him. He did not look like other people," Norman Mailer wrote. "He had the sweet happiness of an adolescent who has just been given his first major kiss."[9] Being infatuated with Stevenson was such a strong leftist theme that the poet John Berryman closed a "Dream Song" criticizing Eisenhower with the humorously romantic quip, "(O Adlai mine)."[10]

Stevenson's intellect and his unabashed defense of liberalism helped draw people eagerly to his side. Political scientist Jonathan Bell has argued that his candidacy benefited from the peculiar culture of 1950s California in which "the state's intensely media-driven, celebrity politics" thrived on politicians who could successfully court the liberal press.[11] In the same way, the 1952 campaign reignited a demoralized state Democratic Party, giving followers, especially in Hollywood, a candidate they could back. Stevenson had a similar impact on supporters across the country. His presidential campaigns gave women significant administrative positions not just as local volunteers but as professionals with national responsibilities.

And yet the passion Stevenson inspired in his admirers often expressed itself in the idiom of a soulful eroticism that the campaign encouraged and cultivated. A 1952 television commercial provides a case in point. A svelte blonde singer in a surprisingly revealing dress belts a jazzy tune about her devotion to the candidate. She sings, "I love the Gov, the Governor of Illinois, / He is the guy that brings the dove of peace—and joy," winking at the camera with the sexy confidence of a Hollywood New Deal dame. "Didn't know much about him before he came / But now my heart's a ballot that bears his name." For months Americans had been declaring, "I like Ike." They had worn the slogan on scarves, sweaters, buttons, and tie clips. The Democrats tried to trump that ubiquitous affection with an odd combination of civic concupiscence. Dwelling on each syncopated syllable as if it were a breath of joy, the singer closed her eyes and delivered the commercial's key contending line, "Adlai, love you madly / And what you did for your own great state / You'll do for the rest of the 48."[12]

The Seraglio of Middle-Aged Ladies

"I have never been able to clarify my feelings about Governor Stevenson," actress Mercedes McCambridge wrote in her 1981 autobiography, *The Quality of Mercy*. "So many were smitten by this small giant from Illinois, so many of us jumped on his bandwagon."[13] Although the actress came from a strongly Democratic family, it wasn't until she heard Stevenson speak over the radio that she felt motivated to become involved in a political campaign. She recalled the moment in the vivid language of an epiphany. Sitting on the beach on a clear San Diego night, she heard Stevenson address the 1952 Democratic National Convention in Chicago: "On that rare California night when there was no fog, no damp chill, when the beach was sleek and glistening, my husband and I and our best friend heard the voice. Heard the speech. Heard the language of civilization as it should be. We were stunned."[14] That night she sent a telegram to Stevenson offering to help. Over the next four months, she barely left the candidate's side. She appeared at rallies and speeches, participated in multiple forms of campaign publicity, and traveled some 25,000 miles introducing voters to the little-known Democratic candidate. Four years later, she committed to the same whirlwind of activities again. At one point, Stevenson turned to her and said, "Dear girl, you are going to kill yourself working for me." And she replied, "I couldn't think of a better way to go."[15]

Mercedes McCambridge is no longer a household name, though her iconic performance as the voice of the demon in *The Exorcist* (1973) remains unforgettable to everyone who has seen the film. In the 1950s, however, McCambridge was a highly touted actress who played important supporting roles in *Johnny Guitar* (1954) and the sprawling Texas epic *Giant* (1956). McCambridge's reputation rested firmly on her Academy Award–winning performance in *All the King's Men* (1949) in which she played Sadie Burke, the hardboiled assistant to a highly charismatic and corrupt Louisiana governor. Based on Robert Penn Warren's novel about the populist Huey Long, the film was interesting preparation for an actress who three years later would find herself on intimate terms with the Democratic nominee for president. While Burke continually suffers under the governor to whom she has devoted much of her life, McCambridge saw only virtue and tenderness in her close friend. There are "only two kinds of people in the world," she told *Time* magazine, "everybody else and Adlai Stevenson." "I realize how poor my life would have been if I had never known Adlai Stevenson," she followed up in her autobiography.[16] To say the two shared complicated feelings would not be an understatement; filled with mash notes and expressions of affection, their correspondence continually underscored the special nature of their relationship. "When Governor Stevenson said, 'I do love you so,'" McCambridge confessed, "there was no category into which such a sweet declaration could fit and be comfortable." The two eventually settled on the Spanish word *emotiva*, a passionate affinity, to capture the intense feelings they had for one another.[17]

McCambridge reluctantly agreed that she was not alone in having powerful feelings for the governor. While she enjoyed unusual access to him, many joined her in worshipping the Illinois statesman. Borrowing a phrase from Connecticut senator William Benton, she numbered herself among Stevenson's "seraglio of middle aged ladies." Wherever the candidate went, he seemed followed by a virtual harem of admirers. "Oh, the women! Oh, my goodness, the women!," McCambridge exclaimed in recalling a party at Stevenson's apartment at the Waldorf-Astoria:

> There were rich women, oh, very rich women, widowed or barely husbanded, brilliant women, philanthropists, scientists, diplomats, actresses, writers, women with titles of lesser nobility, and me, I guess. It was fascinating to watch Adlai make his way around the room, being gracious and charming to each little cluster. I swear every female eye in that handsome salon knew where he was every minute of the evening, including me, I guess. I felt closest to Adlai whenever his eyes found mine across a crowded room: the great Assembly chamber at the UN; the stage of the Cow Palace in San Francisco, in a salon full of his seraglio.[18]

As she was loath to admit, McCambridge's desire to be selected out of the crowd made her more like the other admirers than she originally had thought.

FIGURE 6.1 *In 1950, Mercedes McCambridge won an Academy Award for Best Supporting Actress as Sadie Burke in the political thriller* All the King's Men. *She is pictured here (holding the coffee cup) with John Ireland as Jack Burden, and Broderick Crawford, who won an Oscar for Best Actor for his role as Governor Willie Stark.* Courtesy of Photofest.

Among those other women was actress Lauren Bacall, the great ingénue of mid-century film who, at the age of twenty, had starred with her soon-to-be husband, Humphrey Bogart in the 1944 classic *To Have and Have Not*. Bacall had entered the political world in 1945 when (depending on whom you believe) her agent or a bored White House press corps coaxed her to pose on top of a piano played by Vice President Truman.[19] In 1947, she and Bogie led a group of stars to Washington to protest the beginning of the HUAC hearings, and a year later, the couple endorsed Truman for president. By the beginning of 1952, however, they had become strong supporters of the Draft Eisenhower movement, and news reports about the January rally prominently mentioned their attendance.

Stevenson's speech at the Democratic National Convention changed everything. Bacall withdrew her support from Eisenhower, and Bogart cautiously followed, explaining that he had grown uneasy about the general's new compatibility with the isolationist Senator Robert Taft. Bacall described her decision in more visceral terms. "I adored Adlai Stevenson. I suppose I even worshipped him," she wrote in her autobiography. "His entrance into my life shook me up completely."[20] Like McCambridge, Bacall treasured the intimacy of catching Stevenson's eyes during a rally or meeting, and she recounted how that shared glimpse would set her to fantasizing about how vulnerable and passionate about people he was. Her memoir describes a cartoon that Bogie wanted to draw in which he was left at home with the couple's two children while she was off with Adlai. "Bogie knew that I had been deeply affected by Stevenson and, for that matter, he had too."[21]

That fall, Bogart, Bacall, McCambridge, and actor Robert Ryan accompanied Stevenson on campaign trips across the country. Their first stop was the Cow Palace, San Francisco's massive events arena, where they served as "pot boilers" before the political speeches commenced.[22] "Our job was to help attract crowds as Stevenson was still relatively unknown in much of America," Bacall explained. "I was sure that the more people saw and heard him, the more would vote for him."[23] The stars' "pertinent, rah-rah words" were carefully scripted, and everyone expected them to perform well on stage.[24] The press conferences required more choreography. Following a decades-old custom, Stevenson would appear in the middle of the adoring stars, their presence lending glamour and energy to his modest frame. Although they served as excellent photographic props, the stars' exposure to reporters was limited. In planning the event, the head of the Hollywood Democratic Committee assured a colleague that he would stay close by to "see that the press doesn't murder our actors by throwing framed questions at them."[25]

The twenty-eight-year-old Bacall engrossed herself in the campaign, and at times it became difficult to differentiate the supporter from the candidate. "From the day we went to San Francisco," she wrote, "my life and I myself began to change. I was insanely caught up in the excitement of campaigning—lunches, rallies, motorcades, platforms, college campuses. We were assigned to a car a couple behind Stevenson's. Crowds waving and screaming—it made me feel I was running for office."[26] In October the stars joined Stevenson on a whistle-stop tour of New England. The crowds went crazy for Bogart and Bacall, their cheers and chants occasionally drowning out the proceedings. In New Bedford, more than 5,000 people squeezed into a hotel ballroom where they would be appearing.[27] In town after town, the hoopla delayed the train from leaving. Finally, Stevenson's campaign manager politely asked the stars to take a break and rejoin the campaign in New York City.[28]

The New England tour culminated in a boisterous Madison Square Garden rally on October 28. Like much of the 1952 campaign, the event was designed to establish Stevenson as Franklin Roosevelt's political heir. Eleanor Roosevelt introduced the governor by reminiscing about her husband's appearance in the Garden twenty years before, and *Newsday* reported that across New York City, he had been met by a "Roosevelt-type crowd."[29]

FIGURE 6.2 *Adlai Stevenson surrounded by celebrity supporters, including Fred Clark, Mercedes McCambridge, Lauren Bacall, and Humphrey Bogart. Stevenson signed this photograph, "To Mercedes McCambridge,* she *did her best!! Adlai E. Stevenson, 1952."*
Courtesy of Women and Leadership Archives, Loyola University, Chicago.

Dubbing the program "Stars for Stevenson," the Democrats broadcast an hour of the rally on radio and television. A procession of stars preceded the governor on stage—Richard Rodgers, Oscar Hammerstein, Carl Sandburg, and Will Rogers, Jr. In February, Arthur Schlesinger, Jr., had criticized the emphasis on glamour at the Eisenhower Midnight Serenade, but eight months later, he was slightly infatuated with the Democratic display. "The Garden was crawling with Hollywood and Broadway talent," he recorded in his journal, noting his warm and animated conversation with Bacall. A prominent Harvard historian, Schlesinger had written portions of Stevenson's speech, struggling whether to direct it to the television or the Garden audience. In the end, he was more impressed with a celebrity skit about Republican doublespeak than "the flop" the candidate delivered. Another throwback to the Roosevelt era, the parody seemed at least to have pleased the 22,000 people who had jammed into the rally.[30]

Bacall and McCambridge played prominent roles in another campaign venture, a film put together by the Hollywood committee for Stevenson and his running mate, Alabama senator John Sparkman. Titled *The Stevenson Bandwagon*, the film interspersed a series of skits and advertisements with clips of the candidate sitting at a desk and (dully) repeating excerpts from some of his most successful speeches. Eisenhower's celebrity endorsements directly appealed to independents and swing-voting Democrats, but the Stevenson stars concentrated on the party faithful, reminding them of their victories over Thomas Dewey and Herbert Hoover.[31] The Democrats had designed the program to reach 10 million women voters as they gathered in homes or meeting halls with pro-Stevenson friends. To that end, the campaign made the performances available for mail order purchase in two formats: a 16-millimeter movie reel and a platter-sized phonograph record.[32] McCambridge helped by hosting the program, Bacall by recording a promotional trailer. Volunteers for Stevenson thought so highly of the film that they interrupted the Madison Square Garden speeches to show excerpts from it.

The Stevenson Bandwagon featured an odd collection of political advertisements, stilted speech-making, and anti-Republican sketches.[33] The most content-heavy sketch, "Three Strangers," involved two men stuck in an elevator during an air raid drill with a ditzy female operator. One man supports Eisenhower, the other Stevenson, and the woman (whose squeaky voice provides comic relief) is undecided. The two men talk about the upcoming election and the prominent issues of the day. Should the United States send aid to Korea? How important is a bipartisan approach to foreign policy? What precisely was Eisenhower's relationship to Joseph McCarthy? And what about Richard Nixon? The talk is cordial and friendly, though the Stevenson supporter politely challenges his counterpart to think beyond the sentiment of admiring Ike and begin to question the right-wingers surrounding him. By the time the drill is over and the elevator is moving again, the reasons have become too hard to dismiss, and all three inhabitants support the Democrat's candidacy. The sketch offered a microcosm of what Stevenson hoped voters would find in his campaign: rational discussion overcoming Cold War accusations and Madison Avenue publicity.

In its judicious treatment of the issues, "Three Strangers" stood apart from the other Hollywood material included in *The Stevenson Bandwagon*. A more typical contribution was a fluffy sketch situated at the Republican headquarters. Looking for good songs for the upcoming campaign, the Republicans hire a group of songwriters, but each song the musicians perform turns out to be a disaster. One sheds unflattering light on Eisenhower's relationship with conservative senator Everett Dirksen, as well as McCarthy and Taft. Another suggests that with Taft on board, Eisenhower's White House would be like a "bicycle built for two." The frustration mounts with each attempt. "A Republican song should confuse the people, right?" one of the songwriters asks, to which the dimwitted chairman reluctantly agrees. Eventually the songwriters decide to pull out the really good stuff with a song that "people all around the country are beginning to sing." The Republicans smile at the jazzy opening notes—this is going to be good—and then out flow the words,

"I love the Gov, the Governor of Illinois." Looks of confusion cross their faces, but the song is too catchy to resist. By the second verse, the whole office has joined in, the Eisenhower workers happily giving in to their mad love for Adlai Stevenson.

In a film designed to rally the party faithful, these fantasies about converting the opposition may have been misplaced, though perhaps the scriptwriters believed they would help stave off defections. At the same time, the conversion theme drove to the heart of the Broadway and Hollywood mission. The program was premised on the notion that Republicans would switch their allegiance because, in the end, Democrats had funnier sketches, better songs, and superior talent. The simplicity of this vision has to be understood in the context of an entertainment blacklist that made the discussion of issues difficult, if not perilous. Like dozens of others, Bogart and Bacall had been advised *not* to campaign for Stevenson, and considering the negative response to their 1947 protest of HUAC, it took courage to participate.[34] The dangers for all these stars were real, even when they were only generating publicity and excitement. Although entertainment played a minimal role in the October rally, the Red-baiting magazine *Counterattack* paid careful attention to the program.[35] In 1955, a former assistant at the magazine told the Senate Judiciary Committee that the editors compiled a list of people who had been part of *Stars for Stevenson,* labeling them "left-wingers and controversial, unsuitable people." These well-known personalities received a black mark "on their record," the assistant explained, "because they had supported Adlai Stevenson, the Democratic Party candidate for President of the United States."[36]

As we have seen with McCambridge and Bacall, however, the idea of "conversion" hung heavily about the Stevenson campaign. Working for the Illinois governor was no ordinary experience in the lives of these actresses; it was filled with excitement, devotion, and the ecstasy of personal transformation. The response was on one level peculiar. Stevenson was hardly a feminist, and in 1955, he notoriously told the graduating class of Smith College that their primary role during the Cold War was to provide a stable home for their husbands and children.[37] Nonetheless, Hollywood's hyperbolic sense of what it contributed to the presidential race ultimately mirrored the intensity of the actresses' response. To both women—and the friends who observed them—the pull to Stevenson seemed irrational, mysterious, and profoundly full of meaning. "She was crazy about Stevenson, almost on a sexual level," the screenwriter Milton Sperling said about Lauren Bacall. "She was insane about him, she just adored him."[38] Though their memoirs barely mention each other, Bacall strangely echoed McCambridge when she addressed the bond she felt with the candidate: "It took me a long time to dissect my feelings, but at that moment I felt a combination of hero worship and slight infatuation. The campaign had disrupted my life completely." As if they had taken the allusion to Gethsemane seriously, both women saw themselves as disciples, turning Stevenson into a heroic explainer, a man of consequence who helped them see the world—and themselves—differently. "It wasn't that I was dissatisfied with Bogie or loved him any the less," Bacall later explained, "it was that Stevenson could help a different, unknown, obviously dormant part of me to grow."[39]

What remains so interesting about Stevenson's Hollywood followers was how little he professed to care about glamour, packaging, and image. The 1952 campaign unfolded alongside the transformation of American culture as television began to surpass radio as the primary broadcast medium. Although they represented an industry devoted to the production of image, Bacall, McCambridge, and many others found themselves in awe of Stevenson's voice. As television drew the political world closer to performance, they found in the governor not just a charming, divorced man eager for their attentions, and not just an eloquent defender of liberalism amidst the geopolitical tension of the Cold War. They found in Stevenson a man who defended the value of rational discourse against the seemingly allied threats of military might and visual packaging.

The Things You Don't See

Stevenson's Hollywood supporters had to fit their efforts within a loosely defined organization that was generally uncomfortable with political image-making.[40] While major advertising agencies coordinated the different parts of Eisenhower's campaign, the advocacy groups supporting Stevenson had little connection and oversight. Stevenson had inherited a Democratic establishment that for years had respected newsreels over the upstart technology of television, and he did little to reverse the trend.[41] His own dislike of television (he personally did not own a set until after 1952) led him to adopt a cool, seemingly haphazard approach to the medium.[42] Stevenson's insistence that the presidential race was an opportunity to educate the public was both noble and fatally naïve, for it excused a lack of preparation as evidence of his political integrity. Republican programs offered paeans to TV, pointing to its capacity for elegant transitions and cross-continental camera feeds. Stevenson meanwhile found ways to critique the very medium upon which he was appearing. Will Rogers, the father of one of Stevenson's most recognizable supporters, liked to quip, "I don't belong to any organized party . . . I'm a Democrat." The same thing could be said about Stevenson's advertising and media strategy.

Despite the assistance Roosevelt and Truman had received from Milton Biow's advertising agency (the Biow Company), the party was wholly unprepared for the ways in which the postwar economy had changed public relations. As they got ready for the 1952 elections, the Democrats seemed incapable of recognizing the new horizons of publicity. The Stevenson campaign had only one prominent PR adviser with any commercial experience: Manly Mumford of the Borden food company. Internally, the party favored public relations bureaucrats who had extensive experience with newspapers and government agencies. Sam Brightman, who headed publicity for the DNC, had been trained as a reporter and worked as a special assistant to the Housing Expediter office. Porter McKeever directed public relations for the Volunteers for Stevenson organization after serving for six years as an information officer for the US Mission to the United Nations.[43] These officials understood publicity in narrow, informational terms; their jobs were about overseeing press releases and producing campaign literature rather than creating an aura of likeability. From the beginning, the Volunteers group seemed proud that their decentralized organization would result in a "non-professional ad hoc Stevenson effort."[44] Piecing together the initiatives of state and local committees, the campaign welcomed programs like *The Stevenson Bandwagon,* which would have national appeal and could be used to lighten the "deadliness of straight political speechifying" by local candidates.[45]

Stevenson's distaste for the merchandising of politics filtered into how the Democrats used their advertising firms. The party hired Baltimore's Joseph Katz agency to coordinate its print, radio, and television advertising, and they also received assistance from Chicago's Erwin, Wasey agency. In his study of the 1952 race, Stanley Kelley, Jr., reported that Stevenson's people expected the agencies to serve more as day-to-day tacticians than as comprehensive strategists.[46] In contrast to the broad vision that BBDO and Young & Rubicam brought to Ike's campaigns, the agencies' input was particularly defined and limited. They bought radio and television time, placed advertisements and fundraising appeals in the newspapers, and used their own corporate credit to handle expenses when the Democrats were late paying their bills. After a last-minute change scrambled its newspaper placements, the frustrated media director at Erwin, Wasey gently reminded McKeever that the campaign had to give the agency "sufficient notice" if it wanted its advertisements to run correctly.[47]

The lack of planning and foresight was fatal when it came to television.[48] The Democrats persistently attacked Eisenhower on the topic, but in reality, the party relied on television as much as their Republican counterparts. According to a much-cited Miami University study, the Democrats blanketed the airwaves during the 1952 campaign, but, trying to save money, they advertised during less-expensive periods when viewership was limited.[49] Rosser Reeves had convinced the Republicans that they should try to sandwich their commercial and full-length broadcasts between the nation's most popular shows. Though Stevenson's campaign spent $1.5 million on television advertising, nearly all of it went toward thirty-minute speeches that were broadcast simultaneously on radio.[50] While the Republicans used television to promote Ike's personality, the Democrats tried to air their candidate with as little staging as possible.

As if he were protesting their very existence, Stevenson's commercials were poorly designed and executed. Because the candidate himself was so dismissive, his advisers developed a number of cartoon advertisements with soundtracks designed for radio play. Anxious about running against Eisenhower, the Democrats tried to make the election about Joe McCarthy and Bob Taft. One advertisement played off of Stan Freberg's comedic skit that told an entire story—soap opera style—using just the words *John* and *Marsha*. Depending on the actor's melodramatic tone, the two names conveyed a shifting narrative of love, suspicion, anger, and back again to love. The Democrats' satirical soundtrack featured Bob and Ike muttering the other's name with dreary tenderness, happy to be such good friends after their convention strife. On screen, the static cartoon image underscored the homophobic joke: two hearts joined by a Cupid's arrow, one labeled Bob, the other Ike.[51] This was poor radio and terrible TV, leading one to wonder whether Stevenson would have been better off delegating his television commercials to his spirited Hollywood advocates. When the campaign ended in November, the candidate watched the disappointing results from the governor's mansion with his sister, his sons—and Ryan, Bacall, and McCambridge. He had won only nine states and eighty-nine electoral college votes, though as Stephen Whitfield has observed, Stevenson received more popular votes than any Democrat since 1936.[52]

Stevenson conducted his second campaign more professionally, and with his approval, supporters began organizing themselves a year in advance. By October 1955, ninety people had joined the Hollywood for Stevenson Committee.[53] In January, a group of public relations volunteers was assembled that included TV producers, PR executives from the Ideal Toy and Merck Chemical companies, and an extensive list of writers (the *New Yorker*'s Richard Rovere and John Hersey among them).[54] Recognizing how important television exposure would be, Bacall hosted Stevenson at a "Tea for TV" event at the Beverly Hills Hilton in February 1956. With nearly 1,000 Democratic women in attendance, she presented the candidate with a specially designed lapel pin—a silver shoe with a hole in the sole—as a reminder that he would not make his journey alone.[55] By May, the Democratic National Committee had named Dore Schary of MGM and Cass Canfield of Harper & Brothers publishing as co-chairmen of its Committee for the Arts. The positions were influential enough that Oscar-winning director Joseph L. Mankiewicz tried to take over Schary's position, privately dismissing him (and the Hollywood committee chairman Allen Rivkin) as "second rate."[56] Schary survived the incursion, and after directing the national convention, he helped the committee assemble two pools of talent: an A-list of twenty-four "absolutely top drawer people" and a B-list of the less famous who would work with local committees.[57]

Although the Stevenson camp continued to complain about Madison Avenue, the Democrats recognized that they had to hire a more substantial advertising agency if they were going to prevent another crushing loss. The party faced a serious problem, however, in that fearing a backlash among Republican-headed corporations, the leading firms did not want to work for the Democratic Party. The situation seemed so dire that, according to Vance Packard, there was talk of developing a neutral "anchor" agency that would work for unpopular campaigns. As one proposal explained, the largest agencies would create what amounted to a promotional bailout of the two-party system by anonymously loaning out members of their own staff for the duration of the race.[58] The worry proved to be unnecessary, for in early March, Norman, Craig and Kummel (NCK) took the Democrat's $8 million account.

Formed only the year before, NCK was a young and vibrant agency that was best known for its work on the Maidenform Bra campaign.[59] *Space and Time*, a trade newsletter since 1938, evaluated the agencies as if they were boxers, giving BBDO the advantage in terms of size and experience but seeing potential in Norman, Craig and Kummel's youthful, enterprising, and courageous staff. In its clipped, bulletin style, the newsletter explained, "Issues and personalities may largely determine results, but advertising and public relations are twin locomotives that will propel campaigns. Sleekness, polish and speed with which BBDO and NCK engineer runs may have lots to do with victory."[60] *Time and Space* was right in depicting the showdown as a case of David versus Goliath. Norman, Craig and Kummel had selected one of its best men to lead the Democrats, but fresh off the Blatz Beer account, the thirty-four-year-old executive was hardly a match for BBDO's Bruce Barton and Ben Duffy—not to mention Young & Rubicam's Sig Larmon and McCann-Erickson's Marion Harper. The agency spent the fall dodging punches and picking itself up off the mat.

Norman, Craig and Kummel turned to veteran Reggie Schuebel to develop a Democratic response to the Republican practice of running five-minute spots. A maverick in the male-dominated industry, she purchased her own spots adjacent to popular programs such as *The Arthur Godfrey Show*, *The Red Skelton Hour*, and *The $64,000 Challenge*. Schuebel worked closely with Marciarose Shestack, a student who had taken leave from her doctoral program at the University of Pennsylvania, to give Stevenson the kind of dignified television presence that he admired. In a nod to previous Democratic campaigns, Norman, Craig and Kummel had produced several LP albums with testimonials from entertainers such as Henry Fonda. When it came to filling airtime, however, the Democrats decided to showcase Eleanor Roosevelt and what Shestack called "the stars of the Democratic Party," youthful, handsome senators such as George Smathers (Florida), Scoop Jackson (Washington), John Kennedy (Massachusetts), and Michigan governor Soapy Williams.[61] "In scheduling our five-minute spots," Shestack explained in one memo, "we will try wherever possible to plan live shows utilizing the young, vigorous, 'glamour' figures of the Democratic party." Although they appeared in several prime-time commercials, Shestack preferred to feature her pols before ABC's *Afternoon Film Festival*, a weekday series that broadcast British films in their entirety. "We think this will be most effective during our afternoon schedule," she wrote, "when the audience is primarily composed of women who will be A) the most likely volunteers, and B) the most susceptible to our 'glamour boys.' "[62] These unscripted, live speeches focused on improving the party's visibility rather than commodifying the candidate.

When it came to television, Stevenson may have been the biggest liability to his own campaign. Unlike the president, he had not grown more comfortable performing on television, and on one occasion, he was overheard complaining that he felt as if he were in a beauty contest.[63] "The concept of canned commercials disgusted Adlai," George Ball wrote. "Only the pressure of the pols persuaded him to film a few spots to be used near the end of the campaign. It was an art form for which he had neither liking nor facility."[64] The Democrats asked St. Louis filmmaker Charles Guggenheim to film a series of commercials at the Stevenson farm in Libertyville, Illinois. Guggenheim was a highly skilled filmmaker who would go on to win an Academy Award for his 1964 documentary *Nine from Little Rock*, but the governor proved to be a weak subject. Eager to match the advice Montgomery was giving in the West Wing, Edward R. Murrow volunteered to work with the candidate, but as Ball describes it, just getting Stevenson to meet with the newsman involved a fight. "Murrow spent a long afternoon of patient coaching, but it did no good. In spite of his friendship with and admiration for Murrow, Stevenson hated the whole exercise and did not conceal his distaste; he even chided me about the expense of the studio."[65] As if he were deconstructing the whole enterprise, Stevenson began one of the Libertyville commercials by gesturing off-screen toward all the broadcast equipment crowded into his library. "It's amazing how many things there are in television that you don't see."[66]

Stevenson's speeches were the most powerful aspect of his candidacy, as Bacall and McCambridge would attest, and the campaign sought ways to capture his humor and eloquence in a series of nationally televised primetime broadcasts. The results were often disappointing. Jane Kalmus, a former NBC producer who joined his public relations team, reviewed his television performances after the early primaries and declared that the settings "did nothing to dispel the dangerous misconception of formality, cold intellectuality, lack of personal warmth." Again and again, she noted, "We saw the Candidate in formal attire before a formal podium in the formal setting of a grand ballroom addressing an audience also formally attired."

Though beautifully written, the speeches "were played not to the camera but to the ballroom audiences." Kalmus recommended that Stevenson learn to use a teleprompter and that the campaign employ "extreme camera close-ups to enhance communication between the Governor and the viewer." Better yet, it might situate him in informal conversation with other well-known public figures. "Television is designed to tell its story in sight and sound," Kalmus concluded. "To play to the ear alone and neglect the eye seems a tragic and uneconomical waste of a staggeringly powerful medium."[67]

The DNC adopted many of Kalmus's ideas. The Libertyville commercials included action sequences like Stevenson's pulling a book off the shelf or holding a bag of groceries that created a sense of identification with his family. Another commercial featured the candidate in informal conversation with Kennedy. Despite their perseverance, however, the presence of cameras seemed regularly to jinx the Stevenson team. The Democrats had hoped to kick off the fall campaign with a televised speech at an outdoor amphitheater in Harrisburg, Pennsylvania. They had bussed in thousands of young Stevenson supporters to greet the candidate when he walked on stage, but the organizers introduced him too early. The crowd's boisterous cheers went on for six, maybe eight minutes, with Stevenson basking in the adulation. The program went live, the candidate was introduced again, and amid the confusion, the crowd offered a somewhat half-hearted welcome, leaving the candidate visibly worried and uncertain.[68] In the aftermath, Ball received letters and telegrams from anxious Democrats. Not only had the candidate seemed hesitant and sweaty under the lights, they complained, but the speech itself was monotonous and dreary.

Aside from a lack of funds, the problem that most troubled the campaign was trying to get Stevenson to finish his remarks before such broadcasts expired. In both sight and sound, the story that television repeatedly told was of a man going over time. Advisers begged the candidate to keep a close eye on the clock, but as if the marathon debates of his forefathers exerted too strong an influence, he had difficulty wrapping his comments up before the networks cut away. Stevenson's lack of interest in the camera was a major frustration. The camera's lack of interest in Stevenson was nothing short of catastrophe. Shestack recounts an October 23, 1956, rally in Madison Square Garden at which Sammy Davis, Jr., Mitch Miller, and Alan Lerner appeared. Two days later, Young & Rubicam would hold the Republicans' tightly scripted rally in the same place, stoking the audience's fire and then carefully cooling it down. The Democratic event was supposed to head off the cult of personality that was growing up around Ike. The night was Stevenson's opportunity to talk sense about nuclear testing, the Soviet Union, and American obligations abroad. As Shestack reports, the broadcast of the proceedings fell painfully short.

Shestack would go on to become a broadcasting pioneer. She would be the first woman to anchor a major market news program in the United States and the first to interview Madame Chiang Kai-shek after Nixon opened relations with China in 1972. She would later host a Sunday morning program in New York City that would be the forerunner of the many weekend profile programs we know today. On this October night, however, she anxiously stood with her mentor Reggie Schuebel on the floor beneath the podium as Stevenson delivered a blistering attack on Eisenhower's foreign policy. As hard as they had worked for their candidate, as much as they believed in his cause, they also had a growing sense of alarm. "It became clear that he was going to run over," she recalled. "Terrible. I mean, Madison Square Garden, three networks, and you just say 'Oh God he's going to run over.'" As the speech went on and on, Schuebel, who had not eaten all day, turned to her much younger colleague and said, "I'm going to faint." The emergency personnel ended up carrying her away.[69]

Salesmanship or Sense?

As early as February 1956, the campaign had been interested in organizing another *Stars for Stevenson* extravaganza that might attract widespread interest and publicity. In a harbinger of things to come, the Democrats eventually decided to use their Broadway and Hollywood connections for fundraising rather than votes.[70] Three days after the Madison Square Garden rally, the Arts Committee hosted a coast-to-coast fundraising dinner that was broadcast live over closed-circuit television. In over sixty cities, donors willing to spend $100 a plate were patched into a program of speeches and entertainment that emanated from Washington, New York, Chicago, Indianapolis, and Los Angeles. Along with speeches by Truman, Kennedy, Stevenson, Eleanor Roosevelt, and Estes Kefauver, the diners were treated to "Seventeen Days to Victory," a self-described "spectacular" of political entertainment. Richard Rodgers and Oscar Hammerstein wrote music for the program. Herman Wouk, the author of *The Caine Mutiny*, contributed the script. Applying some of the talent that had turned *Brigadoon, An American in Paris*, and *My Fair Lady* into recent hits, Allen Jay Lerner was part of the directorial team. Combining "the features of a political rally and a Broadway show," the program included performances by over a dozen stars, including Frank Sinatra, Harry Belafonte, Marlon Brando, Henry Fonda, Tallulah Bankhead, Bette Davis, Sammy Davis, Jr., and Yul Brynner. The event raised $750,000 and proved to be an important step in turning the show business community into a regular source of Democratic fundraising.[71]

It is tempting to speculate why officials—two weeks before the election—would put so much time and energy into an event that neither garnered new

FIGURE 6.3 *Adlai Stevenson and Tallulah Bankhead.*
Courtesy of Princeton University Library.

publicity nor directly sought new votes. Why would the Democrats limit their spectacle to 75,000 supporters when a network broadcast would have attracted a much larger audience, something comparable to the 21 million Americans who viewed the Ike Day special on CBS? The planning and logistics were easily transferrable to broadcast television, and the benefits were more tangible. Political and financial pressures may have influenced the decision to scale the program down. Despite a significant thaw, there was still considerable anxiety about the blacklist. Just that summer, HUAC had held Arthur Miller and Paul Robeson in contempt of Congress, and some of the stars may have balked at participating in a more widely publicized performance. The Democrats were also quickly running out of money. Whether on television or in the newspapers, their fall campaign was filled with appeals for donations. Although the dinner's elaborate costs ultimately made it a poor moneymaker, at the very least, it did not push the party further into the red.

In the end, however, the program's relatively low profile may have been the point. From Steinbeck to Ball, the Democrats had made a habit of comparing the Republican presidential strategy to the selling of breakfast cereal and toothpaste. In August, Stevenson accepted the party's nomination by resurrecting his 1952 attack on Madison Avenue and its Corn Flakes campaign.

"What this country needs is not propaganda and a personality cult," Stevenson thundered, "what this country needs is leadership and truth."[72] The censure of Madison Avenue Republicans became a constant refrain, with party officials eager to make voters anxious about the merchandising of democracy. In September, the Democrats published a full-page newspaper advertisement, challenging voters to determine "Which will win—salesmanship or sense?" "Republican money is at work," the text warned. "The commercials have been prepared. The choicest TV time has been reserved for a great selling blitz."[73] To embrace stardom on the mega-stage of network television would be to undercut Stevenson's critique and expose him to charges of hypocrisy only weeks before Election Day. Restricted to donors, the *Stars for Stevenson* dinner remained an open secret, one that received only cursory treatment in newspapers and trade magazines. Whatever glamour the stars brought to the evening would help replenish the party's coffers but not taint the candidate.

For all their complaints, the Stevenson campaign had a bitter fascination with Eisenhower's willingness to associate himself with the feel-good aura of celebrity. On October 20, a week after Ball had mocked the Republicans over Ike Day, the campaign contacted Claude Traverse, an NBC production manager, about developing a televised rally for Election Eve. Since the 1930s, Election Eve broadcasts had become a staple of presidential campaigns, but while Young & Rubicam had been working on Eisenhower's broadcast since early September, the Democrats were starting very late. Traverse had attended the Madison Square Garden rally, and though he had nothing but praise for Stevenson and the Democrats, he worried that they were being overwhelmed. Traverse responded by proposing that the DNC stage a star-studded television rally that would directly address the manipulative nature of Ike's campaign.

A shortage of funds prevented the program from going into production, but Traverse's proposal remains a revealing attempt to shift the focus of celebrity politics from image-making to something like media awareness. As Traverse envisioned it, Eleanor Roosevelt would open the program by announcing "the longest list of distinguished or popular entertainers ever to appear on one show," mentioning that many of them had wanted to work for Stevenson early in the campaign. Traverse had a ready answer for critics who wanted to know why the stars had waited until Election Eve to convey their support. With an implicit attack on Rosser Reeves, Roosevelt would reiterate the Democratic theme that Stevenson did "not feel voters want to be sold candidates like a tube of toothpaste."[74]

A time-honored rhetorical strategy is *occupatio*, in which a speaker overtly declines to engage a subject as a way of raising it clandestinely. ("I come to bury Caesar, not to praise him," Marc Antony says in Shakespeare's *Julius Caesar*, before going on to praise the assassinated leader for nearly one hundred lines.)[75] Traverse's six-page script deftly uses *occupatio*, as it imagines dozens of stars warning the nation against the influence of television, advertising, and celebrity. Serving as a representative of the show business community, Orson Welles explains that "as entertainers we may be best qualified to call your attention to the kind of advertising techniques used during the campaign in an effort to sell their candidates." Bette Davis and Melvyn Douglas follow with a withering critique of Nixon's famous "Checkers" speech. Tallulah Bankhead, Marlene Dietrich, and Henry Fonda demonstrate the blatant deceptions of Ike Day and the People's Press Conference. "We have come forward tonight," Welles explains, "because such methods must be exposed.... Television today plays too great a part in our national life for us to allow it to fall into misuse by unprincipled hucksters. We must demonstrate at the polls tomorrow that we will not be treated like suckers at a nation-wide Republican carnival." As Traverse proposed it, a steady stream of entertainers would then briefly appear—Faye Emerson, Paul Muni, and Edward G. Robinson—with each one saying that while they, too, liked Ike, they would be voting for Stevenson.[76]

The cavalcade of stars was a throwback to the Election Eve program that Hollywood Democrats hosted for FDR in 1944, though Traverse's television script aimed for a different effect. The 1944 radio broadcast produced urgency and momentum, the endorsements and locomotive sounds combining to create a sense of social pressure. In Norman Corwin's script, everyone was boarding the Roosevelt train, everyone understood that his victory was just down the tracks. Traverse hoped the procession of stars would suggest mounting resistance. Their experience with Hollywood publicity would make them ideal voices in the fight against phony advertisements. As star after star appeared on screen, viewers would understand the manipulative quality of Eisenhower's Madison Avenue advisers. They would look to these plain-speaking entertainers for wisdom and enlightenment. In keeping with the pedagogical tenor of his campaigns, the stars supporting Stevenson would emerge as heroes saving voters from their lesser selves. They would bring Eisenhower's momentum to a halt by teaching Americans about the false engine of publicity.

Traverse had faith that viewers would welcome his message, especially if he delivered it using popular culture icons.[77] His script, however, was conflicted about its methods and purpose. Elvis Presley had inadvertently endorsed Stevenson when he remarked to a reporter, "I don't dig the intellectual bit, but I'm telling you, man, he knows the most."[78] Rather than build on that theme, however, Traverse gave Presley the most direct—and frankly bizarre—lines in the script. Representing America's youth, Presley would reflect on popularity as a poor criterion for establishing merit and value:

> I'm young and I admit to knowing very little about politics—some say
> I know very little about singing. And as you know, I have become a rather

controversial personality. However, in my case it doesn't matter much since I'm not likely to become president of our great country. And whether you like me or not you must admit I do attract very large and enthusiastic audiences for which I am very grateful. But I don't kid myself for a second that this popularity makes me the best singer in the country—I know I'm not. And from what I've learned in a short time about advertising and promotion I certainly would hate to see us make the mistake of choosing a president on the basis of a popularity contest.[79]

We have to remember that these remarkable lines exist only in a script, and as such, they reflect not Presley's own thoughts but Traverse's proposal for heading off the disaster facing Stevenson's campaign. As such, there is a rich comedy to Traverse's effort to harness Presley's cultural power, while refusing to acknowledge the singer's talent for anything but controversy. As Traverse would have it, Presley would effectively use his popularity in explaining its irrelevance; he would question his own phenomenal celebrity to puncture the campaign of a sitting president who victoriously commanded the Allied forces in Europe.

The Democrats' repeated attacks on the frivolity of Eisenhower's campaign led Traverse to believe that Stevenson would object to the television program. Anticipating a negative response, he proposed using the allure of celebrity to sell a liberal media education program. It is "proper to use a legitimate degree of showmanship to bring to the attention of the voters the selling techniques used by the opposition," he declared on the opening page, arguing that the show would help unmask the "phony sentimentality" that would appear in the Republican program directly afterwards. The Democrats had found an ally in Jack Gould, television critic for the *New York Times*. Gould had used his review of the Ike Day program to criticize the increasingly heavy-handed influence that show business was exerting on politics. "As the campaign progresses," Gould predicted, "there may be nonpartisan agreement on the wisdom of separating state and theatre."[80] The Democrats were so pleased with the article that Traverse gave Dietrich the role of reading its most stinging paragraphs. Traverse's ambitions were hopelessly divided, however, when it came to the separation of theater and state. He wanted to use the techniques of show business to question its role in presidential politics, dispelling the charm of glamour with a series of sober-minded stars. Traverse would ventriloquize the likes of Welles, Davis, and Presley in order to diminish their power.

Traverse's proposal captured the contradictions inherent in Stevenson's relationship to celebrity. On one hand, there were Stevenson's famous supporters who saw in the campaign's frenzy an opportunity for self-actualization and personal growth. Bacall and McCambridge would remain devoted to Stevenson until his death in 1965, turning to him in moments of personal crisis and dropping romantic hints in typewritten letters, Valentine's cards, and scribbled notes. (After Bogart's death in 1957, Bacall's messages became notably flirtatious and inviting, and gossip columns reported seeing her with Stevenson at restaurants in Chicago and New York.)[81] Aside from their romantic attachments, the actresses' response was characteristic of a larger group of liberal celebrities who found a calling in their political activities and understood them as an extension of what it meant to be artists and performers in the twentieth-century United States. On the other hand, there was the campaign's widespread disgust at the promotional forces that left them yearning for another age. Traverse and Stevenson put themselves in the difficult situation of trying to mount a politically progressive vision while attacking the greatest communications development since the advent of radio.

In the end, the campaigns were divided between the authenticity that celebrities saw in Stevenson and the fraudulence he suspected in certain aspects of their work. Even as they were cautiously calling liberal entertainers onto the public stage, the Democratic leaders remained highly skeptical of the publicity through which they could communicate their support. Although politically hesitant and confused, the skepticism was well-founded, for by the summer of 1956, it was becoming clear that the political influence of advertising agencies extended well beyond the promotion of candidates. Madison Avenue had positioned itself as a major defender of American values.

The Biggest Fan in the World

Throughout 1956, contributors to the *Public Relations Journal* proposed an array of professional strategies for how to make the best use of television. With no mention of the concerns raised by media critics, they looked for new ways to differentiate their strategies from radio and strengthen the connections among television, the image, and publicity. Observing "a cultural lag" in the use of the new medium, Claude Robinson of Opinion Research, Inc., called upon his colleagues to develop a "language of pictures" that would rise to the challenge of the TV screen. George Gallup theorized that a "successful picture language uses the video to communicate specific ideas or sales arguments." Although little understood, he wrote, the visual aspects of television provided a "great new opportunity" to "impress a message on the minds of millions of viewers." Writing more generally, Charles M. Hackett charged professionals with not understanding the "vernacular of the eye" and urged them to regard the image as "the photographic interpretation of an idea."[1]

Many of these authors focused on corporate communications, but James Kelleher extended the call for innovation to the planning of political campaigns. Kelleher was a member of Linder-Scott Associates, an Indiana-based public relations agency, and his accounts ranged from Chrysler and the US Army to local political races in and around the Midwestern college town of South Bend, Indiana. Citing the "tremendous outpouring of voters in off-year municipal and state elections," Kelleher argued that with the emergence of television, politicians would no longer organize their campaigns around mass selling techniques. "Campaigning has become a more personal thing," he explained. "It can once again have the intimate character of the days when every voter 'knew' his candidates."[2] To illustrate this point, the editors positioned a television still of Indiana congressman Shepard Crumpacker alongside "Canvassing for a Vote," George Caleb Bingham's 1852 painting in which a frontier politician huddles outside a tavern with three potential voters.[3] The argument may have been surprising to industry insiders who regularly touted television as a form of mass communication. As Kelleher presented it, however, the challenge for public relations specialists was learning how to adapt "political materials and personalities" to the strange feelings of familiarity that viewers associated with the new medium.[4] Kelleher cautioned that the bombast of political rallies would seem offensive in the privacy of a viewer's living room and urged readers to think about their broadcasts aesthetically. "Restrained underplay, the perennial essential of good drama, must be built into every political show," he counseled.[5] "Each political telecast must combine the intimacy of the stage with the planned perfection of a film and the confidence inspiring quality of radio." Kelleher's title proclaimed the change he was lauding: "TV's Perennial Star: The Political Candidate."

Far from Hollywood or Madison Avenue, Kelleher focused on exploring ways to give local politicians some version of the simulated intimacy that audiences associated with television and movie personalities. By paying attention to "Timing, Taste, Truth and Techniques," a generation of public relations experts could successfully employ television to advance the careers of their political clients.[6] Aside from Richard Nixon's "Checkers" speech, Kelleher did not reference national figures or events, but his thoughts were in step with the preparations his better-known colleagues were making for the 1956 presidential race. As BBDO and J. Walter Thompson developed new strategies for Ike, as the Democrats struggled to hire an agency willing to promote their (then-) unknown candidate, Kelleher was pragmatically thinking about how he could turn the living room into a site of political persuasion and opinion-making. In the age of television, public relations experts could introduce new, more profitable models of consumption, intimacy, and citizenship.[7]

Although Kelleher would have had no way of knowing it at the time, the man who was rapidly coming to realize this new model was the congenial host of a weekly television program on CBS. The program was the *General Electric Theater*, and the host, a forty-five-year-old actor and corporate spokesman named Ronald Reagan. Like his friends Robert Montgomery and George Murphy, Reagan had been the president of the Screen Actors Guild (SAG), a position that put him at the center of the intense political battles that stormed through Hollywood after the Second World War. A lifelong Democrat and admirer of Franklin Roosevelt, he had grown increasingly wary of communism, and in 1947 he joined Murphy and Montgomery in publicly denouncing the efforts of Hollywood radicals to disrupt the Guild's activities. In 1954, BBDO selected Reagan to represent General Electric (GE), its longtime client and one of the nation's largest and most diverse corporations. Over the next eight years, he would host *General Electric Theater*, appear in and produce a number of its dramas, and tour the country as the company's goodwill ambassador. At the same time that Kelleher was thinking about television's power to turn politicians into celebrities, BBDO and GE were turning Reagan's celebrity into a position of political influence and efficacy. Whether visiting the lunchroom of a refrigerator factory or inviting a television audience into his family's ultra-modern, appliance-decorated home, the actor was learning how to use the glamour of stardom for something more serious than entertainment. To borrow from Kelleher, Reagan found a way to combine the intimacy, composure, and confidence of an effective television performance with his increasingly outspoken conservatism.

There were many signal moments in Ronald Reagan's career as the most important American conservative of the late twentieth century: the nationally televised call to arms for Barry Goldwater in 1964; the use of the National Guard to quell the 1968 student protests at the University of California at Berkeley; the militant campaign against the incumbent Gerald Ford in an unsuccessful bid for the 1976 Republican presidential nomination. But the Reagan Revolution would never have happened if General Electric and BBDO had not given the actor an extraordinary opportunity to reinvent himself. Much has been made of the influence that Reagan's cinematic training had on his political vision and policies. Political scientist Michael Rogin has joined biographers Lou Cannon, Gary Wills, and Edmund Morris in making important connections between Reagan's film career and the performative aspects of his presidency.[8] But as scholars Thomas W. Evans and Timothy Raphael have separately demonstrated, the years Reagan worked for GE were crucial to the development of his ideas about taxes, labor relations, and the size of the federal government.[9] Looking back on the experience, Reagan

FIGURE 7.1 *Ronald Reagan as host of General Electric Theater.*
Courtesy of General Electric and The Ronald Reagan Presidential Foundation and Library.

commented that GE provided him with a "postgraduate education in political science" and an "apprenticeship for public life."[10]

Reagan's years with GE offer a similarly valuable window into the history of celebrity politics in the 1950s. Though the legacy would only come to light decades later, Reagan was in many ways an heir to the Eisenhower White House. This claim *does not* mean that he inherited Ike's political vision, or even that their politics always meshed. (The Democrat Reagan supported Eisenhower's presidential bids from the left before he developed a more strident conservatism that questioned him from the right.) The point is that the corporate and promotional forces that touted an Eisenhower presidency discovered in Reagan a remarkably effective voice for spreading their interests—not initially to voters, but to workers, consumers, and the general public. Reagan's transformation owed little (if anything) to the machine-based politics of Republicans such as Robert Taft. Inasmuch as any politician can be the product of an organization or time period, Reagan was a product of the advertising machine that played such an important part in Eisenhower's campaigns. The actor was effectively remade as a public spokesman by the same institutions that transformed General Eisenhower into the presidential candidate Ike.

The Shrewd Use of Glamour

The political activities that Madison Avenue developed for stars such as Reagan and Helen Hayes occurred amid the cloud of suspicion that had settled over liberal entertainers since the end of the Second World War. Eisenhower had tried to keep his distance from the anti-Communist fervor that appeared during Truman's and his own presidency. Although he never publicly challenged Joseph McCarthy (a decision that troubled his advisers), he privately seethed at the senator's demagoguery and troublemaking, describing him as a "pimple" and a "skunk" and comparing him on one occasion to Adolf Hitler.[11] While McCarthy focused on the State Department and the US Army, it was the House Un-American Activities Committee that targeted the entertainment industry, its investigation of Communist activity stretching from 1947 to 1956. The public rituals of confession and the naming of names did much to shame liberal celebrities and to root out the activism of the Roosevelt years. At the same time, the attention HUAC gave to stars ironically underscored the power of art and celebrity to convey political ideas.

In the post-Soviet world, it may be difficult to imagine the government attention that entertainment received at the height of the Cold War and how frequently artists and performers had to defend their beliefs to both their Congressional inquisitors and the public at large. The press was ablaze with rumors about the leftist leanings of movie stars. Responding to charges made by the American Legion, *Photoplay*, a popular fan magazine, published a 1940 piece that openly asked, "Is Melvyn Douglas a Communist?"[12] Four years later, *Time* mocked the pretense of Hollywood activists by contrasting their comfortable lifestyles with their inflated aims.[13] Working with FBI director J. Edgar Hoover, Hedda Hopper used her syndicated gossip column to attack Charlie Chaplin—first for his morals, and then for his alleged Communist sympathies.[14] In August 1947, *Photoplay* asked screenwriter and crime novelist James M. Cain to consider the question "Is Hollywood Red?"[15] In 1951, the *Saturday Evening Post* asked, "What Makes a Hollywood Communist?"[16] Over nearly ten years, HUAC publicized the testimony and political opinions of so-called friendly witnesses like Walt Disney, James Cagney, and Gary Cooper and alleged subversives such as Paul Robeson, Arthur Miller, and Karen Morley who had been summoned before the committee unwillingly. When Humphrey Bogart, Lauren Bacall, Danny Kaye, and a group of stars flew to Washington in October 1947 to protest what they believed was HUAC's infringement of civil liberties, newspapers gave them ample publicity, though many took the opportunity to accuse the protestors themselves of being Red. (Calling them "Demmies," Hopper organized a boycott of the participants' films.)[17] The accusations grew so extreme that, urged on by Ed Sullivan, Bogart took to the pages of *Photoplay* to salvage his career: he denounced HUAC but vigorously explained that he was "about as much in favor of communism as J. Edgar Hoover."[18]

Even as it tarnished many reputations, the publicity had the ironic effect of elevating stardom as an effective (albeit dangerous) vehicle for transmitting radical ideas. *Time* tried to trivialize the politicization of celebrity. ("No Hollywood hostess was safe," the magazine commented. "Try as she might to keep her Max Factor powder dry, her very next swimming-pool party might become tomorrow's ideological battleground.")[19] But the lesson handed down by the committee, the columnists, and the studios was that stardom could be a deviously powerful force. MGM executive James McGuinness reinforced this impression when he appeared before HUAC as a friendly witness: "Glamour is appealing," he told the investigators. "The Communists have made very shrewd and excellent use of that for their purpose."[20] "It would be tragic," Bogart wrote, if the events in Washington caused actors to "withdraw to the political sidelines."[21]

With the attack on activist celebrities also came new fears about the power of cinematic narratives to dramatize issues of social justice and inequality. Despite winning two Academy Awards, John Ford's 1940 film *The Grapes of Wrath* was a key exhibit in the conservative case against Hollywood's subversive messaging. An adaptation of John Steinbeck's best-selling novel, the film sympathetically portrayed the impoverished Joad family as they joined thousands of others migrating to California after being evicted from their Oklahoma farms during the Dust Bowl years. Even before HUAC had begun its investigations, Eric Johnston, the head of the Motion Picture Alliance of America (MPAA), had written screenwriters about the new political climate. "We'll have no more Grapes of Wrath, we'll have no more Tobacco Roads, we'll have no more films that deal with the seamy side of American life."[22] The eventual blacklisting and imprisonment of the "Hollywood Ten," a group of writers, directors, and producers who refused to cooperate during HUAC's 1947 hearings, was on the front page of newspapers around the country.

To writer and Russian émigré Ayn Rand, men such as Johnston were too willing to compromise with Hollywood leftists. After publishing her best-selling novel *The Fountainhead* in 1943, she allied herself with the conservative Motion Picture Alliance for the Preservation of American Ideals, which counted Irene Dunne, Gary Cooper, and John Wayne among its members.[23] Working with the Alliance, Rand anonymously published *Screen Guide for Americans*, a pamphlet that relentlessly attacked the influence of "Red propaganda" in the movie industry. "The purpose of the Communists in Hollywood," she wrote, "is not the production of political movies openly advocating communism. Their purpose is to corrupt our moral premises by corrupting non-political movies." What made the Communists so dangerous, she contended, was that they hoped to introduce "small, casual bits of propaganda into innocent stories—thus making people absorb the basic premises of Collectivism by indirection and implication." Some of Rand's decrees seemed directly aimed at *The Grapes of Wrath*. "Don't Glorify Failure," "Don't Deify 'The Common Man,'" "Make villainy a sign of character not wealth or class." "Only savages and Communists get rich by force," she wrote, "—that is, by looting the property of others." Among Rand's other commandments: "Don't Smear the Free Enterprise System," "Don't Smear Industrialists," "Don't Glorify Depravity," and "When you make pictures with political themes and implications—DON'T hire Communists to write, direct, or produce them."[24]

Perhaps the most lasting effect of the HUAC hearings was the dawning recognition that the investigations had been organized as political theater. Fearing a backlash in public opinion, presidential hopeful Thomas Dewey tried to persuade the committee to cancel the 1947 hearings, but the leadership remained determined to turn them into a publicity-driven spectacle.[25] The proceedings were held in the caucus room of the "old House Office building" with plenty of space to accommodate four newsreel cameras, four radio networks, nearly 100 reporters, and 400 spectators for each session.[26] Bogart compared the hearings to a "vaudeville show," objecting to the Klieg lights, newsreels, and coast-to-coast broadcast of the testimony.[27] Noting the remarkable publicity, the *New York Times* commented that the hearings had "been launched with that ineffable touch of showmanship which the naïve Easterner associates with a Hollywood premiere." The only details missing were "orchids, evening dresses and searchlights crisscrossing the evening sky."[28] The presence of so many stars required Washington authorities to develop new methods of fan control. "A special detail of uniformed police is on hand to handle the throng of spectators who rush the doors as each session opens," the *Times* reported. The police learned to "form a flying wedge to hustle such 'name' witnesses as Gary Cooper and Robert Montgomery through the clamoring ranks of onlookers."[29] When Robert Taylor entered the hearing room, the mostly female spectators "greeted him with an audible ah."[30]

A Democrat with deep ties to the New Deal, Reagan was right in the middle of the battle between Hollywood liberals and Communists. He identified himself as a liberal and had campaigned for Franklin Roosevelt and Harry Truman, but he bitterly objected to the misleading, deceptive methods he believed Communists employed to advance their cause. He recalled traveling with Olivia de Havilland in support of FDR when she discovered that the screenwriter Dalton Trumbo had rewritten parts of her speech to include a tirade against capitalism.[31] When Reagan succeeded Montgomery as SAG president in 1947, Hollywood was in the throes of a violent labor battle sparked by the Conference of Studio Unions (CSU). CSU's call for a general strike among all industry workers deeply divided liberal groups such as the Hollywood Independent Citizens Committee of Arts, Sciences and Professions (HICCASP). Convinced that Communists ran the CSU and wanted to splinter mainstream organizations, Reagan steered the Guild away from supporting the strike and the ideological fissures it created.[32] His resistance to the strikers and ability to protect SAG from a schism earned him the admiration of liberals and conservatives alike. Hopper was so impressed with the skills of the new SAG president that she interviewed him for the *Chicago Tribune*.[33]

In October 1947, Reagan traveled to Washington, DC, with Murphy and Montgomery to appear as friendly witnesses before HUAC. Although earlier that year he had secretly supplied the FBI with names of suspected Communists, Reagan's HUAC testimony was a model of tolerance and equanimity.[34] Under questioning, he acknowledged that Communists had tried to disrupt the Screen Actors Guild and split its membership. Drawing on personal history, he described the way that radicals misled celebrities and other notable figures, persuading them to lend their names to charitable events that were, in fact, run by Communist affiliates. He himself had endorsed a fundraiser for a local hospital only to discover, weeks later, that the event was raising money for the Joint Anti-Fascist League, a remnant of the Popular Front (and favored HUAC target). In Reagan's telling, celebrities had become valuable weapons in the cultural Cold War, as groups across the political spectrum recognized their power to attract attention, create prestige, and communicate ideas.[35]

HUAC traveled to California in 1951 for another round of hearings, and hundreds more industry workers would join the Hollywood Ten on the blacklist. Clifford Odets, Lloyd Bridges, and Elizabeth Wilson followed Elia

Kazan and Budd Schulberg in cooperating with the committee. Edward G. Robinson, Jose Ferrer, and Lucille Ball cleared their names without informing on anybody, Ball's case bolstered by the fact that advertisers continued to support her number-one show on television.[36] Despite their best efforts, Lillian Hellman, Howard DaSilva, and Anne Revere found themselves in contempt of the committee and struggled to find work. Reagan's tenure as president of the Screen Actors Guild had made him increasingly supportive of the hearings.[37] When Academy Award winner Gale Sondergaard took out an advertisement in *Variety* asking for the Guild's help before her HUAC testimony, the Board of Directors responded that she was on her own. In a time of "clear and present danger," they wrote, the Guild would not force the studios to hire "an actor" whose activities had "so offended American public opinion" that he had made himself "unsaleable at the box office."[38] Published in the *Hollywood Reporter*, the response made a finely grained distinction: the board objected to the *secret* blacklisting of actors and actresses, but it had no problem with a studio making market-based decisions based on their controversial pasts.

The irony of this position was that Reagan's own acting career had been dwindling since the Second World War. In 1949, the year he and Jane Wyman divorced, he had appeared in five films. By 1953, he had started a new family with actress Nancy Davis and appeared in only two. Within two years, the number had dropped to one. Reagan had long believed that television was ruining the film industry, and he feared that actors who shifted to the new medium would have difficulty reviving their movie careers.[39] When BBDO contacted his agent about the position with *General Electric Theater*, he had recently returned from a two-week gig at a Las Vegas hotel in which he served as master of ceremonies for a musical show featuring The Continentals, an all-male singing group with a slapstick approach to performance. Much of Reagan's act made fun of the fact that he couldn't dance or sing. "Never again," he told his agent, "will I sell myself so short."[40] For a fading actor with heavy expenses and few professional prospects, the hotel's name must have seemed painfully appropriate: The Last Frontier.[41]

The Little Courthouse on Madison Avenue

General Electric Theater came out of one of the most well-established partnerships in the history of advertising. Bruce Barton had begun writing copy for General Electric in 1920 when he collaborated with illustrator Norman Rockwell on a series of highly successful print advertisements for GE's Edison Mazda Lamps. Like General Motors, another Barton client, GE employed multiple agencies to represent its different product lines, but as it expanded across an astonishing range of industries (from power stations, to trains, to washing machines), the company sought help defining its image not just to the public but to its own far-flung employees. In 1923, the thirty-eight-year-old executive traveled to the company's headquarters in Schenectady, New York and proposed that GE identify itself "with research, innovation, and progress." After listening to two days of presentations from rival agencies, 80 percent of the executives agreed that their corporate account should go to Barton and his agency.[42] (It remains with BBDO today.) Barton was a minister's son, and as Raphael has demonstrated, he had a notably spiritual sense of progress that would shape General Electric's identity throughout the twentieth century. His 1920 advertisements, for example, had suggested that GE did not simply sell light bulbs or lamps; it fulfilled a biblical imperative to create light.[43] Over the years, BBDO would cultivate the sense that GE had a missionary purpose in improving the world. The providential zeal informs such famous company taglines as "Progress is our most important product" and "We bring good things to life."

Under Barton's direction, BBDO developed a special expertise in institutional advertising, and companies such as DuPont and United States Steel came to the agency for help creating, promoting, and protecting their image at the height of the New Deal. Barton had a gift for naturalizing mega-corporations and turning them into familiar parts of everyday life. With its fancy script enclosed by a circle, the ubiquitous GE logo became "the initials of a friend."[44] General Motors's diverse product lines became a "family" of automobiles. Although consumers did not purchase its goods directly, US Steel turned to BBDO in the 1930s to combat its reputation for unfair labor practices, and over the next decades, it would become known for "Helping to Build a Better America."[45] DuPont's history as a manufacturer of explosives had led many to regard it as a war profiteer. Barton and his BBDO partner Ray Durstine supplied DuPont with a slogan the company would use off and on throughout the twentieth century: "Better Things for Better Living ... Through Chemistry."[46] Barton would adapt the same institutional approach to the Republican Party in turning Eisenhower into a familiar, friendly presence in the family living room.

In each of these cases, BBDO steered their clients toward what it called "good will advertising," which focused not on the promotion of specific consumer products but on the creation of positive feelings about the company. BBDO was a pioneer in developing radio and television programs that would help build a corporate image. Under the agency's direction, General Motors sponsored *The Parade of States* and DuPont *The Cavalcade of America*, an exploration of United States culture and history with a special emphasis on scientific discovery. In 1945, US Steel began sponsoring *Theater Guild on the Air* on ABC radio, and in 1953 it transitioned the series to a live television drama, *The United States Steel Hour*. In both incarnations, the program presented hour-long dramas such as *A Doll's House*, *Julius Caesar*, and *The Glass*

Menagerie, interspersed with appealing updates about the work of US Steel.[47] While some questioned the value of these programs, others saw them as a vital part of public and government affairs. CEO Ben Fairless held the Theater Guild program in high regard. It was "not only the finest and most important channel we have to the public," he wrote the agency in 1948, "but it is difficult to imagine a finer one. To keep this program on the air is of vital importance to the Corporation, and we should not question it for a minute."[48]

BBDO's focus throughout these endeavors was to define, promote, and protect the image of its corporate clients. The issue of protection came to a head in June 1950 when the right-wing magazine *Counterattack* published *Red Channels,* a special report listing the names of 151 accused Communists working in radio and television. The disclosure of these names (and the fervent expectation that more would follow) alarmed corporate sponsors, who found themselves exposed on multiple fronts. Not only were corporations responsible for their own employees, but they would potentially have to answer for the actors, actresses, screenwriters, and directors they hired to promote their image. The increased risk underscored how complicated the blacklist was in the East. The Hollywood studio system had centralized its talent in relatively hierarchical organizations, making it efficient for executives to ban anyone from their lots who had run afoul of HUAC or other Red-baiting authorities. Radio and television programs, in contrast, involved a complex web of independent organizations in the 1950s. There were sponsors, networks, talent agencies, and production companies with an ever-changing cast, and all risked a public relations controversy in associating with the others.[49] The job of advertising agencies was to make sure all parties worked together to advance the clients' interests.

BBDO spearheaded the evolution and operation of the radio and television blacklist. Young & Rubicam and McCann-Erickson vigorously completed background checks and refused to hire suspected Communists. But as Barton boasted to a colleague, BBDO was "among the first to recognize the Communist menace," and it took special pride in managing and overseeing the blacklist's operation across the broadcast industries.[50] Clients appreciated this leadership and were persuaded by the agency's confidence in tackling the problem. Rather than presenting itself as bowing to external forces, BBDO actively persuaded clients such as US Steel to see the blacklist as working in their interest.[51] The president of Armstrong Cork Company recommended BBDO to his counterpart at Borden's, noting that with its extensive research and talent vetting, the agency was doing "a fine job keeping Armstrong out of trouble."[52] In his exhaustive 1956 report on the radio and television blacklist, journalist John Cogley drew an implicit connection between BBDO's political and corporate activities. Although it faced wide criticism, the agency happily touted its promotional methods in the Eisenhower campaign. Cogley saw evidence of the same spirit in the way Barton and his colleagues looked upon the blacklist: it provided them with another opportunity to engineer consent among polarized forces. "Rather than sit loose and be buffeted around, BBDO has taken the blacklisting problem for what it is: i.e., a problem in public relations."[53]

The man at BBDO most responsible for this reputation was Jack Wren, a former FBI informant who was widely regarded as the top "security officer" on Madison Avenue.[54] Eschewing the usual accoutrements of an advertising executive—a spacious office, multiple secretaries, a knack for getting his name in the papers—Wren presided over the blacklist with a mysterious, but undeniable, power. Two things differentiated him from the legal and security officials employed at other agencies. Wren's contacts provided him with a steady stream of knowledge about the business. More importantly, he agreed to meet with blacklisted performers and determine whether they should be cleared. Nearly every organization simply enforced the list and then moved on. But, working with a handful of others (among them, top officials at CBS, James Francis O'Neil of the American Legion, and the well-known Eisenhower critic George Sokolsky of Hearst newspapers), Wren quietly exonerated performers he determined were either wrongly accused or expressed enough regret about their past associations that their reputations could be "rehabilitated."[55] If he was convinced of their sincerity, Wren might ask blacklisted performers to deliver a speech apologizing for their past or give a highly repentant interview to a leading conservative magazine.[56] The private consultation, in effect, would prepare the way for a public statement of conversion. In exchange for work, the performer was willing to carry a new political message into the public sphere. According to one blacklisted comedian, working with Wren was "the 'worst part' of the blacklist phenomenon."[57]

This window for discussion created a cottage industry of clearance guides who wrote letters and made contacts on behalf of performers in the hopes that after a series of affidavits and consultations, they might eventually get an audience with Wren and CBS. According to Cogley, no money or favors were exchanged; Wren and his colleagues performed this service out of devotion to their business and their uncompromising conservativism.[58] Wrongfully accused performers took comfort in knowing Wren could help them out, but the informal system of confessions and consultations had a more deleterious effect: it transformed the blacklist from an edict to an institution, a living set of rules and relations that changed over time. The secret negotiations did much to enhance the power of Wren and his agency. As Cogley derisively put it, BBDO became "the little court house on Madison Avenue" and Wren its most powerful judge.[59]

This context helps explain why Ronald Reagan was such an appealing addition to BBDO's partnership with General Electric. Earl Dunckel, one of Reagan's first colleagues at the company, recalled that GE was "very, very definite as to the kind of person" they wanted to host the show: an actor with "good moral character, intelligent," "a good, upright kind of person," someone who did not have a "reputation for the social ramble." "When Ron was suggested," Dunckel recalled, "it went through almost immediately."[60] But of course with his HUAC appearance and SAG presidency, Reagan came with the additional attraction of being fervently anti-Communist. Corporate America had two prominent fears about Hollywood in the 1950s: it was the source of much licentiousness, and it was a hotbed of Communist propaganda. Well-spoken, serious-minded, and doggedly pro-American, Reagan dispelled both of those concerns. In fact, his position in Hollywood resembled the one Wren had defined for himself in Manhattan. Despite SAG's public rebuke to Sondergaard, Reagan did occasionally help clear the names of blacklisted actors so they could return to work. In a story that Nancy Reagan liked to tell, the couple had met when she feared that a case of mistaken identity had landed her on the studio blacklist in 1951. A mutual friend urged her to contact Ron for help.[61]

Although it sponsored a number of product-specific shows, General Electric had struggled to find the right format for its Sunday night institutional program. Prior to *General Electric Theater*, the company had presented *The Fred Waring Show*, which Young & Rubicam had initially produced for the Appliance, Electronics, and Lamps division. Despite its early success, the musical variety program lacked the gravitas to be an effective public relations vehicle, and in conjunction with the Music Corporation of America (MCA), BBDO began developing an anthology drama that would put GE in line with its other institutional clients.[62] The format was ideal "for cultivating a modern, progressive corporate image," media scholar Anna McCarthy has explained, in that it created "the impression that the corporations were 'patrons of the arts.'"[63] Because anthology dramas provided a wide range of entertainment (comedies, Westerns, sentimental holiday tales, adaptations of prominent stories and plays), they could seem inchoate and unfocused. As BBDO and GE envisioned it, Reagan's star power would unify the show from week to week. "He was the continuity, the host, the element that tied the whole thing together," Dunckel recalls. "We needed that, because these [episodes] were so disparate. They were as different as night and day from one week to the next, and we needed a focal force in there to hang them all together, to keep them in line."[64] Reagan would have the opportunity to vet scripts and star in a number of productions, but his primary responsibility was to embody the corporate brand. In 1959, GE would license the cartoon character Mr. Magoo to advertise light bulbs, but it wanted a Ronald Reagan to represent the corporation itself.[65] As the voice and face of General Electric, he would become, as Hackett put it in the *Public Relations Journal*, "the photographic interpretation of an idea."[66]

Reagan's position was considerably more complex than that of other anthology hosts because, in addition to the Sunday evening programs, GE

FIGURE 7.2 *Ronald Reagan visits with employees at the General Electric factory in Danville, Kentucky.*
Courtesy of The Ronald Reagan Presidential Foundation and Library.

asked him to spend several weeks each year visiting its plants and factories. With its decentralized management structure and plants across the country, General Electric was a widely dispersed and disparate company. Much like the program he hosted, Reagan's goodwill tours were meant to create a stronger sense of identity among the multiple divisions and subsidiaries. Whether they were producing turbines in Schenectady, New York, or outdoor lighting fixtures in Hendersonville, North Carolina, workers would receive a common corporate message from its new and friendly spokesman. As it evolved over the course of Eisenhower's presidency, the position began to suggest a mode of celebrity politics that complemented what Robert Montgomery was doing in the White House and Helen Hayes was doing on the campaign trail. Although technically nonpartisan, Reagan would increasingly promote the benevolent vision of corporate America that Republicans such as Eisenhower, Barton, and GE's president Ralph Cordiner were doing so much to define. In 1947 McGuiness had warned HUAC that Communists were using Hollywood glamour to advance their radical cause. Ten years later Reagan was proving that glamour could convey conservative ideas just as well. By then, Cordiner was sitting on Eisenhower's Business Advisory Council and *General Electric Theater* was the third most popular program on television.[67]

The Actor in the Gray Flannel Suit

General Electric Theater was the first television show to alternate between live broadcasts from New York and taped broadcasts from Los Angeles.[68] The format helped the program attract top Hollywood and Broadway entertainers, including Ethel Merman, Natalie Wood, Jack Benny, Angie Dickinson, Charlton Heston, Michael Landon, and Zsa Zsa Gabor. Reagan appeared in a number of these productions, and in the first season alone, he performed alongside James Dean, Cloris Leachman, Charles Bronson, Lionel Barrymore, and Lee Marvin.[69] Sidney Rubin, who directed the program from 1959–1962, complained that Reagan tended to prefer the stories that came from the saccharine magazine *Reader's Digest*, but *General Electric Theater* also attracted remarkable writing talent. Screenwriters adapted stories by William Faulkner, Evelyn Waugh, and William Saroyan. Kurt Vonnegut, who began his professional career in GE's public relations office, saw one of his stories adapted in 1955 and then contributed to a teleplay in 1958. Though Rubin chided Reagan's literary taste, he acknowledged that the actor was "an excellent host" who "delighted in espousing the glories of General Electric."[70]

Reagan's periodic performances eased his transition from a fulltime actor to a corporate personality. In May 1955, BBDO reviewed the previous television season and concluded that the program had revived the host's career: "Ronald Reagan is a far more valuable property than he was one year ago," the agency informed executives at GE. "His weekly appearances on the program, his personal appearance tours and the newspaper publicity he has received as a result of his association with THE GENERAL ELECTRIC THEATER all help make him a more attractive subject for newspaper stories." BBDO proudly tallied up the good press the program had brought to the company. In one year, GE's public relations department had filled eleven scrapbooks with newspaper clippings, and hundreds more awaited them in the BBDO files. *General Electric Theater* had been covered five times in the Sunday *New York Times* and three times in the Sunday *New York Herald Tribune*. Together, the Associated Press and United Press had distributed fourteen stories to papers across the country, and among national magazines, *Life*, *Time*, *Newsweek*, and *TV Guide* had all done features on the show.[71]

To the team at BBDO, "Reagan's name value and the close association which has been established between Reagan and General Electric" meant that more publicity was on the way. With a promotional budget of $74,636.86 for the 1955–1956 season, BBDO identified Reagan's celebrity as the vehicle for delivering the good news about GE. The agency recommended releasing the actor's corporate travel schedule to the trade magazines and arranging for him to publish personal recipes in *Good Housekeeping, McCall's*, and *Ladies Home Journal*. They hoped to turn his background as a football player and baseball announcer into a series of articles in sports magazines. Some of the most iconic impressions we now have of the Reagans originated in BBDO's ideas about how to promote the couple as the new face of GE. Nancy could become an arbiter of style with a series of fashion shoots for *Vogue* or *Harper's Bazaar*. The fact that Ron owned a ranch could form the basis for a story and layout in *Farm Journal* that presented him as a working rancher, a cowboy of the Golden West.[72]

Each of these recommendations aimed to exploit the illusory intimacy that Americans found so attractive in television celebrity. As we have seen, the Eisenhower campaign thought frequently about this tactic during the 1956 presidential race. Young & Rubicam's Preston Wood envisioned a set of commercials in which stars would endorse the president while cameras led viewers on tours of their beautiful homes. The Ike Day special reached for a similar effect when it put Howard Keel and Kathryn Grayson in a reconstructed version of the Eisenhower family's Abilene living room. From features on their garden to tips on how to pack for a day at the beach, BBDO saw numerous possibilities in bringing viewers inside the Reagans' domestic world. Adlai Stevenson's divorce had produced some surreptitious attacks from GOP stalwarts, but Reagan's previous marriage did not matter to GE as long as he and Nancy could display the benefits of living electrically. Using motivational research, Ernest Dichter found that, in contrast to movie stars, an effective television announcer "must be a *real person* who behaves in the same manner as other people do in reality."[73] As *General Electric Theater* became more successful, the agency began to promote the Reagans as an ideal version of the American family, albeit one more coolly elegant than what viewers encountered on the popular ABC sitcom *The Adventures of Ozzie and Harriet*.

The same fall that viewers joined the Eisenhowers in celebrating the president's sixty-sixth birthday, BBDO began arranging for a series of Reagan family commercials that would follow the Sunday program. The Reagans had been building a new home in Pacific Palisades, and these three-and-a-half-minute spots tracked their progress, from the laying of electrical wires to the magic of mood lighting. An especially domestic commercial followed an episode in which Jimmy Stewart was reunited with Beulah Biondi, the actress who had played Jefferson Smith's mother in *Mr. Smith Goes to Washington*. The show gave Stewart the opportunity to reprise his role as Britt Ponsett from the popular radio show *The Six Shooter*. In this episode, the wandering cowboy uses some trickery to resolve a bitter property dispute so that the railroad could come to Virtue City and rejuvenate the town. With Stewart's voice still ringing in the background, viewers were escorted to the Reagans' new California home where Ron and Nancy were standing in their decked-out kitchen explaining the benefits of living better electrically. What the commercial did not reveal was that GE had supplied so many appliances that it was forced to build a 3,000-pound electrical panel alongside the property to service the family's needs.[74]

In the 1940s, Reagan the actor had become Reagan the soldier and then Reagan the union head and bureaucrat. By the middle of Ike's presidency, another shift had taken place as the anti-Communist crusader became the corporate pitchman. Reagan's facility at this kind of work aroused the attention of his contemporaries, and pivoting off the popular novel and movie, Hollywood insiders began referring to him as "The Actor in the Gray Flannel Suit."[75] In reality, though, the message Reagan pitched was more abstract than if he were just touting slide projectors and toaster ovens. While the program's announcer, Don Herbert, often explained the company's technological breakthroughs, Reagan's task was not just to extol the links between innovation and consumption but to lift them to a larger symbolic plane. As Raphael has argued, the *General Electric Theater* featured "the citizen consumer as the protagonist of a heroic drama cosponsored by democracy and capital."[76] The tagline Reagan repeated throughout his GE career ensured that that drama had a moral dimension as well: "Progress in products goes hand in hand with providing progress in the human values that enrich the lives of us all." The pronouncement had the same premise that BBDO had been supplying to GE since the 1920s. Just as Mr. Smith had overcome Senate corruption to build his patriotic boys' camp, just as Ponsett had brought the vigor of progress to Virtue City, General Electric created products that increased everyone's chances to enjoy better values and better living. In this providential scheme, the "electric servants" produced stronger families and stronger citizens, and consumption itself became a coveted form of grassroots democracy.

GE Theater was never identified with a specific partisan vision, and even at the height of the blacklist when caution reigned, the program included such outspoken liberals as Bette Davis, Henry Fonda, and Harry Belafonte. Reagan occasionally did give the program a political bent by reminding his audience that communism constituted a political and moral threat. On February 3, 1957, a week before the Stewart broadcast, he concluded the show by talking about the suffering of refugees who had escaped to Austria after the Soviet invasion of Hungary. Fresh off his position as the national director for Ike Day, Tracy Voorhees was then immersed in the job of finding homes for the thousands of Hungarians who were arriving in the United States. Reagan fixed his viewers' attention not on these resettlement efforts but on the population that remained vulnerable in Europe. "Ladies and gentlemen, about 160,000 Hungarian refugees have reached safety in Austria," he reported. "More are expected to come." Encouraging Americans to send donations to the Red Cross and their local religious organizations, he explained, "These people need food, clothes, medicine, and shelter. You can help."[77] The humanitarian appeal was inseparable from the Cold War context.

FIGURE 7.3 *The Reagan Family frequently appeared in General Electric commercials, urging viewers to "Live Better Electrically."*
Courtesy of General Electric and The Ronald Reagan Presidential Foundation and Library.

Reagan's hatred of communism also shaped the decisions he made on set. In 1962, as the series was winding down, *General Electric Theater* performed a two-part adaptation of Marion Miller's *My Dark Days*, a memoir of her years as an anti-Communist spy. Although the HUAC investigations had long subsided, Reagan fervently battled his colleagues about the script, trying to make Miller's story as hard-edged and polarizing as possible. He boasted about creating the conflict to Lorraine and Elwood Wagner, longtime fans from Philadelphia who had become his regular correspondents:

> At our own studio I had to fight right down to the wire to make the Communists villains. When I say "fight" I mean really that. On our producing staff the liberal view that communism is only something the "Right-wingers" dreamed up prevails and they literally resorted to sabotage to pull the punch out of the show. Two individuals including the director wanted to cut the whole scene about the little girl saying her prayers. Finally in a near knock-down dragout—they admitted their objection was because they were atheists.

> 'Twas a merry time we had but I'd gladly do it all over again. Let me make one thing plain—none of this fight involved GE. They were all for doing an anti-Communist story and knew nothing of the battle I was having out here.[78]

As Americans focused less on their enemies at home and more on their enemies abroad, Reagan grew convinced that the people who disagreed with him
were godless Communists. In a 1960 letter to Vice President Nixon, he privately mocked John Kennedy's nomination acceptance speech. "Under the
tousled boyish haircut," he wrote, "it is still old Karl Marx."[79]

Marinated in Middle America

The ideological roots of Reagan's position with GE lay in a report that Chester
Lang, the company's vice president for public relations, delivered to his fellow executives at the Waldorf-Astoria Hotel. On January 7, 1954, the day of
Eisenhower's second State of the Union address, Lang outlined the company's
strategy for managing public perception and influencing "the traditionally
nebulous area of what people think and feel." In a presentation shared with
BBDO, Lang reiterated the "four major obstacles to growth" that the company had identified in the years before:

Centralized government, chipping away at our traditional freedoms;

Confiscatory taxes, threatening our ability and our customers' ability
to grow;

Politically powerful labor;

And the outmoded, but still potent, fear of big business.

Recognizing that public opinion was changing during the Eisenhower administration and that, by 1964, half of the American population would have had
no direct exposure to the anti-business sentiment of the New Deal, Lang
argued that the time was right to begin shaping the way Americans viewed
General Electric and big business. As good as they were, he explained, the
company's products could never convey the extent to which GE was "a vital
factor in our national life."[80]

Lang suggested that, with BBDO's help, the company develop a public relations campaign to neutralize these threats and prepare for the more favorable climate ahead. Consumers would come to recognize that not only did
GE make outstanding consumer products, but the company was "a leader in
research and engineering" and "vital to our national defense." Perhaps most
significantly, the public would recognize the company as a "good citizen" and
"an inspiring example of free, growing, and profitable enterprise." Describing
television as "the most effective medium ever created by man for the communication of ideas and attitudes," Lang highlighted GE's "Sunday night TV
network time" as "an extremely valuable franchise" that could attract a large
audience while also meeting the company's "basic public relations objectives."

Department managers might protest the program's lack of focus on sales, but as BBDO well understood, the public relations goals had to remain paramount.[81]

Reagan's hiring six months later sent a clear message about these priorities, for both his television and touring responsibilities were dedicated not to selling specific goods but to branding GE as a model corporation. As Anna McCarthy has pointed out, in the 1950s "it became commonplace to describe economic entities as citizens—the corporation, the consumer, and even organized labor—in a conceptual move that transformed production, exchange, and accumulation of goods into a moral and patriotic act."[82] GE, of course, was not unique among the mega-corporations in wanting BBDO to promote it as a generous, friendly neighbor, but the participation of Ronald Reagan gave the company an unusually cogent message. Whether on television or in local communities, the intimacy and glamour of his appearances helped personalize a corporation that had grown so large that even its own employees regarded it as being remote from their daily lives. When he started in September 1954, the actor received a three-inch stack of papers that explained what the company hoped to achieve during these visits.[83] Reagan absorbed the lessons so thoroughly that three years after the show was cancelled, he still touted the company line. General Electric was "a good sponsor," he wrote in his 1965 memoir, "a vast corporation, but as human as the corner grocer."[84]

Soon after hiring Reagan, BBDO began canvassing GE facilities to determine his tour schedule during the 1954–1955 television season.[85] By his estimation, over the next eight years he would visit 135 plants and meet with some 250,000 employees.[86] Dunckel recalled that after some initial missteps he and Reagan quickly developed a rhythm. The morning would often begin with a breakfast meeting in their hotel suite with local politicians and businessmen. Once they arrived at the factory, Reagan would spend four, six, even eight hours touring each line. Like any star, he would pose for pictures, sign autographs, and answer questions about Hollywood, but Reagan had a knack for making small talk and ingratiating himself with different sorts of people. He learned to change and adapt the schedule so nothing became stale or routine. Some days he would tour the entire facility, walking miles of factory floor. Others, he would gather small groups for an informal presentation and Q & A. As the afternoon wore on, he would visit with the plant managers and their wives, the local executives ecstatic about the boost in morale he had provided. Looking back, he calculated that he spent the equivalent of two entire years traveling for the company, oftentimes giving fourteen speeches a day.[87] The advantage to GE was clear: the star served as an agent of cohesion, for "scattered as they were," the employees "would realize that the headquarters knew that they were there because here's that fellow they saw on Sunday night coming to visit them."[88] The advantage to Reagan went well beyond his home and salary: as one colleague put it, he became "marinated in Middle America."[89]

Reagan's celebrity powerfully imparted GE's core values and philosophy, and the appearances were easily absorbed into its employee education program. The program was the brainchild of Lemuel Boulware, the
vice president of employee and public relations. Hired after a long and
costly strike, the influential executive developed a policy by which GE
would bypass union officials and try to influence its workers directly. Like
Cordiner and Lang, Boulware believed that high taxes, excessive government regulation, and the unreasonable demands of labor were hinder-
ing the American economy. As if he were a university dean, Evans has
explained, he created an extensive system of corporate education to promote this perspective to everyone from executives to managers to workers
on the assembly line.[90]

Under Boulware's direction, Reagan became a key figure in this multifac-
eted indoctrination program. The more he traveled, the more responsibility
he took on for selling GE's white-collar philosophy to its blue-collar workers.
The Hollywood anecdotes gave way to informal explanations about unions,
government encroachment, and corporate policy. Reagan's charm nicely
suited Boulware's ambition to think beyond the creation of a compliant and
agreeable workforce. The vice president believed that if GE could properly
educate its workers, they would then become the vanguard of political change
that would sweep conservatives into power. The company offered classes on
grassroots political organizing, and Reagan began fielding questions about
how government policies affected the business climate.[91] "What Boulware
was proposing was a national crusade," Evans writes. "GE's 250,000 employees could use their 'relationships' to influence their fellow citizens toward a
course of right-thinking designed to frustrate and defeat the 'demagogs' who
normally set the agenda in matters of public policy."[92] Having long defended
the right of stars to voice their political opinions, Reagan discovered that his
stardom helped him reach audiences that might otherwise tune his message
out. Reagan's celebrity was "an entrée factor," according to Dunckel. "The fact
that he was a movie star gave him the entrée so people would listen. Then
what he had to say was so compelling that people were for the most part, convinced and supportive."[93]

Reagan liked to downplay BBDO's role in shaping the work he did for
GE, preferring to emphasize his personal relationship with company leaders, but from the beginning, the agency recognized and promoted his value
as a public relations spokesman. A little over a year into the Eisenhower
administration, BBDO began booking Reagan to represent GE at national
conventions.[94] As the press began to cover the factory tours, invitations
flowed in for the actor to address local Rotary Clubs, Kiwanis Clubs, and
Chambers of Commerce. These evening appearances were a hit. Working
what he memorably described as the "mashed potato circuit," Reagan
transferred key elements of Boulware's curriculum into his speeches.[95] He

recounted the battle against Hollywood Communists. He railed against high taxes and the government's wasteful spending. When asked about government deficits, he encouraged audience members to write their congressmen.[96] Sounding like Ayn Rand, he began delivering speeches against the rising tide of collectivism.[97] These after-dinner speeches were not isolated or discrete events; they went hand-in-hand with a larger effort to promote corporate conservativism while Eisenhower was in the White House. *Time, Fortune,* and the Harvard Business School celebrated Boulware and Cordiner for their innovations at GE. As one of the first investors in William F. Buckley's *National Review,* Boulware bought block subscriptions for executives and communicators as a supplement to the materials his office was already producing.[98] Such experiences helped Reagan develop what has come to be known as "The Speech," the hard-edged comments he delivered at hundreds of banquets and GE events and later adapted to Barry Goldwater's presidential campaign.[99]

The circumstances surrounding Reagan's departure from *General Electric Theater* are shrouded in a lot of myth-making. Commentators generally agree that the program had been declining in ratings and that Reagan had become too partisan for the company.[100] Some believe that Reagan's attacks on the Tennessee Valley Authority began to displease BBDO because GE hoped to win a major contract supplying generators to the region.[101] Others point to the federal investigation of a decision Reagan had made during his SAG presidency; in a possible violation of anti-trust statutes, he had granted a special waiver to MCA, his talent agency, to produce its own programming.[102] Reagan acknowledged both of these controversies, but he shifted blame to BBDO for wanting him to depoliticize his speeches after Kennedy's election. The termination, in his account, became another example of liberal censorship and Federal overreach. Edmund Morris's controversial biography reports that the actor was crestfallen when he discovered that *General Electric Theater* had been cancelled, pleading with GE officials to keep him on the air.[103] Reagan described a more amicable departure in which everyone recognized that he couldn't return to speaking about kitchen appliances when audiences expected him to take on the issues of the day. In contrast to the government bureaucrats, he claimed, executives such as Cordiner always upheld the value of free speech, an ironic assertion coming from someone who had been so involved in the blacklisting of his colleagues. In fact, GE emerges from Reagan's memoir *Where's the Rest of Me?* not just as an upstanding corporate citizen but as a model of conservative government—a loosely organized federation of semiautonomous entities held together by affection, self-interest, and celebrity.[104]

Reagan's years at GE marked a new development in the story of celebrity politics during the Eisenhower age. As a corporate spokesman, his initial task had been to identify conservatism with the consumption of commodities rather than Protestant restraint. Congenial and non-polarizing, he fit comfortably alongside the glowing, bipartisan celebrities who helped Madison Avenue sell the Eisenhower presidency. Liking GE, after all, was not dissimilar from liking Ike when one considered the magnitude of both entities. Over the years, however, the actor in the gray flannel suit became the ideologue intent on pressing his advantage against union heads and liberal activists. Reagan's anti-communism allowed him to move celebrity politics beyond the unifying tenor of the Eisenhower campaigns. His speeches had a growing anger and resentment that one did not find in the public comments of Helen Hayes. He delivered lines, as Rick Perlstein has commented, as if they were punches.[105] With liberal entertainers still trying to avoid the hazards of speaking openly, Reagan was reviving the ideological passion and partisanship of another decade.

Where Reagan most differed from Eisenhower and the celebrities who surrounded him was in the recognition that celebrity provided a public calling. Eisenhower was famous in that millions of people celebrated him for his accomplishments and the strong character they revealed. Like Coriolanus, however, his military values made him ambivalent about how his fame had been translated into a political commodity. Reagan did not have the Coriolanus gene. Having grown up with the movies and having spent years in the entertainment industry, he welcomed the rites of stardom. In Reagan's mind, fame was not artificially produced by public relations and publicity. Fame was a genuine accomplishment and, in this respect, a fundamentally populist identity. In 1965, he explicitly compared his twelve-hour days touring the factory floors to those of a candidate looking for votes. There was no doubt in his mind which activity hewed closer to the spirit of democracy. "No barnstorming politician ever met the people on quite such a footing," Reagan wrote. "Sometimes I had an awesome, shivering feeling that America was making a personal appearance for me, and it made me the biggest fan in the world."[106] As he looked to enter politics himself, Reagan retained a faith in celebrity's power to orient his relation to the world, though he cleverly inverted its central dynamic. Fame was not simply about alliance and endorsement: it was a fleeting but privileged view into the nation itself.

Happy Birthday, Mr. President

Consider John F. Kennedy, seated in the presidential box on the north side of Madison Square Garden. In ten days, he will turn forty-five and celebrate with his wife and young children in Washington, DC. But tonight, May 19, 1962, he is being fêted in Manhattan with a birthday fundraiser designed to retire the debts from his presidential campaign and deliver some much-needed cash to the New York Democratic Party.

Though his wife has stayed behind in the White House, he is surrounded by donors, friends, and family. Act after act appears on the Garden's thirty-by-forty-foot stage—Jack Benny, Ella Fitzgerald, the Jerome Robbins Ballet.[1] The president claps along with the crowd as Harry Belafonte sings "Michael, Row the Boat Ashore." He listens intently to Maria Callas's two arias. The president's brother-in-law, actor Peter Lawford, serves as the master of ceremonies. With much fanfare, he introduces a platinum-haired entertainer, but the spotlight marking her entrance remains empty. She is nowhere to be found. At some point, she writes on her call sheet from the evening, "who do you have to be/to ask/who do you think you have to be to be disappointment."[2] Perhaps they are words of solace, or recrimination, or the lyrics to a new song. At this moment, though, she must seem disappointing to the 17,500 Democrats who hear Lawford introduce her again and expect to see her emerge.

Among the showbiz crowd, the missed cue is an old gag, but with the rumors coming from the West Coast about the star's illness and unreliability, no one can be sure whether the absence is awkward or funny. Lawford winds up for another introduction, and mid-sentence she appears, the crowd roaring with approval and relief. "Ladies and gentleman," he announces, "the *late* Marilyn Monroe." The laughter turns to sounds of astonishment and delight, as he unwraps a fur stole to reveal a flesh-toned sequined dress that is so tight she had to be sewn into it. Monroe begins to sing "Happy Birthday" as no one has heard it before. She is all breath and softness and innuendo, her cadence slow and loaded with a drowsy sexuality that Gloria Steinem would later attribute to dope and fear.[3] The Democrats hoot and clap with each pause and gesture. The verse she adds thanking the president for battling US Steel is as incidental as the five-tiered cake that rolls to the stage, both details lost amid the thousands of imagined intimacies that bind the crowd to this moment.

And there sits President Kennedy in the only upholstered chair in the Garden's presidential box. As it does during many of the public events of his presidency, a cocktail of procaine, steroids, and amphetamines probably courses through his veins to soothe his Addison's disease and back pain.[4] His legs propped on the metal rail before him, he puffs contentedly on a cigar, fixing his presidential gaze on the rhinestone singer sparkling in the darkness. When the president comes to the podium afterwards, he will offer many warm comments about the stars who helped him celebrate his birthday. Belafonte came from the tranquil town of Columbus, Ohio, where they hadn't elected a Democrat in sixty years; Peggy Lee valiantly left her sickbed to perform; Jimmy Durante was a fellow godfather to the president's nephew, and a better one at that. And then there is the familiar line, though to much of the public the rest of the night remains vague: "I can now retire from politics after having had 'Happy Birthday' sung to me in such a sweet, wholesome way." Cool, compressed, ironic, it cleverly both acknowledges and denies the secret history betrayed beneath the lights.[5]

What a change from the earnest charm of Ike Day. How far away Ike and Mamie must have seemed from the showy eroticism of the evening. Helen Hayes, Jimmy Stewart, the family gathered around the television in the White House library; Howard Keel and Kathryn Grayson evoking the kind of parlor romance you might find in turn-of-the-century Abilene. After six short years, it is "exit Fred Waring and his tidy Pennsylvanians" and "enter the wig-wearing Norma Jean." Her performance offers a striking contrast to the Eisenhower stars and their efforts to convey the Republican's warmth and likeability. Whether they were in a Washington hotel or on a Los Angeles soundstage, they were meant to be instruments of consensus, drawing the audience into the same comfortable admiration they expressed for Ike. The celebration made Eisenhower seem approachable, down-to-earth, the patriarch of the American family. It is telling that in preparing the birthday tribute, McCann-Erickson asked him to behave like most Americans did: by sitting in front of the television and watching the stars entertain.

The singular quality of Monroe's performance, of course, came in part from her personal connection with Kennedy. The act aroused a cluster of tangled feelings among those in the Garden that night. There was the pleasure of watching, spectating, of being overwhelmed by the glamour and glitter of a show; there was the pleasure of gossip, speculation, of sensing that something scandalous was being revealed. And with such feelings came a hunger to know more, to access the hidden narrative, to understand what had happened backstage. The exceptional nature of the moment has only grown over the decades as evidence suggests that Monroe probably did have an affair

with the president and that the hooting Democrats were right in seeing something daring and flirtatiously self-destructive in her performance.[6] Watching
video of the festivities today, we cannot help remembering that the birthday
party was the actress's last public appearance before she died of an overdose
later that year and that Kennedy himself would be killed by an assassin on
November 22, 1963. To those of us on the other side of history, there is something darkly prophetic in Lawford's joke about "the late Marilyn Monroe."

But no matter how distinctively personal it seemed to be, Monroe's appearance powerfully conveyed the role that stardom and glamour played in
Kennedy's political career. Kennedy's birthday gala was not a nationally televised event (news channels carried live reports to local New York residents),
and strictly speaking, it was not part of a campaign. Nonetheless, the performance was a fitting, though hyperbolic, expression of the aura of celebrity
politics that had hung over Kennedy since the mid-1950s. While Americans
were used to the charm of the Eisenhower years, Kennedy and the stars who
surrounded him buzzed with desire. Their cool bonhomie gave the impression
that politicians circulated in separate company—whether it was the rarified
world of American aristocracy (Jacqueline Bouvier) or the boisterous, swanky
world of show business celebrities (Marilyn Monroe). When Kennedy sat in
the upholstered chair and watched the events onstage, he was not a spectator
in the way that Ike and Mamie presented themselves as being. He was watching his friends and intimates, appreciating the inside jokes, acknowledging
the public and private histories. From Monroe, to Lawford, to Durante, these
relationships were part of the show. Indeed, as if he were a member of the
company, the president had been informed earlier that Monroe's rehearsal
had been shaky. He confidently dismissed the concerns with, "Oh, I think
she'll be very good."[7]

Unlike Eisenhower's carefully orchestrated Madison Square Garden rallies, Kennedy's birthday fundraiser was not organized by advertising agencies. Arthur Krim, the head of United Artists (and a prominent Democratic
financier), had hired Richard Adler to produce the evening's entertainment.
Although Adler was part of the songwriting team behind the Broadway
hits *Pajama Game* and *Damn Yankees*, Monroe quarreled with him during
rehearsals, resisting his pleas to drop the baby-soft voice and sing the tune
outright. Years later, he readily admitted that her willful, astonishing performance provoked an immediate response. "The crowd was yelling and screaming for her," he recalled. "It was like a mass seduction."[8] That Monroe had
publicly come on to the president was memorable enough, but as Adler suggests, she had simultaneously come on to every audience member and camera
in the building. The breathiness, the revealing gown, the hand moving up
the torso, they all contributed to the idiom of desire in which Monroe's performance took place—a desire that connects the 17,500 faithful in Madison
Square Garden to the millions who have since watched the clip on television

and the Internet. Though lust may be its most obvious and identifiable form, the response encompassed other yearnings as well—among them, the wish for luxury, for public intimacy, and for the magnetism of fame itself.

Cold War intellectuals were fascinated by the complex power of desire. Whether seeking treatment from Freudian therapists or reading Vladimir Nabokov's 1955 novel *Lolita*, they regarded the many permutations of desire as being an integral part of their times. Since the 1958 publication of *The Affluent Society*, the Harvard economist John Kenneth Galbraith had been one of the nation's leading thinkers on the topic. (Galbraith would later serve as Kennedy's ambassador to India.) Reviewing the booming postwar economy, Galbraith argued that the United States had based its economic and cultural success on the creation of consumer wants. Throughout history, governments had tried to increase production to meet their material needs, but with improvements in manufacturing, the situation in America was reversed. Producers had unprecedented capacity, and the nation's prosperity depended on consumers purchasing the seemingly endless supply of goods. Like many of his contemporaries, Galbraith named BBDO in critiquing the role that advertising agencies played in this new economy. The primary job of Madison Avenue, he wrote, was "to create desires—to bring into being wants that did not previously exist."[9] Elegant automobiles, shiny barbeque pits, exotic food, wall-to-wall carpeting, erotic clothing, expansive television screens—"consumer wants are created by the process by which they are satisfied," Galbraith explained. "Production creates its own demand."[10] The glamorization of desire awakened consumers to the things they lacked, turning not just the market but the culture at large into a spectacle of seduction and longing.

In many ways, celebrities personify the economy of desire that Galbraith saw operating in the United States. They serve as both commodities and advertisements, wooing the public's attention toward the products and people they want to promote. Working in what Christine Gledhill has called an "industry of desire," stars have been effective in promoting versions of themselves that appeal to consumers but never fully satisfy. From the earliest kinescopes to the latest Twitter feeds, the production of fame has created more and more cultural demand.[11] No single person demonstrates this commodification more than Monroe, whose untimely death spawned a virtual industry of products inviting consumers to possess her by proxy. Represented by the posters, coffee mugs, and T-shirts that have taken the place of her body, she has become an icon of inexhaustible commercial longing: to covet her is to covet the world of relentless production and publicity.

Having basked in the glow of celebrity since he was a young man, Kennedy carefully constructed his political identity around stardom and sex appeal. Although party stalwarts doubted his liberal convictions, JFK was widely celebrated as a new kind of candidate, one so thrillingly "glamorous" that his contemporaries forgot that in 1952, Robert Taft's supporters had used the same adjective to disparage Ike.[12] Just as conservatives worried that Eisenhower's media personality would gloss over a basic indifference to the Republican Party, liberals worried that the photogenic young senator would threaten the Democratic establishment. To some, Kennedy seemed more a candidate of the media than of a particular political party, his glamour effectively superseding any sense of ideology.[13]

The work JFK did to support Adlai Stevenson made his comfort with the media especially apparent. As one of the Democrats' designated "glamour boys," the Massachusetts senator was keenly aware of the excitement Stevenson aroused among Democratic women such as Lauren Bacall and Mercedes McCambridge. Years later, in a conversation knowingly recorded for posterity, Jackie Kennedy felt the need to differentiate her husband's sexual persona from that of his Democratic predecessor. Stevenson's supporters, she recalled, included a group of "violently liberal women" who would always prefer the governor to Kennedy. Why? "Jack so obviously demanded from a woman—a relationship between a man and a woman where a man would be the leader and a woman be his wife," she demurely explained. "With Adlai you could have another relationship where—you know, he'd sort of be sweet and you could talk, but you wouldn't ever. . . ." She stumbled into her answer: "I always thought women who were scared of sex loved Adlai."[14]

The comment underscores the degree to which Jackie saw the drama of sexuality as being vital to her late husband's public persona. The mad devotion that Stevenson aroused in his supporters was inextricably tied to his person, to the way he thought, spoke, listened, wrote letters, and conducted his daily life. As attractive as it was on the radio, however, the power of Stevenson's voice dissipated on TV. Kennedy, on the other hand, was remarkably skilled at using visual media to project his youth and virility. Norman Mailer compared him to Marlon Brando in marveling at his ability to shift appearances from one moment to the next. Put JFK in front of three microphones and a television camera, Mailer wrote, and this pleasant, sunburned professor was immediately transformed into "a movie star, his coloring vivid, his manner rich, his gestures strong and quick, alive with that concentration of vitality a successful actor always seems to radiate."[15] Like Monroe, Kennedy recognized that the interplay between star and spectator involved its own erotic message.

The combination of sexual scandal, tragic death, and mega-celebrity have enshrined the Kennedy fundraiser in cultural memory. With tickets ranging from $3–$1,000, the party raised $1 million—by all accounts a fundraising success, though as the *New York Times* pointed out, the Democrats were unable to match the $2.5 million the Republicans had raised during Young & Rubicam's 1956 Madison Square Garden rally.[16] And yet, the Eisenhower stars have become historical footnotes compared to the lavish attention Americans have given to Kennedy's forty-fifth birthday. Over time, the vision of Helen Hayes cutting a piece of cake has not competed well with that of a sparkling Marilyn Monroe interpreting "Happy Birthday" as a torch song. In 1999, Christie's auctioned forty-five lots of Monroe's memorabilia on live television. Her Bible fetched $37,950, while a diamond eternity band, a gift from Joe DiMaggio, went for $772,500. An anonymous bidder spent $115,000 for Monroe's invitation to the Madison Square Garden party. And finally, a group of investors paid close to $1.27 million for the beaded rhinestone dress, its value obviously enhanced by the man who had seen her wear it.[17] By contrast, we might turn to Alexander Autographs, which in 2010 conducted an online auction of the four-star general's helmet Eisenhower had used for much of World War II. The company could certify that Ike had worn the helmet in North Africa, and he had worn it when the Allies stormed the Normandy coast. He had worn it as the army pushed across France and into the Low Countries. The helmet sold for $47,800.[18]

Kennedy eroticized the political spectacle that Eisenhower and his advisers introduced to civic life. In 1956, that spectacle revolved around the new

FIGURE 8.1 *Marilyn Monroe speaks with Robert Kennedy, Jack Kennedy, and Arthur Schlesinger after the May 19, 1962, birthday gala.*
Courtesy of John F. Kennedy Library, PX2000-2:1.

institutional alignment of politics, television, and advertising. Critics saw danger in the rise of celebrity endorsements because they worried that television would turn politics into a popularity contest and leave voters confused and dazed. By the 1960s, the cultural import of celebrity had begun to change. Commentators began to think that celebrities functioned as symbols of deeper conflicts and desires. People did not see Monroe singing "Happy Birthday" to the president and fret about the presence of Communists or advertising's influence on American political life. Nor did they vociferously complain, as later generations would, about the money Hollywood insiders gave to Democratic candidates. Like another 1950s icon, Elvis Presley, Monroe came to represent the unfettering of national desire and a loosening of moral constraints. As one historian has commented, she became the body politic, her personality receding further and further into what she signified.[19] (The actress seemed to recognize this drift when she asked a designer to create a dress for the performance "that only Marilyn Monroe would wear.")[20] The merger of politics and celebrity was no longer seen as a group of allied institutions that threatened to act as an integrated whole; it became a problem of psychoanalytical depths, a knot of unconscious impulses, emotions, and ideas that revealed secret truths about American life.

All the Way

The Kennedy family had a lucrative history with the movie industry. In the 1920s, Joseph Kennedy, the president's father, had been one of the first Wall Street bankers to recognize the investment potential in the film industry, and leaving his family behind, he moved to California in 1926. Though his Hollywood sojourn is perhaps most remembered for his steamy affair with the actress Gloria Swanson, it also proved him to be a shrewd and tireless businessman. In five short years, Kennedy entered into a financial partnership with Swanson; financed, bought, and merged a string of small studios; and acquired a national theater chain and distribution network. With RCA's David Sarnoff as his partner, he created RKO Pictures, the first studio devoted exclusively to producing talking pictures. By 1931, he had returned home and sold nearly all of his Hollywood investments, making millions in the process.[21]

Joseph Kennedy's work helped spur his son's lifelong engagement with stardom and the movies. As a young man recuperating from back surgery and preparing for his first congressional race, Jack traveled to Los Angeles where he hung out on movie sets, romanced starlets, and socialized with the likes of Olivia de Havilland and Gary Cooper.[22] His sister Pat's 1954 marriage to Peter Lawford gave him a convenient base of operations in southern California and deepened his ties to actors, musicians, and producers. In 1957, the young senator's presidential ambitions were boosted by a half-hour television program called *Navy Log* that dramatically recreated his heroic efforts to rescue his crew after their PT boat was rammed by a Japanese destroyer in the South Pacific. Having been involved in the episode's writing and production, Kennedy flew to San Diego to meet the actors and serve as a technical adviser.[23]

Kennedy's fascination with Hollywood continued in the White House. Adler recalls the president regularly reading *Variety* magazine and asking to hear stories about moviemaking and show folk. At parties after galas and benefits, he gossiped with the stars and encouraged them to do impromptu performances for the assembled guests.[24] Lawford was astonished by the president's grasp of the industry and the way he tracked box office numbers as films opened around the country.[25] When he heard that Richard Condon's novel *The Manchurian Candidate* was being turned into a movie, he pumped its star, Frank Sinatra, for news from the set and wondered who would play the role of Raymond Shaw's mother.[26] When Hollywood began plans to produce the 1963 feature film *PT-109*, the president not only reviewed the script, he also suggested Warren Beatty to play the role of his younger self.[27]

JFK's star quality made national news during the 1960 Wisconsin Democratic primary when he took on the longtime Minnesota senator Hubert Humphrey. Kennedy's win in the New Hampshire primary had not impressed many, but the six-week battle in Humphrey's neighboring state would prove to party bosses that JFK could overcome anti-Catholic bias and connect with rural voters. The campaign ran from mid-February to early April, and in the snow and slush of Wisconsin's "mud season," Kennedy began to attract crowds hungry for personal contact. The Kennedy campaign was unusually well organized, and in each contest, he sent scores of advance men who spread across the state making contacts with county chairmen and assessing the local media. The files from the Wisconsin primary reveal the staff's voluminous and detailed attention to hardnosed, precinct-based politicking, and it is hard not to attribute Kennedy's winning 56 percent of the vote to the power of his political machine.

Amid all this intensive grassroots organizing, however, the campaign realized the power of its glamorous candidate and his family. Kennedy's siblings appeared throughout the state, courting the media and drawing excited crowds. From the beginning, Kennedy was beset by hundreds of young women who showed up at campaign events to get a glimpse of the young candidate. (He and Jackie eventually nicknamed these women "jumpers" in reference to their constant hopping up and down around his motorcade.)[28] Patrick J. Lucey managed JFK's Wisconsin campaign before going on to his own high-profile career in Democratic politics. Asked in 1964 to reflect on the strategy in the Wisconsin primary, he explained that, while Humphrey did more to target traditional voting blocs, Kennedy devised a broad appeal that focused on young people: "The Kennedy campaign was, for a very large part, just an effective presentation of a celebrity."[29]

Robert Drew's documentary film *Primary* vividly captures the energy and excitement of the Wisconsin campaign. Liberated by the invention of hand-held mobile cameras, the crew followed the candidates through the crowds and captured their preparations backstage. (In one remarkable scene, the camera focuses on Jackie's nervous, shifting fingers as she addresses a Polish-American audience in Milwaukee.) The film reveals two markedly different political operations: one rooted in neighborly affection, the other in magnetism and celebrity. In a hotel lobby, a group of children play accordions while a dozen or so supporters sing "Hubert, Hubert Humphrey" to the tune of "Davy Crocket," the theme song to Walt Disney's hit television show and movie. Humphrey walks the streets of the small Wisconsin town Thoma, shaking hands with pedestrians and passing out business cards. He likes to congratulate the husbands on having had the good sense to marry such excellent wives. He sits in the front seat of a campaign car, shaking hands with the farmers and laborers who trudge by. Standing in a half-empty gym on the Minnesota border, he extols the virtues of a Norwegian cup of coffee and explains that, against the wishes of the New York media, he remains committed to the government's support of dairy farmers.[30]

The Kennedy scenes are claustrophobic. (The few times he appears visually alone are when he stands at a microphone or sits in a photography studio waiting for his portrait to be taken.) Again and again, we see the candidate working his way through large, at times giddy, crowds, the camera jostled by the rush toward him. "Please don't crowd the senator," a man repeats to no avail. "The hardest thing to do in a Kennedy campaign," a worker tells us, "is to properly harness the enthusiasm he generates." Compared to the drawn faces of Humphrey's farmers, Kennedy's supporters look animated, and though the camera focuses on the pretty young women in the front rows, even the older Polish matrons exude nervous anticipation. When Kennedy hits the streets after an event, he is mobbed by adolescents seeking autographs and struggles to get into his vehicle and be driven away.

Adding to the pressure of such campaign scenes is the music that blares incessantly from loudspeakers, Frank Sinatra's 1959 hit "High Hopes." To help support his friend, Sinatra had recorded the song with new lyrics that substituted the Massachusetts senator for the gutsy rubber tree ant:

> Nineteen-sixty's the year for his high hopes.
> Come on and vote for Kennedy
> Vote for Kennedy
> And we'll come out on top![31]

The release of "High Hopes" epitomized the campaign's blend of grassroots outreach and celebrity style. The idea for the song had originated in the California Democratic community that had risen up around Kennedy's sister and brother-in-law. Although Kennedy's supporters had to pay union rates

for the musicians, Sinatra and the lyricist Sammy Cahn donated their services for "High Hopes" and its B-side, a rewritten version of another Sinatra/
Cahn hit, "All the Way." For the cost of about ten to eleven cents per unit, the
campaign distributed the record to donors around the country.[32]

Kennedy premiered the song at the start of his Wisconsin campaign, and
of the 100,000 records made in February 1960, 25,000 were sent to the headquarters in Milwaukee.[33] From Whitewater, to Elkhorn, to Lake Geneva, a
station wagon equipped with loudspeakers rolled down the streets, Sinatra's
upbeat voice following the candidate and his advocates as they greeted pass-
ersby.[34] Within days, Kennedy's supporters knew the lyrics themselves, and
they broke out in song as they waited for him at speeches and rallies. "Senator
Kennedy, supported by a slick high octane machine, is a 'celebrity' to folks
here," the New York Times reported from Milwaukee, adding that supporters had taken to dressing for his meetings as if they were attending "a major
society event."[35] The influx of glamour irritated the earnest Humphrey, who
accused the Massachusetts senator of being bought and sold by Hollywood.
Though Kennedy assiduously avoided bringing celebrities directly into the
Wisconsin campaign, Humphrey was quick to condemn his opponent's glitzy
friends and family. A steady public servant with a bald head and little pizzazz,
he found himself echoing the Democrats' complaints about Eisenhower in
1952 and 1956. "Beware of these orderly campaigns," he warned voters. "They
are ordered, bought, and paid for. We are not selling cornflakes or some
Hollywood production."[36] In this new Democratic formulation of politics
and celebrity, Humphrey became the scolding Adlai Stevenson and JFK the
photogenic Ike.

But unlike Eisenhower, Kennedy did not need popular culture to make
him seem younger or more in touch with common men and women. Kennedy
liked to pal around with entertainers, and he reveled in the gossip, camaraderie, and looseness of Hollywood relationships. He turned to friends like
Sinatra and Monroe less for their cultural prestige than for his own personal
relaxation. A week before he embarked on the Wisconsin campaign, Kennedy
scheduled a brief stop in Las Vegas to visit Lawford, Sinatra, Sammy Davis,
Jr., and Dean Martin. The four friends were filming Ocean's 11, and their "hell-
blazing antics,"—what one reporter summarized as "booze, broads, dice,
broads, cards, broads"—were already becoming legendary. Taking a suite at
the Sands Hotel, Kennedy immersed himself in the atmosphere, speaking
with the press one moment and gossiping with the Rat Pack the next. He was
in the audience when the stars joined Joey Bishop's standup routine, the five
men engaging in a clamorous caricature of their boozy, ribald selves. A gossip
column captures Kennedy laughing "in mock-delight as his well-lubricated
brother-in-law went through a semi-strip tease" and Bishop bantered about
the ambassadorships he and his buddies expected. As if it offered a warning,

someone from the California headquarters cut the article out of the newspaper and carefully preserved it for office reading.[37]

The danger of celebrity was that it risked compromising the seriousness of Kennedy's candidacy. With voters concerned about his age and religion, and party officials questioning his true commitments, the long trail of Hollywood friends could leave Kennedy appearing callow, immature, and lacking substance. While aides fanned out across Wisconsin preparing for the six-week campaign, Kennedy arrived in Vegas with an entourage ready to party, and Sinatra promptly introduced him to Judith Campbell, the Mob-associated woman with whom he conducted a two-year love affair.[38] Perhaps not wanting the fun to end, he left for Oregon with more folks in tow, including Gloria Cahn, the wife of the songwriter who had collaborated with Sinatra on the "High Hopes" and "All the Way" recordings. In Las Vegas, Cahn was rumored to have clashed with Campbell as both women vied for the senator's attentions.[39] Whatever happened in Oregon, the trip seemed to soothe Cahn's injured feelings. The next week, she wrote Kennedy with an easy, flirtatious intimacy, dubbing herself " 'ye ole' campaigner.' " "I am at your service," she promised, "whenever duty calls."[40] Kennedy's reply was archly suggestive: "I must say, you went 'all the way' and all out on our trip to Oregon."[41]

A Ready-Made Spectacle

The 1960 Democratic National Convention in Los Angeles proved to be a coming-out party for a generation of Hollywood liberals who had spent much of the 1950s dodging HUAC's inquiries. The city had a long tradition of staging star-studded political events. In 1932, studio chief Jack Warner organized "the Motion Picture Electrical Parade and Sports Pageant" in honor of the candidate Franklin Roosevelt, promising that he would provide "the spectacle of spectacles, the show of shows."[42] In 1944, 93,000 people crowded into the Los Angeles Coliseum to join such stars as Ginger Rogers, Gary Cooper, Clark Gable, and Barbara Stanwyck in supporting Thomas Dewey.[43] And as recently as 1956, George Murphy had organized a massive event at the Hollywood Bowl to support Eisenhower's reelection. With the Soviet Union threatening to invade Poland and Egypt's seizure of the Suez Canal, Eisenhower delivered a blistering attack on Adlai Stevenson that was followed by a televised rally in which dozens of stars took the stage to announce their support.[44] The city had to wait until the summer of 1960, however, to host the nominating convention of a major political party, and combined with the new openness, the organizers made sure to highlight its most attractive and famous industry. Over forty stars showed up at the Los Angeles Airport to greet their favorite candidates.[45] Even fervent Republicans such as Bob Hope,

Gary Cooper, Ann Miller, and Irene Dunne could not resist the dinners and events that had sprung up around the convention.[46]

Kennedy was in an excellent position to capitalize on the city's excitement and energy. With an eye toward the nomination, the Lawfords had hosted a dinner party for members of the convention planning committee in 1959, and as Kennedy inched closer to victory, they served as valuable emissaries between established party officials and his local supporters.[47] While the stars had been kept in the wings during the Wisconsin and West Virginia primaries, Kennedy's advisers began carefully recruiting talent for the convention. They turned to June Lockhart Lindsay to compile a list of actors and actresses who would be willing to participate, apparently hoping that her role as the mother in the wholesome television drama *Lassie* would stave off any controversy or criticism.[48]

As both parties had in 1956, the Democrats viewed the Los Angeles convention as a combination of political meeting and choreographed show. They hired longtime radio and television producer Leonard Reinsch to be the executive director, an enormous job that included organizing the hotel accommodations for nearly 30,000 people and staging the five-day meeting so that it would hold the interest of a television audience. (Reinsch compared his job to "producing 'Ben-Hur' for a one-night stand.")[49] The proximity to Hollywood gave Reinsch an extensive supporting cast. Sinatra, Martin, and Judy Garland entertained 2,600 guests at a $100-a-plate fundraising dinner the night before the official proceedings.[50] The next night, Edward G. Robinson, Vincent Price, Tony Curtis, Shelly Winters, and the Ike Day veteran Nat King Cole joined other entertainers in taking the stage.[51] Each night produced more personalities until, on the final day, the convention moved outdoors to the Los Angeles Sports Coliseum, where the pageantry continued with a large cast of actors, actresses, singers, and dancers.

As industry executives flooded the hotel lobbies and the studios expanded their tour schedules to accommodate delegates, *The Hollywood Reporter* asked entertainers such as Janet Leigh and Milton Berle to contribute to a rotating column about the proceedings.[52] The most exuberant of these columns came from Frank Capra. The director had taken great pains to make the political scenes in *Mr. Smith Goes to Washington* seem as realistic as possible, as he hoped the film would provide the audience with a helpful civics lesson. Twenty-one years later, he presented the 1960 Democratic National Convention as a lesson not in politics but in movie-making. Brushing aside "egghead analysis," he wrote that the scene before him was a director's dream:

> I see here a ready-made spectacle—a tight and suspenseful script—a starring cast of the most important political figures (of at least one major party) in the country—thousands of extras representing all walks of life and drawn from all sections of the country—bands and orchestras contributing

an exciting musical score—and evidence of an almost unlimited amount of money to spend on a production.[53]

For Capra, the convention took place in the increasingly blurred space between reality and fiction, one in which politics and aesthetics worked symbiotically. The director openly cheered the ways in which the convention lent itself to a Hollywood picture he would title *Politics USA*: "Here is contained drama of the highest order, deep and moving suspense and 'story values' which affect the life, if not the very fate, of every individual in the United States." All a director would need to create a box office hit, he noted, was a competent film crew.[54]

As vapid and myopic as these columns could be, they reinforced a broader narrative that it was reasonable to see the convention as a political entertainment. Some observers did not share Capra's enthusiasm, but their complaints centered on the feeling that the political action could not compete with the surrounding pageantry. "The CONVENTION—needed a Pilot," an article in *The Hollywood Reporter* declared, complaining that it was draggy, repetitive, and filled with old material.[55] Even veteran reporter Russell Baker could not help presenting the convention as a show: "The Democrats finally lifted the curtain on what was once billed as the most daring political drama of the age," he wrote in the *New York Times*. "All signs suggested that they have a turkey on their hands." Baker was referring to the fact that the great issue of the convention—whether Kennedy would secure the nomination—had been settled in a series of private meetings with Lyndon Johnson at the Biltmore Hotel. With the ticket already decided, Baker noted, the delegates' interest collapsed whenever the movie stars left the stage.[56]

In the absence of suspense-filled votes and stunning swings of support, the convention generated excitement through the buildup of personality. In this respect, both supporters and detractors could agree that the candidate and his star-studded convention fit each other well. Kennedy's magnetism, combined with the omnipresent entertainment industry, underscored the political value of glamour and celebrity. Eisenhower, of course, had received worldwide publicity for nearly twenty years, but he was ultimately promoted as an object of affection rather than desire, the heroic grandfather whose personality comforted and charmed the nation without necessarily inspiring it. The 1960 Los Angeles convention suggested that politicians could be commended for their attractive lifestyles as much as their accomplishments. In the new environment created by television, even the delegates were more than activists, voters, minions, and cronies. They were televised performers (whose responses had to be managed) and members of an audience (whose responses had to be gauged). As if only an insider could recognize the humor of the scene, a writer for the *Hollywood Reporter* wryly noted what Lawford, Sinatra, and Shirley MacLaine were doing on the convention floor during the nominating speeches: they were holding stopwatches and timing the applause each candidate received.[57]

The Psychic Loins

The convention's emphasis on politics as a glamorized performance both alarmed and excited its participants. Norman Mailer, whose *Esquire* essay "Superman Comes to the Supermarket" helped establish a new school of political writing, found himself curiously attracted to a convention that could be so dull and uneventful on one hand and yet so monumentally historical on the other.[58] Amid all the "pig-rooting, horse-snorting, band-playing, voice-screaming" of the American political carnival, he noted a mysterious sense of depression and, above all, panic among the delegates. When he saw the crowd at Pershing Square nearly carry Kennedy into the Biltmore Hotel, he had an epiphany as powerful as *déjà-vu*: he had seen this moment before in a dozen musical comedies. It was the scene in which, buoyed by hundreds of well-wishers, the football star arrives at the dean's house to ask his daughter for a kiss:

> And suddenly I saw the convention, it came into focus for me, and I under-stood the mood of depression which had lain over the convention, because finally it was simple: the Democrats were going to nominate a man who, no matter how serious his political dedication might be, was indisputably and willy-nilly going to be seen as a great box-office actor, and the conse-quences of that were staggering and not at all easy to calculate.

Mailer carefully acknowledges Kennedy's talents, and the delegates he describes are no less aware of his political acumen and organizational supremacy. They nonetheless worry about what the candidate's star qual-ity bodes for their own understanding of politics. "America's politics would now be also America's favorite movie," Mailer explains, "America's first soap opera, America's best-seller."

Mailer's portrait of Kennedy as a leading man had little sense of the *Camelot*-inspired idealism that many associate with his presidency.[59] The writer saw in Kennedy's rise a return of the deepest (and sometimes darkest) mythic forces in American political culture:

> Since the First World War Americans have been leading a double life, and our history has moved on two rivers, one visible, the other underground; there has been the history of politics which is concrete, factual, practical and unbelievably dull if not for the consequences of the actions of some of these men; and there is a subterranean river of untapped, ferocious, lonely and romantic desires, that concentration of ecstasy and violence which is the dream life of the nation.

During the 1950s, he explained, the life of politics and the life of myth had diverged, as Ike governed the nation with the small-town mindset of a committee. Eisenhower's pragmatism had given rise to the triumph of corporations and a culture marked by a "tasteless, sexless, odorless sanctity." The false, superficial desires that Galbraith identified with Madison Avenue neatly matched such an environment. Mailer saw something existential, however, in the way Kennedy's candidacy invited the nation to confront the nightmare of history and summon the more extraordinary and adventurous aspects of itself. The Democrat was "the edge of the mystery," an open invitation to merge the nation's political life with the vibrant collisions of its unconscious. With his suntan and white teeth, Kennedy may have looked like a ski instructor or Broadway king, but he represented something else: he was a hipster. Even his "good, sound, conventional liberal record [had] a patina of that other life," Mailer wrote, "the second American life, the long electric night with the fires of neon leading down the highway to the murmur of jazz."

The distinction, of course, says as much about Norman Mailer in 1960 as it does John F. Kennedy. Only three years before the Los Angeles convention, *Dissent* magazine had published Mailer's essay "The White Negro," and he was still working out his theory that "the hipster" was a repository of subconscious cultural desires. In a series of essays, interviews, and stories, he had explored the significance of this new personality on the American scene, taking it upon himself to chart the differences between "hipsters," "beatniks," and "squares."[60] As "the fissure in the national psyche widened to the danger point" in the 1950s, he admired the way hipsters turned their alienation into a daring ethic of limitless and primal possibility.[61] Literary critic Michael Szalay has written that in the 1960s the concept of "hip" became a way of dramatizing consumer tensions between the old Protestant work ethic and the new vibrant marketplace. Hip "transformed the white insider into a black outsider," allowing consumption to be ironic, liberated, and deeply symbolic at the same time. Hip shifted the basis of Galbraith's marketplace from needs to wants.[62]

To Mailer, what depressed the delegates and excited the crowds was that Kennedy represented a potential fusion of the mythic and political worlds: his highly professional campaign seemed as skilled at awakening desires as it was at securing votes. Thinking about the imminent Kennedy–Nixon showdown, Mailer saw a battle of monumental significance—not in the policy decisions it would dictate, but in the alternatives it offered the nation:

> So, finally, would come a choice which history had never presented to a nation before—one could vote for glamour or for ugliness, a staggering and most stunning choice—would the nation be brave enough to enlist the romantic dream of itself, would it vote for the image in the mirror of its unconscious, were the people indeed brave enough to hope for an

acceleration of Time, for that new life of drama which would come from choosing a son to lead them who was heir apparent to the psychic loins?

In his relentlessly hyperbolic style, Mailer widened the meaning of glamour, associating its various surface pleasures with existential bravery. Glamour invited Americans not to gild the political world but to aggressively and *carnally* embrace a politics of meaning. To vote for Kennedy was to vote "for the image in the mirror" of the nation's unconscious; it was to embrace the challenge to self-knowledge.

The extravagance of Mailer's vision, of course, is rather gloriously his own, but in many ways, he dramatizes the rhetoric of desire that had circulated around Kennedy since the beginning of his career. As a young senator, he had appeared on the cover of *Life* magazine with his fiancée Jackie, the bare-legged couple grinning as their sailboat coursed through the Atlantic surf. As if they were models in an advertisement for cigarettes or scotch, the image promoted the couple's exclusive, enviable lifestyle, while also inviting viewers to take in their attractive sexuality.[63] (On Jackie's image in postwar magazines, Gay Talese once quipped, "Never before in American history have so many men privately craved a President's wife.")[64] From his showbiz friendships, to his secret liaisons, to the crushing, exuberant crowds, Kennedy brought Eros into the merger of politics and celebrity, thus creating a sense of longing for him and his family but also eroticizing the spectacle of politics in the commercial media age. When Mailer described him in *Esquire* as the "heir apparent to the psychic loins," he was building on an image of the rakish, virile Kennedy that was already prevalent in the cultural marketplace. Seen in this light, Marilyn Monroe's shimmering performance three years later was neither scandalous nor shocking. Her skintight dress and drowsy voice complemented the president's image almost to the point of parody.

The Distinction of Celebrity

Mailer did not explore the relationship between the mythic, dream life of Kennedy's celebrity and the candidate's advertising. The oversight was surprising, for Mailer had long been fascinated with the language of promotion and publicity. In an age when intellectuals saw Madison Avenue as a threat to creative and political life, he gave his 1959 collection of stories, essays, and autobiographical writings the notorious title *Advertisements for Myself*. As Mailer presented it in "Superman Comes to the Supermarket," Kennedy's stardom revealed much about his personal character and the secret yearnings of the American unconscious, but it was not a strategic product of his exceptional campaign. Mailer seemed as stupefied as the Democratic bosses who pondered how their princely candidate could have created such "a jewel of a political machine." "It is as good as a crack Notre Dame team," he explained, "all discipline and savvy and go-go-go." He found evidence of the superiority in everything from the models hired to politick for the candidate to the speed and *élan* of his top lieutenants. If Stevenson's floor demonstration was filled with nostalgia for the 1930s and Johnson's seemed dominated by football players shaking loose their limbs, the Kennedy demonstration was jazzy, fashionable, and filled with Madison Avenue cachet. In Mailer's analysis, however, the quality of Kennedy's campaign had little to do with the erotic mystery he represented to the nation. It was as if the admen and the depth psychologists were headed to the same station on different trains.

Much of this neglect may have come from the fact that Kennedy's tight-knit organization left the broad symbolism to others and focused instead on connecting with members of the party hierarchy. Despite its extensive Hollywood supporters, when it came to endorsements in California, the campaign meticulously tallied the names of county commissioners and labor leaders, making no mention of ball players and movie stars. The Democratic National Committee (DNC) made a similar choice when it put together its Speakers Bureau. The list of potential speakers was composed almost entirely of politicians (e.g., senators Estes Kefauver, Frank Church, and Stuart Symington) and the members of political families (Franklin Delano Roosevelt, Jr., and his mother, Eleanor). There were no stars or celebrities. Rather than Mrs. Babe Ruth professing her ignorance of current events, the DNC offered academics such as Galbraith, Schlesinger, and Williams College political scientist James MacGregor Burns.[65]

The shift in focus was evident in the Democrats' advertising strategy. Despite the many embarrassments of the 1956 presidential race, the party was flooded with agency bids to take its account after the Democrats' liberal wing captured Congress in 1958. The party eventually chose Guild, Bascom, and Bonfigli, a San Francisco agency. One might think that the move from an East to a West Coast agency made for softer, more lifestyle-oriented advertisements, but that was not the case. Guild, Bascom, and Bonfigli promised a technical, scientifically based mode of advertising that included a careful study of demographics. The agency's president, Walter Guild, had headed up the Skippy peanut butter account, but unlike Rosser Reeves, he made sure the press understood that he did not plan to sell his candidate the same way he would sell cereal or cat food. "In selling a highly competitive product like peanut butter, the public is used to a certain amount of—let's say, hyperbole," Guild explained. "That wouldn't be right for a political campaign."[66] His focus would be on providing technical assistance and making sure that the lighting and sound were of high quality. After Kennedy won the nomination, the agency coordinated with local television stations to ensure maximum coverage and determined the appropriate issues-based ads to run in different states. As the election headed into the crucial month of October, Kennedy was filmed at New York's Biltmore Hotel for a series of advertisements targeting voters in Hawaii, Louisiana, Mississippi, Arkansas, Alabama, and Nevada. Humphrey and Kennedy appeared together in two film spots about agricultural policy.[67]

Sensitive to the complaints about salesmanship in the Eisenhower campaigns, Nixon had chosen a different approach that the Democrats easily exploited. Rather than hire one of the Republicans' many outside agencies, he created an in-house advertising team led by Carroll Newton, a BBDO executive who had developed sophisticated audience analysis tools for Eisenhower in 1952 and 1956.[68] Nixon had little respect for his advisers' expertise, however, and he insisted that all decisions about advertising would come through him. "You couldn't talk to him," Newton confessed in an interview with media scholar Kathleen Hall Jamieson. "Nixon wouldn't take advice about what to say or how." Preferring to improvise his own comments in a series of five-minute spots, Nixon spoke directly to the camera in a nondescript office. In the eight years since his "Checkers" speech, he seemed to have forgotten that television was primarily an entertainment medium and that it was especially effective in demonstrating social interaction and ease.[69] The dull and prosaic set of advertisements culminated in Nixon's disastrous appearance in the presidential debates. Come November, he would win his home state of California by less than 37,000 votes.[70]

Kennedy had a similarly complicated relationship with Guild, Bascom, and Bonfigli—not because of any micromanaging but because he preferred Jack Denove, a Hollywood producer who had been the senator's filmmaker during the primaries. Denove was a television veteran who had worked with such stars as Barbara Stanwyck and Bing Crosby when producing *The Christophers Show* and *Cavalcade of America*. Although the party was under contract with Guild's agency, Kennedy insisted that Denove produce most of the television advertisements in the general campaign. The tension led to a confusing, redundant process that left many of the principals unhappy and many of the bills unpaid. Denove's cameras were crucial to the most memorable advertisements of the race—chief among them, Kennedy's discussion of his Catholicism in a speech before the Greater Houston Ministerial Association, a Baptist organization. Kennedy's speech had been carried live in the state of Texas, but the campaign resourcefully turned his spirited argument for religious tolerance into a series of advertisements ranging from a full half-hour program to five- and one-minute spots. It was so successful that the United Auto Workers ordered 100 prints to use in their own advertisements.[71]

From his attractive, wealthy family to his call for a "new frontier," Kennedy brought so much glamour to the election that it was neither necessary nor advisable to surround him with the hoopla of the entertainment industry. At forty-three, he was the youngest man to ever run for president, and among a large portion of the electorate, his age and relative inexperience were cause for some concern. While Young & Rubicam had viewed celebrities as a way to associate vigor and bipartisanship with Ike, Kennedy's advisers cautiously used his well-known supporters to vouch for his character and political loyalties. Harry Belafonte, for example, appeared in several spots for the campaign, including one in which Jack and Jackie visited a Harlem couple to talk about the anti-colonial fervor in Africa and civil rights. The spot presented Belafonte as an emissary to the black community, introducing Kennedy to African Americans (and in the process introducing the white electorate to black American concerns). The advertisement recalled Eddie Fisher's and Nat King Cole's performances during the Ike Day telecast and Marian Anderson's rendition of "God Bless America" during the 1940 radio program "Salute to Roosevelt." The stars signified the candidates' commitment to specific constituencies and voting blocs; they helped acknowledge a broader, more inclusive America than what might conventionally be thought.

Belafonte's appearance, however, represented a significant change from the artists before him, for he did not sing, dance, or in any way perform as he would at the inauguration and the Madison Square Garden birthday party. Wearing a business suit and tie, he looked directly into the camera

FIGURE 8.2 *Singer Harry Belafonte made frequent appearances on behalf of John F. Kennedy. Here the two are joined by Belafonte's wife, Diane Robinson Belafonte, after the Madison Square Garden birthday gala.*
Courtesy of John F. Kennedy Library, ST-A47-7-62.

and framed Kennedy's "unrehearsed, impromptu conversation" with Mr. and Mrs. Boyden. His stardom was part of his ethos, an attribute meant to convince other African Americans that the candidate could be trusted on civil rights. "There are many negroes in America who still do not have the right to vote and many of us who do," Belafonte concluded. "And I think we should use that right. I am voting for Senator Jack Kennedy. How about you?"[72]

While Belafonte's advertisements addressed a specific political group, the campaign used actor Henry Fonda to reach a broader Democratic constituency. Fonda was a longtime friend of Jimmy Stewart's, and like Stewart, he possessed an earnest likeability. The star of such classics as *Young Mr. Lincoln* and *Twelve Angry Men*, he was widely known for playing forceful, resolute idealists committed to the common man—idealists like the character Tom Joad, whom he played in John Ford's 1940 adaptation of John Steinbeck's *The Grapes of Wrath*. If Stewart's Mr. Smith was naïve about the forces of corruption, Fonda's Joad was keenly aware of the world's injustices—a trait that annoyed Hollywood conservatives. "I'll be around in the dark. I'll be everywhere," he pledges in *The Grapes of Wrath*. "Wherever you can look, wherever there's a fight so hungry people can eat, I'll be there. Wherever there's a cop beating up a guy, I'll be there." With the outbreak of World War II, Fonda teamed up with Stewart to raise money for victims of the London bombings. In 1942, just days after he finished filming *The Ox-Bow Incident*, he enlisted in the US Navy and served three years as an intelligence officer in the South Pacific. When he returned, he renewed his friendship with Stewart, while also becoming active in Democratic politics. As Stewart campaigned for Eisenhower, Fonda barnstormed the East Coast, giving speeches for Stevenson that Steinbeck had written.[73]

Fonda's reputation made him a natural choice for an electorate that admired and, in some cases, revered Roosevelt but had reservations about Kennedy. Sitting beneath a portrait of FDR, Fonda described how the courage and endurance Roosevelt had developed as a young man fighting polio had prepared him to lead the country when "it was hurt and stricken, when we all needed courage and endurance." "I know another man like that," Fonda transitioned, "with the same strong character and indomitable will to live." Opening a copy of *Reader's Digest*, he proceeded to summarize the story of PT-109, which the magazine had excerpted from John Hersey's 1944 article in the *New Yorker*. With movie images of warring battleships, Japanese destroyers, and a young seaman swimming his injured crewmate through the water, Fonda dramatically described how Kennedy's determination had saved lives and been a beacon of heroism in the war's darkest moments. After three minutes, he brought the story of PT-109 back to Roosevelt:

Courage. Endurance. Leadership. John F. Kennedy has them all the way. And the way has been the hard way. As president, John F. Kennedy will have the courage to meet the greatest challenge our country has ever faced. He'll have the endurance to do the work, to maintain the patience, to possess the raw nerve we need in a world where our enemies would like to win by wearing us down. And he will give us leadership for the '60s, a new American leadership for the world beyond the seas to honor and respect. FDR, a man who loved the sea. John F. Kennedy, another man of the sea. His hand will be a strong hand on the ship of state.

The conclusion managed to combine a reference to the Kennedy theme song ("All the Way") with the nautical imagery the campaign had been developing since the Los Angeles convention. More importantly, by transforming the polio-stricken Roosevelt into a heroic survivor and fellow "man of the sea," it brought JFK's uniqueness into line with his Democratic heritage.[74]

What made this advertisement so remarkable is the way that it used a celebrity to add gravitas to Kennedy's campaign. Rather than "leaven the loaf" of politics (as Preston Wood had proposed in 1956), Fonda's presence gave Kennedy the aura of wisdom and authenticity. The movie star reminded voters that for all his charisma and photogenic appeal, Kennedy was a battle-tested hero and the political heir to the most beloved president the party had ever elected. To the image of that glamorous young couple sailing off the coast of Massachusetts, Americans could now add a determined lieutenant braving the South Seas.

As counterintuitive as it may seem, the campaign turned to celebrities in the final weeks both to demystify and to elevate the candidate and his family. Actress Myrna Loy appeared in a four-minute spot in which she presented excerpts from a prerecorded interview with Mrs. Kennedy. With three-year-old Caroline seated next to her, Jackie answered questions about raising children, her pregnancy, and the satisfactions of being a political wife. "Every woman wants to feel needed, and in politics you are," she explained. Addressing the audience, Loy responded, "Isn't she charming?" Another spot presented Jackie meeting with Dr. Benjamin Spock in the Kennedys' Washington home. While Jackie's stilted questions betrayed her discomfort with the medium, Spock seemed thrilled to be on television with the future First Lady. The four-minute commercial gave him the opportunity to explain Kennedy's commitment to education and medical care for the aged, while also addressing common misconceptions about the funding for his legislative proposals.[75]

The advertisements tempered the glamour with domestic and political talk. Perhaps because she herself was so awkward on screen, Jackie thought these celebrity appearances were important to the campaign. Although they had been sidelined for much of the race, Guild, Bascom, and Bonfigli produced a thirty-minute commercial with Fonda that appeared on November 2 on CBS. The program evolved as an informal conversation between Fonda in New York, Jackie in Washington, and later, Jack in California. Directed at women voters, it began with Jackie's sharing family photographs and home movies and ended with her husband responding to the issues she told him most concerned American women. The agency had given Fonda a minimal role: he emceed the production, asked questions about the photographs, and chatted politely about the campaign.[76] And yet, Jackie credited the actor with bringing the program a unique sense of respectability. As she later wrote him, "I feel so strongly that your participation gave it the distinction it so badly needed—it could have been a corny amateurish home-movie sort of thing where we could have looked like fools, and given people something like Checkers to laugh about—."[77]

It is surprising that Jackie would express such fears, for she hardly needed the company of entertainers to bring eminence to her public activities. In many ways, Jackie Kennedy was the most significant endorsement of the 1960 presidential race, as she learned to use the "media halo" that seemed to float above her.[78] No matter how different her life was from that of average Americans, the public identified with (and often copied) the young Mrs. Kennedy. To use a neologism that came into vogue in the 1960s, she worked hard to be *relatable*.[79] She often greeted ethnic audiences in their native tongue, speaking a few words in Polish or filming a commercial in Spanish to reach out to different constituencies. On television, she described the relief she felt in learning that, like her daughter Caroline, other people's children misbehaved. Such gestures are typically the stuff of political pandering, but with Jackie, they came off as sincere and endearing.

Jackie was especially valuable in suggesting to voters that her husband was no longer the wealthy young playboy they had read about in news and gossip magazines. Kennedy had cultivated his reputation as a philanderer, and he delayed announcing the couple's engagement in June 1953 until after the *Saturday Evening Post* had published a profile about him titled "The Senate's Gay Young Bachelor."[80] The transformation of JFK into a family man began just one month later, when his father arranged the *Life* cover story about his relationship with Jackie. As if there were uncertainty about this identity shift, the magazine had titled the piece "Senator Kennedy Goes A-Courtin'," though officially the impending nuptials had ended his courting days. Jackie's refinement and sophistication helped create a more acceptable narrative than the ones that circulated about Las Vegas, Hollywood, and the various socialites eager to go "all the way." If only in appearance, she helped tame and domesticate her husband's ribald sexuality, channeling it into the image of a vibrant and fertile monogamy. In the sublimated world of American publicity, the "heir to the psychic loins" could become a devoted husband and father, a man whose frequently pregnant wife liked to read Dr. Spock's baby and childcare book.

Limited though they were, the Jackie Kennedy spots heralded what would happen to celebrity politics over the next decade. She bridged the likeable, consensus-building entertainers who assembled around Ike and the irrepressibly partisan stars who dominated campaigns in the late 1960s and early '70s. Eisenhower's Madison Avenue advisers had created spectacles that elevated personality and good feelings over actual discussions of policy. Kennedy's advisers asked Jackie to turn her Washington home into a televised salon, a place where the public might hear Democratic proposals and concerns. More than Jimmy Stewart, Irene Dunne, and Mamie Eisenhower, Jackie and her husband's famous supporters spoke about real issues: there was a shortage of teachers and schools; women had to sacrifice their children's education in order to pay their aging parents' medical bills; peace was of vital importance, and yet disarmament negotiations had failed. There is no doubt that, like Hayes, Stewart, and Dunne, Jackie was meant to soften the presidential campaign, but within the narrow frame afforded her, there was new space for political opinions and ideas. In 1956, BBDO had celebrated the First Lady's birthday with dance and music, treating her admirers across the nation to fluffy afternoon entertainment. In giving Mrs. Kennedy a forum for public discussion, Guild, Bascom, and Bonfigli had suggested that glamour, style, and fame could be both persuasive and instructive.

Even as it augured a world in which celebrities would become more politically outspoken and divisive, the Kennedy campaign effortlessly expanded on Eisenhower's recognition that politicians also had to be performers. Eisenhower had tackled the demands of the televised presidency with a soldier's perseverance; while his 1952 commercials for Rosser Reeves were wooden and constrained, by 1956 he had learned to use the medium to convey the force of his personality.[81] With the persistent help of Robert Montgomery, he projected the aura of an experienced father amiably presiding over a nation of living rooms. Four years later, Kennedy offered a new presidential identity. He was "wise to the game," an actor who accepted his role with cool detachment. Kennedy's comfort with the performative demands of political life impressed the people around him. "He appeared to be beautifully on to himself," Gore Vidal later wrote. As president, he "seemed always to be standing at a certain remove from himself, watching himself with amusement at his own performance." If Eisenhower practiced a kind of paternal congeniality, Kennedy, as Vidal put it, "was an ironist in a profession where the prize usually goes to the cornball."[82] It was the ironist who greeted the Madison Square Garden audience in 1962, the connoisseur of desire who had watched Monroe's mass seduction and then appeared on stage clever, amused, and unfazed.

Kennedy's ability to distance himself from public performance, to see it as a game, made him an alluring politician for the television age, but it also raised a significant problem for the next decades. Voters expected more out

of presidential candidates. They still looked for good government and ideological compatibility, but they also wanted the pleasure of entertainment
and the satisfaction of choosing new political personalities. First awakened
during the Eisenhower years, these desires became increasingly stylized,
and by 1968, even Nixon was striving to meet the demand. Before long,
the idea that politics was a series of calculated, even cynical, performances
had moved into the culture at large. "Politics is just like show business,"
Ronald Reagan told his gubernatorial staff in California. "You have a hell
of an opening, coast for a while, and then have a hell of a close."[83] In 1995,
John F. Kennedy, Jr., premised his glossy magazine *George* on the idea that
politics was a glamorous lifestyle to be coveted and displayed. "Much of
politics, like the movies, is about star power," he gratuitously explained in
the inaugural issue.[84] By then, the merger of celebrity and politics was so
commonplace that few recalled how much of it came from teams of advertising executives discussing how to sell their reluctant candidate.

{ Conclusion }

THE GLAMOUR REPUBLIC

Television glamorized politics in the middle of the twentieth century, revolutionizing the way that politicians and their advisers thought about campaigns. Broadway and Hollywood stars had obviously ventured into politics before the 1950s, but with the rise of television and the rapid expansion of advertising, glamour became a fixture in American political life. Politicians and entertainers did not just recognize their symbiotic relationship; they increasingly saw (and occasionally protested) the ways in which their professions overlapped. Emboldened by the changing media environment, advertising and media experts sought new ways to mix politics and entertainment, focusing not just on drawing crowds but on broadcasting appealing images and personalities. They speculated how stars might attract different segments of the electorate and how politicians might learn to project amiable, stylized versions of themselves. The change was so comprehensive that political glamour became the subject of public debate, an issue observed, analyzed, and parodied by politicians, journalists, academics, novelists, filmmakers, and Broadway lyricists. In 1950, Irving Berlin's *Call Me Madam* praised Ike for being "good on a mike." By 1956, Johnny Mercer would mock the president's television training in another musical, *Li'l Abner*. "My friends say I could run for any office I seek," the character General Bullmoose laments. "But first I'd have to brush up on my TV technique / I plan to get in touch with Bob Montgomery next week. / Bring back the good old days!"[1]

From Robert Taft to Adlai Stevenson, Eisenhower's opponents charged him with being a glamour candidate. Although it ignored his many accomplishments, the label loosely came to fit the most dominant political figure of the age. With friends in publishing, television, and advertising, Eisenhower arguably remains the most media-connected public servant in the history of the United States. His well-known resistance to politicians and electioneering, his insistence that he would "recognize a 'duty' " without seeking the presidency himself, paradoxically contributed to the profusion of spectacle and celebrity in his campaigns. Stationed in Europe as the Draft Eisenhower movements got underway, he allowed advertising and media executives to fashion his public relations strategies, and they eagerly adapted the promotional methods that had made them successful in the marketplace. Ike's absence added to the glamorous feel of his campaign, for, with no candidate on the program, the movement counted on a steady stream of famous personalities to appear at major events. By the time Eisenhower returned from Paris in June 1952, the campaign's tone and tenor were already in place.

Ironically, Eisenhower had minimal interest in celebrities and deep reservations about the entertainment industry. The general who warned Americans against the military-industrial complex also had strong feelings about Hollywood's values and priorities. We can see these concerns in Eisenhower's lengthy response to a 1953 bill to repeal the sales tax on movie tickets. As part of a comprehensive effort to manage wartime deficits, Congress had instituted a 10 percent federal excise tax in 1919 and then doubled it during World War II. The law taxed a wide range of businesses (from furriers, to jewelers, to whiskey makers), but Hollywood and the nation's theater owners felt particularly hard hit. By 1953, the Council of Motion Picture Organizations was blaming the tax for declining movie attendance and the serious financial crisis that ensued. Over six years, it argued, profits across the industry had fallen from $201 million to $25 million. Five thousand theaters had closed, and another 5,000 would follow if relief did not come soon. In a massive lobbying effort, the Council urged lawmakers to exempt movie theaters—and movie theaters alone—from the admissions tax, even though it would cost the government over $100 million in annual revenue. Afraid of the specter of "a bankrupt and paralyzed disaster," Congress overwhelmingly voted to support the bill just days before its August recess.[2]

Writing in the privacy of his diary, the president unleashed what he called "a tirade" about the theater owners' request. Ike described the excise taxes as "onerous," "heavy," and "positively stupid," but he also thought that Hollywood's problems largely stemmed from mismanagement and the competition from television. "The movies ran the old-fashioned vaudeville practically off the stage," he recalled. "They enjoyed for many years practically a monopoly in popular indoor entertainment. Both the legitimate theater, and the opera and the concert companies were hard put to it to stay in business." As Eisenhower described the problem, the motion picture industry wanted government protection from television after years of scant competition, huge profits, and lavish expenditures. "If a citizen has to be bored to death," he seethed, "it is cheaper and more comfortable to sit at home and look at television than it is to go outside and pay a dollar for a ticket." He pocket-vetoed the bill and called for a broader range of tax reforms the next year.[3]

Extending to almost 1,500 words, the diary entry criticized Hollywood for being selfish and insular. Eisenhower noted that the nation's steelmakers also wanted tax relief, but they recognized that the administration could not "favor one group in the country at the expense of another." Presenting his industry as part of the solution, the chairman of US Steel had suggested that the government prolong the taxes for another six months until it developed a more comprehensive and equitable system. ("There is no future prosperity for any except as the whole shall prosper," Ike commented.) Without regard for other segments of the economy, the film and theater executives came to the White House demanding nothing short of a complete repeal. Their basic unfairness and lack of perspective turned him off.

Eisenhower's annoyance went well beyond the tax question, however. In a remarkable passage, he criticized the industry's manufacture of glamour and celebrity:

> It is true that the motion picture industry has gone through a very hard time because of the competition of television, as well as other influences. Nevertheless, the American public is still keenly aware of the fact that much of the cost of motion pictures has gone into extravagant and almost senseless competition, and the salaries of the so-called "stars" whose qualifications were normally nothing more (in the case of the women) than platinum hair and shapely legs, or men with good profiles and vibrating voices.

> I have personally met a number of these people. Those with whom it is a pleasure to talk informally constitute a very small portion of the whole. I think one out of ten would be an exaggeration. Yet these people have been reported constantly in the public prints as having incomes of half a million a year, or at least in the hundreds of thousands; fabulous salaries of directors, producers, and so on have likewise been publicized.

Eisenhower was troubled by Hollywood's "salary binges" for celebrities who possessed neither talent nor even conversational interest. More importantly, he saw their superficial attractions as embodying misplaced cultural values. The publicity the studios generated for their leading directors and stars had made extravagance part of the show. For a government still recovering from economic depression and two world wars, the lack of perspective was more than misguided: it lacked even the veneer of public spiritedness.

Figures such as Ronald Reagan and Al Jolson believed that performers were "in more intimate touch with the people than any other profession," that they inhabited a particularly meaningful category of democratic citizenship.[4] Eisenhower saw the situation differently. Celebrities might enhance a candidate's profile or attract public attention, but outside a well-defined public relations strategy, they had limited political value. It is no accident that among the handful of stars whose company he enjoyed, Ike particularly respected George Murphy, who was director of public relations for MGM and the chairman of the California State Republican Party. Murphy's background and character gave him a legitimacy that other stars did not possess, and on several occasions, Ike encouraged advisers to recruit the actor for a position on the White House staff.[5] Eisenhower had more ambivalent feelings about Robert Montgomery. Although he depended on Montgomery's television expertise, he made a point of not involving him in policy decisions and, fearing a backlash, ultimately did not support his 1958 request for a paid position with the Federal Communications Commission (FCC).[6] This does not mean that Ike relegated Montgomery to the television studio, only that he saw him in terms of communications and publicity. The president sent Montgomery, in his official role as White House consultant, to address the 1954 conference of the Public Relations Society of America, where he conveyed the administration's belief that the industry would play an important role in defeating Soviet communism.[7] The appearance went so well that the organizers expected Eisenhower himself to deliver the keynote address the next year. When his heart attack prevented the president from attending, the Society replaced him with another prominent Republican, director Cecil B. DeMille.[8]

The substitution said a lot about the breezy relations between Madison Avenue, the Eisenhower administration, and the show business community. Although he disdained celebrity excess, the president happily sought advice about how to sell and promote his policies, and from Ben Duffy to Darryl Zanuck, executives welcomed the distinction of being asked for help. (The PR industry was as eager to align itself with Eisenhower as Hollywood had been with Roosevelt. Amid a slew of articles about the 1956 election, the *Public Relations Journal* featured a long story touting the White House's public relations team.)[9] Whether they came from Broadway, Hollywood, television, or the sports page, the famous could persuade audiences through spectacle and image rather than ideology. By depoliticizing conservatives such as Irene Dunne and Jimmy Stewart, by softening their advocacy for specific policies, Madison Avenue expected to increase their effectiveness in reaching the middle of the electorate.

These events, of course, did not overrun traditional politicking, but as a calculated addition to Eisenhower's campaigns, celebrities formed the heart of what the writer George Trow memorably described as "the context of no context." Like television, their presence momentarily stripped the candidates of history, politics, and ideology and promoted them instead within the frame of glamour and personality.[10] In this Madison Avenue version of democracy, celebrity endorsements cleverly identified the illusion of consensus with commercial publicity. Over time, the star-studded Eisenhower moments developed the look and feel of a Golden Age musical comedy. There was Ethel Merman dancing with Fred Waring around the Madison Square Garden boxing ring in 1952. There were the dancers at Mamie's 1956 televised birthday party, their dresses and parasols streaming in and out of the picture to the backdrop of romantic music. And there was Kathryn Grayson trading verses with Howard Keel on a soundstage facsimile of the Eisenhower family living room. To borrow from film critic Richard Dyer's analysis of Hollywood musicals, the Eisenhower campaign created an image of utopia that was more felt than organized, one that dissolved debate in the overwhelming force of capital and entertainment.[11]

As the 1950s wore on, several factors made it difficult to contain celebrity politics within the realm of public relations and advertising. Perhaps most importantly, television vastly increased the number and visibility of celebrities in American society. Although movie executives complained of shrinking profits, television had created an unprecedented platform for publicity—not just for actors and actresses, but for a new generation of cultural personalities. Novelists, musicians, singers, comedians, journalists, academics, cartoonists, politicians, religious leaders, and athletes appeared on network TV, their faces and mannerisms broadcast—and subsequently recognized—across the country. Television's capacity to create and disseminate stardom was so powerful that other forms of media such as magazines quickly adapted to cover the interests and tastes that the new medium had stimulated.[12] Drawn from

FIGURE 9.1 *Jules Alberti, president of Endorsements, Inc., with George Murphy, Helen Hayes, and Mervyn LeRoy as they announced their support for Richard Nixon in August 1960. Days later, conservative George Sokolsky would denounce celebrity politics in his nationally syndicated column.*

Courtesy of National Archives Center, A10-024-74-14-2.

widely diverse fields, this new generation of celebrities was increasingly free of the studio structures that jealously guarded their reputations. By the decade's end, celebrities had become a ubiquitous national presence, more open about their opinions and attracting the attention of multiple media outlets.

To veteran cold warrior George Sokolsky, this new visibility was cause for alarm. Sokolsky had disliked the infusion of celebrity into Eisenhower's 1952 campaign, claiming it was a threat not only to stalwarts like Robert Taft but also to the dignity of the political process. Working with BBDO, the American Legion, and CBS, he had monitored the radio and television blacklist through 1956, deciding the fates of performers who wanted to return to work.[13] Not surprisingly, Sokolsky was appalled by the openness of the 1960 presidential election. When stars such as Murphy and Frank Sinatra took prominent roles in the Nixon and Kennedy campaigns, Sokolsky compared them to socialites and caustically dismissed them as coming from "the land of make believe." "What is a celebrity?" he repeatedly asked in his syndicated column, as if the emergence of these Hollywood politicos had disrupted his sense of the term.[14]

As they became more visible, the consensus prudently crafted by Young & Rubicam and McCann-Erickson gave way to the candor of both right- and left-wing celebrities who saw themselves in the vanguard of political change. In 1960, Reagan presented himself as a crossover Democrat supporting the Richard Nixon–Henry Cabot Lodge ticket, but by 1964, he was a revolutionary Republican campaigning for Barry Goldwater and warning his audiences that he spoke of "controversial things."[15] Veterans of the Kennedy campaign Harry Belafonte, Charlton Heston, and Diahann Carroll joined the civil rights movement and in 1963 marched on Washington with Martin Luther King, Jr. Though Belafonte promised they would create a festive atmosphere, the stars aggressively challenged the status quo. When an official from the US Information Agency reminded him that such marches did not occur in Moscow or Peking, Belafonte disputed his self-congratulatory tone. "It is long since past the time when we can measure our own sense of conscience and our own morality based on what some decayed society refuses to give their own."[16] The activism shifted from corporate image-making and the polite "distinction" that Jackie Kennedy valued in Henry Fonda's political work. No longer limited to merchandising candidates, celebrities could publicize cultural conflict and dissent. Having retired from public life, even Robert Montgomery condemned advertising's capacity to create "phony" political attitudes and impressions.[17]

By 1968, so many celebrities were working in the Democratic and Republican primaries that *Life* magazine published a lengthy story on the topic.[18] Assembling photographs and quotations from over fifteen entertainers, the magazine focused on the dueling Democratic campaigns of New York's Robert Kennedy and Minnesota's Eugene McCarthy. Lacking both funds and name recognition, McCarthy gave stars a critical role in reaching out to young voters. In a throwback to the Franklin Roosevelt caravan shows,

FIGURE 9.2 *James Baldwin and Marlon Brando at the March on Washington on August 28, 1963.*

Courtesy of National Archives Center, 306-SSM-4D-99-10.

Paul Newman was one of numerous actors who traveled to college campuses to explain the candidate's opposition to the Vietnam War. (The appeal of celebrity led *Life*'s editors to put Newman on the cover rather than an image from its lead story on the student takeover at Columbia University.) To raise money, other entertainers established temporary nightclubs in Manhattan, East Hampton, and Los Angeles in which guests could see the likes of Hal Holbrook, Alan Alda, and Elaine May perform.[19] The association of celebrities with fundraising carried over to the general election when Frank Sinatra appeared in a TV spot asking viewers to donate money to the Democratic ticket of Hubert Humphrey and Edmund Muskie.[20]

From the advertising experts at Young & Rubicam to the organizers of Ike Day, Eisenhower's advisers wanted to match his celebrity supporters with a grassroots concern for volunteerism and the "little people." In the eyes of their organizers, these star-inflected programs had a familiar, populist appeal that would help the candidates appear accessible, down-to-earth, and ordinary. Although the tone had changed considerably, Nixon and Humphrey both returned to this strategy in a set of telethons broadcast on Election Eve. Newman joined Danny Thomas in emceeing a show on ABC in which several dozen celebrities (including actress Joanne Woodward, comedian Bill Cosby, and actor Burt Lancaster) answered phone calls from viewers who had questions for the candidates. In a typical exchange, singer Nancy Sinatra

FIGURE 9.3 *Marching for civil rights, Sidney Poitier, Harry Belafonte, and Charlton Heston at the Lincoln Memorial on August 28, 1963.*

Courtesy of National Archives Center, 306-SSM-4D-99-22.

summoned Humphrey to her desk and relayed a question about tax relief from a Mr. Stan Green in Florida. As Humphrey responded, the star nodded enthusiastically as if she were an intermediary between the people and the candidate.[21]

The Republicans revisited a format they had successfully used earlier in the campaign, in which Bud Wilkinson, a former University of Oklahoma football coach, moderated questions from a panel of community members.[22] Broadcast on NBC, the Election Eve telethon began with a prerecorded message from comedian Jackie Gleason and then transitioned to a studio where about fifty young women answered viewers' calls. Vetted and perhaps rewritten off set, the questions were then carried to Wilkinson, who sat downstage in conversation with Nixon.[23] Designed to protect him from the unpredictability of a live call, the format showcased the Republican's earnest interaction with the coach, a proxy for the white male voters he needed to attract. Though his advisers complained (as they had for months) about Wilkinson's wooden delivery, the filtering mechanisms worked, and Nixon credited the show with his victory.[24]

The remaking of Nixon into a glossy, media-friendly candidate was the subject of great interest in a country that had changed dramatically since his 1960 loss to John Kennedy. In his classic book *The Selling of the President, 1968*, journalist Joe McGinniss offered an insider's account of the campaign's efforts to glamorize Nixon with a supporting cast of television producers, consultants, and admen. Nixon had little affinity for the big Madison Avenue agencies, and, having been shut out of Eisenhower's meetings about the 1952 and 1956 campaigns, he had little respect for their expertise.[25] In 1968, he put together his own advertising team, which included Harry Treleaven, an executive on leave from the J. Walter Thompson Agency; Frank Shakespeare, an eighteen-year veteran of CBS; and Roger Ailes, a young television producer who would go on to become the chairman and CEO of Fox News. Sixteen years after Rosser Reeves compared politicians to toothpaste, Treleaven shared the insights he had gathered from running George H. W. Bush's 1966 congressional race: "Political candidates are celebrities, and today with television taking them into everybody's home right along with Johnny Carson and Batman, they're more of a public attraction than ever."[26] Offered without apology or fanfare, the statement pervaded the team's yearlong effort to give Nixon the movie star "aura" of a JFK.[27]

As improbable as it may seem, selling Nixon as a vibrant, charismatic leader fit the campaign's goal of appealing to the decade's burgeoning youth culture. Rather than pledge a return to the comfort of Eisenhower's America, Nixon and his advisers tapped into Madison Avenue's growing emphasis on vigor and change. Journalist Thomas Frank has argued that, during the 1960s, the advertising industry worked to infuse commerce with a "countercultural" spirit. Led by new boutique agencies, the industry helped create a world of "hip consumerism" in which the purchase of commodities became identified with asserting one's independence from the mainstream. From whiskey and lipstick to soda, air conditioners, and automobiles, "products existed to facilitate our rebellion against the soul-deadening world of products, to put us in touch with our authentic selves, to distinguish us from the mass-produced herd."[28] "'Youth,'" Frank writes, "was a sort of consumer fantasy that admen would make available to older Americans."[29] For all their emphasis on law, order, and traditional Republican values, Nixon's advisers adapted this theme as a way of attracting the middle-aged. From the earliest days of the Republican primary, his advisers obsessed about the candidate's need to appear active, energetic, new, and *with it*. "To be self-satisfied is to be old," one adviser wrote. "Searching is a posture of youth. Youth moves."[30]

Although Nixon's advisers associated this spirit with the Kennedys, the grandfatherly Ike helped lay the foundation for the pervasive student culture of the 1960s. In 1954, Eisenhower called for a constitutional amendment reducing the voting age to eighteen because he recognized that the burden of America's wars fell disproportionately upon its youth.[31] Though many of them could not vote, his campaigns regularly identified young people as an important constituency. Raised on television, they responded well to advertising, popular culture, and celebrity, and as McCann-Erickson and the RNC discovered, they were happy to sponsor campaign activities that conveyed their admiration for Eisenhower. The Ike Day telecast on CBS returned to the Statler Hotel gala not just to showcase Eddie Fisher, Fred Waring, and Helen Hayes, but also to share the exuberance that the College Republicans brought to the campaign. When Young & Rubicam closed out the presidential race with another coast-to-coast program, the producers featured boisterous students cheering for the president at a University of Pennsylvania bonfire rally. The broadcasts complemented the campaign in foregrounding college and even high school campuses as potent sites for the display of political feeling.[32]

What JFK added to Eisenhower's appeal to young people was a sense of possibility, and as the postwar Baby Boomers transitioned into adolescence and adulthood, their reverence evolved into aspiration and fantasy. In 1960, Norman Mailer associated the glamour of Kennedy's campaign with the drive toward self-realization that he identified at the heart of the American dream. Kennedy made youthfulness erotic and hip, turning it into a heroic desire to embrace the unconscious and outstrip conventional modes of being. We can debate whether Kennedy actually embodied those qualities, but the values Mailer saw in the candidate spread profusely across the decade. Searching became the "posture of youth," as Nixon's adviser explained, and advertisers soon followed with an attractive commercial myth that stylized the quest for authenticity as a demographic rather than a personal desire. By the time she addressed her graduating class in 1969, a former president of Wellesley College's Young Republicans Club described her generation in strikingly similar terms: "We are, all of us, exploring a world that none of us understands and attempting to create within that uncertainty." As if Mailer had been part of the curriculum, she added, "We're searching for more immediate, ecstatic and penetrating modes of living." Americans would come to know that young woman as Hillary Rodham Clinton.[33]

Treleaven hoped that a series of powerful endorsements would give Nixon a fresh, contemporary feel. Like Young & Rubicam's Preston Wood, he concluded that voters looked upon the famous as trusted friends and intimates. "Getting back to building Nixon's acceptability," he wrote in a campaign memo, "we should strongly consider the use of high-level endorsements. The opinion of someone you respect has more meaning than the most soundly constructed argument." The trick, as he explained it, was to get a star's " 'prior approval' factor" to rub off on the notoriously stodgy candidate. "*He* likes him," Treleaven's ideal voter would conclude, "so maybe *I* would (or should)."[34] But while the Democrats could depend on scores of celebrities to advocate for their candidates, Nixon's advisers struggled to get beyond a dozen key supporters, a rather humble list of mostly older celebrities that included singers Connie Francis and Rudy Vallee, comedians Bob Hope and Jackie Gleason, actor John Wayne, and basketball player Wilt Chamberlain.[35] The desire to seem new and up-to-date led Nixon to appear on NBC's popular sketch show *Laugh-In,* where, amid the zany nonsequiturs and double entendres, he delivered the show's trademark punchline, "Sock it to me." Humphrey thought the gag helped Nixon get elected, but nobody was really fooled.[36] Six months into his presidency, *Esquire* winked at the rupture between style and substance; it celebrated the "hep" new Nixon by putting him on the cover with Vallee, orchestra director Lawrence Welk, TV personality Art Linkletter, and evangelist Billy Graham.[37]

Faced with a candidate who had little in common with the prevailing commercial mood, Nixon's advisers found a way to incorporate the energy of youth culture while also maintaining a prudent presidential distance. In a highly touted commercial titled "Youth," the Republican proclaimed his confidence in young people above a swirling rock 'n' roll soundtrack. In a minute's time, the spot flashed some forty photographic stills: a couple dancing in a psychedelic nightclub, a contemplative student sitting on her bed, a group of studious young chemists, a cheerleader, a smiling young man in a baseball cap. "American youth today has its fringes," Nixon explained, "but that's part of the greatness of our country. I have great faith in American youth."[38] Amid this cavalcade of imagery (and directly on the word "fringes"), Nixon's team curiously included a photograph of the Grateful Dead guitarist Jerry Garcia wearing an Uncle Sam hat. It is possible that the campaign had no idea who Garcia was. Containing no identifying details, no T-shirts or guitars that would suggest membership in a rock 'n' roll band, the image could easily have been filed under the stock heading "San Francisco hippie." The mistake, if it was a mistake, produced a comedy worthy of the Merry Pranksters.

It is more likely, however, that Shakespeare and Treleaven recognized Garcia and believed his image would help them adorn the campaign with a few countercultural trappings. The odd juxtaposition cleverly stood the notion of celebrity endorsement on its head. Rather than resist the radical elements of young America, the commercial transformed its heroes into icons of amusing, but benign excess—the implication being that Nixon's nation was big enough to incorporate the fringe in its quest for new energy and creativity. To accomplish this goal, the advertisement elevated the creation of compelling visual effects over an expression of coherent political beliefs. Removing the musician from time and place, it situated him in a world of other televised images. Posters of the original photograph had earned Garcia the nickname "Captain Trips" in his Haight-Ashbury neighborhood; the commercial slickly transformed him into a purveyor of Nixon's trendy youth motif.[39]

In this confusion of categories, the Nixon team bridged the celebrity politics of the 1950s and 1960s with Ronald Reagan and the present age. In some ways Reagan exemplified the themes that came out of Eisenhower's engagement with Madison Avenue. He had taken a long and circuitous path to the Republican Party, and on the way, he became a deep admirer of corporate and executive power. Though an active member of the Hollywood scene (he reportedly spent about $750 a month in nightclubs after separating from his first wife, Jane Wyman, in 1948), he came to value celebrity less as a lavish lifestyle and more as a public relations tool.[40] In broadcasting from the Reagans' home, General Electric promoted the family as a model of aspirant consumption and conventional domesticity. But rather than follow the consensus-building spirit of Ike, Reagan pursued a more partisan path, adopting right-wing language about lowering "confiscatory taxes" and resisting "socialized medicine." In an era when stars like Heston were fighting for civil rights, Reagan was fighting for GE and learning that a touch of glamour went a long way in selling corporate ideas to a broad audience.[41] His ability to convey a partisan platform to an ultimately bipartisan following was a credit to his powers as a performer. "How can a president not be an actor?" he asked a series of skeptical journalists in the 1980s.[42]

Reagan's comfort with merging these two occupations set him far apart from Ike. When Robert Montgomery addressed the Public Relations Society in 1954, he praised the industry's role in combating Soviet propaganda. To send reliable, convincing information overseas, he explained, the nation would need a "merchandising program of the first magnitude." In the administration's corporate parlance, the statement captured Eisenhower's willingness to engage a series of partners—from Hollywood to Madison Avenue—to better sell the product of the United States. In fact, the man Eisenhower twice asked to head the newly formed US Information Agency was Young & Rubicam's Sig Larmon.[43] For the anti-Washington Reagan, however, governing *was* a form of public relations and not especially distinct from performance and advertising. Timothy Raphael has demonstrated that the language of Hollywood permeated Reagan's administration: the president's staff developed "scripts" for his appearances, described meetings with foreign leaders as "scenes," and wrote their issues-oriented memos in the form of "movie treatments."[44] Rather than dodge the questions about show business and television that sometimes vexed Eisenhower's relationship with Montgomery, Reagan embraced his cinematic past, regularly alluding to his film roles and inviting Americans to see the overlap between theatrical and political performance. As the president applied movie lines and scenes to actual circumstances, the border between cinematic and political images blurred.[45] In moving detail, he several times recounted his experience photographing Nazi death camps after Allied troops had liberated them in April 1945. Reporters later discovered, however, that Reagan never left the United States during World War II: he had seen those images on film.[46]

Critics in Eisenhower's time worried that television and fame would produce new forms of demagoguery. By the 1980s, the fears focused not on the next Stalin or Mao but on the media's systemic power. Media scholar Neil Postman concluded that Americans were "amusing themselves to death" and pointed to the glut of images that emotionalized public discourse and blocked critical thought. Political figures, he argued, had "become assimilated into the general television culture as celebrities," and politics had devolved into a form of therapy rooted in symbolism and audience feeling.[47] Though obviously piqued by Reagan's presidency, Postman's concerns reverberate through twenty-first-century discussions about the politics of media fame. "Celebrity is part of the culture of distraction," sociologist Chris Rojek warned in 2001; it deflects "public consciousness away from structural inequality" and the decline of religious meaning.[48] The following year, Todd Gitlin, a prominent cultural critic and sociologist, described how the torrent of media entertainment creates a sideshow democracy built on evanescence and disposable feelings.[49] In the aftermath of the 2008 economic collapse, journalist Chris Hedges cultivated a more conspiratorial tone: "The fantasy of celebrity culture is not designed simply to entertain. It is designed to keep us from fighting back."[50] To summarize this line of thinking, we might look to musician Gil Scott-Heron, whose satire of Reagan's 1980 victory remains equally powerful today: Americans aren't living their lives so much as they are starring in a B-movie.[51]

Eisenhower's Madison Avenue experts turned to celebrities to break the old ideological barriers and gain wider support for their candidate. With its capacity to convey personality and generate feelings of public intimacy, they welcomed television as an opportunity to reinvent the Republican Party and create what seemed to them a more consensus-based political culture. The confidence was both opportunistic and short-lived. Amid discussions about its impact on the 1956 presidential election, film critic Richard Dyer

MacCann predicted that television would eventually intensify partisanship in the United States:

> The essence of drama is conflict. The conflict between parties, of course, is part of the American way of life. It is built-in, indispensable. But TV redoubles and glamorizes the conflict—makes it into something unreal—makes it part of the restless search for dramatic excitement in an increasingly visual age.

At the very moment that voters were tranquilly moving into "the middle of the road," MacCann feared television would lead to a spectacle of disagreement that pulled the nation into ever-more-polarized camps.[52]

Sixty years after the Republicans' musical set pieces, MacCann's prediction seems as prescient as the optimism of Ike's advisers seems naïve. In an era of dueling news channels with their glib put-downs, self-righteous anger, and distorted storylines, television thrives on amplified conflict, though on prominent channels, the winners of that conflict are rarely, if ever, in doubt. Television's ability to commodify disagreement has helped transform Congress from a body of lawmakers into cheerleaders and hecklers committed to thwarting their opponents at all costs. Substituting controversy for debate, it encourages Americans to view the president as a hero or a villain singularly capable of either saving the country or bringing about its collapse. The hyperbole makes for erratic government but dependable TV.

The media climate has made it easy to resurrect the old resentments about activist stars whose wealth and access to publicity appear to give them undue influence over the nation's political and social mores. One can understand the frustration of private citizens who, noting the outsized press attention that celebrity opinions receive, dejectedly conclude that while speech in the United States may be free, it is also terribly unequal. Bitterness about celebrity politics tends to rise and fall with divisions in the electorate, however, and it is never so vitriolic as when the nation is contemplating or engaging in war. Politically active stars may feel especially motivated to speak out during these crises, but the press and political opponents will almost assuredly punish them for their dissent. The actress Helen Gahagan Douglas discovered that this was doubly true for women when Nixon tagged her as being "pink right down to her underwear" during their 1950 US Senate race.[53] The label managed to smear the congresswoman's politics while also presenting her as a scandalously sexual object. Perhaps one reason Helen Hayes does not appear among the list of actresses reviled after advocating peace is that she cast herself as a mother who completely trusted the ultimate in patriarchal figures—a general turned president.

Female celebrities have also had to contend with the effort to trivialize their opinions, to make them seem more frivolous and insubstantial than those of their male counterparts. Oddly enough, Republican media strategist Fred Davis employed a version of this tactic when attacking Democratic presidential candidate Barack Obama in the summer of 2008. As Davis explains it, exasperated by the rapt, enthusiastic crowds that greeted Obama around the world, John McCain's top advisers were willing to do "anything to change the game" after Obama had become an "international media star." In perhaps the most provocative advertisement of the 2008 campaign, Davis responded by comparing Obama to heiress Paris Hilton and singer Britney Spears. "He's the biggest celebrity in the world," a narrator asked as flash bulbs popped and the women's images dissolved into the candidate's, "but is he ready to lead?" Neither woman was known to have strong political views, but as Davis later explained, their reputation for superficiality, for being "blonde bombshell airheads," helped the campaign feminize Obama and sow doubts about his fitness for the presidency. The advertisement received so much attention—and proved to be so effective when followed by a policy statement—that Davis developed an entire series of celebrity-themed commercials for McCain.[54]

Although they were two dramatically different men with unique paths to the presidency, Davis effectively leveled the same charge at Obama that Robert Taft's people had leveled at Ike: they were glamour candidates. Obama's eloquence and ability to inspire young people inevitably recalled his fellow Democrats Adlai Stevenson and John Kennedy, but the comparison to Eisenhower may be more revealing. When Susan Eisenhower endorsed Obama in 2008, she saw something of her grandfather in his political courage, ability to inspire, and willingness to pursue "genuine bipartisan cooperation" in the midst of "angry, noisy extremists." Eisenhower, she explained, had reached the presidency with the help of the "Democrats for Eisenhower" movement, and following "this great tradition of crossover voters," she supported Obama in 2008 and again in 2012.[55] The endorsement reminds us how successfully Obama replicated the same triangle of forces that brought Eisenhower to office: a celebrated, larger-than-life personality, a deep and reciprocal relationship with popular culture, and a fervent bipartisan following. Like Eisenhower, Obama received numerous celebrity endorsements, including one from Oprah Winfrey that, according to one academic study, brought him over 1 million votes in the 2008 Democratic primaries.[56] Like Young & Rubicam and BBDO, the Obama Media Team was exceptionally skilled in using new forms of media. From Internet videos, to social networking sites, to the placement of advertisements in the virtual world of video games, the campaign created an aura of likeability around its candidate.[57] As with Eisenhower sixty years before, Obama's likeability was premised on a uniquely personal story that beckoned a triumphant new chapter in the national story.

Studying Eisenhower and the 1950s can add some useful perspective on the glamorization of politics today. Critics will continue to fret about the role of celebrity activists. Others will lament that around the world, television has turned leaders into actors on the public stage. As playwright Arthur Miller said in 2001, "Whether for good or evil, it is sadly inevitable that all political leadership requires the artifice of theatrical illusion."[58] John McCain may have tried to label Obama a celebrity, but as countless observers pointed out, in addition to the customary news programs, he himself was known for his appearances on the television shows *24* and *Saturday Night Live* and in the movie *The Wedding Crashers*. Nearly a hundred years after Warren Harding greeted Al Jolson and his Broadway contingent during the Front Porch campaign, it is unrealistic, and perhaps even simpleminded, to expect the alliance between politicians and actors to go away.

At the same time, our public life seems increasingly reliant on celebrity. Celebrities are no longer just heroes, entertainers, role models, sex symbols, sources of gossip, and democratic royalty. They bring issues and concerns into public consciousness and provide us with satirical versions of the news on late night TV. They are walking publicity machines who command immediate notice and visibility. Recognizing their promotional value, some stars travel the world, bringing attention to an array of exigencies, from human trafficking, to debt relief, to the cessation of armed conflicts. This work differs from recording a consciousness-raising protest song or starring in a revelatory film. The political act lies not in the stars' creation of art but in the civic use of celebrity and the skillful wielding of publicity for the causes in which they believe.

There is no doubt that such acts are often noble and humanitarian, and they can bring much-needed help. But if previous generations worried about politics as salesmanship and branding, it is reasonable to ask whether our public life will become so enmeshed in spectacle that someday we will have difficulty attending to issues and ideas that do not come to us through the unblinking eye of fame. We have largely acclimated to a media landscape that distracts us from seeing the world clearly. To what extent will we eventually depend on advertising and celebrity to show us what is valuable, meaningful, ethical, unifying, and, simply, worth seeing? As we look deeper into our own century, we might remember Eisenhower's skepticism about the changes made in his name.

{ ABBREVIATIONS }

DUL   Duke University Libraries
DDEL   Dwight David Eisenhower Presidential Library
FDRL   Franklin D. Roosevelt Presidential Library
JFKL   John F. Kennedy Presidential Library
PUL   Princeton University Library
RAC   Rockefeller Archive Center
RUL   Rutgers University Libraries
WHS   Wisconsin Historical Society

{ NOTES }

Preface

1. "President's Left Eye Inflamed by Confetti," *New York Times*, September 20, 1956, 10. Online. Accessed January 25, 2016.

2. Eisenhower's attending cardiologist originally supplied this detail, thinking that physicians around the country would be relieved to know that the stroke had not hindered a basic bodily function. About the incident and Eisenhower's response, see Robert E. Gilbert, *The Mortal Presidency: Illness and Anguish in the White House* (New York: Fordham University Press, 1998), 92.

3. Dwight David Eisenhower, *Mandate for Change, 1953–1956* (Garden City, NY: Doubleday, 1963), 45.

Introduction

1. Mission Statement, Dwight D. Eisenhower Memorial Commission. Available at http://www.eisenhowermemorial.org/#/commission/mission. Accessed November 12, 2013.

2. U.S. Congress, House of Representatives, Hearings Before the Subcommittee on National Parks, Forests and Public Lands of the Committee on Natural Resources, *The Proposed Dwight D. Eisenhower Memorial*, 112th Cong., 2nd sess., March 20, 2012. Available at http://www.gpo.gov/fdsys/pkg/CHRG-112hhrg73488/pdf/CHRG-112hhrg73488.pdf. Accessed April 25, 2014.

3. As if representing the Eisenhower presidency were an impossibly difficult task, the composition of this sculpture has changed many times. In March 2010, Gehry proposed an image of Eisenhower as an elder statesman with his hand on the globe; by October 13, 2010, the image had become the president signing the 1957 Civil Rights Act. On July 9, 2015, the National Capital Planning Commission approved the symbolic image of Eisenhower balancing military and civilian life. The image of the young man sitting on the stone ledge has also gone through several iterations as well, including one in which Eisenhower was depicted as a West Point cadet.

4. Eisenhower was honored with an Emmy "For His Distinguished Use and Encouragement of the Television Medium." Not only did Eisenhower make frequent use of television, the Academy of Television Arts and Sciences explained, but he encouraged his Cabinet and Congress to adapt to the new medium. The award came in 1956 but recognized his achievements for the previous season. See Pam Parry, Eisenhower: *The Public Relations President* (Lanham, MD: Lexington, 2014), 2–3.

5. "Let's Keep It Dignified," *New York Journal-American*, February 23, 1952. Henry Cabot Lodge Papers, Scrapbooks from Eisenhower Campaign, vol. 2, Carton 61. Massachusetts Historical Society.

6. Neal Gabler, "Toward a New Definition of Celebrity," 4. The Norman Lear Center, USC–Annenberg. Available at http://learcenter.org/pdf/Gabler.pdf. Accessed October 10, 2010.

7. Barack Obama, "Remarks at a Memorial Service for Walter L. Cronkite in New York City," September 9, 2009. Online by Gerhard Peters and John T. Woolley, The American Presidency Project. Available at http://www.presidency.ucsb.edu/ws/?pid=86597. Accessed January 30, 2014. For a similar perspective, see Al Gore, The Assault on Reason (New York: Penguin, 2007), 2–6.

8. See, for example, Ken Auletta, "Non-Stop News: With Cable, the Web, and Tweets, Can the President—or the Press—Still Control the Story?" *New Yorker*, January 10, 2010. Available at http://www.newyorker.com/magazine/2010/01/25/non-stop-news. Accessed July 21, 2015.

9. Chris Hedges, *Empire of Illusion: The End of Literacy and the Triumph of Spectacle* (New York: Nation Books, 2010), 47, 49.

10. "Election of 1952" and "Election of 1956." Online by Gerhard Peters and John T. Woolley. The American Presidency Project. Available at http://www.presidency.ucsb.edu/showelection.php?year=1956. Accessed January 30, 2014.

11. The phrase comes from Adlai Stevenson's "Address Accepting the Presidential Nomination at the Democratic National Convention in Chicago," July 26, 1952. Online by Gerhard Peters and John T. Woolley, The American Presidency Project. Available at http://www.presidency.ucsb.edu/ws/?pid=75173. Accessed August 3, 2014.

12. "Television." American Women, American Memory, The Library of Congress. Available at http://memory.loc.gov/ammem/awhhtml/awmi10/television.html. Accessed July 21, 2015.

13. On Kefauver's organized crime hearings, see Greg Lisby, "Early Television on Public Watch: Kefauver and His Crime Investigation," *Journalism Quarterly*, 62:2 (Summer 1985), 236–42. Commentators noted that Senator Kefauver became an overnight celebrity during the fifteen-day hearing, going on to appear on the cover of *Time* magazine and a television game show. More disturbing to journalist Alan Barth was the way that "each day's curtain came down with a promise of fresh sensations in the next installment," as if the proceedings were pegged to a daily television schedule (Lisby, op. cit., 240). New York governor Thomas Dewey had mixed feelings about the hearings. Comparing television to an X-ray machine, he argued that it was useful in helping the public assess the qualities of political candidates. On the other hand, he thought the klieg lights and spectacle of the hearings were too reminiscent of the Soviet Union and showed little respect for the dignity of individuals. See Jack Gould, "Political Leaders Acclaim TV But Warn Against Its Misuse," *New York Times*, June 25, 1951, 27. Accessed July 20, 2015.

14. Jack Gould, "What TV Is Doing to Us: A Survey of the Effects of Television on American Life," *New York Times*, June 24–June 30, 1954. Individual articles about the effects of television, politics, sports, radio, reading comprehension, education, and cultural knowledge can be accessed online.

15. Charles A. H. Thomson, *Television and Presidential Politics: The Experience in 1952 and the Problems Ahead* (Washington, DC: Brookings Institute, 1956); Charles A. H. Thomson and Frances M. Shattuck, *The 1956 Presidential Campaign* (Washington, DC: Brookings Institute, 1960).

16. Richard Dyer MacCann, "Viewing with Alarm—on TV," *Christian Science Monitor*, November 5, 1956, 16. ProQuest Historical Newspapers. Electronic Database. Accessed January 9, 2008.

17. Senator John F. Kennedy, "Television as I See It: A Force That Has Changed the Political Scene." *TV Guide*, November 14–20, 1959. As reproduced by the Museum of Broadcast Communications. Available at http://www.museum.tv/debateweb/html/equalizer/print/tvguide_jfkforce.htm. Accessed October 12, 2015.

18. Lizabeth Cohen, *A Consumer's Republic: The Politics of Mass Consumption in Postwar America* (New York: Vintage, 2003), 302.

19. Gail Collins, *Scorpion Tongues: The Irresistible History of Gossip in American Politics* (New York: Harcourt Brace, 1999), 157.

20. See Virginia Postrel, *The Power of Glamour: Longing and the Art of Visual Persuasion* (New York: Simon and Schuster, 2013), 6, 172.

21. On the responses to Presley's appearance on *The Milton Berle Show*, see Peter Guarlinick, *Last Train to Memphis: The Rise of Elvis Presley* (Boston: Back Bay Books, 1995), 184.

22. On *The Ed Sullivan Show* lineup, see http://www.tv.com/the-ed-sullivan-show/elvis-presley-2nd-appearance---senior-wences---joyce-grenfell/episode/106974/summary.html. Accessed July 20, 2015.

23. Tab Hunter with Eddie Muller, *Tab Hunter Confidential: The Making of a Movie Star* (New York: Algonquin, 2005), 117–118.

24. On the outing of lesbian and gay actors in Hollywood, see Samuel Bernstein, *Mr. Confidential: The Man, the Magazine and the Movieland Massacre* (New York: Walford, 2006). On the popularity of celebrity magazines in the 1950s, see Anthony Slide, *Inside the Hollywood Fan Magazine: A History of Star Makers, Fabricators, and Gossip Mongers* (Oxford, MS: University of Mississippi Press, 2010).

25. Laura Ingraham, *Shut Up and Sing: How Elites from Hollywood, Politics, and the UN Are Subverting America* (New York: Regnery, 2006).

26. Ronald Brownstein, *The Power and the Glitter: The Hollywood–Washington Connection* (New York: Pantheon, 1990); Steven J. Ross, *Hollywood Left and Right: How Movie Stars Shaped American Politics* (New York: Oxford University Press, 2011). Other important books include Alan Schroeder's *Celebrity-in-Chief: How Show Business Took Over the White House* (Boulder, CO: Westview Press, 2004), which provides an anatomy of the different ways in which presidents interacted with celebrities and the political benefits (and costs) of those relationships. Donald T. Critchlow's *When Hollywood Was Right: How Movie Stars, Studio Moguls, and Big Business Remade American Politics* (New York: Cambridge University Press, 2013) focuses on the rise of conservative celebrities. Critchlow masterfully explains how Hollywood conservatives rebuilt the California Republican Party from the end of World War II to Ronald Reagan's election as governor and president. Kathryn Cramer Brownell's *Showbiz Politics: Hollywood in American Political Life* (Chapel Hill, NC: University of North Carolina Press, 2014) examines how the turn toward entertainment as a form of political communication has occupied both studio heads and politicians for over forty years. Brownell's extraordinary research makes her study an essential contribution to the field. See also Kathryn Cramer Brownell, "The Making of the Celebrity Presidency," in *Recapturing the Oval Office: New Historical Approaches to the American Presidency*, ed. Brian Balogh and Bruce J. Schulman (Ithaca,

NY: Cornell University Press, 2015), 162–174. For analyses that focus more on contemporary (and international) politics, see Mark Wheeler, *Celebrity Politics* (Malden, MA: Polity, 2013) and Darrell M. West and John Orman's textbook, *Celebrity Politics* (Upper Saddle River, NJ: Prentice Hall, 2003). A valuable related study is David T. Canon's *Actors, Athletes, and Astronauts: Political Amateurs in the United States Congress* (Chicago: University of Chicago Press, 1990).

27. George W. S. Trow, *My Pilgrim's Progress: Media Studies 1950–1998* (New York: Random House, 1999), 139–188.

28. See "The Man from Libertyville: TV Campaigning," Democratic National Committee, 1956. Maker: Charles Guggenheim Video, courtesy of the John F. Kennedy Presidential Library (hereafter JFKL). From the Museum of the Moving Image, The Living Room Candidate: Presidential Campaign Commercials 1952–2012. Available at www.livingroomcandidate.org/commercials/1956/the-man-from-libertyville-tv-campaigning. Accessed April 25, 2014.

29. Bernard Rosenberg, "Mass Culture in America," in Bernard Rosenberg and David Manning White, *Mass Culture: The Popular Arts in America* (Glencoe, IL: Free Press, 1957), 9.

30. C. Wright Mills, *The Power Elite* (New York: Oxford University Press, 1956), 71.

31. Ibid., 85.

32. Ralph Waldo Emerson, "The Poet," in *Essays and Lectures* (New York: The Library of America, 1983), 454. Emerson is referring to political symbols associated with Andrew Jackson (hickory stick), William Henry Harrison (log cabin and cider barrel), and John Calhoun's state of South Carolina (palmetto). He overlooks the role that political supporters had in introducing these symbols to the populace.

Chapter 1

1. Craig Allen, *Eisenhower and the Mass Media: Peace, Prosperity and Prime-Time TV* (Chapel Hill: University of North Carolina Press, 1993), 141–142. The "Mamie" advertisement is available at http://www.c-span.org/video/?c4471925/clip-9. Accessed July 21, 2015.

2. Tracy Voorhees to Anne Whitman, October 19, 1956. PPF 1-N-3, Box 339, White House Central, Dwight David Eisenhower Presidential Library (hereafter DDEL).

3. Eisenhower expressed the desire to rebuild the GOP frequently in both private correspondence and public statements. See Daniel J. Galvin, *Presidential Party Building: Dwight D. Eisenhower to George W. Bush* (Princeton, NJ: Princeton University Press, 2010), 41–69. Among his activities were a series of GOP fundraising dinners for state and local committees, the creation of a campaign school for Republican candidates, and the creation of a party-wide public relations strategy board. For a contemporary assessment of Eisenhower's party building, see John G. Schneider, "'56: Show-Biz Flop," *The Nation*, November 24, 1956, 451.

4. "National Ike Day Celebration," October 13, 1956, Motion Picture Film (CBS Telecast), Audio-Visual Department, DDEL. All references to the Ike Day television program will be made to this film.

5. John Reed Kilpatrick, Summary Report 1956, National Citizens for Eisenhower–Nixon, Box 6, Young & Rubicam, Records of Citizens for Eisenhower, 1949–1960. DDEL.

6. David A. Nichols' *Eisenhower 1956: The President's Year of Crisis, Suez and the Brink of War* (New York: Simon and Schuster, 2011) expertly describes how conflict in the Middle East unfolded against the backdrop of the 1956 presidential campaign. On Eisenhower's vacillating stance on what became the 1957 Civil Rights Act, see David A. Nichols, *A Matter of Justice: Eisenhower and the Beginning of the Civil Rights Revolution* (New York: Simon and Schuster, 2007), 120–142. For a less sympathetic view, see Piers Brendon, *Ike: His Life and Times* (New York: Harper and Row, 1986), 320, 342–43.

7. "Whole Nation Will Join President Eisenhower in Celebrating His Birthday via Television, October 12, Over CBS-TV," press release, n.d., News Bureau Communications Counselors, Folder: Ike Day, 1956—Planning Material (1)(2), Box 20, Katherine Howard Papers, DDEL. The press release describes "Swing Low, Sweet Chariot" and "The World Is Waiting for the Sunrise" as "having special personal meaning for Mr. and Mrs. Eisenhower."

8. See, for example, Harriet Van Horne, "Ike Birthday Party Most Effective," *New York World–Telegram and Sun*, October 15, 1956, 20; and Lawrence Laurent, "Both Parties Tailoring Speeches to TV Size," *The Washington Post and Times Herald*, October 15, 1956, 21. Both of these articles were included in the files of the National Ike Day Committee, Tracy S. Voorhees papers, Rutgers University Libraries (hereafter RUL).

9. On the program's viewership, see Katherine Howard to Sherman Adams, December 7, 1956, PPF 1-N-3, Box 339, White House Central, DDEL. Census data and contemporary reports suggest that there were 37–38 million television sets in the United States in 1956; see *Historical Statistics of the United States, Colonial Times to 1970*, Part II (US Department of Commerce: Bureau of the Census, 1975), 793; as well as Robert S. Bird, "This Will Be a 5-Minute Campaign," *Washington Post*, September 9, 1956. E3. ProQuest Historical Newspapers. Electronic Database. Accessed January 9, 2008.

10. "Election of 1956." Online by Gerhard Peters and John T. Woolley, The American Presidency Project. Available at http://www.presidency.ucsb.edu/showelection.php?year=1956. Accessed April 17, 2015.

11. Richard Butsch, *The Making of American Audiences: From Stage to Television, 1750–1990* (New York: Cambridge University Press, 2000), 235, 236–40, 249–50. See also William Boddy, *Fifties Television: The Industry and Its Critics* (Champagne/Urbana: University of Illinois Press, 1992), 78.

12. Butsch, *Making of American Audiences*, 236.

13. Kevin Mattson, *Just Plain Dick: Richard Nixon's Checkers Speech and the "Rocking, Socking" Election of 1952* (New York: Bloomsbury, 2012), 154.

14. On the decade's fixation on the nuclear family, see Stephanie Coontz, *The Way We Never Were: American Families and the Nostalgia Trap* (New York: Basic, 1993; 2006), 23–41.

15. "The President's Birthday Party," press release, October 4, 1956, News Bureau/Communications Counselors; "Today is Ike Day," press release, October 13, 1956, Folder: National Ike Day Committee, Box V, Tracy S. Voorhees Papers, RUL.

16. As reported in Voorhees to Whitman, October 19, 1956, DDEL.

17. As reported in Voorhees to Whitman, October 19, 1956, DDEL.

18. Richard Severo, "Harriet Van Horne, 77, Critic of Early TV and Radio Shows," January 17, 1998. Available at http://www.nytimes.com/1998/01/17/arts/harriet-van-horne-77-critic-of-early-tv-and-radio-shows.html. Accessed on January 26, 2016.

19. Guy Debord, *The Society of the Spectacle*. Trans. Donald Nicholson-Smith (New York: Zone Books, 1967, 1995), 24.

20. Ibid., 12. Debord explains on pages 16–20 that, as the economy of appearances increasingly dominated social life, the spectacle produced and transmitted a self-portrait of the ruling elite.

21. Dunne's work for Catholic charities resulted in her being awarded the University of Notre Dame's prestigious Laetare Medal, "the highest possible honor for a Catholic layperson." See Wes D. Gehring, *Irene Dunne: First Lady of Hollywood* (Lanham, MD: Scarecrow Press, 2006), 9, 148.

22. "Former Illinois Sen. Charles Percy dies at age 91," Neil Steinberg, *Chicago Sun Times*, September 17, 2011. Available at http://www.suntimes.com/news/metro/7711024-418/former-illinois-sen-charles-percy-dies-at-age-of-91.html. Accessed July 1, 2015. On Percy's nickname as the "Whiz Kid of U.S. Business," see "Profile of Charles H. Percy," Institute of Government Studies, University of California, Berkeley. Available at https://igs.berkeley.edu/research/csr/percy/profile. Accessed July 28, 2015. See also David Kenney and Robert E. Hartley, *An Uncertain Tradition: U.S. Senators from Illinois, 1818–2003* (Edwardsville, IL: Southern Illinois University Press, 2003), 175.

23. See Republican Committee on Program and Progress, *Decisions for a Better America* (Garden City, NY: Doubleday, 1960).

24. "Irene Dunne Among 10 Proposed As U.S. Delegation to the U.N.," *New York Times*, August 10, 1957, 6. Online. Accessed January 26, 2016.

25. Steven J. Ross, *Hollywood Left and Right: How Movie Stars Shaped American Politics* (New York: Oxford University Press, 2011), 150.

26. On Voorhees, see W. H. Lawrence, "President Names Aide to Expedite Refugees' Entry," *New York Times*, November 30, 1956, 1, 14. "Tracy Voorhees Dead at 84," *New York Times*, September 26, 1974, 32. Online. Accessed January 26, 2016.

27. Charles Percy to Tracy Voorhees, October 24, 1956, Folder: National Ike Day Committee, Box V, Tracy S. Voorhees Papers, RUL.

28. "Hurry-Up Man," *Time*, December 20, 1948, 90. History of Interpublic Group. Funding Universe: Available at http://www.fundinguniverse.com/company-histories/the-interpublic-group-of-companies-inc-history/. Accessed February 19, 2013.

29. Russ Johnston, *Marion Harper: An Unauthorized Biography* (Chicago: Crain, 1982), 109.

30. McCann-Erickson billing statement, November 20, 1956, Folder: National Ike Day Committee, Box V, Tracy S. Voorhees Papers, RUL.

31. Jay Donahue to Dwight Eisenhower, October 24, 1956, Folder: PPF 1-N-3, Box 339, White House Central Files, DDEL; "Round Up of Highlights, Nation-Wide Ike Day Celebration," October 9, 1956, Box 20, Katherine Howard Papers; "Bulletin: Ike Day in Washington and Youth Salutes the President," October 3, 1956, Folder: PPF 1-N-3, Box 339, White House Central Files DDEL.

32. *Life Magazine*, November 5, 1956, 58.

33. C. Langhorne Washburn, Memorandum to Tracy Voorhees, September 15, 1956, "IKE Day National Program," Folder: Ike Day, Box 13, C. Langhorne Washburn Papers, 1952–1964, DDEL.

34. "Round Up of Highlights, Nation-Wide Ike Day Celebration," October 9, 1956, Box 20, Katherine Howard Papers, DDEL.

35. Patty Phillipp, "Suggested Format for Ike's Birthday Party," pamphlet, Folder: "Ideas Kan Elect," Box 13, C. Langhorne Washburn Papers, 1952–1964, DDEL.

36. Biehl P. Clarke, publicity director, Youth Salutes the President, Memorandum to Bernard M. Shanley, Secretary to the President, October 1, 1956, PPF 1-N-3, Box 339, White House Central, DDEL. See also "Youth Salutes the President," press release, October 4, 1956, DDEL.

37. C. Langhorne Washburn to Mark Gill, September 18, 1956, Folder: Ike Day, Box 13, C. Langhorne Washburn Papers, 1952–1964, DDEL.

38. "Format for President's Birthday," October 13, 1956, Folder: Ike Day, Box 13, C. Langhorne Washburn Papers, 1952–1964, DDEL; C. Langhorne Washburn to Tracy Voorhees, September 15, 1956, Folder: National Ike Day Committee, Box V, Tracy S. Voorhees Papers, RUL.

39. C. Langhorne Washburn to D. B. Johnson, October 22, 1956, Folder: Ike Day, Box 13, C. Langhorne Washburn Papers, 1952–1964, DDEL.

40. As they did in Washington, the RNC screened Washburn's documentary at the more prominent galas held around the country.

41. McCann-Erickson Billing Statement, November 20, 1956, Folder: National Ike Day Committee, Box V, Tracy S. Voorhees Papers, RUL.

42. On the family contributions, see Francis A. Jamieson, Memorandum to Mr. Nelson A. Rockefeller, October 10, 1956; and Francis A. Jamieson to Mr. Nelson A. Rockefeller, October 19, 1956, both in Folder: 552, Box 65, RG 4, Series A, Rockefeller Archive Center (hereafter RAC). On the finances of the National Ike Day Committee, see "Statement by the Treasurer . . . filed with the Clerk of the House of Representatives," n.d., Folder: National Ike Day Committee, Box V, Tracy S. Voorhees Papers, RUL.

43. Dwight David Eisenhower to Nelson A. Rockefeller, October 25, 1956, Folder: 552, Box 65, RG 4, Series A, RAC.

44. Nelson A. Rockefeller to President Dwight Eisenhower, October 31, 1956, Folder: 552, Box 65, RG 4, Series A, RAC.

45. On Voorhees, see Lawrence, "President Names Aide," *New York Times*, 1, 14. "Tracy Voorhees Dead at 84," *New York Times*, 1, 14. "Tracy Voorhees Dead at 84," *New York Times*.

46. Dwight D. Eisenhower to William Edward Robinson, March 24, 1958, *The Papers of Dwight David Eisenhower*, Vol. 19, ed. Louis Galambos and Daun van Ee (Baltimore: Johns Hopkins University Press, 2003), 795–796. Electronic Database: Available at http://eisenhower.press.jhu.edu/. Accessed September 14, 2014.

47. Johnston, *Marion Harper*, 103.

48. Debord, *Society of the Spectacle*, 19.

49. Charles Percy to Tracy Voorhees, October 24, 1956, Folder: National Ike Day Committee, Box V, Tracy S. Voorhees Papers, RUL.

50. Tracy Voorhees to Nelson Rockefeller, November 1, 1956, Folder: 552, Box 65, RG 4, Series A, RAC.

51. Rockefeller had advocated public diplomacy since the 1930s and 1940s when he headed up Franklin Delano Roosevelt's Office of the Coordinator of Inter-American Affairs (OCIAA) in Latin America. See Justin Hart, *Empire of Ideas: The Origins of Public Diplomacy and the Transformation of United States Information Agency* (New York: Oxford University Press, 2013), 32. It should be noted that the US Information Service was the cultural arm of the United States Information Agency. As Pam Parry explains, Eisenhower

opened the United States Information Agency in August 1953 and saw it as a critical part of his public relations diplomacy. See Pam Parry, *Eisenhower: The Public Relations President* (Lanham, MD: Lexington Books, 2014), 119–135.

52. Debord, *Society of the Spectacle*, 38.

53. Colleen Glenn, "The Traumatized Veteran: A New Look at Jimmy Stewart's Post-WWII *Vertigo*," *Quarterly Review of Film and Video*, 31.1, 2014, 27–41.

54. "James Stewart, the Hesitant Hero, Dies at 89," *New York Times*, July 3, 1997. Available at http://www.nytimes.com/1997/07/03/movies/james-stewart-the-hesitant-hero-dies-at-89.html. Accessed January 13, 2016.

55. Jim Cullen, *Sensing the Past: Hollywood Stars and Historical Visions* (New York: Oxford University Press, 2013), 176–177. Cullen defines "institutionalism" as a belief in "the need for a strong institutional presence in everyday life" (13).

56. The Ike Day program carefully obscured the political opinions of its stars in favor of building Ike's personality. Dunne was one of the most fiscally savvy actresses of her age and had deep concerns about protecting her wealth from taxes. With the help of her agent, Charles Feldman, she carefully acted in only a few pictures each year and structured her contracts to avoid reaching the 80 percent tax bracket. Dunne's strong opinions are noticeably absent from the Ike Day telecast, although her volunteer work is prominently featured. On Hollywood and taxes, see Eric Hoyt, "Hollywood and the Income Tax, 1929–1955," *Film History: An International Journal*, 22, 1, 8–9. On Dunne's business acumen and relationship with her manager Charles Feldman, see Thomas Kempler's important book *Hidden Talent: The Emergence of Hollywood Agents* (Berkeley and Los Angeles: University of California Press, 2010), 82–93.

57. "Ike Day Surprise Birthday Party," *Variety*, October 17, 1956, electrostatic copy included in Voorhees to Whitman, October 19, 1956, DDEL. *Variety*'s full-throated enthusiasm for the program is worth recording here: "Chalk up one of the smartest political time buys in this year's election campaign to the National Ike Day Committee, which in a 'surprise birthday party' for the President, probably accomplished more in a half-hour telecast than most of the straight political speech expenditures by the Republican National Committee. The Ike Day group accomplished two things with this 'entertainment' styled show—it caught Ike at his most gracious and most natural, surrounded by family and glowing in humor, and it subtly wrapped a political pitch in terms of an entertainment for an ostensibly non-partisan occasion. // End result was to supply a fairly entertaining show with lotsa top name stars, along with a sugar-coated political message that could hardly have failed to register. With the genuine admiration expressed by the stars for Ike, along with his modest and gracious acceptance of the situation, this show was easily a bigger voter getter than a half dozen speeches. It was genuine and believable and couldn't fail to register. Just what the Dems can do to counter this is a toughie, but they'd better do something."

Chapter 2

1. George W. Ball, "Remarks to the Women's National Democratic Club," October 15, 1956, Folder: 1, Box 133, George W. Ball Papers, Seeley G. Mudd Manuscript Library, Princeton University Library (hereafter PUL).

2. Evan Thomas, *Ike's Bluff: President Eisenhower's Secret Battle to Save the World* (New York: Little, Brown, 2012), 209.

3. Eisenhower received 62,026,908 total votes, compared to Stevenson's 35,590,472. "Election of 1956." Online by Gerhard Peters and John T. Woolley. The American Presidency Project. Available at http://www.presidency.ucsb.edu/showelection.php?year= 1956. Accessed April 17, 2015.

4. David L. Sills, *The Volunteers, Means and Ends in a National Organization, A Report of the Columbia University Bureau of Applied Social Research* (n.p.: Ayer Publishing, 1980), 43–44.

5. Keith Morgan to Grace Tully, December 10, 1937, PPF 4885: Committee for Celebration of the President's Birthday; Nicholas M. Schenck to Franklin Delano Roosevelt, September 6, 1944, PPF 4885: Committee for Celebration of the President's Birthday; International Bakers Union to Franklin Roosevelt, January 21, 1944, PPF 4885: Committee for Celebration of the President's Birthday. All these letters are found in the President's Personal File, Franklin D. Roosevelt Presidential Library (hereafter FDRL).

6. Folder: Luncheon, Saturday, January 29, 1938, 1 p.m., Box 55, Office of Social Entertainments; Folder: Luncheon, Movie Stars, January 30, 1941, 1 p.m., Box 93, Office of Social Entertainments; Folder: Luncheon, Movie Stars, January 30, 1944, 1 p.m., Box 110, Office of Social Entertainments, FDRL. See also Scott M. Cutlip's chapter titled "F.D.R., Polio, and the March of Dimes" in *Fund Raising in the United States: Its Role in America's Philanthropy* (New Brunswick, NJ: Transaction Publishers, 1990), 351–397.

7. On Disney and Cantor, see Morgan to Tully, December 10, 1937, FDRL. On Stewart, see Folder: Luncheon, Movie Stars, January 30, 1942, 1 p.m., Box 102, Office of Social Entertainments, FDRL.

8. David M. Oshinsky, *Polio: An American Story* (New York: Oxford University Press, 2005), 52.

9. For the sake of clarity, I refer to the committee by its more common name, the House Un-American Activities Committee. The committee was also known as the House Committee on Un-American Activities.

10. On Lasker's involvement, see John Morello, *Selling the President, 1920: Albert D. Lasker, Advertising, and the Election of Warren G. Harding* (New York: Praeger, 2001).

11. "Harding Demands Team Government," *New York Times*, September 3, 1920, 3. Online. Accessed November 13, 2013.

12. On the involvement of Frances Harding, see Carl Sferrazza Anthony, *Florence Harding: The First Lady, the Jazz Age, and the Death of America's Most Scandalous President* (New York: William Morrow, 1998), 219–220.

13. "Hughes Declares Harding Best Man," *New York Times*, August 25, 1920, 3. Online. Accessed November 13, 2013; Harry N. Price, "Actors Stir Marion," *The Washington Post*, August 25, 1920, 1. ProQuest Historical Newspapers. Electronic Database. Accessed January 9, 2008.

14. Price, "Actors Stir Marion," *Washington Post*.

15. Ibid.

16. On the "Jazz Campaign," see "Harding Speech to Actors and Actresses Will Begin Republican Jazz Campaign," *Macon Daily Telegraph*, August 22, 1920, 9. ProQuest Historical Newspapers. Electronic Database. Accessed January 9, 2008. See also "Hughes Declares Harding," *New York Times*.

17. "Hughes Declares Harding," *New York Times*.

18. Ibid.

19. "Players' Day in Marion," *New York Times*, August 26, 1920, 10. Online. Accessed November 13, 2013.

20. For Jolson's comment, see "Actors Eat Cake with the Coolidges," *New York Times*, October 18, 1924, 1. Online. Accessed November 13, 2013; on the congressional investigation, see Ronald Brownstein, *The Power and the Glitter: The Hollywood–Washington Connection* (New York: Pantheon, 1990), 29.

21. Franklin Roosevelt, "Address of President Franklin Roosevelt to Thirteenth Annual Awards Dinner of the Academy of Motion Picture Arts and Sciences, Hollywood, California, February 27, 1941," Press Release, PPF 7410: Academy of Motion Picture Arts and Sciences, President's Personal Files, FDRL.

22. Kathryn Cramer Brownell, *Show Biz Politics: Hollywood in American Political Life* (Chapel Hill: University of North Carolina Press, 2014), 71.

23. See the correspondence with Bette Davis in PPF 8922: Davis, Bette, President's Personal File, FDRL.

24. Franklin Delano Roosevelt to Hollywood Victory Caravan, April 22, 1942, PPF 8030: Hollywood [California] Victory Caravan, President's Personal File, FDRL. For other activities, see Koppes and Black, *Hollywood Goes to War* (Berkeley: University of California Press, 1990).

25. Bryan Foy and Ralph Block, Letter to Members of Hollywood for Roosevelt, n.d. [1940], PPF 7024: Hollywood for Roosevelt Committee, President's Personal Files, FDRL.

26. Sally Denton, *The Pink Lady: The Many Lives of Helen Gahagan Douglas* (New York: Bloomsbury, 2009), 63.

27. The literature on Douglas is deep. In addition to Denton, see Ingrid Scobie, *Center Stage: Helen Gahagan Douglas, A Life* (New York: Oxford University Press, 1992). On the 1950 California Senate race, see Greg Mitchell, *Tricky Dick and the Pink Lady: Richard Nixon vs. Helen Gahagan Douglas—Sexual Politics and the Red Scare, 1950* (New York: Random House, 1998).

28. Compare the correspondence in PPF 7024: Hollywood for Roosevelt Committee (including Franklin Delano Roosevelt to Charles L. O'Reilly, October 31, 1940; and Charles L. O'Reilly to Franklin Delano Roosevelt, December 16, 1940) with the correspondence in PPF 7028: United Retail, Wholesale and Department Store Employees of America, President's Personal Files, FDRL.

29. On the emergence of right-wing groups in Hollywood before World War II, see Donald T. Critchlow, *When Hollywood Was Right: How Movie Stars, Studio Moguls, and Big Business Remade American Politics* (New York: Cambridge University Press, 2013), 42–65.

30. Steven J. Ross, *Hollywood Left and Right: How Movie Stars Shape American Politics* (New York: Oxford University Press, 2012), 52.

31. Ibid., 66.

32. Ibid., 56, 69.

33. Brownstein, *The Power and the Glitter*, 35.

34. An excellent study of Sinclair's E.P.I.C. campaign is Greg Mitchell's *The Campaign of the Century: Upton Sinclair's E.P.I.C. Race for Governor of California and the Birth of Media Politics* (New York: Random House, 1992).

35. Ross, *Hollywood Left and Right*, 78–79.

36. Critchlow, *When Hollywood Was Right*, 45–46.

37. "The Truth About Hollywood!" Advertisement. *New York Times*, November 4, 1940. ProQuest Historical Newspapers. Electronic Database. Accessed January 9, 2008. Endorsements were important across professional lines. On the same day, a similar advertisement appeared in the *Times* from twelve American authors and editors warning about the dangers of a third-term presidency.

38. Ross, *Hollywood Left and Right*, 79–80.

39. Democratic State Committee of New York, "Salute to Roosevelt," November 4, 1940, NBC Radio Broadcast, Audio Visual Department, FDRL.

40. Mitchell was also coming off of his role as "Diz" Moore, a jaded political reporter, in Frank Capra's *Mr. Smith Goes to Washington*.

41. Independent Voters Committee of the Arts and Sciences for Roosevelt, "Report of Election Campaign Activities" [pamphlet], 1944, Folder: Campaign Literature, 1944, Vertical File, FDRL.

42. Ibid.

43. On Welles's work on the Roosevelt Victory Caravan, see Mr. Biow Memorandum to Mr. Hamm, August 28, 1944, Folder 20: Democratic National Committee, Box 2, Hollywood Democratic Committee Records, 1942–1950, Wisconsin Historical Society (hereafter WHS); Franklin Delano Roosevelt to Orson Welles, November 25, 1944, PPF 8921: Welles, Orson, President's Personal Files, FDRL.

44. Brownstein, *The Power and the Glitter*, 92.

45. "Democrats Close Major Drive Here," *New York Times*, November 4, 1944, 11. Online. Accessed April 27, 2014.

46. "Report of Election Campaign Activities," FDRL.

47. Ibid.

48. Milton H. Biow, *Butting In: An Ad Man Speaks Out* (New York: Doubleday, 1964), 171.

49. Ibid., 24.

50. David Everitt, *A Shadow of Red: Communism and the Blacklist in Radio and Television* (Chicago: Ivan R. Dee, 2007), 107.

51. Hollywood Democratic Committee, "FDR Radio Program Election Eve," November 6, 1944, Audio Broadcast, Hollywood Democratic Committee Records, 1942–1950, WHS.

52. Brownstein offers an appreciative discussion of Corwin's role in creating the FDR program in *The Power and Glitter*, 100–102.

Chapter 3

1. On the founding of Citizens for Eisenhower, see Stanley M. Rumbough, Jr., *Citizens for Eisenhower: The 1952 Presidential Campaign: Lessons for the Future?* (McLean, VA: International Publishers, 2013), 17–24. The Citizens group would eventually be led by the Wall Street investor Cliff Roberts (a co-founder of the Augusta National Golf Club and, for over forty years, the chairman of the Masters Tournament). See Piers Brendon, *Ike: His Life and Times* (New York: Harper & Row, 1986), 208–213.

2. Dwight Eisenhower, January 10, 1952, diary entry, *The Eisenhower Diaries*, ed. Robert H. Ferrell (New York: W.W. Norton, 1981), 209.

3. See Henry Cabot Lodge, *The Storm Has Many Eyes: A Personal Narrative* (New York: W.W. Norton, 1973), 93–98.

4. Arthur Krock, "Eisenhower in a Battle That He Tried to Avoid," *New York Times*, June 1, 1952, E3. Online. Accessed September 5, 2013.

5. William Shakespeare, *Coriolanus*, ed. Peter Holland, *The Arden Shakespeare* (New York: Bloomsbury, 2013), Act 2, scene 1, line 199.

6. *Coriolanus*, 2.1.254–262.

7. *Coriolanus*, 1.1.174–175.

8. *Coriolanus*, 3.2.73–79.

9. *Coriolanus*, 5.3.36.

10. On Shakespeare's revision of Plutarch, see Peter Holland, "Introduction," *Coriolanus*, 31–49.

11. "Truman Wrote of '48 Offer to Eisenhower," *New York Times*, July 11, 2003. Available at http://www.nytimes.com/2003/07/11/us/truman-wrote-of-48-offer-to-eisenhower.html. Accessed September 5, 2013.

12. Brendon, *Ike: His Life and Times*, 25–26.

13. Merriman Smith, *Meet Mr. Eisenhower* (New York: Harper and Row, 1955), 3. Jefferson explained his concept of a natural aristocracy in an October 28, 1813, letter to John Adams. See *The Adams–Jefferson Letters*, ed. Lester J. Cappon (Chapel Hill: University of North Carolina Press, 1987), 387–389.

14. Merlo J. Pusey, *Eisenhower the President* (New York: Macmillan, 1956), 3. See also Early Swift, *The Big Roads: The Untold Story of the Engineers, Visionaries, and Trailblazers Who Created the American Superhighways* (New York: Houghton-Mifflin, 2011). William Safire's *Political Dictionary* (New York: Oxford University Press, revised 2008) describes this as a "Sherman Statement," 653.

15. David Halberstam, *The Fifties* (New York: Ballantine, 1954), 229.

16. Evan Thomas, *Ike's Bluff: President Eisenhower's Secret Battle to Save the World* (New York: Little Brown, 2012), 117.

17. Halberstam, *Fifties*, 230.

18. See the Broadway Internet Database, http://www.ibdb.com/show.php?id=2358, as well as Brian Kellow, *Ethel Merman: A Life* (New York: Viking Press, 2007), 141–142. A well-researched and good narrative on this topic is Carl Anthony's "Ike, Irving, Mamie and Merman: The Hit Song Which Elected a President." Available at http://carlanthonyonline.com/2012/08/02/ike-irving-mamie-merman-evolution-of-a-catchy-campaign-tune/. Accessed April 26, 2013.

19. Inez Robb, "If Nomination Goes to Ike, Irving Berlin Rates Assist," *Cedar Rapids Gazette*, October 19, 1950, 14. Available at http://newspaperarchive.com/cedar-rapids-gazette/1950-10-19/page-14 Newspaper Archive. Accessed July 11, 2013.

20. "Repercussion," *New Yorker*, January 19, 1952, 20–21. Digital edition. Accessed October 30, 2012.

21. Irving Berlin, "They Like Ike," *Call Me Madam* (Piano-Vocal Scores), Holograph, Folder 2, Box 78., Irving Berlin Collection, Library of Congress.

22. Ibid.

23. Irving Berlin, "They Like Ike," *Call Me Madam* (Piano-Vocal Scores), Holograph, Folder 1, Box 31, Irving Berlin Collection, Library of Congress.

24. On the release of Berlin's "I Like Ike," see *The Billboard*, March 22, 1952, 15. Google Books. Online. Available at https://books.google.com/books?id=hx4EAAAAMBAJ&q=berlin#v=snippet&q=berlin&f=false. Accessed July 30, 2014.

25. George W. S. Trow, *Within the Context of No Context* (New York: Atlantic Monthly Press, 1981), 46.

26. Roman Jakobson, "Closing Statement: Linguistics and Poetics," *Style in Language*, ed. Thomas Sebeok (New York: MIT and Wiley, 1961), 357.

27. See William L. Bird, Jr., "TV and the Ike Age," *Hail to the Candidate: Presidential Campaigns from Banners to Broadcasts*, ed. Keith Melder (Washington, DC: Smithsonian Press, 1992), 169; and "I Like Ike: Election Fashion from 1952," *Time*, November 6, 2012. Available at http://style.time.com/2012/11/06/i-like-ike-election-fashion-from-1952/. Accessed July 31, 2014.

28. Herbert Brownell with John P. Burke, *Advising Ike: Memoirs of Attorney General Herbert Brownell* (Lawrence: University Press of Kansas, 1993), 101.

29. The Eisenhower Campaign, January 8, 1952, Folder: Correspondence of Sig Larmon and Others, Box 1, Young & Rubicam, Records of Citizens for Eisenhower, 1949–1960. DDEL.

30. Ibid.

31. The details of Serenade to Ike come from James A. Hagerty, "A 'Serenade to Ike' is Theme at Rally of 15,000 in Garden," *New York Times*, February 9, 1952, 1, 3. Online. Accessed July 22, 2015. It should be noted that the reporter who wrote this article was the father of James C. Hagerty, who headed press operations for Ike's 1952 campaign and became his White House Press Secretary.

32. Ibid.

33. George E. Sokolsky, "Eisenhower's Campaign Reduced to Vaudeville," *New York Journal American*, February 15, 1952, press clipping; Arthur B. Schlesinger, Jr., "History of the Week," *New York Post*, February 17, 1952, press clipping; "Show-Time," *New Bedford Standard Times*, February 11, 1952, press clipping. All of these items come from Vol. 2, Scrapbooks from Eisenhower Campaign, Carton 61, Henry Cabot Lodge Papers, Jr. Massachusetts Historical Society.

34. Lodge, *Storm Has Many Eyes*, 98–99.

35. Hagerty, "Serenade," *New York Times*, 1, 3.

36. The Eisenhower Campaign, January 8, 1952, Young & Rubicam, DDEL.

37. Martin Post, "Midnight Serenaders Want Ike at Helm," *Pacific Stars and Stripes*, February 10, 1952, 4. Available at http://newspaperarchive.com/pacific-stars-and-stripes/1952-02-10/page-4. Newspaper Archive. Accessed August 15, 2013.

38. Richard Severo, "Tex McCrary Dies at 92: Public Relations Man Who Helped Create Talk-Show Format," *New York Times*, July 30, 2003. Available at http://www.nytimes.com/2003/07/30/arts/tex-mccrary-dies-at-92-public-relations-man-who-helped-create-talk-show-format.html?pagewanted=all. Accessed July 22, 2015.

39. *Eisenhower Diary*, February 11, 1952, 214.

40. Ibid. On Ike's not using the diary to reflect on his campaign, see the headnote on 217–218.

41. Samuel L. Popkin, *The Candidate: What It Takes to Win and Hold the White House* (New York: Oxford University Press, 2012), 82.

42. Dwight D. Eisenhower, *Mandate for Change* (New York: Doubleday, 1963), 22.

43. "Seymour's Speeches and Grant's Silence," *New York Times*, October 24, 1868, 6. Online. Accessed February 17, 2011.

44. "Gen. Grant's Sayings and Doings," *New York Times*, October 11, 1868, 4. Online. Accessed February 17, 2011.

45. Craig Allen, *Eisenhower and the Mass Media: Peace, Prosperity and Prime-Time TV* (Chapel Hill: University of North Carolina Press, 1993), 14–16. On October 24, 1952, Eisenhower promised to "forego the diversions of politics and to concentrate on the job of ending the Korean war—until that job is honorably done. That job requires a personal trip to Korea. I shall make that trip. Only in that way could I learn how best to serve the American people in the cause of peace. I shall go to Korea." On the crafting of this statement, see Jeffrey Frank, *Ike and Dick: Portrait of a Strange Political Marriage* (New York: Simon and Schuster, 2013), 63–64.

46. On the smearing of CBS as the "Communist Broadcast System," see David Everitt, *A Shadow of Red: Communism and the Blacklist in Radio and Television* (Chicago: Ivan R. Dee, 2007), 71.

47. On IKE-TV, see Steve M. Barkin, "Eisenhower's Secret Strategy: Television Planning in the 1952 Campaign," *European Journal of Marketing*, 20.5 (May 30, 1986), 18–28, especially 19–21.

48. Jacqueline Cochran to General Dwight D. Eisenhower, February 15, 1952. DDEL. Available at http://www.eisenhower.archives.gov/research/online_documents/jacqueline_cochran/BinderP.pdf. Accessed September 6, 2013.

49. Sigurd Larmon to Dwight D. Eisenhower, July 18, 1952. Folder: Sigurd Larmon, Box 9, William E. Robinson Papers, DDEL.

50. The Eisenhower Campaign, January 8, 1952, Young & Rubicam, DDEL.

51. Ibid.

52. Ibid.

53. Frederick A. Zaghi, Oral history interview with John E. Wickman, November 5, 1968, OH-107, DDEL.

54. Ibid.

55. Frank G. Prial, "Kate Smith, All-American Singer, Dies at 79," *New York Times*, June 18, 1986. Available at http://www.nytimes.com/learning/general/onthisday/bday/0501.html. Accessed July 22, 2015.

56. Zaghi, Wickman interview. Unless otherwise noted, all details in this paragraph come from this source.

57. Jack Gould, "Gen. Eisenhower's Video Appearance Discloses Screen Appeal and Naturalness for Medium," *New York Times*, June 4, 1952, Sports section, 38. Online. Accessed September 6, 2013.

58. Lodge, *Storm Has Many Eyes*, 109. Eisenhower would later cause controversy when he got frustrated with a slow teleprompter technician in Indianapolis and could be heard cursing over the radio, "Go ahead, go ahead, yeah, damn it, I want him to move up!" Eisenhower's first weeks as a candidate included many of the pitfalls that Samuel Popkin has associated with hero candidates who have to adjust to new kinds of media and new expectations as they enter a presidential race. See Popkin, *The Candidate*, 82–85.

59. Michael D. Bowen, *The Roots of Modern Conservatism: Dewey, Taft, and the Battle for the Soul of the Republican Party* (Chapel Hill: University of North Carolina Press, 2011), 131.

60. Lawrence E. Davies, "Gabrielson Ouster Defeated by an Overwhelming Vote," *New York Times*, January 18, 1952, 19. Online. Accessed January 28, 2016.

61. Zaghi, as quoted in Bowen, *Roots of Modern Conservatism*, 142.

62. On Young & Rubicam activities, see Zaghi, Wickman interview.

63. Jack Gould, "Radio and Television: Video Suffers Temporary Setback," *New York Times*, July 2, 1952, 33. Online. Accessed July 30, 2013.

64. Steve Neal, *Harry and Ike: The Partnership That Remade the Postwar World* (New York: Simon and Schuster, 2002), 248.

65. Zaghi, Wickman interview.

66. Arthur Krock, "In the Nation: The Reckoning That Could Not Be Evaded," *New York Times*, July 10, 1952, 30. Online. Accessed July 30, 2013.

67. Jeff Kisseloff, *The Box: An Oral History of Television, 1920–1961* (New York: Viking, 1995), 380.

68. "International Film Set Beats Drum for Ike: Profits from Sales Abroad," *Chicago Daily Tribune*, July 3, 1952, Part 1, 5. Online. Accessed May 13, 2015.

69. On Zanuck's role in creating the Entertainment Industry's Joint Committee for Eisenhower–Nixon, see Kathryn Cramer Brownell, *Show-Biz Politics: Hollywood in American Political Life* (Chapel Hill: University of North Carolina Press, 2014), 136–138.

70. Zanuck's July 9, 1952, letter to the *Chicago Tribune* is collected in *Memo from Darryl F. Zanuck: The Golden Years at Twentieth Century-Fox*, ed. Rudy Behlmer (New York: Grove Press, 1995), 209–214.

71. Phyllis Schlafly, *A Choice, Not an Echo: The Inside Story of How American Presidents Are Chosen* (Alton, IL: Pere Marquette Press, 1964), 53.

72. Schlafly, *A Choice*, 57. Schlafly quoted from Allen Drury's novel *Advise and Consent* to amplify the grievance conservatives had against New York media elites: "All the vast publicity machine that always goes into concerted action for a liberal cause had gone to work . . . an operation so honed and smoothed and refined over the years that none of its proprietors even had to consult with one another. The instinct had been alerted, the bell had rung, the national salivations had come forth on schedule." What we know from the archive, however, is that such consultations did take place and that they extended from Larmon and Zaghi to Lodge, Brownell, and Luce.

73. "The Eye of the Nation," *Time*, July 14, 1952, 23. Ebsco Host. Electronic Database. Accessed June 1, 2013.

74. Charles A. H. Thomson, *Television and Presidential Politics: The Experience in 1952 and the Problems Ahead* (Washington, DC: Brookings Institution, 1956), 137, 158.

75. Kurt Lang and Gladys Engel Lang, "The Televised Conventions: 1952," *Politics and Television* (Chicago: Quadrangle, 1968), 101–103. The study was originally published as an article in *Public Opinion Quarterly* (Fall 1955) 19(3).

76. Frank, *Ike and Dick: Portrait*, 47.

77. As cited in Thomson, *Television and Presidential Politics*, 60.

78. Zanuck's zeal was at times bewildering to Eisenhower's inner circle, who tended to ignore his advice. See Ronald Brownstein, *The Power and the Glitter: The Hollywood-Washington Connection* (New York: Pantheon, 1990), 134.

79. On Zanuck's reaction, see Burton W. Peretti, *The Leading Man: Hollywood and the Presidential Image* (New Brunswick, NJ: Rutgers University Press, 2012), 107. Mattson recounts how Eisenhower followed the advice of BBDO's Bruce Barton and Ben Duffy about how to respond to Nixon's speech. See Kevin Mattson, *Just Plain Dick: Richard Nixon's Checkers Speech and the "Rocking, Socking" Election of 1952* (New York: Bloomsbury, 2013), 157–158.

80. Thomson, *Television and Presidential Politics*, 70.

81. Ibid., 137.

82. Richard M. Fried, *The Man Everybody Knew: Bruce Barton and the Making of Modern America* (Chicago: Ivan R. Dee, 2005), 102–103.

83. Ibid., 128.

84. Ibid., 157.

85. Dwight Eisenhower to Bruce Barton, September 2, 1950, Bruce Barton Papers, Folder: Eisenhower, Dwight D., Box 19, Bruce Barton Papers, 1881–1967, WHS.

86. Fried, *Man Everybody Knew,* 217.

87. John E. Hollitz, "Eisenhower and the Admen: The Television 'Spot' Campaign of 1952," *The Wisconsin Magazine of History* 66, 1, Autumn 1982, 27.

88. The BBDO website directs visitors to a Wikipedia page as the official history of the company. Available at http://en.wikipedia.org/wiki/BBDO. Accessed September 6, 2013.

89. As quoted in Stanley Kelley, Jr., *Professional Public Relations and Political Power* (Baltimore: Johns Hopkins University Press, 1956), 156.

90. Bruce Barton to John Haynes, September 8, 1952, on fundraising letter to the Republican Women's Division. Folder: Eisenhower Campaign, Box 19, Bruce Barton Papers, WHS.

91. Kelley, *Professional Public Relations,* 156.

92. Alex Osborn is widely credited with bringing brainstorming techniques to BBDO in the 1940s. See Jonah Lehrer, "Groupthink: The Brainstorming Myth," *New Yorker,* January 30, 2012, 22–23.

93. Barton to Haynes, September 8, 1952, Barton Papers, WHS.

94. Bernard C. Duffy to Stanley High, Republican National Committee, September 19, 1952, Folder: Eisenhower Campaign, Box 19, Bruce Barton Papers, WHS.

95. Bruce Barton, Memorandum to B. C. Duffy, October 22, 1952, Folder: Eisenhower Campaign, Box 19, Bruce Barton Papers, WHS.

96. "World Sports Champions Select Eisenhower and Nixon," Pamphlet, Folder: Advertisements, 1952, Box 19, Politics Series, Rosser Reeves Papers, 1927–1971, WHS.

97. Thomas Whiteside, "Annals of Television: The Man from Iron City," *New Yorker,* September 27, 1969, 60. Digital Edition. See also Halberstam, *Fifties,* 225–227.

98. Whiteside, "Annals of Television," 47.

99. Ibid., 64, 69.

100. On the funding for the spots, see Hollitz, "Eisenhower and the Admen," 27. On Biow's development of the radio spot, see Milton H. Biow, *Butting In: An Ad Man Speaks Out* (New York: Doubleday, 1964), Burton Lindheim, "Milton Biow Dies: Headed Ad Agency," *New York Times,* February 3, 1976, 34. Online. Arthur Krock wrote about the Democratic radio spots in "Various New Devices to Capture the Vote," *New York Times,* November 2, 1944, 18. Online. Both articles accessed January 28, 2016. The first television spot, according to Bird, was used by Bill Benton in the 1950 Connecticut senate race. See Bird, "TV and the Ike Age," 164.

101. On Reeves and the Eisenhower spots, see Whiteside, "Annals of Television," 86; Halberstam, *Fifties,* 227–231; and Kathleen Hall Jamieson, *Packaging the Presidency: A History and Criticism of Presidential Campaign Advertising,* third edition (New York: Oxford University Press, 1996), 83–86. Sample Eisenhower spots (including the one I quote from) can be found online at the Museum of the Moving Image, *The Living*

Room Candidate: Presidential Campaign Commercials 1952–2012. Available at http://www. livingroomcandidate.org/commercials/1952. Accessed September 7, 2013.

102. "Program to Guarantee an Eisenhower Victory," Folder: Reports, August 1952, Box 19, Politics Series, Rosser Reeves Papers, 1927–1971, WHS. On the directing of the commercials, see Bird, "TV and the Ike Age," 165.

103. "Program to Guarantee," Reeves Papers, 2. WHS.

104. The convention statistics come from Thomson, *Television and Presidential Politics*, 43. The *I Love Lucy* and Inauguration statistics come from Jeff Kisseloff, *The Box: An Oral History of Television, 1920–1961* (New York: Viking, 1995), 302.

105. On the Eisenhower mistake, see Jamieson, *Packaging the Presidency*, 44. On Stevenson, see Erik Barnouw, *Tube of Plenty: The Evolution of American Television* (New York: Oxford University Press, 1990), 210.

106. George Murphy with Victor Lasky, *Say . . . Didn't You Used to Be George Murphy?* (New York: Bartholomew House, 1970), 319.

107. Ibid., 265.

108. Richard English, "Hollywood's Yankee-Doodle Dandy," *Saturday Evening Post*, July 2, 1955, 72.

109. Murphy, *Say . . . Didn't You Used*, 326. On Taft supporters in Hollywood, see Donald T. Critchlow, *When Hollywood Was Right: How Movie Stars, Studio Moguls, and Big Business Remade American Politics* (New York: Cambridge University Press, 2013), 124–125. Critchlow credits Eisenhower's selection of Nixon to be his running mate with his winning over Murphy and other ardent Hollywood conservatives.

110. On Zanuck and Murphy's relationship, see Brownell, *Show Biz Politics*, 136–138; and Brownstein, *Power and the Glitter*, 129, 133–134.

111. Murphy, *Say . . . Didn't You Used*, 331–332.

112. See Dwight David Eisenhower to Edward John Bermingham, November 24, 1953, *The Papers of Dwight David Eisenhower*, vol. 14, ed. Louis Galambos and Daun Van Ee (Baltimore: Johns Hopkins University Press, 1996), 693–694; and Dwight David Eisenhower to Edward John Bermingham, January 26, 1954, *The Papers of Dwight David Eisenhower*, vol. 15, ed. Louis Galambos and Daun Van Ee (Baltimore: Johns Hopkins University Press, 1996), 853. Electronic Database: Available at http://eisenhower.press.jhu. edu/. Accessed September 14, 2014.

113. English, "Hollywood's Yankee-Doodle," 71.

114. Steven J. Ross, *Hollywood Left and Right: How Movie Stars Shaped American Politics* (New York: Oxford University Press, 2011), 153.

115. Ibid., 154.

116. Ibid.

117. Murphy, *Say . . . Didn't You Used*, 135. BBDO's Arthur Pryor, Jr., produced the Election Eve broadcast. See Bird, "TV and the Ike Age," 166.

Chapter 4

1. "Tony Martin, Marion Marlow, et al., in Musical Tribute to Mrs. Eisenhower March 22," CBS News press release, March 16, 1956, Folder: Eisenhower, Mamie—Television Birthday, Box 378, Norman, Craig and Kummel, Papers of the Democratic National Committee, John Fitzgerald Kennedy Presidential Library (hereafter JFKL). The show itself can be found

as "To Our First Lady, with Music," presented by the Wives of the Federal Independent Agencies, of the United States Government, March 22, 1956, 16 RNC 47, CBS. Audio-Visual Department, JFKL.

2. Cy Anderson, phone message for Paul Butler, March 15, 1956; and Paul M. Butler to Jack Christie, both in Folder: Eisenhower, Mamie—Television Birthday, Box 378, Norman, Craig and Kummel, Papers of the Democratic National Committee, JFKL.

3. Reggie Schuebel to Mr. Paul Butler, March 28, 1956; and Paul M. Butler to Jack Christie, both in Folder: Eisenhower, Mamie—Television Birthday, Box 378, Norman, Craig and Kummel, Papers of the Democratic National Committee, JFKL.

4. In its statement to the US Senate Committee on Elections, BBDO cited several figures from *Printer's Ink* to demonstrate the growth in advertising. In 1940, total advertising expenditures were $2,087,600,000. In 1955, they were $9,039,000,000. See "Statement of Carroll P. Newton of Batten, Barton, Durstine & Osborn, Inc. Before the United States Senate Committee on Rules and Administration, Subcommittee on Privileges and Elections," October 1956. Folder: "Correspondence with Carroll P. Newton," Box, 49, Bruce Barton Papers, WHS. My thanks to Professor Cynthia Meyers for bringing this document to my attention.

5. [TV Plans Board], A Proposal: Television Campaigning for President Eisenhower, Folder: 1956 Campaign Ideas, Box 12, C. Langhorne Washburn Papers, 1952–1964, DDEL.

6. Ibid. The numbers here reflect the board's understanding of television's growth in 1956 and are not necessarily consistent with subsequent census and scholarly figures.

7. See Statement of Carroll P. Newton of Batten, Barton, Durstine & Osborn, Inc., Bruce Barton Papers, WHS.

8. On Montgomery's pay and commute, see "Behind the Scenes: Robert Montgomery," *New York Times*, March 1, 1956, 18. Online. Accessed September 17, 2013. Montgomery himself insisted that it would have been "an impertinence" to influence President Eisenhower's relationship to the people. In 1968, he described his activities in modest—and perhaps too modest—terms. "What I did attempt to do was, in a sense, to educate him about the uses of television, a medium unfamiliar to him except as a casual viewer when he entered the White House." See Robert Montgomery, *Open Letter from a Television Viewer* (New York: Heineman, 1968), 62.

9. On Montgomery's TV expertise, see Craig Allen, *Eisenhower and the Mass Media: Peace, Prosperity, and Prime-Time TV* (Chapel Hill: University of North Carolina Press, 1993), 32–33; and Evan Thomas, *Ike's Bluff: President Eisenhower's Secret Battle to Save the World* (New York: Little Brown, 2012), 117.

10. Allen, *Eisenhower and the Mass Media*, 34.

11. Ibid., 32–33. Confronting rampant fears about communism and the hydrogen bomb, Eisenhower's "Radio and Television Address to the American People on the State of the Nation" is justly regarded as one of the most successful speeches of his presidency. See Dwight Eisenhower, "Radio and Television Address to the American People on the State of the Nation," April 5, 1954. Online by Gerhard Peters and John T. Woolley, *The American Presidency Project*. Available at http://www.presidency.ucsb.edu/ws/?pid=10201. Accessed January 29, 2016.

12. "Television Campaigning for President Eisenhower," C. Langhorne Washburn Papers, DDEL. Emphasis is in the original.

13. C. Langhorne Washburn, Memorandum to National Citizens for Eisenhower, Recommended program for 1956 campaign operations, March 6[?], 1956, Folder: 1956 Campaign Ideas, Box 12, C. Langhorne Washburn Papers, 1952–1964, DDEL.

14. On the bandwagon, see William L. Bird, Jr., "TV and the Ike Age," *Hail to the Candidate: Presidential Campaigns from Banners to Broadcasts*, ed. Keith Melder (Washington, DC: Smithsonian Press, 1992), 169–173; and Stanley M. Rumbough, Jr., *Citizens for Eisenhower: The 1952 Presidential Campaign: Lessons for the Future?* (McLean, VA: International Publishers, 2013), 21, 77–81.

15. "A Salute to Ike" dinner, January 20, 1956, Closed Circuit Television Broadcast, 16 RNC: 26, Audio-Visual Collections, JFKL.

16. "Television Campaigning for President Eisenhower," C. Langhorne Washburn Papers, DDEL.

17. Hugh C. Foster, Memorandum to C. Langhorne Washburn, July 29, 1956, "Random Thoughts on Special Campaign Events," Folder: 1956 Campaign Ideas, Box 12, C. Langhorne Washburn Papers, 1952–1964, DDEL.

18. "Television Campaigning for President Eisenhower," C. Langhorne Washburn Papers, DDEL.

19. Ibid.

20. Ibid. Although the context does not necessarily suggest it, the phrase "inferred integration of the political personality" may refer to the psychoanalytic concept that motivational researchers found so intriguing. See Chapter 5.

21. Dwight D. Eisenhower to Sigurd Stanton Larmon, January 15, 1954, *The Papers of Dwight David Eisenhower*, Vol. 15, ed. Louis Galambos and Daun van Ee. (Baltimore: Johns Hopkins University Press, 1996), 817–818. Electronic database. Available at http://eisenhower.press.jhu.edu/. Accessed September 14, 2014.

22. Frederick A. Zaghi, oral history interview with John E. Wickman, November 5, 1968, OH-107, DDEL.

23. "Sigurd Larmon, 95, Guided Ad Agency Into Television Age," *New York Times*, January 7, 1987. Available at http://www.nytimes.com/1987/01/07/obituaries/sigurd-larmon-95-guided-ad-agency-into-television-age.html. Accessed July 14, 2012.

24. Preston Wood, telephone interview with author, February 6, 2010.

25. All details in this paragraph come from Wood, telephone interview.

26. "David Levy, 87, TV Executive Who Produced 'Addams Family,'" *New York Times*, February 6, 2000. Available at http://www.nytimes.com/2000/02/06/nyregion/david-levy-87-tv-executive-who-produced-addams-family.html. Accessed July 14, 2012; Allen, *Eisenhower and the Mass Media*, 16.

27. On Young & Rubicam's focus during the 1956 campaign, see Robert S. Bird, "This Will Be a 5-Minute Campaign," *The Washington Post*, September 9, 1956, E3. ProQuest Historical Newspapers. Electronic database. Accessed July 7, 2011. David Levy to Messrs. Hanker and Crider, September 4, 1956, Box 7, Young & Rubicam, Records of Citizens for Eisenhower, 1949–1960. DDEL.

28. William Morris Agency, telex to Preston Wood, September 12, 1956, Box 9, Young & Rubicam, Records of Citizens for Eisenhower, 1949–1960. DDEL.

29. Mildred Fox, memo to Messrs. Harding, Barnes, Levy, et al., Daily Progress Report—Citizens for Eisenhower TV Comm., September 12, 1956, Box 1, Young & Rubicam, Records of Citizens for Eisenhower, 1949–1960. DDEL.

30. Richard Dana, Memorandum to Messrs. P. Wood, A. Guire, E. Snowden, et al., September 14, 1956, Citizens for Eisenhower, Box 1, Young & Rubicam, Records of Citizens for Eisenhower, 1949–1960. DDEL.

31. Citizens for Eisenhower–Nixon, TV Operations, September 12, 1956, Box 6, Young & Rubicam, Records of Citizens for Eisenhower, 1949–1960. DDEL. On Cooper, see Donald Higgins to David Levy, September 17, 1956, and accompanying script, "Four Full Years," Box 6, Young & Rubicam, Records of Citizens for Eisenhower, 1949–1960. DDEL.

32. Washburn, memo to National Citizens for Eisenhower, March 6[?], 1956, Washburn Papers, 1952–1964, DDEL.

33. C. Langhorne Washburn, Action Plan and Garden Rally Check-off Sheet, October 25, 1956, Folder: Madison Square Garden Rally, Oct. 25, Box 13, C. Langhorne Washburn Papers, 1952–1964, DDEL.

34. K. A. Wood, Jr., Memorandum to David Levy, Citizens for Eisenhower TV Show, October 17, 1956, Box 9, Young & Rubicam, Records of Citizens for Eisenhower, 1949–1960. DDEL.

35. Philip Benjamin, "G.O.P. Loves Show at Garden Rally," *New York Times*, October 26, 1956, 18. Online. Accessed July 23, 2015.

36. Peter Kihss, "President to Visit City Today for Garden Rally," *New York Times*, October 25, 1956, 22. Online. Accessed July 23, 2015.

37. For example, the campaign had 20,000 tickets for a mezzanine that only fit 1,200 guests, and 40,000 tickets for the balcony (when the arena itself only held about 20,000 seats). See A. Fred Williamson to C. Langhorne Washburn, November 16, 1956, Folder: Madison Square Garden Rally Oct. 25, Box 13, C. Langhorne Washburn Papers, 1952–1964, DDEL.

38. David Levy, Memorandum to Messrs. J. Roosevelt, R. Tobin, L. Washburn, R. Montgomery, et al., October 25th Show, October 23, 1956, Folder: Madison Square Garden Rally Oct. 25, Box 13, C. Langhorne Washburn Papers, 1952–1964, DDEL.

39. Alistair Cook[e], "Contented Republicans Wait for Victory," *The Guardian*, October 25, 1956. Available at http://www.theguardian.com/world/1956/oct/25/usa.fromthearchive. Accessed September 26, 2013.

40. "Helen Hayes Is Back to Lead G.O.P. Drive," *New York Times*, August 22, 1956, 59. Online. Accessed July 23, 2015.

41. Fred Rayfield, "TV or Not TV: Mary Martin Likes Ike, But What Does Ike Like?" *New York Daily Compass*, February 12, 1952. Vol. 2, Scrapbooks from Eisenhower Campaign, Carton 61, Henry Cabot Lodge Papers, Massachusetts Historical Society.

42. On Waring, see "The History of Fred Waring," Fred Waring's America. Pennsylvania State University Libraries. Available at http://www.libraries.psu.edu/psul/digital/fwa.html. Accessed November 12, 2013.

43. Therese Lewis to Mrs. W. E. Dunkle, September 18, 1956, Box 1, Young & Rubicam, Records of Citizens for Eisenhower, 1949–1960. DDEL.

44. Compare Hayes's replies to Dorothy Townsend of the *Los Angeles Times* and to Winzola McLendon of the *Washington Post*. Dorothy Townsend, "Actress in Drive for G.O.P.," *Los Angeles Times*, September 22, 1956, 10; and Winzola McLendon, "Helen Hayes Does Some 'Ike-Liking,'" *Washington Post*, October 12, 1956, 43. ProQuest Historical Newspapers. Electronic database. Accessed July 7, 2011.

45. McLendon, "Helen Hayes," *Washington Post*, 43.

46. Townsend, "Actress," *Los Angeles Times*, 10.

47. Richard L. Coe, "Service Life on Two Fronts," *Washington Post*, October 5, 1956, 56. ProQuest Historical Newspapers. Electronic database. Accessed July 7, 2011. Michael Rogin connects *My Son John* with the concept of "Momism" that Philip Wylie discussed in his best-selling book *A Generation of Vipers* (1942). See Rogin, *Reagan: The Movie and Other Episodes In Political Demonology* (Berkeley: University of California Press, 1987), 240–244, 250–252.

48. David Levy, Memorandum, to Mr. Preston Wood, Citizens for Eisenhower, September 4, 1956; Alice B. Morgan to Preston Wood, September 6, 1956, Box 1, Young & Rubicam, Records of Citizens for Eisenhower, 1949–1960. DDEL.

49. "A Meeting with Lewis Douglas," October 30, 1956, 9:25–9:30 p.m., CBS-TV, Script, Box 6, Young & Rubicam, Records of Citizens for Eisenhower, 1949–1960. DDEL.

50. C. Langhorne Washburn to National Citizens for Eisenhower, March 6[?], 1956, C. Langhorne Washburn Papers, 1952–1964, DDEL.

51. Ibid., 4.

52. All quotations from Preston Wood to David Levy, August 3, 1956, Box 7, Young & Rubicam, Records of Citizens for Eisenhower, 1949–1960. DDEL.

53. Townsend, "Actress," *Los Angeles Times*, 10.

54. Theresa Lewis to Mrs. W. E. Dunkle, September 18, 1956, Young & Rubicam, Records of Citizens for Eisenhower, 1949–1960. DDEL.

55. Wood, telephone interview. See also biographical information collected at the Belknap Collection for the Performing Arts, University of Florida Libraries. Available at http://web.uflib.ufl.edu/spec/belknap/tvradio/wood.htm#table. Accessed July 22, 2015.

56. Ibid. Additional information supplied by the collections catalogue of the Paley Center for Media, New York, NY.

57. Wood to Levy, August 3, 1956, Young & Rubicam, DDEL.

58. See Daniel J. Galvin, *Presidential Party Building: Dwight D. Eisenhower to George W. Bush* (Princeton, NJ: Princeton University Press, 2010), 50–57.

59. Ibid., 49; Kihss, "President to Visit," *New York Times*, 22.

60. George Murphy to James Hagerty, April 24, 1953, as cited in Kathryn Cramer Brownell, "The Entertainment Estate: Hollywood in American Politics, 1932–1972," dissertation, Boston University, 2011, 220.

61. Wood to Levy, August 3, 1956, DDEL.

62. Wood, telephone interview.

63. My point here draws on Richard Schickel's book *Intimate Strangers: The Culture of Celebrity in America* (1985 orig.; Chicago: Ivan R. Dee, Revised 2000).

64. "Taxi Driver and Dog," Citizens for Eisenhower, video courtesy DDEL. From Museum of the Moving Image. *The Living Room Candidate: Presidential Campaign Commercials 1952–2012*. Available at www.livingroomcandidate.org/commercials/1956/taxi-driver-and-dog. Accessed July 26, 2015.

65. David Levy, Memorandum to Messrs. Harding, Zaghi, et al., Citizens TV, August 28, 1956, Box 7, Young & Rubicam, Records of Citizens for Eisenhower, 1949–1960. DDEL.

66. Peter Lisagor, "His TV Program Warms Ike's Heart," *Chicago Daily News*, October 13, 1956, 14. As clipped and collected in Box 6, Young & Rubicam, Records of Citizens for Eisenhower, 1949–1960. DDEL.

67. Mrs. and Mrs. J. H. Odin to Dwight Eisenhower, n.d., Folder: PPF 1-N-3, Box 339, White House Central Files, DDEL.

68. As quoted in Jeffrey Frank, *Ike and Dick: Portrait of a Strange Political Marriage* (New York: Simon & Schuster, 2013), 122.

69. Dwight Eisenhower to Mr. Sigurd S. Larmon, October 13, 1956, Box 6, Young & Rubicam, Records of Citizens for Eisenhower, 1949–1960. DDEL.

70. For a complete transcript, see Dwight D. Eisenhower, "The People Ask the President," CBS Television Broadcast, October 12, 1956. Online by Gerhard Peters and John T. Woolley, The American Presidency Project. Available at http://www.presidency.ucsb.edu/ws/?pid=10640. Accessed July 26, 2015. For plans and scripts, see "A National Town Meeting: Suggested Routine," Box 6, Young & Rubicam, Records of Citizens for Eisenhower, 1949–1960. DDEL.

71. Katherine Howard to Sherman Adams, December 7, 1956, PPF 1-N-3, Box 339, White House Central, DDEL.

72. See correspondence regarding this request in Folder: PPF 1-N-3, Box 339, White House Central Files, DDEL. Stanley Rumbough tells a similar story about the 1952 campaign, in which three unnamed movie moguls fought over who would be named the head of the Hollywood chapter of Citizens for Eisenhower; in the end, the campaign decided to name all three of them co-chairmen while expecting none of them to be actively involved in fundraising. See Stanley M. Rumbough, Jr., *Citizens for Eisenhower: The 1952 Presidential Campaign: Lessons for the Future?* (McLean, VA: International Publishers, 2013), 105.

73. Chris Rojek, *Celebrity* (London: Reaktion, 2001), 52.

74. Network Television for National Citizens for Eisenhower–Nixon, September 10, 1956, Box 7, Young & Rubicam, Records of Citizens for Eisenhower, 1949–1960. DDEL.

75. See Chapter 5 on the findings of these analysts.

76. James Reston, "Washington; 1956 and All That in Minnesota," *New York Times,* March 25, 1956, E10. Online. Accessed July 26, 2015.

77. "Television Campaigning for President Eisenhower," C. Langhorne Washburn Papers, DDEL.

Chapter 5

1. David Riesman, *The Lonely Crowd: A Study of the Changing American Character* (New Haven, CT: Yale University Press, 1950), 214.

2. Ibid., 215.

3. Charles McGrath, "The Lives They Lived: Big Thinkster," *New York Times Magazine,* December 29, 2002. Available at http://www.nytimes.com/2002/12/29/magazine/the-lives-they-lived-big-thinkster.html. Accessed October 8, 2013.

4. On the popularity of *The Lonely Crowd,* see Todd Gitlin's "Foreword" to *The Lonely Crowd, A Study of the Changing American Character* (New Haven, CT: Yale University Press, 2001), xii.

5. See Margaret Mead, "National Character and the Science of Anthropology," in *Culture and Social Character: The Work of David Riesman,* ed. Seymour Martin Lipset and Leo Lowenthal (New York: The Free Press of Glencoe, 1961), 15–26.

6. On Riesman's impact, see "David Riesman, obituary," *The Telegraph* (UK), May 13, 2002. Available at http://www.telegraph.co.uk/news/obituaries/1394001/David-Riesman. html. Accessed October 8, 2013; see *Time* magazine, September 27, 1954, cover page.

7. Riesman, *Lonely Crowd*, 215.

8. See Brownstein, *Power and the Glitter*, 93.

9. Dwight MacDonald, "Masscult & Midcult" (1960), *Against the American Grain* (New York: DaCapo, 1962; 1983 reprint), 74.

10. George W. Ball, "The Corn Flakes Campaign" (address to National Volunteers for Stevenson, Springfield), October 1, 1952, Folder 1; Public Policy Papers, Box 133, George W. Ball Papers, Seeley G. Mudd Manuscript Library, Princeton University Library (hereafter PUL.) All quotations from the speech refer to this document. Nixon's Checkers speech, Ball pointed out, was produced by the man responsible for *The Lone Ranger* and *Double or Nothing* TV series.

11. Since the 19th century, the Proctor & Gamble company had advertised the fact that Ivory Soap could float. My thanks to Gail Scott for this background information.

12. Stanley Kelley, Jr., *Professional Public Relations and Political Power* (Baltimore: Johns Hopkins University Press, 1956), 156.

13. As quoted in Vance Packard, *The Hidden Persuaders* (New York: David McKay, 1957), 193.

14. Ball, "Corn Flakes Campaign," George W. Ball Papers, Seeley G. Mudd Manuscript Library, PUL.

15. George Ball, *The Past Has Another Pattern* (New York: W. W. Norton, 1982), 144.

16. Philip Benjamin, "Truman Derides TV NATO Report," *New York Times*, December 27, 1957, 4. Online. Accessed November 14, 2013.

17. David Halberstam, *The Powers That Be* (Champagne, IL: University of Illinois Press, 1975), 236.

18. Bob Garfield, "The Top 100 Advertising Campaigns of the Century," *Advertising Age*. Available at http://adage.com/century/campaigns.html. Accessed July 25, 2015.

19. David Ogilvy, *Confessions of an Advertising Man* (London: Southbank, 2004), 190.

20. John G. Schneider, *The Golden Kazoo* (New York: Rinehart, 1956), 7–8.

21. Ibid., 3.

22. Ibid., 22–23.

23. Ibid., 82.

24. John G. Schneider, "'56: Show-Biz Flop," *The Nation*, November 24, 1956, 451.

25. Adlai Stevenson: "Address Accepting the Presidential Nomination at the Democratic National Convention in Chicago," August 17, 1956. Online by Gerhard Peters and John T. Woolley, The American Presidency Project. Available at http://www.presidency.ucsb.edu/ws/?pid=75172. Accessed July 25, 2015.

26. Elvin T. Lim, *The Anti-Intellectual Presidency: The Decline of Presidential Rhetoric from George Washington to George W. Bush* (New York: Oxford University Press, 2008), 43–44.

27. Jean H. Baker, *The Stevensons: A Biography of an American Family* (New York: W.W. Norton, 1997), 322.

28. All quotations come from George W. Ball, "Remarks to the Women's National Democratic Club," October 15, 1956, Folder 1, Box 133, George W. Ball Papers, Seeley G. Mudd Manuscript Library, Princeton University.

29. On the problem of affluence in the 1950s, see Daniel Horowitz, *The Anxieties of Affluence: Critiques of American Consumer Culture, 1939–1979* (Amherst: University of Massachusetts Press, 2005), 48–78 and 101–128.

30. "The Kitchen Debate," Teaching American History website. Available at http:// teachingamericanhistory.org/library/document/the-kitchen-debate/. Accessed November 15, 2013.

31. Riesman, *Lonely Crowd*, 215.

32. "Taxi Driver and Dog," 1956. From Museum of the Moving Image, *The Living Room Candidate: Presidential Campaign Commercials 1952–2012*. Available at http://livingroomcandidate.movingimage.us/election/index.php?nav_action=election&nav_subaction=overview&campaign_id=166. Accessed July 17, 2015.

33. John Steinbeck, "Madison Avenue and the Election," *Saturday Review*, March 31, 1956, 11. By the Fall of 1956, *The Jackie Gleason Show* had morphed into *The Honeymooners*, the half-hour sitcom about a belligerent New York bus driver and his friends and family. (The concept had evolved from a popular sketch on the Gleason show.) When Steinbeck was writing in March 1956, however, *The Jackie Gleason Show* was on the air.

34. Steinbeck, "Madison Avenue," 11.

35. Steinbeck's critique, as well as those of other writers in this chapter, may recall the academic attack on mass culture offered by the Marxist intellectuals who made up the Frankfurt School in the mid–20th century. In a series of brilliant, though dense, analyses, scholars such as Theodor Adorno, Max Horkheimer, and Leo Lowenthal critiqued the rise of the culture industry for its role in affirming and legitimizing oppressive societies, be they Fascist, Communist, or capitalist. See Max Horkheimer and Theodor Adorno, *Dialectic of Enlightenment*, ed. Gunzelin Schmid Noerr, trans. Edmund Jephcot (1947; Palo Alto, CA: Stanford University Press, 2007) and Leo Lowenthal, "The Triumph of Mass Idols" (1944) in *Literature, Popular Culture, and Society* (Englewood Cliffs, NJ: Prentice-Hall, 1961). Critics of the Frankfurt School have emphasized the ways in which audiences actively receive and critique popular culture, using it as the basis for their own meaning-making activities.

36. Eisenhower, as quoted in Lizabeth Cohen, *A Consumers' Republic: The Politics of Mass Consumption in Postwar America* (New York: W.W. Norton, 2003), 133. Inger L. Stole discusses the development of differentiated advertising groups in "Televised Consumption: Women, Advertisers, and the Early Daytime Television Industry," in *The Advertising and Consumer Culture Reader*, ed. Joseph Turow and Matthew P. McAllister (New York: Routledge, 2009), 59–75.

37. As quoted in Anna McCarthy, *The Citizen Machine: Governing by Television in 1950s America* (New York: New Press, 2010), 23.

38. See Edward L. Bernays, "The Engineering of Consent," *The Annals of the American Academy of Political and Social Science*, March 1947, 250: 113–20. Sage Premier Journals. Electronic Database. Accessed June 15, 2013.

39. As quoted in Steven J. Whitfield, *The Culture of the Cold War*, 2nd ed. (Baltimore: Johns Hopkins University Press, 1996), 177.

40. Packard, *Hidden Persuaders*, 7.

41. Ibid., 87, 80–81, 102.

42. Whitfield, *Culture of the Cold War*, 177.

43. Packard, *Hidden Persuaders*, 45: "*Sales Management* printed one estimate that $12,000,000 would be spent by marketers in 1956 for research in motivations."

44. Ibid., 27.

45. Ibid., 57.

46. Stephen Fox, *The Mirror Makers: A History of American Advertising and Its Creators* (New York: William Morrow, 1984), 186; Mark Crispin Miller, "Introduction," *The Hidden Persuaders* (Brooklyn: Ig Publishing, 2007), 19, 21.

47. Other important films of the period include Billy Wilder's World War II drama *Stalag 17* (1953), and, only because of its lead, *Prisoner of War* (1953), starring Ronald Reagan. See Charles S. Young, "Missing Action: POW Films, Brainwashing and the Korean War, 1954–1968," *Historical Journal of Film, Radio & Television*, March 1998. Academic Search Elite. Electronic Database. Accessed November 13, 2003.

48. See Daniel Horowitz, *Vance Packard and American Social Criticism* (Chapel Hill: University of North Carolina Press, 1994), 133 and Richard Severo, "Vance Packard, 82, Challenger of Consumerism, Dies," *New York Times*, December 13, 1996. Available at http://www.nytimes.com/1996/12/13/arts/vance-packard-82-challenger-of-consumerism-dies.html. Accessed February 1, 2016.

49. Phyllis Schlafly, *A Choice, Not an Echo: The Inside Story of How American Presidents Are Chosen* (Alton, IL: Pere Marquette Press, 1964), 55.

50. Packard, *Hidden Persuaders*, 183.

51. Institute for Motivational Research, Inc., "Emotions, Not Issues Will Decide Presidential Election the Institute for Motivational Research Finds," 5–9 and pretest appendix, American Consumer Culture: Market Research and American Business, 1935–1965. Website and Electronic Database. Available at http://www.consumerculture.amdigital.co.uk/Home/index. Accessed July 24, 2015.

52. David Levy, Memorandum to Mr. Harding, Mr. Zaghi, et al., Citizens TV, August 28, 1956, Box 6, Young & Rubicam, Records of Citizens for Eisenhower, 1949–1960. DDEL.

53. Network Television for National Citizens for Eisenhower–Nixon, September 10, 1956, Box 7, Young & Rubicam, Records of Citizens for Eisenhower, 1949–1960. DDEL.

54. Institute, "Emotions, Not Issues," 1.

55. Network Television for National Citizens, DDEL. Emphasis in the original.

56. Ernest Dichter, "The Psychology of T.V. Commercials: A Report," 24, 45, 56. October 1952, American Consumer Culture: Market Research and American Business, 1935–1965. Website and Electronic Database. Available at http://www.consumerculture.amdigital.co.uk/Home/index. Accessed July 24, 2015.

57. As quoted in Packard, *Hidden Persuaders*, 185.

58. Burdick as quoted in Packard, *Hidden Persuaders*, 185–86.

59. Ibid.

60. Mead, as quoted in Fox, *Mirror Makers*, 200.

61. Daniel J. Boorstin, *The Image: A Guide to Pseudo-Events in America* (1961 orig.; New York: Vintage, 1992), 11.

62. Ibid., 41.

63. Ibid., 44.

64. Ibid., 57.

65. Horowitz, *Anxieties of Affluence*, 59, 111.

66. Ibid., 37.

67. Schulberg developed the screenplay for *A Face in the Crowd* from his 1953 short story "Your Arkansas Traveler." A self-described "Hollywood prince," he had risen to prominence when he published his 1941 novel *What Makes Sammy Run?* an exposé based on his father's notorious career as the head of Paramount Pictures.

68. Advertising and PR executives were quick to defend their professions with a series of books and editorials mocking their critics. Frederick Manchee's *The Huckster's Revenge: The Truth About Life on Madison Avenue* (New York: Nelson, 1959) explicitly countered Packard's book. The editors of *Public Relations Journal* published an editorial titled "Hollywood's Version of the Public Relations Man," which castigated the film *The Man in the Gray Flannel Suit*. See *Public Relations Journal* (12) June 1956, 2.

69. In all actuality, the orphan Don Draper has many fathers. On advertising novels, see Fox, *Mirror Makers*, 199–216.

70. See Elia Kazan, *A Life* (New York: Knopf, 1988), 500.

71. "A Slick Performance: George Murphy," *New York Times*, August 24, 1956, 9. Online. Accessed July 17, 2015.

72. Richard Schickel, *Elia Kazan: A Biography* (New York: Harper Perennial, 2005), 336. Schulberg warned the *New Yorker* not to identify the blues-singing, charisma-exuding Rhodes with Elvis Presley, as if he were afraid that the controversies surrounding rock 'n' roll would quickly obscure the film's serious engagement with politics and the media. John McCarten, "Transfer to the East," *New Yorker*, December 1, 1956, 42. Digital Edition. Accessed January 22, 2011.

73. On Eisenhower's interest in Godfrey, see Craig Allen, *Eisenhower and the Mass Media: Peace, Prosperity, and Prime-Time TV* (Chapel Hill: University of North Carolina Press, 1993), 31.

74. Elia Kazan, "Introduction," *A Face in the Crowd: A Play for the Screen*, 16. *The Arthur Godfrey Show* was also sponsored by Lipton Tea.

75. Budd Schulberg, "Preface," *A Face in the Crowd: A Play for the Screen*, Introduction by Elia Kazan (New York: Bantam Books, 1957), 21.

76. Dichter, "Psychology of T.V. Commercials," 26, American Consumer Culture. Website and Electronic Database.

77. Mary Ann Watson, "Television and the Presidency: Eisenhower and Kennedy," in Gary R. Edgerton, ed., *The Columbia History of American Television* (New York: Columbia University Press, 2007), 214. In 1992, *Time* magazine reported that, at Eisenhower's request, Godfrey had recorded a public service announcement to be played over American radio and television in the event of a nuclear attack. See Ted Gup, "The Doomsday Blueprints," *Time*, August 10, 1992. Available at http://content.time.com/time/magazine/article/0,9171,976187,00.html. Accessed June 10, 2010.

78. Jeff Young, *Kazan: The Master Director Discusses His Films* (New York: New Market Press, 1999), 233–234.

79. Francois Truffaut, *The Films in My Life*, trans. Leonard Mayhew (New York: Simon and Schuster, 1978), 114.

80. Leonard Quart, "A Second Look: *A Face in the Crowd*," *Cineaste* (17:2) 1989, 31.

81. Young, *Kazan*, 235.

82. Michael Ciment, *Kazan on Kazan* (New York: Viking, 1974), 113.

83. Elia Kazan, "Introduction," Budd Schulberg, *A Face in the Crowd: A Play for the Screen* (New York: Bantam Books, 1957), 16.

84. Schickel, *Elia Kazan*, 342.

85. Ciment, *Kazan on Kazan*, 113.

86. Young, *Kazan*, 244.

87. Schickel, *Elia Kazan*, 337.

88. Denise Mann, *Hollywood Independents: The Postwar Talent Takeover* (Minneapolis: University of Minnesota Press, 2008), 170.

89. Ibid., 173.

90. Ibid., 177–178.

91. The coast-to-coast broadcast required extensive planning and took up space throughout the White House. "I was up to my neck in production on that one," Preston Wood recalled. Doing pick-up in the library and placing the president and his wife in the China Room, the Young & Rubicam team "wound up doing a lot of work in the ladies room on the 1st floor." The agency originally planned to have Ike and Mamie watching the festivities on a television screen, but they had to cancel that idea because the space was too tight. Preston Wood, telephone interview with author, February 6, 2010. See also Allen, *Eisenhower and the Mass Media*, 148.

92. Ciment, *Kazan on Kazan*, 115. See also the comments of Richard Sylbert, the film's designer, who described the film as a critique of the president's well-publicized congeniality. Eisenhower, he wrote, "was the first example I can remember of TV image making, which would in time become the hallmark of American politics; the triumph of the image over substance." Richard Sylbert and Sylvia Townsend, *Designing Movies: Portrait of a Hollywood Artist* (Westport, CT: Praeger, 2006), 65.

93. William F. Buckley, Jr., *National Review*, November 24, 1955, p. 5.

94. Alistair Cook[e], "Contented Republicans Wait for Victory," *The Guardian*, October 25, 1956. Available at http://www.theguardian.com/world/1956/oct/25/usa.fromthearchive. Accessed September 26, 2013.

95. Young, *Kazan*, 235.

96. Schickel, *Elia Kazan*, 343.

97. See Truffaut's comment that "Demagoguery, because it contains a certain euphoria, a good-guy aspect, is pre-eminently American. It is slowly but surely gaining a foothold in France in journalism, radio, and television by dint of the fact that the media are more and more inspired by American methods every day." Truffaut, *Films in My Life*, 113.

98. Bernays, "Engineering of Consent," 114. For more on Bernays's authoritarianism, see Stuart Ewen, *PR! A Social History of Spin* (New York: Basic Books, 1996), 9.

99. J. Hoberman, "The Long Road of Lonesome Rhodes," *Virginia Quarterly Review*, Fall 2008. Available at http://www.vqronline.org/articles/2008/fall/hoberman-lonesome-rhodes/. Accessed July 25, 2015.

100. Rhodes's confidence that his 65 million viewers will translate into electoral power anticipates the comments made by reality television star and businessman Donald Trump throughout the 2016 Republican presidential primary season. Among many examples, see the following statement from Trump's campaign on September 23, 2015: "As a candidate for president of the United States and the definitive front-runner in every poll, both nationally and state wide, including the just released poll in the state of Florida, Mr. Trump expects to be treated fairly. All you have to do is look at the tremendous ratings last night from 'The Late Show' with Stephen Colbert, where Mr. Trump was the guest, or the ratings from both debates, to fully understand the facts." Ashley Parker, First Draft, September 23, 2015: "Donald Trump Quits Fox News (Again) After O'Reilly Appearance Is Canceled," *New York Times*, September 23, 2015. Available at http://www.nytimes.com/politics/first-draft/2015/09/23/?_r=0. Accessed September 27, 2015.

101. Kazan, *A Life*, 567.

102. Packard, *Hidden Persuaders*, 181.

103. Robert Montgomery, *Open Letter from a Television Viewer* (New York: Heineman, 1968), 60, 72.

Chapter 6

1. The phrase comes from Adlai Stevenson, "Address Accepting the Presidential Nomination at the Democratic National Convention in Chicago," July 26, 1952. Online by Gerhard Peters and John T. Woolley, The American Presidency Project. Available at http://www.presidency.ucsb.edu/ws/?pid=75173. Accessed August 3, 2014.

2. Walter Lippmann, "Adlai Stevenson: A Model for Americans," *Milwaukee Sentinel*, July 21, 1965, 5. Google Newspapers. Available at http://news.google.com/newspapers?nid=1368&dat=19650721&id=_lMxAAAAIBAJ&sjid=QREEAAAAIBAJ&pg=7490,3213197. Accessed August 3, 2014.

3. On Stevenson's relationship to Princeton University, see "Stevenson, Adlai Ewing." Princeton University Companion: http://etcweb.princeton.edu/CampusWWW/Companion/stevenson_adlai.html. Accessed August 3, 2014.

4. Adlai Stevenson, "Address Accepting the Presidential Nomination at the Democratic National Convention in Chicago," July 26, 1952. Online by Gerhard Peters and John T. Woolley, The American Presidency Project. Available at http://www.presidency.ucsb.edu/ws/?pid=75173. Accessed July 31, 2015.

5. On the Internal Revenue scandal, see "Internal Revenue Bureau Revamped," in *CQ Almanac 1952*, 8th ed., 240–243. Washington, DC: *Congressional Quarterly*, 1953. Available at http://library.cqpress.com/cqalmanac/cqal52-1381321. Accessed January 30, 2016. In response to the scandal, the Bureau of Internal Revenue was reorganized as the Internal Revenue Service in 1953.

6. See "By the Numbers." National World War II Museum. Available at http://www.nationalww2museum.org/learn/education/for-students/ww2-history/ww2-by-the-numbers/us-military.html. Accessed August 5, 2014.

7. J. Leonard Reinsch, oral history interview with J. R. Fuchs, March 13–14, 1967, Atlanta, Georgia; Harry S. Truman Library and Museum. Available at https://www.trumanlibrary.org/oralhist/reinsch.htm. Accessed May 3, 2013.

8. Ronald Brownstein, *The Power and the Glitter: The Hollywood–Washington Connection* (New York: Pantheon, 1990), 124.

9. Norman Mailer, "Superman Comes to the Supermarket," *Esquire*, November 1960. Available at http://www.esquire.com/features/superman-supermarket?click=main_sr. Accessed April 22, 2014.

10. John Berryman, "23, The Lay of Ike," *The Dream Songs* (New York: Macmillan, 2007), 25.

11. Jonathan Bell, *California Crucible: The Forging of American Liberalism* (Philadelphia: University of Pennsylvania Press, 2012), 64.

12. "I Love the Gov," Stevenson, 1952. Video courtesy of the John F. Kennedy Presidential Library. From Museum of the Moving Image, *The Living Room Candidate: Presidential Campaign Commercials 1952–2012*. Available at www.livingroomcandidate.org/commercials/1952/i-love-the-gov. Accessed April 22, 2015.

13. Mercedes McCambridge, *The Quality of Mercy* (New York: Times Books, 1981), 191–92.

14. Ibid.

15. Ibid., 193.

16. Ibid., 191. After alcoholism led McCambridge to attempt suicide in 1959, Stevenson wrote his friend urging her to "Remember the words of St. Luke. 'It is only through endurance that we gain possession of our souls' " (ibid., 191).

17. Ibid., 202.

18. Ibid., 197–198.

19. This event was later widely reported to be a publicity stunt organized by Bacall's agent, though veteran reporter Anthony Leviero participated in the event and saw it differently. Anthony Leviero, "How to Live in a Fish Bowl: Some advice about this fish bowl—and prison—which is called the White House. . . ." *New York Times Sunday Magazine*, November 30, 1952, 33. ProQuest Historical Newspapers. Electronic Database. Accessed January 22, 2014. On the publicity stunt story, see Stuart Elliott, "Lauren Bacall Photo with Harry Truman Was Selfie Gone Viral for 1945," *New York Times*, August 14, 2014. Available at http://www.nytimes.com/2014/08/15/business/media/piano-photo-was-selfie-gone-viral-for-1945.html. Accessed October 13, 2015.

20. Lauren Bacall, *Lauren Bacall by Myself* (New York: Knopf, 1979), 202–203.

21. Ibid., 200–201.

22. McCambridge, *The Quality of Mercy*, 193–194.

23. Bacall, *Lauren Bacall by Myself*, 200.

24. Ibid., 201.

25. Bell, *California Crucible*, 65.

26. Bacall, *Lauren Bacall by Myself*, 200.

27. John H. Fenton, "Stevenson Favors Bureaucracy Curb," *New York Times*, October 27, 1952, 16. Online. Accessed January 18, 2014.

28. See Brownstein, *Power and the Glitter*, 130.

29. Virginia Pasley, "NYC Gives Adlai 'FDR' Greeting," *Newsday*, October 29, 1952, 4. ProQuest Historical Newspapers. Electronic Database. Accessed August 13, 2013.

30. Arthur M. Schlesinger, Jr., *Journals, 1952–2000* (New York: Penguin, 2007), 19.

31. Bob Thomas's syndicated "Hollywood" column quotes Allen Rivkin at length about the campaign strategy: "We are organizing a mass media campaign that would cost any commercial advertiser a million dollars. . . . But all of the services involved are donated and the costs are absorbed by our Hollywood contributors. Unlike the GOP group, which is concentrating on star appearances at rallies, the Democrats are mainly concerned with radio transcriptions and TV films. On his trip here last month, Stevenson spent an hour and a half before the movie cameras. The Hollywood volunteers are producing four 15-minute films and transcriptions and 25 one-minute shorts. Stevenson appears on three-fourths of them. This campaign material is sent on a mail-order basis by the Volunteers for Stevenson Committee in Chicago and the Democratic headquarters in Washington. The Hollywood group has also provided skits and songs, such as 'Sing a Song for Stevenson' and 'Ballots and Votes.' The latter is a parody on 'Buttons and Bows' by its authors, Ray Evans and Jay Livingstone." Bob Thomas, "Hollywood," (AP) *The Niagara Falls Gazette*, October 7, 1952, 20. Available at http://www.fultonhistory.com/Fulton.html. Accessed October 13, 2015.

32. Earnest Pascal, Memorandum to Tom Durrance, "The Women," September 22, 1952, Folder 12, Box 243, Adlai Stevenson Papers, Seeley G. Mudd Manuscript Library, PUL; Thomas, "Hollywood," 20.

33. "Stevenson Bandwagon," 1952, Hollywood for Stevenson, Kinescope, MR2007-46, Audio-Visual Collections, JFKL.

34. During a garden party organized to introduce Stevenson to people from the film industry, a producer told Bacall, "If you're smart, you'll keep your mouth shut and take no sides." See Bacall, *Lauren Bacall by Myself*, 199. On Bacall's and Bogart's involvement in the HUAC protest, see Chapter 7.

35. At one point, the Madison Square Garden audience was shown a film clip of the Republican songwriters skit.

36. Harvey Matusow, *False Witness* (New York: Cameron & Kahn, 1955), 111. Matusow reprints his testimony in front of the Senate Judiciary Committee in the book as follows: "I had been assistant to the editor of a blacklisting publication called *Counterattack*, which, through devious means, obtains information which is based on hearsay and surmise and not on fact. They claim it to be fact, but I worked there, and I believe it is surmise and hearsay and, for instance, in 1952 they compiled a list of people 'Stars for Stevenson,' for Adlai Stevenson, and these Hollywood stars are now listed in the files of Counterattack as left-wingers and controversial, unsuitable people."

37. Adlai Stevenson, "A Purpose for Modern Woman," Smith College commencement address. W.W. Norton College History Resources. Available at http://www.wwnorton.com/college/history/archive/resources/documents/ch32_04.htm. Accessed January 30, 2016.

38. Ronald Brownstein, *Power and the Glitter*, 126.

39. Bacall, *Lauren Bacall by Myself*, 204. The erotic idiom in which stars such as Bacall and McCambridge understood their attraction to Stevenson occurred in the midst of a well-orchestrated whisper campaign (conducted by J. Edgar Hoover's FBI) that the Illinois governor was a homosexual. See Jean Harvey Baker, *The Stevensons: A Biography of an American Family* (New York: W. W. Norton, 1997), 329–331.

40. On the lack of coordination in the Stevenson campaign, see Stanley Kelley, Jr., *Professional Public Relations and Political Power* (Baltimore: Johns Hopkins University Press, 1956), 157. Part of this stemmed from the Democrat's late entry into the presidential race, part from the governor's own leadership style and priorities.

41. On tensions between the newsreel and television people during the Truman administration, see Reinsch, Fuchs interview.

42. On Stevenson's not owning a TV, see Baker, *The Stevensons*, 321.

43. Kenan Heise, "U.N. Friend, Critic Porter McKeever," *Chicago Tribune*, March 5, 1992. Available at http://articles.chicagotribune.com/1992-03-05/news/9201210028_1_chicago-council-korean-war-state-james-f-byrnes. Accessed July 26, 2015.

44. Dick Babcock, Memorandum to Porter McKeever, n.d., Background information relative to Publicity and Public Relations job., Folder 14, Box 243, Adlai Stevenson Papers, Seeley G. Mudd Manuscript Library, PUL.

45. Hollywood for Stevenson-Sparkman, Memorandum to Tom Durrance, Distribution, September 22, 1952, Adlai Stevenson Papers, Folder 12, Box 243, Seeley G. Mudd Manuscript Library, PUL.

46. Kelley, *Professional Public Relations*, 160.

47. John L. Gwynn to Porter McKeever, September 17, 1952, Adlai Stevenson Papers, Folder 11, Box 243, MC 124, Seeley G. Mudd Manuscript Library, PUL. This letter complains about the agency's having to pay the DNC's bills.

48. On the lack of planning, see Kelley, *Professional Public Relations*, 158.

49. See Kathryn Cramer Brownell, *Show Biz Politics: Hollywood in American Political Life* (Chapel Hill: University of North Carolina Press, 2014), 153.

50. Edwin Diamond and Stephen Bates, *The Spot: The Rise of Political Advertising on Television* (Cambridge, MA: MIT Press, 1992), 46.

51. "Ike . . . Bob," Stevenson, 1952. Video courtesy of the John F. Kennedy Presidential Library. From Museum of the Moving Image, *The Living Room Candidate: Presidential Campaign Commercials 1952–2012*. Available at www.livingroomcandidate.org/commercials/1952/ikebob. Accessed April 22, 2014.

52. Stephen F. Whitfield, *The Culture of the Cold War* (Baltimore: Johns Hopkins University Press, 1996), 17. For statistics, see "Election of 1956," Online by Gerhard Peters and John T. Woolley, The American Presidency Project. Available at http://www.presidency.ucsb.edu/showelection.php?year=1956. Accessed April 25, 2014.

53. Robert Blanchard, "Stevenson Boom Starts in California," *Los Angeles Times*, October 14, 1955, 2. ProQuest Historical Newspapers. Electronic Database. Accessed July 7, 2014.

54. Richard Brown, Memorandum to John J. B. Shea et al., Public Relations Department, January 23, 1956, Folder 23, "Stars for Stevenson" and the Press, Box 7, J. B. Shea Papers on Adlai Stevenson, Seeley G. Mudd Manuscript Library, PUL.

55. "Stevenson Bids for Women's Vote in '56," *Los Angeles Times*, February 8, 1956, B3. ProQuest Historical Newspapers. Electronic Database. Accessed July 13, 2014.

56. Cass Canfield to Barry Bingham, March 23, 1956, including Memorandum from Joseph L. Mankiewicz, Project for Enlisting Talent on National Scale for Stevenson, Folder 13, National Talent Ideas, March 1956–April 1956, Box 7, J. B. Shea Papers on Adlai Stevenson, Seeley G. Mudd Manuscript Library, PUL.

57. Cass Canfield to Allan Jay Lerner, Oscar Hammerstein et al., August 31, 1956, Folder 13, National Talent Ideas, March 1956–April 1956, Box 7, J. B. Shea Papers on Adlai Stevenson, Seeley G. Mudd Manuscript Library, PUL.

58. Vance Packard, *The Hidden Persuaders* (New York: David McKay, 1957), 198–199.

59. On the "I Dreamed I Went . . . In My Maidenform Bra" campaign, see the Smithsonian Institution's History Wired website: http://historywired.si.edu/object.cfm?ID=294. Accessed July 27, 2015.

60. "Norman, Craig and Kummel, BBDO Square Off For Natl. Elections," *Space & Time: Inside Advertising*, March 5, 1956, Folder: Norman, Craig and Kummel, Box 384, Democratic National Committee, TV and Radio Division, JFKL; see also Packard, *Hidden Persuaders*, 199.

61. Marciarose Shestack, interview with author, Philadelphia, PA, May 12, 2012. See also Eugene Kummel to George Ball, August 29, 1956, Folder 3, Box 166, George W. Ball Papers, Seeley G. Mudd Manuscript Library, PUL.

62. Marciarose Shestack, Memorandum to Mr. Finnegan and Mr. McCloskey, Explanation of Schedule October 3, 1956. Folder: Norman, Craig and Kummel—Five Minute Spot Plans folder, Box 384, Democratic National Committee, Television and Radio Division, JFKL.

63. Packard, *Hidden Persuaders*, 200.

64. George W. Ball, *The Past Has Another Pattern* (New York: W.W. Norton, 1982), 144.

65. Ibid.

66. "The Man from Libertyville: TV Campaigning," Democratic National Committee, 1956, from Museum of the Moving Image, *The Living Room Candidate: Presidential Campaign Commercials 1952–2012*. Available at www.livingroomcandidate.org/commercials/1956/the-man-from-libertyville-tv-campaigning. Accessed April 11, 2014.

67. Jane Kalmus, Memorandum to Jack Shea, Personal, June 11, 1956, Folder 20, Publicity and Television Projects, May–August 1956, Box 7, J. B. Shea Papers on Adlai Stevenson, Seeley G. Mudd Manuscript Library, PUL.

68. Shestack interview.

69. Shestack interview. See also Harrison E. Salisbury, "Nixon Is Assailed: Stevenson Asks Help to Poland and Israel—Critical in Suez," *New York Times*, October 24, 1956, 1. Online. Accessed April 17, 2014.

70. See Leonard Levinson to Allen Rivkin, February 21, 1956, Folder 23, "Stars for Stevenson" and the Press, Box 7, J. B. Shea Papers on Adlai Stevenson, Seeley G. Mudd Manuscript Library, PUL.

71. "Democrats Stage 'Tele-Rally' on TNT Closed Circuit TV," *Broadcasting Telecasting*, October 22, 1956, 34. American Radio History. Available at http://americanradiohistory.com/Archive-BC/BC-1956/1956-10-22-BC.pdf Accessed March 7, 2014. See also "Democrats Plan Closed TV Show," *New York Times*, October 18, 1956. Online. Accessed March 7, 2014.

72. Adlai Stevenson: "Address Accepting the Presidential Nomination at the Democratic National Convention in Chicago," August 17, 1956. Online by Gerhard Peters and John T. Woolley, The American Presidency Project. Available at http://www.presidency.ucsb.edu/ws/?pid=75172. Accessed August 3, 2014.

73. "Which will win—salesmanship or sense?" Newspaper advertisement. Folder 1, Advertisements, 1956, Box 7, J. B. Shea Papers on Adlai Stevenson, Seeley G. Mudd Manuscript Library, PUL.

74. All quotes are from Claude Traverse to John H. Sharon, October 24, 1956, Folder 9, Public Policy Papers, Box 167, George W. Ball Papers, Seeley G. Mudd Manuscript Library, PUL.

75. William Shakespeare, *Julius Caesar*, ed. David Daniell (New York: Bloomsbury Arden, 1998), Act 3, Scene 3, line 75.

76. Traverse to Sharon, October 24, 1956, PUL.

77. Democrats had made a similar argument in 1940 when they attacked Montgomery's "We the People" for its portrait of Wendell Willkie as a man of the people. "As makers of entertainment," they proclaimed in a *New York Times* advertisement, "we are experts in the art of make-believe. . . . We of the films also know how to make a 'star' overnight." "Why We of Hollywood Will Vote for Roosevelt," *New York Times*, October 31, 1940, p. 26. ProQuest Historical Newspapers. Electronic Database. Accessed January 9, 2008.

78. Quoted in Peter Guralnick, *Last Train to Memphis: The Rise of Elvis Presley* (New York: Little, Brown, 1994), 327.

79. Traverse to Sharon, October 24, 1956, PUL.

80. Jack Gould, "TV: Campaign Highlights," *New York Times*, October 15, 1956, 5. Online. Accessed October 5, 2010.

81. See Herb Lyon, "Tower Ticker," *Chicago Daily Tribune*, July 1, 1958, A4; and Dorothy Kilgallen, "Star Sleeps Through Show!" *Washington Post*, September 11, 1958, C10. ProQuest Historical Newspapers. Electronic Database. Accessed July 13, 2014.

Chapter 7

1. Claude Robinson, "The Gentle Art of Persuasion," *Public Relations Journal*, vol. 12, November 1956, 15; George H. Gallup with Leyton E. Carter, "TV's Sorriest Commercials," *Public Relations Journal*, vol. 12, August 1956, 9; Charles M. Hackett, vol. 12, "The Forceful and Vivid Vernacular of the Eye," *Public Relations Journal*, November 1956, 15–16. My thanks to Stuart Ewen's *PR! A Social History of Spin* (New York: Basic Books, 1996) for leading me to these sources.

2. James F. Kelleher, "TV's Perennial Star: The Political Candidate," *Public Relations Journal*, vol. 12, April 1956, 6.

3. Ibid., 7.

4. Ibid., 6–7.

5. Ibid., 18.

6. Ibid., 6.

7. Five months later, the *Journal* would publish an article on public relations in Eisenhower's White House. Fletcher Knedsel, "Public Relations at the White House," *Public Relations Journal*, vol. 12, September 1956, 3.

8. Michael Rogin, *Reagan: The Movie and Other Episodes in Political Demonology* (Berkeley: University of California Press, 1987); Lou Cannon, *Reagan* (New York: Perigee, 1982); Gary Wills, *Reagan's America: Innocents at Home*, (New York: Penguin, 2000); Edmund Morris, *Dutch: A Memoir of Ronald Reagan* (New York: Random House, 1999). Another valuable interpretation of Reagan and Hollywood is Anthony Lane's "The Method President: Ronald Reagan and the Movies," *New Yorker*, October 18, 2004. Available at http://www.newyorker.com/magazine/2004/10/18/the-method-president. Accessed January 22, 2016.

9. Thomas W. Evans, *The Education of Ronald Reagan: The General Electric Years and the Untold Story of His Conversion to Conservatism* (New York: Columbia University Press, 2006); Timothy Raphael, *The President Electric: Ronald Reagan and the Politics of Performance* (Ann Arbor: University of Michigan Press, 2009).

10. Reagan as quoted in Evans, *Education of Ronald Reagan*, 13.

11. Piers Brendon, *Ike: His Life and Times* (New York: Harper and Row, 1986), 245, 248.

12. See Anthony Slide, *Inside the Hollywood Fan Magazine: A History of Star Makers, Fabricators, and Gossip Mongers* (Oxford: University of Mississippi Press, 2010), 160.

13. "The Battle of Hollywood," *Time* 43.7, February 14, 1944, 25. Academic Search Premier. Electronic Database. Accessed December 17, 2013.

14. See Jennifer Frost, *Hedda Hopper's Hollywood: Celebrity Gossip and American Conservatism* (New York: New York University Press, 2011), 82–88, 131.

15. James M. Cain, "Is Hollywood Red?" *Photoplay*, August 1947, 21, 105.

16. The article was meant to rehabilitate the reputation of the director Edward Dymytryk after he had appeared before HUAC and "named names." Richard English, "What Makes a Hollywood Communist?" *Saturday Evening Post*, May 19, 1951, 30. Available

at http://www.saturdayeveningpost.com/wp-content/uploads/satevepost/what_makes_ a_hollywood_communist_by_richard_english.pdf. Accessed July 26, 2015.

17. Frost, *Hedda Hopper's Hollywood*, 123–124.

18. Humphrey Bogart, "I'm No Communist," *Photoplay*, May 1948, 86.

19. "Battle of Hollywood," *Time*, 25.

20. As quoted in Kathryn Cramer Brownell, *Show Biz Politics: Hollywood in American Political Life* (Chapel Hill: University of North Carolina Press, 2014), 117.

21. Bogart, "I'm No Communist," 87.

22. Lary May, *The Big Tomorrow: Hollywood and the Politics of the American Way* (Chicago: University of Chicago Press, 2000), 177.

23. On the founding of the Motion Picture Alliance for the Preservation of American Ideals, see Steven J. Ross, *Hollywood Left and Right*, 140–141; Larry Ceplair and Steven Englund, *The Inquisition in Hollywood: Politics in the Film Community, 1930–1960* (Garden City, NY: Anchor Press, 1980), 209–210.

24. [Ayn Rand], *Screen Guide for Americans* (Beverly Hills, CA: Motion Picture Alliance for the Preservation of American Ideals, n.d.). Available at http://archive.lib. msu.edu/DMC/AmRad/screenguideamericans.pdf. Accessed February 14, 2014.

25. See Donald T. Critchlow, *When Hollywood Was Right: How Movie Stars, Studio Moguls, and Big Business Remade American Politics* (New York: Cambridge University Press, 2013), 84–85.

26. Ibid., 94; and "Radio, Television and Floodlights Will Open Red Film Inquiry Today," *New York Times*, October 19, 1947, 14. Online. Accessed February 14, 2014.

27. Bogart, "I'm No Communist," 87.

28. Cabell Phillips, "Un-American Committee Puts on its 'Big Show,'" *New York Times*, October 28, 1947, E7. Online. Accessed February 14, 2014.

29. Ibid.

30. Samuel A. Tower, "79 in Hollywood Found Subversive, Inquiry Head Says," *New York Times*, October 23, 1947, 1. Accessed February 1, 2014.

31. Ronald Reagan with Richard G. Hubler, *Where's the Rest of Me? The Autobiography of Ronald Reagan* (New York: Dell, 1965), 192.

32. The literature on Reagan and HICCASP is extensive. Good summaries include Steven J. Ross, *Hollywood Left and Right: How Movie Stars Shapes American Politics* (New York: Oxford University Press, 2012), 143–148; and Brownell, *Show Biz Politics*, 106–107.

33. See Ross, *Hollywood Left and Right*, 148.

34. On Reagan's cooperation with the FBI, Critchlow, *When Hollywood Was Right*, 83–84; and Anne Edwards, *Early Reagan: The Rise to Power* (Lanham, MD: Taylor Trade, 2012), 304–307.

35. "The Testimony of Ronald Reagan and Walter Disney." From George Mason University. History Matters. Available at http://historymatters.gmu.edu/d/6458. Accessed February 14, 2014. Reagan insisted that celebrities retain their political voice, and he skillfully deflected the committee's concern that Communists exerted undue influence over the Screen Actors Guild and entertainment industry. "99 percent of us are pretty well aware of what is going on," he told the congressmen, "and I think within the bounds of our democratic rights, and never once stepping over the rights given us by democracy, we have done a pretty good job in our business of keeping those people's activities curtailed."

Citing Thomas Jefferson, Reagan argued that Americans should focus on exposing the truth rather than trying to outlaw disagreeable organizations and activities. "I happen to be very proud of the industry in which I work; I happen to be very proud of the way in which we conducted the fight. I do not believe the Communists have ever at any time been able to use the motion-picture screen as a sounding board for their philosophy or ideology."

36. See Ceplair and Englund, *Inquisition in Hollywood*, 373–374. On Robinson's circumstances, see Ross, *Hollywood Left and Right*, 116–124. On Lucille Ball, see Thomas Doherty, *Cold War, Cool Medium: Television, McCarthyism, and American Culture* (New York: Columbia University Press, 2003), 49–59.

37. For a list of Hollywood workers who were named in the HUAC hearings or interviewed by the committee itself, see U.S. Congress, House of Representatives, Annual Report for the Committee on Un-American Activities for the Year 1952, 82nd Cong., 2nd sess., December 28, 1952. Available at https://archive.org/details/annualreportfory1952unit. Accessed on December 20, 2014.

38. See Edwards, *Early Reagan*, 425–28.

39. Cannon, *Reagan*, 92.

40. See Edwards, *Early Reagan*, 447.

41. Reagan, *Where's the Rest of Me?* 250.

42. Richard M. Fried, *The Man Everybody Knew: Bruce Barton and the Making of Modern America* (Chicago: Ivan R. Dee, 2005), 61.

43. Raphael, *President Electric*, 166–167.

44. Fried, *Man Everybody Knew*, 59–62.

45. Ibid., 145.

46. Ibid., 146. On DuPont and BBDO, see William L. Bird, *"Better Living": Advertising, Media, and the New Vocabulary of Business Leadership, 1935–1955* (Chicago: Northwestern University Press, 1999), 62–85.

47. Cynthia B. Meyers, "BBDO and US Steel on Radio and Television, 1948–53: The Problems of Sponsorship, New Media, and the Communist Threat," 4. Presented at On Archives! Conference, July 9, 2010. My thanks to Professor Meyers for sharing this paper with me.

48. Ibid., 5.

49. See David Everitt, *A Shadow of Red: Communism and the Blacklist in Radio and Television* (Chicago: Ivan R. Dee, 2007), 133.

50. Fried, *Man Everybody Knew*, 206.

51. Meyers, "BBDO and US Steel," 13.

52. Fried, *Man Everybody Knew*, 206.

53. John Cogley, *Report on Blacklisting*, Vol. II: *Radio-Television* (New York: Fund for the Republic, 1956), 118.

54. Cogley, *Report on Blacklisting*, 115. On Wren's background, see Everitt, *Shadow of Red*, 14.

55. Cogley, *Report on Blacklisting*, 62. Sponsored by the Fund for the Republic, Cogley's report produced its own HUAC investigation. The committee had two motives when it asked Cogley, a *Commonweal* columnist and former editor of the *Chicago Catholic Worker*, to appear in July 1956: one, to follow up on the relationships he revealed about blacklisted stars; and two, to determine whether his publication was "a friend or foe in America's

struggle against Communism." "House Group Inquires into Blacklisting Report," *Los Angeles Times*, July 11, 1956, 23. ProQuest Historical Newspapers. Online. Accessed December 10, 2014. During the three days of hearings, George Sokolsky and American Legion president James F. O'Neil acknowledged that they worked to "rehabilitate" stars but denied being part of a "clearance board" that engaged in blacklisting. See Anthony Lewis, "'Clearing' Board on Actors Denied," *New York Times*, July 12, 1956, 10. Online. Accessed December 8, 2014.

56. See Cogley, *Report on Blacklisting*, 60–62.

57. Everitt, *Shadow of Red*, 106.

58. Cogley, *Report on Blacklisting*, 62.

59. Ibid., 120.

60. Earl B. Dunckel, "Ronald Reagan and The General Electric Theater, 1954–1955," oral history interview with Gabrielle Morris, Regional Oral History Office, The Bancroft Library, University of California, 1982. Oral history transcript, University of California Libraries (Berkeley, 1982). Available at https://archive.org/stream/reagangetheatre-00duncrich/reagangetheatre00duncrich_djvu.txt. Accessed November 10, 2014.

61. The story has several variants and has become part of the Reagan mythology. In one version, Nancy used Ron's anti-communism as a screen to get a date with the handsome and recently divorced actor; in another, their relationship took root amid the confusion of the Cold War with Ron acting as a guardian and hero. For an official version, see the Reagan Foundation website: Available at http://www.reaganfoundation.org/nancy-reagan-life-and-times.aspx. Accessed July 26, 2015. Edwards casts suspicion on Nancy's preferred story in *Early Reagan*, 400–403.

62. See Bird, "*Better Living*," 201.

63. Anna McCarthy, *The Citizen Machine: Governing by Television in 1950s America* (New York: New Press, 2010), 39.

64. Dunckel, "Ronald Reagan."

65. Fried, *Man Everybody Knew*, 210.

66. Hackett, "Vernacular of the Eye," 15–16.

67. See Cabell Phillips, "The Eisenhower 'Inner Circle'; No President before has created such an elaborate apparatus of aides and advisers. Here are the men around Eisenhower and the roles they play," *New York Times Magazine*, February 3, 1957, 175. ProQuest Historical Newspapers. Accessed November 12, 2014.

68. In 1956, the year that BBDO opened an office in Los Angeles, the producers moved the show full-time to Los Angeles, where the program was produced by MCA, the production company run by Reagan's talent agent, Lew Wasserman. The reason for the move was that live television took more airtime, and the company discovered that they could get through nine more pages of material when the episode was taped. Nine pages meant richer stories with more complex characters and plot lines.

69. For a complete list of the cast, crew, and writers of *The General Electric Theater*, see General Electric Theater (1953–1962) on the IMDb website. Available at http://www.imdb.com/title/tt0045395/.

70. Stanley Rubin, video interview with Gary Rutkowski, Century City, CA, June 17, 2004, Archive of American Television website. Available at http://emmytvlegends.org/interviews/people/stanley-rubin#. Accessed July 26, 2015.

71. Public Relations Department, Batten, Barton, Durstine & Osborn, Inc., "A Recommended Audience Promotion Plan for The General Electric Theater," May 17, 1955,

Folder: Recommended audience promotion plan, Box 1, Jim Brown Papers, 1945–1959, David M. Rubenstein Rare Book & Manuscript Library, Duke University Libraries (hereafter DUL).

72. Ibid. The promotional budget of $74,636.86 would be the equivalent of about $651,000 today.

73. Ernest Dichter, "The Psychology of T.V. Commercials: A Report," 25. October 1952, American Consumer Culture: Market Research and American Business, 1935–1965. Electronic Database and website. Available at http://www.consumerculture.amdigital. co.uk/Home/index. Accessed July 24, 2015. Dichter's use of the term "announcer" encompasses a variety of roles on TV, including those of personalities such as Arthur Godfrey, spokespersons such as Westinghouse's Betty Furness and the GE Theater's "Progress Reporter" Don Herbert, and hosts such as Reagan.

74. "Electric Servants," *General Electric Theater*, television commercial. Available at http://www.youtube.com/watch?v=u5Lz1C53RwI. Accessed April 2, 2015. On the dating of the program, see Bird, *"Better Living,"* 205–206. The story of the electrical panel comes from Reagan, *Where's the Rest of Me?* 273.

75. Edwards, *Early Reagan*, 461.

76. Raphael, *President Electric*, 159–60.

77. Paul Kengor, *The Crusader: Ronald Reagan and the Fall of Communism* (New York: Harper Collins, 2007), 24.

78. Ronald Reagan to Lorraine and Elwood Wagner, June 3, 1962, in *Reagan: A Life in Letters*, ed. Kiron Skinner, Annelise Anderson, and Martin Anderson (New York: Free Press, 2003), 145.

79. Ibid., Ronald Reagan to Richard Nixon, July 15, 1960, 705.

80. Dave Danforth to Bruce Barton, January 19, 1954 with attached document: Chester H. Lang, "Business Review: Public Relations Services Division," January 7, 1954, client presentation, Folder: General Electric, 1940, 1948–1958, Box 76, Correspondence, Bruce Barton Papers, WHS.

81. Ibid.

82. McCarthy, *Citizen Machine*, 11.

83. Dunckel, "Ronald Reagan," 9.

84. Reagan, *Where's the Rest of Me?* 257.

85. [BBDO], All Activities Report for the BBDO General Electric Institutional Account, Report #3, June 15, 1954. Folder: General Electric, 1940, 1948–1958, Box 76, Correspondence, Bruce Barton Papers, WHS.

86. Reagan, *Where's the Rest of Me?* 257.

87. Reagan describes his GE tours in *Where's the Rest of Me?* 257–61. His account should be read in the context of the accounts by Dunckel, "Ronald Reagan" and Evans, *Education of Ronald Reagan*.

88. Reagan as quoted in Cannon, *Reagan*, 93.

89. Edward Langley, "Reagan Philosophy Changed by GE Years," *Knoxville Journal*, July 14, 1980, p. 4.

90. The details of Boulware's activities are interesting. For managers, there was a special GE school in Crotonville, New York, to teach the company's leadership philosophy. Factory book clubs invited employees to discuss pro-business writings and then participate in surveys to track what information they had gleaned. Boulware's operation produced a library of publications that addressed corporate and economic policy. There were newsletters,

magazines, break-room posters, and pamphlets inserted into paychecks. The ostensibly nonpartisan material focused on the need to establish a "better business climate." An employee newspaper, *Works News*, featured such articles as "General Electric Keeps Trying to Make Jobs Better," "Should Pay Be Equal Everywhere?" and "What Is Communism? What Is Capitalism? What Is the Difference to You?" See Evans, 69–80, 50–51.

91. Ibid., 68.

92. Ibid., 91.

93. Dunckel, "Ronald Reagan," 30.

94. [BBDO], All Activities Report for the BBDO General Electric Institutional Account, Report #2, May 15, 1954. Folder: General Electric, 1940, 1948–1958, Box 76, Correspondence, Bruce Barton Papers, WHS.

95. Reagan, *Where's the Rest of Me?* 263.

96. Evans, *Education of Ronald Reagan*, 96–7.

97. Reagan, *Where's the Rest of Me?* 266.

98. On Boulware's financial support, see Evans, *Education of Ronald Reagan*, 106. On Reagan's subscription, see Langley, "Reagan Philosophy," 4. When Reagan left GE in 1962, he wrote Buckley a lugubrious letter apologizing that he was "between engagements" and would no longer be able to donate funds to *National Review*. See Ronald Reagan to William F. Buckley, Jr., June 16, 1962, in *Reagan: Letters*, 281.

99. Titled "A Time for Choosing," but commonly called "The Speech," Reagan's televised speech for Barry Goldwater on the night of October 27, 1964, is widely thought to have established him as a national political figure. On the drama of the speech, see Rick Perlstein, *Before the Storm: Barry Goldwater and the Unmaking of the American Consensus* (New York: Nation Books, 2009), 500–504.

100. In the early 1960s, Reagan's power still rested on his being perceived as a cross-over Democrat. When he officially endorsed Nixon in 1960, he offered to switch his membership to the Republican Party. The Nixon campaign gratefully accepted the endorsement but asked Reagan to remain a member of the Democratic Party. His endorsement would be more valuable that way. See Cannon, *Reagan*, 96.

101. See Rubin, video interview with Rutkowski; and Morris, *Dutch*, 313–314.

102. See William L. Bird, "General Electric Theater," Museum of Broadcast Communications website. Available at http://www.museum.tv/eotv/generalelect.htm. Accessed July 26, 2015.

103. Morris, *Dutch*, 321.

104. On the TVA dam speech, the Kennedy administration, and the cancellation of *GE Theater*, see Reagan, *Where's the Rest of Me?* 268–273.

105. Perlstein, *Before the Storm*, 501.

106. Reagan, *Where's the Rest of Me?* 261.

Chapter 8

1. Stage and event details from Jerome Robbins, Folder 4, New York's Salute to the President, May 3, 1962, Box 137, Jerome Robbins Papers, Jerome Robbins Dance Division, The New York Public Library for the Performing Arts.

2. "Happy Birthday, Mr. President" Invitation, Sale 9216, Lot 54, Christie's Auction House. Available at http://www.christies.com/LotFinder/lot_details.aspx?intObjectID=1646518. Accessed February 26, 2009.

3. Gloria Steinem, as quoted in Sarah Churchwell, *The Many Lives of Marilyn Monroe* (New York: Metropolitan Books, 2004), 273.

4. Robert Dallek, *J.F.K.: An Unfinished Life, 1917–1963* (New York: Little, Brown, 2003), 398–399, 472–473.

5. Leo Egan, "Kennedy, at 'Salute' Here, Asks Voters to Back Party," *New York Times*, May 20, 1962, 1; "Text of President's Garden Address," *New York Times*, May 20, 1962, 63. Both accessed February 26, 2009.

6. See Dallek, *J.F.K.: An Unfinished Life*, 613.

7. Fred Lawrence Guiles, *Legend: The Life and Death of Marilyn Monroe* (New York: Stein and Day, 1984), 423. Kennedy's showmanship impressed Richard Adler, the songwriter who produced "New York's Salute to the President." In the 1950s, Adler had co-written the music and lyrics for the Broadway hits *The Pajama Game* and *Damn Yankees*, both of which also produced top-selling singles for the likes of Rosemary Clooney, Eddie Fisher, and Sarah Vaughn. With Kennedy's election (and the death of his writing partner, Jerry Ross), Adler began producing and directing celebrity-themed events for the president. He retained his position as Arts Consultant to the White House through all of Lyndon Johnson's administration. In his 1990 autobiography, Adler wrote that Kennedy "was insatiably fascinated with show business and the people who worked in it." See Richard Adler (with Lee Davis), *You Gotta Have Heart* (New York: Dutton, 1990), 228.

8. Guiles, *Legend*, 423.

9. John Kenneth Galbraith, *The Affluent Society* (Boston: Houghton-Mifflin, 1958), 147, 155.

10. Ibid., 140, 193, 260.

11. See Christine Gledhill, ed., *Stardom: Industry of Desire* (New York: Routledge, 1991).

12. Eleanor Roosevelt was perhaps the most prominent figure to doubt Kennedy's liberalism and pointed to his equivocation about confronting Joseph McCarthy as evidence of his lack of political commitment. She led a sizeable group that hoped Stevenson would defeat Kennedy in 1960 and only helped Kennedy late in the campaign. See Joseph P. Lash, *Eleanor: The Years Alone* (New York: W. W. Norton, 2014), 261, 382–408.

13. Monroe had experienced a similar phenomenon during her years with playwright Arthur Miller. The night before his 1956 HUAC testimony, the playwright received word that the committee would withdraw its subpoena if Monroe agreed to be photographed shaking hands with its chairman. Miller declined, and on July 25, the House of Representatives found him in contempt of Congress for refusing to give the names of other writers who had attended Communist Party meetings with him in the 1940s. See Arthur Miller, *Timebends: A Life* (1987; New York: Penguin, 1995), 406; and Allen Drury, "House Votes 373–9 for Citing Miller," *New York Times*, July 26, 1956, 7. Online. Accessed July 10, 2011.

14. In conversation with Arthur B. Schelsinger, Jr., *Jacqueline Kennedy: Historic Conversations on Life with John F. Kennedy*, ed. Caroline Kennedy and Michael Beschloss (New York: Hyperion, 2011), 241–242. Jackie's comments may also reflect the Kennedy family's suspicion that Stevenson was a closeted homosexual. See Jean Harvey Baker, *The Stevensons: A Biography of an American Family* (New York: W. W. Norton, 1997), 329–331.

15. Norman Mailer, "Superman Comes to the Supermarket," *Esquire*, November 1960. Available at http://www.esquire.com/features/superman-supermarket?click=main_sr. Accessed April 22, 2014.

16. Egan, "Kennedy," *New York Times*, May 20, 1962; Monroe bought two $1,000 tickets and was accompanied by Isidore Miller, the father of her former husband, playwright

Arthur Miller. For a discussion of Young & Rubicam and the 1956 Eisenhower rally, see chapter 4.

17. "Monroe 'Happy Birthday, Mr. President' Dress Brings $1.27 Million at Christie's," Press release, PSA/ DNA Authentication Services, October 28, 1999. Available at www. psadna.com. Accessed January 4, 2010.

18. Alexander Autographs, "Gen. Dwight D. Eisenhower's Four-Star General's Helmet," Sale 41, Lot 797. Available at www.alexanderautographs.com. Accessed May 28, 2010. The sale price comes from Peter Klarnet, Alexander Autographs, email message to author, June 11, 2010.

19. See S. Paige Baty, *American Monroe: The Making of a Body Politic* (Berkeley: University of California Press, 1995).

20. J. Randy Taraborrelli, *The Secret Life of Marilyn Monroe* (New York: Rose Books, 2009), 433.

21. Although estimates vary widely, all agree that Joseph Kennedy's time in Hollywood produced the bulk of his family's wealth. The *Boston Globe* estimated he had made as much as $12 million; *Fortune* $8.5 million. See Cari Beauchamp, *Joseph P. Kennedy Presents: The Hollywood Years* (New York: Knopf, 2009), 324. See also Beauchamp, "The Mogul in Mr. Kennedy," *Vanity Fair*, April 2002. Available at http://www.vanityfair.com/politics/features/2002/04/joekennedy200204?currentPage=1. Accessed January 4, 2010.

22. Beauchamp, *Kennedy Presents*, 380.

23. Alan Schroeder, *Celebrity-in-Chief: How Show Business Took Over the White House* (Boulder, CO: Westview, 2004), 288.

24. Adler, *You Gotta Have Heart*, 228–229.

25. Peter Lawford, oral history interview with John F. Stewart, Los Angeles, CA, February 23, 1968, Oral History Program, JFKL.

26. "Interview with Frank Sinatra, George Axelrod, and John Frankenheimer" (supplementary material). *The Manchurian Candidate*, Special Edition DVD, 20th-Century Fox, 2004.

27. Beatty declined the offer. David M. Lubin, *Shooting Kennedy: JFK and the Culture of Images* (Berkeley: University of California Press, 2003), 225–226.

28. Lubin, *Shooting Kennedy*, 124.

29. Patrick J. Lucey, oral history interview with Leon D. Epstein, Madison, WI, August 1, 1964, Oral History Program, JFKL.

30. Robert Drew, *Primary*, DVD, Docurama, 1960.

31. Samuel Cahn and Frank Sinatra, "High Hopes with John Kennedy," 1960. The complete lyrics can be found at http://www.jfklibrary.org/Research/Research-Aids/Ready-Reference/JFK-Fast-Facts/High-Hopes.aspx. Accessed July 27, 2015.

32. Pat Lawford to Steven Smith, February 17, 1960; Stephen E. Smith to Mrs. Peter Lawford, February 20, 1960, Folder: Lawford, Patricia, Box 927 California, Pre-Presidential Papers, Presidential Campaign Files, 1960, JFKL.

33. Stephen Smith, Telegram to Mrs. Peter Lawford, February 23, 1960, Folder: Lawford, Patricia, Box 927 California, Pre-Presidential Papers, Presidential Campaign Files, 1960, JFKL.

34. Austin C. Wehrwein, "Kennedy Opens Wisconsin Drive with Handshakes and a Record," *New York Times*, February 17, 1960, 25. Online. Accessed March 15, 2011.

35. Austin Wehrwein, "Wisconsin Battle One of Contrasts," *New York Times*, February 21, 1960, 55. Online. Accessed March 15, 2011.

36. Dallek, *J.F.K.: An Unfinished Life*, 249.

37. All details come from Michael V. Kelly, "Off the Record." N.d. or source. Folder: Sinatra et al., Box 927 California, Pre-Presidential Papers, Presidential Campaign Files, 1960, JFKL.

38. The Kennedy–Campbell relationship has been the source of tremendous speculation and intrigue. I take the details of their meeting from the 2002 edition of Arthur M. Schlesinger Jr.'s *A Thousand Days: John F. Kennedy in the White House* (1965; reprint New York: Houghton-Mifflin, 2002), xii. Using phone records and FBI files, Robert Dallek has confirmed Kennedy's relationship with Judith Campbell in *JFK: An Unfinished Life*, 476–479. Some journalists and historians refer to Campbell by her married name, Judith Campbell Exner.

39. On the much-rumored friction between Cahn and Campbell, see Douglas Thompson et al., "The President, the Lady, and the Godfather: A Story of Intrigue and Corruption at the Center of Political Power, Part II" *Daily Mail*, September 21, 1976. Available at http://www.dougiethompson.com/kennedy-mafia2.html. Accessed July 23, 2012.

40. Gloria Cahn to John F. Kennedy, Sunday, [February 14, 1960], Folder: Sinatra et al., Box 927 California, Pre-Presidential Papers, Presidential Campaign Files, 1960, JFKL.

41. John F. Kennedy to Mrs. Gloria Cahn, February 27, 1960. Folder: Sinatra et al., Box 927 California, Pre-Presidential Papers, Presidential Campaign Files, 1960, JFKL. In 1964, the Cahns would divorce, Gloria citing her husband's extreme jealousy as the cause. *Palm Beach Daily News*, April 15, 1964, 6.

42. Kathryn Cramer Brownell, *Show Biz Politics: Hollywood in American Political Life* (Chapel Hill: University of North Carolina Press, 2014), 21.

43. Donald T. Critchlow, *When Hollywood Was Right: How Movie Stars, Studio Moguls, and Big Business Remade American Politics* (New York: Cambridge University Press, 2013), 69.

44. On Murphy, see Brownell, *Show Biz Politics*, 145. On the political message of Eisenhower's speech, see Russell Baker, "Eisenhower Turns Corruption Issue Upon Democrats," and "Text of Eisenhower Speech Accusing Democrats of Corruption," *New York Times* October 20, 1956, 1, 10. Online. Accessed March 15, 2011.

45. "Hollywood at Convention," *The Hollywood Reporter*, July 11, 1960, 3.

46. Radie Harris, "Broadway Ballyhoo," *The Hollywood Reporter*, July 12, 1960, 4.

47. See Folder: Convention, 1960, Site Convention Committee, Box 394, TV and Radio Division, 1956–60, Records of the Democratic National Committee, JFKL.

48. June Lockhart Lindsay to Senator Kennedy, June 13, 1960. Folder: Convention Arrangements, Box 927 California, Pre-Presidential Papers, Presidential Campaign Files, 1960, JFKL.

49. "Democrats' Major-Domo: James Leonard Reinsch," *New York Times*, July 8, 1960, 10. Accessed March 17, 2011.

50. Murray Shumbach, "Democrats to Get Hollywood Help," *New York Times*, June 30, 1960, 22. Accessed March 17, 2011.

51. Russell Baker, "Daring Democratic Drama Opens to Big Stretches of Empty Seats," *New York Times*, July 12, 1960, 1. Accessed March 17, 2011.

52. Schumbach, "Democrats to Get," *New York Times*, 22.

53. Frank Capra, "The Convention—A Director's View," *The Hollywood Reporter*, July 13, 1960, 3. Writing at the beginning of the week, actor Anthony Franciosa pronounced the event a sure hit: "The Convention getting under way today is the kind of a show that Oscars and box office blockbusters are made of!" Actress Janet Leigh proclaimed the convention "the greatest show in the world" and a "major production with an 'A' budget and an all-star cast." She marveled at the way the politicians exhibited the same magnetism that made other people Hollywood stars. Although he himself had publicly come out for Kennedy, Milton Berle made light of Hollywood endorsements. "At one high point in the convention, Dean Martin climbed on the Kennedy bandwagon. The Senator must have a lot of influence," Berle cracked. "No one else ever got Dino on the wagon." See Anthony Franciosa, "The Political Drama—A Blockbuster Show," *The Hollywood Reporter*, July 11, 1960; Janet Leigh, "The Convention—A Glamorous View," *The Hollywood Reporter*, July 12, 1960, 3.3; Milton Berle, "Berle's Eye View of the Democratic Convention," *The Hollywood Reporter*, July 15, 1960, 3.

54. Ibid.

55. Jim Henaghan, "The Convention Needed a Pilot," *The Hollywood Reporter*, July 14, 1960, 3.

56. Baker, "Daring Democratic," *New York Times*, 1.

57. Hank Grant, "On the Air," *The Hollywood Reporter*, July 15, 1960, 10.

58. By 1960, Mailer was a well-known writer whose novel *The Naked and the Dead* had been widely celebrated for its gritty evocation of World War II. Although he continued to publish novels throughout the 1950s, Mailer increasingly brought his elaborate literary style to bear on nonfiction. He is often considered one of the early voices in the so-called New Journalism style of reporting that writers such as Truman Capote, Tom Wolfe, Joan Didion, and Gay Talese would practice in the coming years. All quotations from "Superman Comes to the Supermarket" come from the online text previously cited in note 15.

59. The image of an Arthurian president who for three short years presided over an American Camelot came from Jackie Kennedy several weeks after her husband's death. The musical *Camelot* had been a Broadway hit since the start of the Kennedy administration, winning four Tony awards and spawning a best-selling LP. In an interview with Theodore White that was published in *Life* magazine, Jackie recounted how her husband liked to listen to the recording before going to bed. He especially admired the final song in which playing the role of King Arthur, Richard Burton sings "Don't let it be forgot, / that once there was a spot, / for one brief shining moment that was known as Camelot." No matter how historically misleading, the image of an idealistic young president who built a fleeting utopia devoted to noble causes has remained with us ever since. Theodore H. White, "For President Kennedy: An Epilogue," *Life*, December 6, 1963, 159.

60. See, for example, all three parts of "The Hip and the Square" in *Advertisements for Myself* (1959: reprint Cambridge, MA: Harvard University Press, 1992), 424–430; and the short story "The Time of Her Time" also collected in *Advertisements*, 478–503. In "Superman Comes to the Supermarket," Mailer compared Kennedy to the story's main character, Sergius O'Shaugnessy, who runs a bullfighting school in Greenwich Village. It is telling that "The Time of Her Time" concludes with O'Shaugnessy's rape of a woman he is dating.

61. Norman Mailer, "The White Negro: Superficial Reflections on the Hipster," *Advertisements for Myself*, 354. On Mailer as the "philosopher of hip," see Fred Kaplan, *1959: The Year that Changed Everything* (Hoboken, NJ: John Wiley & Sons, 2009), 15–26.

62. Michael Szalay, *Hip Figures: A Literary History of the Democratic Party* (Palo Alto, CA: Stanford University Press, 2012), 116–117, 121.

63. *Life*, July 20, 1953.

64. Gay Talese, *The Neighbor's Wife* (1980: reprint New York: Harper Collins, 2009), 127.

65. DNC Speakers Bureau, Folder: General Subject Index, 1959–1960, Box 48 Pre-Administration Political Files, Robert F. Kennedy Papers, John F. Kennedy Presidential Library. Organized by an independent national committee, the list of artists, scientists, and intellectuals endorsing Kennedy grew so long that their all their names could not be included in a series of advertisements published in the nation's leading newspapers. The abridgement prompted at least one supporter to write a curt letter protesting that he had contributed his money but was disappointed that his name had not appeared in the advertisements. See Dr. R. W. Gerard to John L. Saltonstall, n.d. Folder: Committee of Arts, Letters, and Sciences for Kennedy for President: Correspondence of Director, Box 1, 1960 Campaign Files, 1959–60, John L. Saltonstall Personal Papers, John F. Kennedy Presidential Library.

66. Michael Harris, "He'll 'Sell' for the Democrats," *San Francisco Sunday Chronicle*, November 15, 1959, 10.

67. Filming of Senator Kennedy, Tuesday, October 11, 1960, Box 38, Pre-Administration Political Files, General Subject Index, 1959–1960, Robert F. Kennedy Papers, JFKL.

68. Craig Allen, *Eisenhower and the Mass Media: Peace, Prosperity, and Prime-Time TV* (Chapel Hill: University of North Carolina Press, 1993), 38, 168–171, and photograph captions.

69. Kathleen Hall Jamieson, *Packaging the Presidency: A History and Criticism of Presidential Campaign Advertising* (New York: Oxford University Press, 1996), 150–151.

70. "Election of 1960." Online by Gerhard Peters and John T. Woolley, The American Presidency Project. Available at http://www.presidency.ucsb.edu/showelection.php?year=1960. Accessed July 26, 2015.

71. On the speech to Baptist ministers and Denove's role in the Kennedy campaign, see Jamieson, *Packaging the Presidency*, 129–133 and 166–168.

72. "Harry Belafonte Spot for John F. Kennedy—1960." Television commercial. IFP: 125 F78-5M. Audio-Visual Collection, JFKL.

73. Henry Fonda, *My Life*, as told to Howard Teichmann (New York: New American Library, 1981), 271.

74. "Henry Fonda," Citizens for Kennedy-Johnson, 1960. Video courtesy of JFKL. From the Museum of the Moving Image, *The Living Room Candidate: Presidential Campaign Commercials 1952–2008*. Available at www.livingroomcandidate.org/commercials/1960/henry-fonda. Accessed March 29, 2011.

75. "Jacqueline Kennedy Talks with Dr. Benjamin Spock," Citizens for Kennedy-Johnson, 1960. Video courtesy of JFKL: https://www.youtube.com/watch?v=A_lkd-EbZK8. Accessed July 28, 2015.

76. "John F. Kennedy, "Interview with Senator and Mrs. John F. Kennedy by Henry Fonda, CBS-TV," November 2, 1960. Transcript online by Gerhard Peters and John T. Woolley, The American Presidency Project. Available at http://www.presidency.ucsb.edu/ws/?pid=25929. Accessed July 22, 2015.

77. Fonda, *My Life*, 272.

78. I borrow the phrase from Daniel Herwitz, *The Star as Icon: Media Celebrity in the Age of Mass Consumption* (New York: Columbia University Press, 2008), 14.

79. See Ben Zimmer, "The Origins of 'Relatable,'" *New York Times Sunday Magazine*, August 13, 2010. Available at http://www.nytimes.com/2010/08/15/magazine/15onlanguage.html. Accessed June 7, 2015.

80. Dallek, *J.F.K.: An Unfinished Life*, 192; and Paul Healy, "The Senate's Gay Young Bachelor," *Saturday Evening Post*, June 1953, 192.

81. Allen, *Eisenhower and the Mass Media*, 33–34.

82. Gore Vidal in "The Holy Family" (1967), *United States: Essays, 1952–1992* (New York: Broadway Books, 2001), 810.

83. Gil Troy, "Ronald Reagan," *The American Presidency: The Authoritative Reference*, ed. Alan Brinkley and Davis Dyer (New York: Houghton-Mifflin, 2004), 482.

84. John F. Kennedy, [Jr.], "Editor's Letter." *George*. December 1995/January 1996, 7.

Conclusion

1. *Li'l Abner* was based on the comic strip of the same name by Al Capp, a well-known supporter of Adlai Stevenson. In 1953, Capp created the character of General Bullmoose as a parody not of Eisenhower himself but of his first Secretary of Defense, Charles Erwin Wilson, the longtime CEO of General Motors. In his Senate confirmation, Wilson was reputed to have said, "What's good for General Motors is good for the country." Bullmoose's tagline (in both the comic strip and the musical) is "What's good for General Bullmoose is good for the USA!" Lyrics from Johnny Mercer and Robert Kimball, *The Complete Lyrics of Johnny Mercer* (New York: Knopf, 2009), 253. On Mercer, Capp, and Wilson, see Glenn T. Eskew, *Johnny Mercer: Southern Songwriter for the World* (Athens, GA: University of Georgia Press, 2013), 445n. My thanks to Ron Mandelbaum of Photofest for making me aware of these lyrics.

2. For financial details, see John D. Morris, "Movie Tax Repeal Is Vetoed; Eisenhower for Cuts in 1954," *New York Times*, August 7, 1953, 1, 8. Online. On the state of the industry, see Bosley Crowther, "Money for Movies: Considering the Tax Relief Measure and the State of the Industry," *New York Times*, August 2, 1953, Sec. 2, 1. Online. Both accessed October 6, 2014.

3. Dwight David Eisenhower, *The Eisenhower Diaries*, ed. Robert H. Ferrell (New York: W.W. Norton, 1981), 250–252. All cited passages come from this entry.

4. "Actors Eat Cake with the Coolidges," *New York Times*, October 18, 1924, 1. Online. Accessed September 15, 2010. Jolson's notion was most notably echoed in actress Shirley MacLaine's editorial "Politics and Performers" in the *New York Times*, May 18, 1972, 47. Defending her role in George McGovern's campaign, MacLaine wrote: "Large numbers of Americans seem to understand now that we are in an age when all citizens must participate if we are to fulfill the original intentions of participatory democracy—that it is the responsibility of everyone, including artists, to search for humane solutions to society's problems. Somehow they sense that artists can be both companions and prophets of social change because they are so inextricably involved with the full range of human life. It is the actor's special task to emulate life with as much power and faithfulness as he or she can command. Our perceptions and knowledge of human motivation govern how good we are at what we do. Those same perceptions should help determine the quality of

our politics. Politics that are void of the insight of art—its compassion, humor and laughter—are doomed to sterility and abstractions." Online. Accessed July 16, 2010.

5. See Dwight David Eisenhower to Edward John Bermingham, November 24, 1953, *The Papers of Dwight David Eisenhower*, vol. 14, ed. Louis Galambos and Daun Van Ee (Baltimore: Johns Hopkins University Press, 1996), 694; and Dwight David Eisenhower to Edward John Bermingham, January 26, 1954, *The Papers of Dwight David Eisenhower*, vol. 15, ed. Louis Galambos and Daun Van Ee (Baltimore: Johns Hopkins University Press, 1996), 853. Electronic Database. Accessed September 14, 2015.

6. As Craig Allen has remarked, "Montgomery sensed clearly what Eisenhower never told him directly: that a TV adviser was not qualified for a policy-making position." Craig Allen, *Eisenhower and the Mass Media: Peace, Prosperity, and Prime-Time TV* (Chapel Hill: University of North Carolina Press, 1993), 159. In gratitude for his years of service, Eisenhower granted Montgomery the literary and movie rights to his life story in 1958. He would eventually curtail these rights as he prepared to leave office, however. On the revision of literary and dramatic rights, see Dwight David Eisenhower to Robert Montgomery, July 3, 1958, *The Papers of Dwight David Eisenhower*, vol. 19, ed. Louis Galambos and Daun Van Ee (Baltimore: Johns Hopkins University Press, 2003), 979; and Dwight David Eisenhower to Robert Montgomery, January 3, 1961, *The Papers of Dwight David Eisenhower*, vol. 21, ed. Louis Galambos and Daun Van Ee (Baltimore: Johns Hopkins University Press, 2003), 2232–2233. Electronic Database. Accessed September 14, 2015.

7. See Robert Montgomery, "Public Relations and Private Obligations," *The Public Relations Journal*, vol. 11, January 1955, 4.

8. See Cecil B. DeMille, "Proclaim Liberty," *The Public Relations Journal*, vol. 12, January 1956, 12.

9. See Clem Whitaker and Leone Baxter, "Campaign Blunders Can Change History," *The Public Relations Journal*, vol. 12, August 1956, 4; Fletcher Knebel, "Public Relations at the White House," *The Public Relations Journal*, vol. 12, September 1956, 3.

10. George W. S. Trow, *Within the Context of No Context* (New York: Atlantic Monthly Press, 1997), 84.

11. I refer here to Richard Dyer's useful assertion that musicals embody "what utopia would feel like rather than how it would be organized." See Dyer's chapter "Entertainment and Utopia" in *Only Entertainment* (New York: Routledge, 1992), 20.

12. As Neil Postman has commented, "Television arranges our communications environment for us in ways that no other medium has the power to do." See Neil Postman, *Amusing Ourselves to Death: Public Discourse in the Age of Show Business*, 20th anniversary edition (New York: Penguin Books, 1985, 2006), 78. See also David E. Sumner, *The Magazine Century: American Magazines Since 1900* (Peter Lang International Academic Publishers, 2010), 117–138.

13. On Sokolsky's ability to clear people from the blacklist, see John Cogley, *Report on Blacklisting*, Vol. II: *Radio-Television* (New York: Fund for the Republic, 1956), 60–63, 113–114.

14. George E. Sokolsky, "Celebrities Support Both Candidates: What Is One?" *The Milwaukee Sentinel*, August 24, 1960, Part 1, 9. Google newspapers. Available at http://news.google.com/newspapers?id=6ykxAAAAIBAJ&sjid=NhAEAAAAIBAJ&pg=7492%2C2158505. Accessed July 25, 2015.

15. Reagan had offered to switch parties prior to the 1960 presidential election and declare himself a Republican, but he was convinced that his endorsement was more valuable to Nixon coming as a Democrat. See Ronald Reagan, "A Time for Choosing" (The Speech) in Thomas W. Evans, *The Education of Ronald Reagan: The General Electric Years and the Untold Story of His Conversion to Conservatism* (New York: Columbia University Press, 2006), 238.

16. "Hollywood Roundtable," August 23, 1963, U.S. Information Agency Film. Available at http://unwritten-record.blogs.archives.gov/2012/09/21/hollywood-roundtable/ Accessed June 18, 2015. Belafonte has been an outspoken activist since the middle of the 1950s and rarely shied away from expressing his political opinions in the most candid manner possible. For more on Belafonte, see Stephen J. Ross, *Hollywood Left and Right: How Movie Stars Shaped American Politics* (New York: Oxford University Press, 2011), 185–226.

17. Robert Montgomery, *Open Letter From a Television Viewer* (New York: J. H. Heineman, 1968), 74.

18. [Anonymous], "The Star Spangled Look of the '68 Campaign," *Life* (64:19), May 10, 1968, pp. 64–69. The cover headline was "The Stars Leap into Politics."

19. "Political Cabaret Opens with Tribute to Dr. King," *New York Times*, April 9, 1968, 49; Deirdre Carmody, "Eugene's Facing State Tax Check," *New York Times*, April 25, 1968, 31; "A Second Eugene's Is Opened on the Coast," *New York Times*, May 12, 1968, 65; Francis X. Clines, "On Fridays, Celebrities Transform L.I. Café into Eugene's East," *New York Times*, August 4, 1968, 48. All online and accessed November 2, 2011.

20. "Frank Sinatra," Citizens for Humphrey-Muskie, 1968, Video courtesy of the Minnesota Historical Society. From Museum of the Moving Image, *The Living Room Candidate: Presidential Campaign Commercials 1952–2012*. Available at www.livingroom-candidate.org/commercials/1968/frank-sinatra. Accessed July 15, 2015.

21. "Nancy Sinatra on ABC's "Humphrey/Muskie Telethon," November 4, 1968. From "Nancy Works for Peace and Hubert Humphrey," NancySinatra.com, web. Available at http://nancysinatra.com/blog/2013/05/nancy-works-peace-hubert-humphrey/. Accessed July 3, 2015.

22. It is worth pointing out that, in 1964, Wilkinson had used his celebrity to win the Republican nomination for the US Senate from the state of Oklahoma. That fall he lost to his Democratic opponent, Fred Harris.

23. On the mechanics of the show, see Edwin Diamond and Robert A. Silverman, *White House to Your House: Media and Politics in Virtual America* (Cambridge: MIT Press, 1997), 26. Kathleen Hall Jamieson has a useful discussion about the various conflicting opinions about the rewriting of questions backstage. See Joe McGinniss, *The Selling of the President 1968* (Trident Press: New York, 1969), 149; and Kathleen Hall Jamieson, *Packaging the Presidency: A History and Criticism of Presidential Campaign Advertising* (New York: Oxford University Press, 1996), 273.

24. On Wilkinson's woodenness, see *Selling of the President*, 102. On the victory, see Richard Nixon, *RN: The Memoirs of Richard Nixon* (New York: Simon and Schuster), 329–330.

25. See Allen, *Eisenhower and the Mass Media*, 178–180.

26. McGinniss, *Selling of the President*, 45.

27. On candidates as actors, see Roger Ailes's comment during the Election Eve telethon: "This is the beginning of a whole new concept. This is it. This is the way they'll be

elected forevermore. The next guys will have to be performers." See McGinniss, *Selling of the President*, 155. On the importance of "aura," see the campaign memorandum that McGinniss publishes by Nixon staffer William Gavin: "People are stirred by the legend, including the living legend, not by the man himself. It's the aura that surrounds the charismatic figure more than it is the figure itself, that draws the followers. Our task is to build that aura. *Attention begets attention.* People who wouldn't look twice at something happening in the street will if they see a crowd gathered to watch. People pant over movie stars in person not because they're inherently any more interesting than the person next door, but because they're a focus of public attention, of adulation. They're events, happenings, institutions, legends," McGinniss, *Selling of the President*, 208. Having deeply resented the press' glowing attention to Jack and Bobby Kennedy, Nixon hoped to approximate the energy and glamour of the brothers' campaigns, rather than the paternal likeability of Ike's. See McGinniss, op. cit., 201, especially this passage: "This was the great source of Kennedy's appeal—the king bit. identify. jfk's ideal. Clean, handsome, witty, articulate, rich, sure, pacesetter, stylesetter, elan, verve, guts, pushing ahead without being pushy" (210).

28. Thomas Frank, *The Conquest of Cool: Business Culture, Counterculture, and the Rise of Hip Consumerism* (Chicago: University of Chicago Press 1997), 157, 239.

29. Ibid., 119. See also Michael Szalay's discussion of how a countercultural hipster style proved to be crucial to the branding of the Democratic Party in the 1960s in *Hip Figures: A Literary History of the Democratic Party* (Palo Alto, CA: Stanford University Press, 2012).

30. McGinniss, *Selling of the President*, 207.

31. See Dwight D. Eisenhower, "Annual Message to the Congress on the State of the Union, January 7, 1954." Online, by Gerhard Peters and John T. Woolley, The American Presidency Project. Available at http://www.presidency.ucsb.edu/ws/?pid=10096. Accessed June 27, 2015.

32. The Eisenhower campaign made numerous attempts to engage youths of all ages. The *New York Times* reported on the formation of a David Eisenhower Club in Houston, Texas, in honor of the president's grandson. The boys and girls who belonged to the club would receive specially made license plates for their bikes reading "IM4IKE2." See "To Ride a Bike for Ike," *New York Times*, October 20, 1956, 10. Online. Accessed July 14, 2015.

33. Hillary D. Rodham, 1969 Commencement Speech, Wellesley College. Available at http://www.wellesley.edu/events/commencement/archives/1969commencement/studentspeech. Accessed April 30, 2011.

34. McGinniss, *Selling of the President*, 235.

35. McGinniss, *Selling of the President*, 77–78, 151.

36. On Nixon's appearance on *Laugh-In*, see Jack Gould, "'Laugh-In' Team Back with a Nixon Line," *New York Times*, September 7, 1968, 95. Online. Accessed April 30, 2011; Elizabeth Kolbert, "Stooping to Conquer," *New Yorker*, April 19, 2004. Available at http://www.newyorker.com/magazine/2004/04/19/stooping-to-conquer. Accessed April 30, 2011.

37. See *Esquire*, June 1969, cover.

38. "Youth," Nixon–Agnew TV Committee, 1968. From Museum of the Moving Image, *The Living Room Candidate: Presidential Campaign Commercials 1952–2008*. Available at www.livingroomcandidate.org/commercials/1968/youth. Accessed November 15, 2011.

39. On television's ability to remove individuals from context, see Joshua Meyrowitz, *No Sense of Place: The Impact of Electronic Media on Social Behavior* (New York: Oxford University Press, 1986).

40. Howell Raines, "From Film Star to Candidate; Ronald Wilson Reagan," *New York Times*, July 17, 1980, B8. Online. Accessed July 4, 2015.

41. Heston had been involved in the civil rights struggle since the 1961 protests against segregation in Oklahoma City.

42. Reagan is widely reported to have offered the quip in 1980 when a reporter asked him about being an actor and the president. Reagan returned to the line in his autobiography. "For years, I've hear the question: how could you, an actor, be president? I've sometimes wondered how you could be president and not be an actor." Ronald Reagan, *An American Life: The Autobiography* (New York: Simon and Schuster, 1990). Electronic edition.

43. See Montgomery, "Public Relations and Private Obligations," 4. Pam Parry explores Eisenhower's interest in applying Madison Avenue sales techniques to Cold War foreign policy. See Pam Parry, *Eisenhower: The Public Relations President* (Lanham, MD: Lexington Books, 2014), 119–135; on Larmon as Ike's hope for the USIA head, see Parry, op. cit., 120–121.

44. Timothy Raphael, *The President Electric: Ronald Reagan and the Politics of Performance* (Ann Arbor: University of Michigan Press, 2009), 13–15.

45. See Michael Rogin, *Ronald Reagan, the Movie and Other Episodes in Political Demonology* (Berkeley, CA: University of California Press, 1987), 7–8, 14–17.

46. See Lou Cannon, *President Reagan, The Role of a Lifetime* (New York: Public Affairs, 2000, 2008 reprint), 426–431.

47. Postman, *Amusing Ourselves to Death*, 132, 135.

48. Chris Rojek, *Celebrity* (London: Reaktion Books, 2001), 90.

49. Todd Gitlin, *Media Unlimited: How the Torrent of Images and Sounds Overwhelms Our Lives* (New York: Henry Holt, 2002), 172.

50. Chris Hedges, *Empire of Illusion: The End of Literacy and the Triumph of Spectacle* (New York: Perseus, 2009), 38.

51. I refer, of course, to Gil Scott Heron's "B Movie," *Reflections*, Arista Records, 1981.

52. Richard Dyer MacCann, "Viewing with Alarm—on TV," *Christian Science Monitor*, November 5, 1956, p. 16. ProQuest Historical Newspapers. Electronic Database. Accessed April 2, 2014.

53. See Greg Mitchell, *Tricky Dick and the Pink Lady: Richard Nixon vs. Helen Gahagan Douglas—Sexual Politics and the Red Scare, 1950* (New York: Random House, 1998). According to Evan Thomas, Nixon claimed to have never said the line. *Being Nixon: A Man Divided* (New York: Random House, 2015), 60.

54. Fred Davis, CEO of Strategic Perception Inc., telephone interview with author, February 5, 2010. The ad itself can be seen at "Celeb," John McCain 2008. From Museum of the Moving Image, *The Living Room Candidate: Presidential Campaign Commercials 1952–2012*. Available at www.livingroomcandidate.org/commercials/2008/celeb. Accessed July 15, 2015. Ed O'Keefe notes that the video received over 1.6 million YouTube hits in the first week. See Ed O'Keefe, "Ad Wars: Is 'Celebrity' the New 'Flip-Flop'? *The Washington Post*, August 6, 2008. Available at http://voices.washingtonpost.com/thefix/ad-wars/mccain-distances-himself-from.html. Accessed August 10, 2008. It is worth pointing out

that some commentators saw the commercial as subtly tapping into racial fears as the image of two blonde white women dissolved into the smiling Obama.

55. Susan Eisenhower, "Why I'm Backing Obama," *Washington Post*, February 2, 2008. Available at http://www.washingtonpost.com/wp-dyn/content/article/2008/02/01/AR2008020102621.html. Accessed July 10, 2015.

56. See Craig Garthwaite and Tim Moore, "The Role of Celebrity Endorsements in Politics: Oprah, Obama, and the 2008 Democratic Primary." Unpublished. September 2008. Available at http://www.stat.columbia.edu/~gelman/stuff_for_blog/celebrityendorsements_garthwaitemoore.pdf. Accessed January 23, 2016.

57. Dave Itzoff, "Obama Ads Appear in Video Game," *New York Times*, October 14, 2008, C2.

58. Arthur Miller, "On Politics and Acting," Jefferson Lecture, National Endowment for the Humanities, March 26, 2001. Available at http://www.neh.gov/about/awards/jefferson-lecture/arthur-miller-lecture. Accessed July 14, 2015.

{ INDEX }